TORTURE, POWER

This volume brings together the most important writing on torture and the "war on terrorism" by one of the leading US voices in the torture debate. Philosopher and legal ethicist David Luban reflects on this contentious topic in a powerful sequence of essays including two new and previously unpublished pieces. He analyzes the trade-offs between security and human rights, as well as the connection between torture, humiliation, and human dignity; the fallacy of using ticking-bomb scenarios in debates about torture; and the ethics of government lawyers. The book develops an illuminating and novel conception of torture as the use of pain and suffering to communicate absolute dominance over the victim. Factually stimulating and legally informed, this volume provides the clearest analysis to date of the torture debate. It brings the story up to date by discussing the Obama administration's failure to hold torturers accountable.

DAVID LUBAN is University Professor in Law and Philosophy at Georgetown University. His many publications include *Lawyers and Justice: An Ethical Study* (1988), *Legal Modernism* (1994), *Legal Ethics and Human Dignity* (2007), and well-known essays on just-war theory and international criminal law.

TORTURE, POWER, AND LAW

DAVID LUBAN
Georgetown University

CAMBRIDGE
UNIVERSITY PRESS

CAMBRIDGE
UNIVERSITY PRESS

University Printing House, Cambridge CB2 8BS, United Kingdom

Cambridge University Press is part of the University of Cambridge.

It furthers the University's mission by disseminating knowledge in the pursuit of
education, learning and research at the highest international levels of excellence.

www.cambridge.org
Information on this title: www.cambridge.org/9781107656291

© David Luban 2014

First published 2014

Printed in the United Kingdom by CPI Group Ltd, Croydon CR0 4YY

A catalogue record for this publication is available from the British Library

Library of Congress Cataloging-in-Publication Data
Luban, David, 1949– author.
Torture, power, and law / David Luban.
pages cm
ISBN 978-1-107-05109-6 (Hardback) – ISBN 978-1-107-65629-1 (Paperback)
1. Torture (International law). 2. Torture–United States. I. Title.
KZ7170.L83 2014
341.6'5–dc23 2014004590

ISBN 978-1-107-05109-6 Hardback
ISBN 978-1-107-65629-1 Paperback

For Daniel and Rachel, who came of age in a confusing world
without becoming confused

CONTENTS

PREFACE

The chapters in this volume represent my major writing over the twelve years since September 11, 2001 on topics surrounding the "war on terrorism," particularly the torture debate. The earliest appeared in summer 2002, barely nine months after 9/11; the latest are Chapter 5 and the final chapter, which I wrote for this volume. The book focuses on three themes: the alleged "trade-off" between national security and human rights, the torture debate itself, and the ways law was manipulated to legitimize torture and ensure there would be no accountability for it.

Obviously, the three topics are tightly connected. If rights must give way to security in times of emergency, those may include the right against torture, at least in "ticking-bomb" cases. Because torture is illegal, leaders who want to torture terrorism suspects for information must manipulate the law. And if the emergency persists for years, guaranteeing the absolute prohibition on torture as a fundamental human right may be a luxury societies think they cannot afford.

The book offers an extended critique of this reasoning. Its first two chapters examine whether the fight against terrorism really does require the sacrifice of major rights, and warn that such sacrifices are likely to become dangerously normalized. Chapter 2 emphasizes that talk of "trade-offs" and "sacrifices" of rights for security is a grotesque euphemism if all we really mean is that we will cheerfully sacrifice other people's rights for our own security. It also argues that the separation of powers and civilian control of the military require a stringently limited commander-in-chief power, just the opposite of the nearly unbounded presidential power to override the law claimed by the George W. Bush administration.

Succeeding chapters criticize the ubiquitous use of imaginary "ticking-bomb" scenarios as justification for torture. The argument is both philosophical and political. I criticize the philosophical strategy of testing moral principles by posing improbable extreme cases, and I argue that ticking-bomb arguments deflect public reflection from actual practices of torture to a make-believe world. In this connection, Chapter 4 examines the handful of supposedly genuine ticking-bomb cases often cited to prove that torture saves lives, and demonstrates that they show nothing of the sort. On the philosophical side,

Chapter 4 raises two objections to investigating morality through extreme cases. First, the cases are often so cartoonish that they transform moral reflection into puzzle-solving of brainteasers; second, the procedure wrongly assumes that moral rationality is equipped to deliver principled verdicts on all possible sets of facts. In my view, moral theories codify rules of thumb useful in many cases but not all possible cases, and there is no reason to suppose that either deductions from general theories or analogical thinking from easy cases to hard ones will reliably deliver rational answers.

The book next turns from the critique of ticking-bomb arguments to investigate more deeply the evils of torture. The newly written Chapter 5 develops a conception of torture as the use of pain and suffering to communicate the torturer's absolute dominance over the victim's absolute helplessness. This is one of the book's central ideas. It adds to the legal definition of torture as the intentional infliction of severe pain or suffering an additional insight into the practice of torture: that the pain and suffering are not simply neurological experiences of a certain intensity – they are *contentful* experiences, and their content is that the absolutely helpless victim is under the total domination of a cruel and merciless master. Analyzing and unpacking this "communicative" conception of torture allows us to see more precisely why torture belongs on the short list of archetypal evils that should properly be regarded as unthinkable. The analysis shows how tightly connected torture is with other forms of humiliating and degrading treatment. Torture is totalitarianism in miniature. To treat torture as merely one option among many for combating terrorism, to be used whenever the benefits outweigh the costs, is to devalue core liberal values of dignity, equal human worth, and antisubordination into matters of mere convenience. To open the question of torture is therefore to call all those commitments into question as well. Instead, I argue that torture belongs in the same moral category as slavery, military massacres, and the subordination of women. Like torture, the latter are all practices taken for granted through most of human history. All are now forbidden (even though they have by no means disappeared from practice). And they are not merely forbidden – they are forbidden in the strong sense that to put back on the table the question of whether their utility might sometimes justify them is itself morally odious. The communicative conception of torture explains why torture belongs in the same category, which for short I call the category of the unthinkable. I do not propose the communicative conception as a substitute for the broader legal definition. To serve its practical ends, the legal definition must remain broad. Rather, the communicative conception aims to provide a deeper understanding of torture, as a step in a moral argument for including torture in the category of the unthinkable.

The next two chapters analyze humiliation and mental torture as fundamental affronts to human dignity. Chapter 6 explores the resources that religious traditions can offer to the defense of human rights, taking as its example the treatment of human dignity in Jewish law. Chapter 7 examines mental torture, and demonstrates how US legislators, determined to shield law-enforcement personnel from potential accusations of torture, wrote convoluted and incoherent law that makes mental torture nearly impossible to prosecute.

The following chapters describe how government lawyers abused the law to get around essential prohibitions on torture, and explore the ethical obligations of professionals in government service. A concluding chapter brings the story up to date (to mid 2013), and analyzes the morality of the Obama administration's decision to "look forward, not back" by not seeking accountability for the US government's descent into torture.

Before 9/11, I never imagined that I would devote ten years to something called the "torture debate." I never imagined there would *be* a torture debate. Debating torture was not how I would have chosen to spend my time. But somehow I did find myself immersed in the debate, not only as a scholar but also as an occasional journalist, radio commentator, Congressional witness, and blogger, as well as a frequent speaker both in and out of the academy.

I felt impelled to speak out on these issues whenever I could. Several of the chapters of this book originated as speeches, and preserve some of the less formal style of writing intended to be spoken. One chapter includes as an appendix my testimony to the US Senate Judiciary Committee on the role of lawyers in legitimizing torture. Whenever I spoke, I tried to supply the background necessary to make my arguments self-contained. As a result, some of these chapters repeat bits of information that also appear in others. Because one aim of this book is to make this writing conveniently available in one place, I have left most of the chapters in their original form, despite minor overlaps; only Chapter 6 has been rewritten to eliminate redundancies, and I have also made stylistic revisions to Chapter 9.[1] Despite the overlaps, each chapter contains distinct and unique material that does not appear in the others. The arguments are cumulative, and my hope is that the questions each chapter leaves in readers' minds will be answered by others.

Some chapters develop and expand on brief ideas from an earlier chapter. For example, Chapter 4 revisits, expands, and provides a philosophical basis for the critique of ticking-bomb arguments in Chapter 3. The newly written Chapter 5 provides an analysis of torture and its evils that I was only groping towards in Chapters 4 and 6.

[1] In two other chapters originally published in law reviews, I have removed some footnotes and consolidated others (and, even so, the chapters remain heavily footnoted). The conventions of law review citation require a footnote every time a document is mentioned, and a source citation to support every factual assertion, including minor or uncontroversial assertions. There are reasons for this convention, but it multiplies footnotes that readers of this book would likely find more distracting than helpful.

The issue that most preoccupied me is the conduct of the "torture lawyers" – the US government lawyers whose legal opinions opened the door to torture. The issue lies directly at the intersection of my work on the "war on terrorism" and my career-long interest in the professional ethics of lawyers. The torture lawyers' role first came into the open in 2004, soon after the revelations about Abu Ghraib, the US military prison in Baghdad, and it prompted my best-known paper on torture, "Liberalism, Torture, and the Ticking Bomb" (Chapter 3). But the full extent of the torture lawyers' activities did not come out until April 2009, when the Obama administration released hitherto secret torture memos, and again in February 2010, when the administration released documents from an internal investigation by the Office of Professional Responsibility (OPR), the Justice Department's internal ethics watchdog.

That investigation lasted for nearly six years. I was stunned to discover from one of these released documents that the OPR had been influenced by my writings. A letter from US Attorney General Michael Mukasey to the head of the OPR complains that "as confirmed in our meeting, the Draft Report draws substantially from Professor Luban's work." Mr. Mukasey continues:

> We are not personally familiar with all of Professor Luban's work, and have nothing bad to say about him, but commentators, like witnesses, typically have certain seeming biases that are conveyed so as to inform a reader or jury or decision-maker. Thus, for example, it would appear at least worth mentioning that, while Professor Luban seems to be a very thoughtful and prolific scholar, he is a trained philosopher, not an attorney; and he has not practiced law. He also appears to be a longtime—to be sure, thoughtful and sincere, but longtime—critic of the Bush Administration and of the War on Terror in general. These facts about Professor Luban do not make him wrong necessarily, of course.[2]

It seems to me that Mr. Mukasey's warning about commentators' biases is exactly right. One of my hopes is that reading these chapters together will reveal a coherent line of argument, and demonstrate that my conclusions are based on reasons and not biases. Of course, that is something readers will judge for themselves.

All the chapters were responses to unfolding events, written in something close to real time, and fuelled by a sense of urgency. From the beginning, the whole story of the war on terrorism and the torture program was blanketed in secrecy. Two weeks after 9/11, US Secretary of Defense Donald Rumsfeld gave journalists fair warning to expect government reticence and disinformation:

---

[2] Letter from Michael B. Mukasey, Attorney General, and Mark Filip, Deputy Attorney General, to H. Marshall Jarrett, Counsel, Office of Professional Responsibility, Jan. 19, 2009 (www2.nationalreview.com/dest/2010/02/20/description011909.mukaseyfilipletter-toopr.pdf). In fact, I never had any contact with the OPR, and had no advance notice that its report drew on the arguments I had been urging in print since 2005.

"Of course, this conjures up Winston Churchill's famous phrase when he said, '[S]ometimes the truth is so precious it must be accompanied by a bodyguard of lies.'"[3]

Secrecy meant that information trickled out, and these essays necessarily relied on incomplete or superseded information. To adapt another Rumsfeld aphorism, you write with the information you have, not the information you might want to have.[4] For example, Chapter 1 reports that Sweden had rendered a Muslim cleric to Egypt, where he was tortured. Years later it came out that actually it was the CIA that carried out the rendition. Chapter 8 describes the CIA's interrogation techniques based on a 2005 news report that listed six of them; when the torture memos were finally released, there turned out to be thirteen. There are other such examples in this book. In addition, the book discusses legal decisions that were sometimes overtaken by higher court decisions or new legislation.

To several chapters I have therefore added prefaces to frame the issues and bring the story up to date. The prefaces (all written in 2013) add significant new material. Writing them, I found that to a dismaying extent the worries I voiced a decade ago remain just as worrisome now.

By now, there is a large library of books and articles on the topics of this book, especially the torture issue. Many of them are very good. For the sake of readability, I have chosen not to add discussions of this literature to the prefaces, or to address disagreements between other authors and my own viewpoint. These omissions should not be taken to indicate disregard for the work of others, but only a desire to keep the prefaces brief and focused.

A note on terminology

Chapters in this book will discuss interrogation practices of a kind sometimes described as "torture lite," sometimes as "bloodless torture," and sometimes – in the official terminology of the US government – as "enhanced interrogation techniques." These include subjecting people to extremes of hot or cold, prolonged isolation, sleep deprivation, humiliations, threats, stress positions, slaps, bombardment with loud music, and nonlethal water suffocation.

Several of the chapters analyze official opinions by US government lawyers declaring that these techniques, singly or in combination, do not cross the legal line into torture. I criticize those opinions and reject their conclusions. For reasons that the book sets out at length, I maintain that US interrogators did,

---

[3] Defense Department Briefing, Sept. 25, 2001. According to some sources, Churchill's quotation is, "In time of war, when truth is so precious, it must be attended by a sturdy bodyguard of lies."

[4] "As you know, you go to war with the army you have, not the army you might want or wish to have at a later time." Wolf Blitzer Reports staff, *CNN*, "Troops Put Rumsfeld in the Hot Seat," Dec. 8, 2004 (http://edition.cnn.com/2004/US/12/08/rumsfeld.kuwait/index.html).

in fact, torture detainees. Recently, a comprehensive report by the bipartisan Constitution Project Task Force on Detainee Treatment reached the same conclusion, after a two-year-long investigation. They report that torture "occurred in many instances and across a wide range of theaters," not only in the three cases in which the US government admittedly waterboarded prisoners.[5] Significantly, President Barack Obama has publicly described the interrogation program as torture.

Journalists who write about these issues face a dilemma: to use the T-word or not? To call these practices "torture" amounts to rejecting the Bush administration's position that they are not torture. But to withhold the word "torture," or to adopt the euphemism of "enhanced interrogation," acquiesces in the Bush administration's legal arguments, and rejects the views of those of us who believe the practices *are* torture and that it is important to call a spade a spade.[6] Either choice begs the question. "Harsh tactics" works a bit better, but it still begs the question of whether the tactics are harsh enough to be torture – in which case, why settle for "harsh tactics"? After a few years of bumbling around the issue, US newspapers hit on a clumsy but suitably noncommittal formula: "techniques that some critics describe as torture."

As a scholar, I dislike begging questions, and begging one of a book's central questions through conclusory word choices seems downright sinful. That might recommend a similarly noncommittal strategy. But the journalists' formula, used throughout this book, would be a mortal sin against English prose. It would also put the author in the bizarre position of writing badly in order to sound noncommittal about his own conclusions.[7]

---

[5] The Constitution Project, Report of the Constitution Project's Task Force on Detainee Treatment 3 (2013) (http://detaineetaskforce.org/read/).

[6] "Enhanced techniques," by the way, literally translates a euphemism coined by the Gestapo in 1937 for similar interrogation methods. Andrew Sullivan, "Verschärfte Vernehmung," The Daily Dish (*The Atlantic*), May 29, 2007 (www.theatlantic.com/daily-dish/archive/2007/05/-versch-auml-rfte-vernehmung/228158/). Sullivan reproduces the Gestapo's order.

[7] The Constitution Project Task Force noted that it faced the same problem. They write:

> The question as to whether U.S. forces and agents engaged in torture has been complicated by the existence of two vocal camps in the public debate. This has been particularly vexing for traditional journalists accustomed to recording the arguments of both sides in a dispute without declaring one right and the other wrong. The public may simply perceive that there is no right side, as there are two equally fervent views held views [*sic*] on a subject, with substantially credentialed people on both sides...
>
> But this Task Force is not bound by this convention.
>
> The members, coming from a wide political spectrum, believe that arguments that the nation did not engage in torture and that much of what occurred should be defined as something less than torture are not credible.

Report of the Task Force on Detainee Treatment, at pp. 3–4.

For these reasons, I will usually forge ahead with the T-word and its cognates: *torture, torturer, torture memos, torture program, torture lawyers* (who wrote the torture memos), *torture doctors* (who assisted at torture sessions), and so on. Given that all terminologies beg the question, I might as well beg it in the direction my arguments support, not the direction they criticize. But readers must understand that when I say "torture" I am saying something that will seem like a tendentious and infuriating provocation to those who reject the label. Provocation is not my reason for using the language.

ACKNOWLEDGMENTS

A great many people have read and commented on these chapters in draft; many of them are acknowledged below. And more commentators than I can possibly remember, in audiences from San Marcos, Texas, to Saskatoon, from Ankara to Australia, from Amnesty International events to the US Military Academy, have influenced their final form. I owe thanks to all of them.

My Georgetown colleagues have been indispensable. I would like to single out Marty Lederman, with whom I have spent long hours discussing the issues in this book. On top of his breadth of knowledge and astounding skill as a lawyer and analyst, Lederman has a special knack of clarifying other people's thinking and making their work better. His detailed comments on several of these chapters saved me from mistakes and changed my thinking, sometimes dramatically; his help was indispensable on Chapters 4, 7, 8, and 10, even though he strongly disagrees with me on some issues. I am also deeply grateful to Julie O'Sullivan for years of illuminating discussions on the topics of the book, as well as her constant moral support and friendship. Discussions with David Cole, Laura Donohue, John Mikhail, Mike Seidman, and Carlos Vázquez have been extremely helpful. Robin West has been a friend as well as an inspiration for twenty-five years. And the encouragement of Naomi Mezey and Nina Pillard has been especially gratifying. Georgetown's research librarians provided indispensable help.

Henry Shue's influence on these pages will be clear. It is most obvious in Chapter 7, which we wrote together, and Chapter 5 (written originally for a *Festschrift* for Henry), which uses two of his important papers as my point of departure. I read drafts of his foundational work on human rights even before he and Peter Brown hired me at the University of Maryland's Center for Philosophy and Public Policy in 1979, and his ideas about basic rights have shaped my thinking ever since, in great and small ways.

My greatest debt is a collective one. Early in 2005, Lederman and Kim Lane Scheppele began the *Law of Torture* listserv, a forum for lawyers, activists, scholars, psychologists, journalists, military officers, and former interrogators to exchange information, documents, news, and analyses. List members often argue sharply with each other, but the arguments are conducted in a splendidly collegial spirit. Eight years after the forum began, I find three thousand of its sometimes lengthy e-mail exchanges in my archive; and I archived only a fraction of what I read. Most of what I know came originally from the forum, and much of what I think was tested there. I have never met many of my most constant correspondents, but very little of this book could exist without them.

Friends and colleagues (and family members) who read and commented on one or more individual chapters, or provided other help, include Gabriella Blum, David Cole, Michael Froomkin, Jack Goldsmith, Katherine Hawkins, Lynne Henderson, Vicki Jackson, Paul Kahn, Sandy Levinson, Judith Lichtenberg, Rachel Luban, Jamie Mayerfeld, Stephen Nathanson, Katherine Newell, David Rodin, Amy Sepinwall, Nancy Sherman, Saul Smilansky, and Kieran Tranter. I am especially grateful to Eric Fair and William Quinn for discussions of their experiences as interrogators. Others whose comments and conversations have found their way into the book include Jean Maria Arrigo, Gregg Bloche, James Forman, Jr., Louis Frankenthaler, Lisa Hajjar, Scott Horton, Christopher Kutz, Carmi Lecker, Jenny Martinez, Ken Pope, Deborah Popowski, Jose Quiroga, David Remes, Deborah Rhode, Kim Lane Scheppele, John Sifton, Stephen Soldz, Gary Solis, Jeremy Waldron, and Brad Wendel; without a doubt, I have forgotten others, to whom I must combine thanks with apology. I would also like to thank the talented and committed research assistants at Georgetown and Stanford who helped at various stages along the way: Mark Aziz, Devon Chaffee, Catherine Foster, Daniel Hornal, Sophia Heller, Sebastian Kaplan-Sears, Matthew King, Anna Melamud, and John Partridge.

Preparing these chapters for publication has made me intensely aware of the incalculable debt that all of us owe to the remarkable corps of journalists whose investigative efforts brought to light virtually everything the world knows about the topics of this book. I don't know them personally (I have met some of them on occasions) – but they deserve acknowledgment here for their influence, which readers will perceive from the names that appear again and again in footnotes.

I have enjoyed great institutional support at Georgetown, but also at Stanford Law School, where I visited in 2005–6; the Institute for Advanced Studies at The Hebrew University in Jerusalem (spring 2011); Fordham Law School, where I taught in spring 2012; and the Center for Transnational Legal Studies in London, where I completed this book in 2013. The support of my deans – Alex Aleinikoff, Judy Areen, Larry Kramer, and Bill Treanor – has been extraordinary. I also wish to thank Hilary Gaskin, my editor at Cambridge University Press, who proposed this book and supported it throughout. Elle Augustson prepared the index of legal authorities and Rachel Luban provided the subject index.

As always, I have leaned on my family, Judith Lichtenberg, Daniel Luban, and Rachel Luban. Daniel and Rachel, who were in high school and middle school when 9/11 transformed our world, are now old enough to have provided invaluable comments on ideas in this book; and Judy has sustained me in every personal as well as professional way I can think of.

xviii   ACKNOWLEDGMENTS

Versions of Chapter 1 were previously published in

Philosophy and Public Policy Quarterly, 22(3) (Summer 2002), 9–14; reprinted in Verna V. Gehring, Ed., *War After September 11* (Rowman & Littlefield, 2002).
Mark V. Tushnet, Ed., *The Constitution in Wartime* (Duke University Press, 2005), pp. 219–31.
The versions differ only in their citation format. This book uses the second version. Reprinted with permission of the publisher.

Chapter 2 was previously published in

Richard Ashby Wilson, Ed., *Human Rights in the War on Terror* (Cambridge University Press, 2005), pp. 242–57. Reprinted with permission of the publisher.

Versions of Chapter 3 were previously published in

Virginia Law Review, 91(6) (2005), 1425–61.
Karen Greenberg, Ed., *The Torture Debate in America* (Cambridge University Press, 2005), pp. 35–83.
Steven Lee, Ed., *Intervention, Terrorism, and Torture: Challenges to Just War Theory in the 21st Century* (Springer Verlag, 2007).
The book uses the *Virginia Law Review* version. Reprinted with permission of the *Virginia Law Review*.

Chapter 4 was originally published in

Charles Beitz and Robert Goodin, Eds., *Global Basic Rights* (Oxford University Press, 2009), pp. 181–206. Reprinted with permission of the publisher.

Chapter 6 was originally published in

Kennedy Institute of Ethics Journal, 19(3) (2009), 211–30. Reprinted with permission of the *Kennedy Institute of Ethics Journal*.

Chapter 7 was originally published in

Georgetown Law Journal, 100 (2012), 823–63. Reprinted with permission of my co-author and of the *Georgetown Law Journal*.

Chapter 8 was originally published in

David Luban, *Legal Ethics and Human Dignity* (Cambridge University Press, 2007), ch. 6. Reprinted with permission of the publisher.

The appendix to Chapter 8 was originally published as

Testimony of David Luban, What Went Wrong: Torture and the Office of Legal Counsel in the Bush Administration: Hearing Before the Subcommittee on Administrative Oversight and the Courts of the Senate Committee on the Judiciary, 111th Congress 11–14, 47–50, 290–5 (May 13, 2009).

A version of Chapter 9 was originally published in

Kieran Tranter *et al.*, Eds., *Reaffirming Legal Ethics: Taking Stock and New Ideas* (Routledge, 2010), pp. 56–72. Reprinted with permission of the publisher.

Chapters 5 and 10 are published here for the first time, as are the prefaces to all chapters that have them.

I

Downgrading rights and expanding power during post-9/11 panic

The war on terrorism and the end of human rights

Preface

This chapter was written in spring and summer 2002, responding to momentous developments in the previous six months, both "on the ground" and in the US government's legal strategy. When I wrote it, the ashes of the World Trade Center had not yet settled. Speaking personally, I can report daily fear of another attack as I drove to work on Capitol Hill in Washington; it felt as though I had a target painted on the roof of my car. I was not the only one; public fear was palpable and pervasive. So were the grief and the anger. I shared, and share, that grief and anger.

Five people in my own tiny neighborhood in suburban Maryland died in the September 11 attack. It seemed clear that ideological suicide bombers cannot be deterred by the threat of criminal punishment, and that fact lent force to the government's aggressive, military-focused strategy. Facing the nightmare scenario in which terrorists acquire weapons of mass destruction, no possible step seemed too drastic.

Of course, this was an entirely me- and us-centered reaction. (More on this point in Chapter 2.) Reading news reports in a more objective spirit, I saw mounting evidence that the government's response posed a menace to human rights wherever the global war on terrorism was being waged. Within the United States, it began with a post-9/11 dragnet of young men from Muslim countries, some held incommunicado for months, and none of whom ever received an apology after their release. Outside the United States, it was hard to ignore news of civilian casualties in Afghanistan and initial reports of harsh treatment of captives. I wanted to present both sides of the argument – the reasons for a militarized policy and the dangers it posed to human rights – as fairly as possible.

On the ground, the United States had recently opened the Guantánamo Bay prison for men suspected of being Al Qaeda or Taliban fighters. The image of prisoners stepping off the planes in orange jumpsuits, blinded by hoods and deafened by headsets, was horrifying. The aim of sensory deprivation, we

The main text of this chapter was first published in 2002 – see Acknowledgments.

already understood, was to disorient the men; a few years later, journalists and academics discovered that the US government had adopted a strategy of psychological torture based on research into how to break down a human personality for interrogation purposes.[1] Sensory deprivation was part of that program. Although I wrote this chapter before the first intimations of torture at Guantánamo, or any hint of CIA "black sites," the media was already filled with talk of torture. Vice President Dick Cheney warned early on that US strategy would move to the "dark side."[2] Everyone knew what Cheney meant.

The US Congress's Authorization for the Use of Military Force (AUMF) granted the president authority "to use all necessary and appropriate force against those nations, organizations, or persons he determines planned, authorized, committed, or aided the terrorist attacks that occurred on September 11, 2001, or harbored such organizations or persons."[3] This is a limited authority, subsequently interpreted by the US government to include Al Qaeda and "associated forces." But two days later, President Bush announced in a famous speech before both houses of the US Congress, "Our war on terror begins with Al Qaida, but it does not end there. It will not end until every terrorist group of global reach has been found, stopped, and defeated."[4] This speech originated the famous phrase "war on terror," and it is why I wrote in this chapter that "terrorists who had nothing to do with September 11, even indirectly, have been earmarked as enemies."

The chapter also responds to legal developments. In early 2002, the government adopted a maximally hard line, stripping away all the detainees' rights. This was the "limbo of rightlessness" I speak of in the chapter. In February, a secret memorandum from the Office of Legal Counsel (OLC) in the Justice Department argued that the Geneva Conventions do not cover either Al Qaeda or Taliban captives. President George W. Bush accepted this conclusion. The president publicly issued an order to that effect, which cleared the path to the harsh interrogation strategies that followed by removing Geneva

---

[1] See Chapter 7 below.

[2] Interview of Vice President Dick Cheney by Tim Russert, NBC, *Meet the Press*, Sept. 16, 2001: "I'm going to be careful here, Tim, because I – clearly, it would be inappropriate for me to talk about operational matters, specific options or the kinds of activities we might undertake going forward . . . We also have to work, though, sort of the dark side, if you will. We've got to spend time in the shadows in the intelligence world. A lot of what needs to be done here will have to be done quietly, without any discussion, using sources and methods that are available to our intelligence agencies, if we're going to be successful. That's the world these folks operate in, and so it's going to be vital for us to use any means at our disposal, basically, to achieve our objective."

[3] Joint Resolution to authorize the use of United States Armed Forces against those responsible for the recent attacks launched against the United States, Public Law 107-40 (Sept. 18, 2001), 115 Stat. 224.

[4] Address to a Joint Session of Congress and the American People, Sept. 20, 2001 (http://georgewbush-whitehouse.archives.gov/news/releases/2001/09/20010920-8.html).

protections against abusive treatment. The government also asserted half a dozen other hyperaggressive legal positions designed to maximize presidential power over the detainees and minimize their rights and recourse. These maintained:

(1) that Guantánamo lies entirely outside the jurisdiction of the federal courts, so no court could hold legal proceedings on behalf of the detainees;

(2) that even though the detainees do not enjoy prisoner-of-war (POW) status and the protections associated with it, they are indeed military captives who can be detained without charges or trial until the war is over – whenever that might be;

(3) that they are entitled to no process to review their status, even if some protested that they were cases of mistaken identity or even innocent victims of mercenary Afghans who denounced them to the United States for financial bounties;

(4) that the detainees have no right to counsel or to visits by the Red Cross;

(5) that the US government lay under no obligation to reveal their identities (and in fact their identities were not revealed until an outraged military lawyer leaked them);

(6) and that those detainees charged with crimes would be tried before special, newly created military commissions, with minimal procedural protections, rather than domestic courts or military courts-martial. Notably, the military commissions would not need a unanimous jury vote to impose the death penalty.

According to the government, the cases even of two US citizens held within the United States – Yaser Hamdi and Jose Padilla – were not justiciable, and the courts must butt out.

In short, the detainees disappeared into a legal black hole, possessing no rights either as POWs or criminal suspects; and no form or forum of legal recourse was available to them.

The US interpretation of the Geneva Conventions put it at odds with the International Committee of the Red Cross (ICRC) and human-rights organiza-tions. According to the ICRC, everyone captured in a combat zone is either a combatant or a civilian, and therefore protected either by the Third Geneva Convention (governing treatment of POWs) or the Fourth Convention (governing treatment of civilians). The ICRC and human-rights groups view the Geneva regime as gapless, protecting every captive in an armed conflict.

The OLC saw matters differently. They noticed that the Geneva Conventions provide broad protections for POWs and civilians in international armed con-flicts (IACs) – armed conflicts among states. The Geneva Conventions also provide more minimal but still significant protections in "armed conflicts not of international character" (noninternational armed conflicts (NIACs)). But in their view, the global war on terrorism was neither. Al Qaeda is not a state, and NIACs, in the OLC's view, include only internal armed conflicts like civil wars, within the borders of a single state. The war on terrorism was novel and unique: an armed conflict with a nonstate organization operating across borders. Reportedly, Al Qaeda had operatives in sixty countries, and all these countries were potential battlefields.

Today, such conflicts are sometimes called *transnational armed conflicts*. This is not terminology recognized by international law, but it is a useful way of distinguishing internal from cross-border NIACs. In the OLC's legal theory, transnational armed conflicts are neither IACs nor NIACs, and therefore none of the Geneva Conventions apply to them.[5] As it concerns Al Qaeda, this was by no means a frivolous position. A fair (if debatable) reading of the Geneva text and negotiating history could be marshaled in its support, and the question of how to classify the "global war on terrorism" remained unanswered for the next four years, at least in US law. Eventually, the landmark 2006 Supreme Court decision *Hamdan* v. *Rumsfeld* rejected the OLC's theory and declared the war on terrorism to be a NIAC, covered by the Geneva Conventions.[6]

As for the Taliban, which had some claim to being Afghanistan's national army, the OLC argued that Afghanistan was a failed state that could no longer be counted as a party to the Geneva Conventions. Unlike the OLC's theory about Geneva protections for Al Qaeda, the failed-state argument was absurd, as the State Department legal adviser argued in an angry and frustrated secret memorandum, because international law does not recognize a category of "failed states," and does not allow one state to declare that another is no longer party to a treaty. But the White House, bent on asserting its own power to do what it wished in the name of national security, sided with the OLC against the State Department.

Given the boldness of the government's legal positions – not to mention the seeming indifference of the American public to civilian casualties in Afghanistan – at the moment I wrote this chapter, "the end of human rights" was not merely a rhetorical flourish. On the surface, everything has changed since then, so readers may think that the concerns I raised in 2002 no longer need trouble us. Alas, it is not so.

To be sure, almost all of the hyperaggressive Bush legal positions have fallen in the courts. Lower courts quickly rejected the claim that they lack authority to hear detainee cases, and one federal judge also rejected the administration's fallback position that courts must defer to the commander in chief's factual

---

[5] Curiously, some human-rights groups agreed with the Bush administration that the conflict with Al Qaeda is not an IAC or NIAC, but for different reasons. Where the OLC saw the conflict as a novel kind of war not anticipated or covered by the treaties, human-rights groups were skeptical that the campaign against Al Qaeda should be thought of as an armed conflict at all. They still are. In their eyes it is a matter for law enforcement. Of course, none doubted that the Afghanistan war was an armed conflict.

[6] *Hamdan* v. *Rumsfeld*, 548 U.S. 557 (2006).

representations about detainees. A few cases began winding their way through the judicial system, and eventually they reached the Supreme Court. Dramatically, in 2004, the Supreme Court rebuffed the administration. The Court held that Guantánamo falls under US jurisdiction, and that the habeas corpus statute applies to the detainees there (*Rasul* v. *Bush*).[7] The same day, the Court held that Guantánamo detainees deserve some form of process to review their detention (*Hamdi* v. *Rumsfeld*).[8] Guantánamo was rescued from limbo and moved back into a legal system of sorts.

The Republican-controlled Congress responded by stripping habeas corpus jurisdiction over Guantánamo from the federal courts, but in 2006 the *Hamdan* court held that this legislation applied only to future detainees, not those currently in Guantánamo. Their cases remained alive. Again, Congress responded with jurisdiction-stripping legislation, but in 2008 the Supreme Court found a constitutional right to habeas corpus that no legislation could extinguish (*Boumediene* v. *Bush*).[9] The dynamic was striking: each time the Court determined that the president had overreached, the Congress – controlled by President Bush's party – rebuked the Court and tried to wrest the Guantánamo cases out of its hands, only to have the Court push back. What remained unclear was whether any of this had to do with the detainees rather than with competition among the branches of the US government.

Shortly before the 2004 oral arguments in *Hamdi* and *Rasul*, the government permitted Yaser Hamdi and Jose Padilla to meet with lawyers (after nearly two years of isolation); this concession was an unavailing public-relations effort to reassure the Court that the detention policy was not the cesspool of lawlessness that its opponents portrayed. After the *Hamdi* decision granted Yaser Hamdi review of his detention, the government in effect conceded that it never had a factual basis for holding him. Instead of submitting his case for review and fighting his release, the government sent Hamdi home to Saudi Arabia, on condition that he renounce his US citizenship.

After the 2004 decisions moved the Guantánamo detention facility back into the ambit of the courts, the other detainees were grudgingly given access to lawyers. The lawyers never succeeded in litigating any of them out of Guantánamo, but they did something else that was immensely valuable: they told the detainees' stories to the outside world. The black hole had become less black. Now, for the first time, news of torture and inhumane treatment filtered out of Guantánamo, and the world learned of the sleep deprivation, temperature manipulation, bombardment with loud offensive music, and force-feeding the detainees were subjected to.

The 2006 *Hamdan* decision not only granted Geneva protections to detainees, but it also found that the Bush military commissions did not meet Geneva's

[7] *Rasul* v. *Bush*, 542 U.S. 466 (2004). [8] *Hamdi* v. *Rumsfeld* 542 U.S. 547 (2004).
[9] *Boumediene* v. *Bush*, 553 U.S. 723 (2008).

minimal standard of "a regularly constituted court ... affording all the judicial guarantees which are recognized as indispensable by civilized peoples" and terminated them. (President Barack Obama subsequently resurrected them.) Since the 2008 *Boumediene* decision guaranteed habeas corpus to detainees as a matter of constitutional right, there have been regular habeas corpus hearings in the lower courts, which the detainees mostly won. And upon assuming office in 2009, President Obama banned torture and rescinded all the OLC's controversial interrogation opinions. Meanwhile, most Guantánamo inmates have been released to other countries.

And yet in reality not so much has changed. Even though detainees won most of their habeas corpus proceedings in lower courts, the District of Columbia (DC) Court of Appeals has reversed every decision that came before it. Indeed, one pugnacious judge on that court wrote in 2011 that

> candor obliges me to admit that one can not help but be conscious of the infinitely greater downside risk to our country, and its people, of an order releasing a detainee who is likely to return to terrorism... I doubt any of my colleagues will vote to grant a petition if he or she believes that it is somewhat likely that the petitioner is an al Qaeda adherent or an active supporter... [T]he whole process ... becomes a charade prompted by the Supreme Court's defiant if only theoretical assertion of judicial supremacy, sustained by posturing on the part of the Justice Department, and providing litigation exercise for the detainee bar.[10]

"Defiant" Supreme Court decisions granting detainee rights do not matter – if we fear the detainees, we will never let them go. Hard words indeed from a judge who is legally obligated to follow, not defy, Supreme Court decisions.

Even if a court does order release, the detainee must remain in Guantánamo if no other country will accept him, because the US courts held that they lack authority to order his release within the United States.[11] Habeas corpus turns out to be a right with no remedy. Just as significantly, the DC Court of Appeals found that even though the courts have jurisdiction over Guantánamo, that is for reasons unique to Guantánamo, which the US government has leased in perpetuity from Cuba, and over which it has legislative authority. Conspicuously, the courts lack jurisdiction over the US prison in Bagram, Afghanistan, where more than a thousand men are detained, including prisoners captured in other countries and shipped to Bagram.[12] Bagram became the new Guantánamo. In 2012 plans were made to turn Bagram over to the Afghan government. That leaves the question of whether another site will become the new Guantánamo.

Meanwhile, the US Congress has forbidden the President to close the old Guantánamo – not that closing Guantánamo would help the remaining

---

[10] *Esmail* v. *Obama*, 639 F.3d 1075, 1078 (D.C. Cir. 2011) (Silberman J. concurring).
[11] *Kiyemba* v. *Obama*, 605 F.3d 1046, 1048 (D.C. Cir. 2010).
[12] *Maqaleh* v. *Gates*, 605 F.3d 84 (D.C. Cir. 2010).

prisoners, who would be transferred to harsher conditions in a super-maximum-security prison within the United States. President Obama himself has continued the policy of holding detainees deemed dangerous in indefinite preventive detention, although he has instituted periodic review of whether they still pose danger.[13] As I write this preface in May 2013, more than 100 Guantánamo prisoners are engaged in a prolonged hunger strike to protest their endless incarceration.

In other words, the chapter remains as relevant today as when I wrote it.

One further update: the chapter notes that Sweden – a supposed bastion of pro-human-rights sentiment – rendered an Egyptian asylum-seeker back to Egypt, where he was reportedly tortured. After I wrote the chapter it emerged that it was not Sweden but the CIA who rendered Mohammed al-Zari (or Alzery) to Egypt, although the Swedish government cooperated by turning him over to the CIA.[14]

THE WAR ON TERRORISM AND THE END OF HUMAN RIGHTS

In the immediate aftermath of 9/11, President Bush stated that the perpetrators of the deed would be brought to justice. Soon afterwards, the president announced that the United States would engage in a war on terrorism. The first of these statements adopts the familiar language of criminal law and criminal justice. It treats the 9/11 attacks as horrific crimes – mass murders – and the government's mission as apprehending and punishing the surviving planners and conspirators for their roles in the crimes. The war on terrorism is a different proposition, however, and a different model of governmental action – not law but war. Most obviously, it dramatically broadens the scope of action, because now terrorists who had nothing to do with 9/11, even indirectly, have been earmarked as enemies. But that is only the beginning.

The hybrid war–law approach

The model of war offers much freer rein than that of law, and therein lies its appeal in the wake of 9/11. First, in war, but not in law, it is permissible to use lethal force on enemy troops regardless of their degree of personal involvement with the adversary. The conscripted cook is as legitimate a target as the enemy general. Second, in war, but not in law, "collateral damage," that is, foreseen but unintended killing of noncombatants, is permissible. (Police cannot blow up an apartment building full of people because a murderer is inside, but an air force

---

[13] Executive Order 13567, Mar. 7, 2011.
[14] *Mohammed Alzery* v. *Sweden*, CCPR/C/88/D/1416/2005, UN Human Rights Committee (HRC), Nov. 10, 2006 (www.unhcr.org/refworld/docid/47975afa21.html).

can bomb the building if it contains a military target.) Third, the requirements of evidence and proof are drastically weaker in war than in criminal justice. Soldiers do not need proof beyond a reasonable doubt, or even proof by a preponderance of evidence, that someone is an enemy soldier before firing on him or capturing and imprisoning him. They do not need proof at all, merely plausible intelligence. Thus, the US military remains regretful but unapologetic about its January 2002 attack on the Afghani town of Uruzgan, in which twenty-one innocent civilians were killed, based on faulty intelligence that they were Al Qaeda fighters.[15] Fourth, in war one can attack an enemy without concern over whether he has done anything. Legitimate targets are those who in the course of combat *might* harm us, not those who *have* harmed us. No doubt there are other significant differences as well. But the basic point should be clear: given Washington's mandate to eliminate the danger of future 9/11s, so far as humanly possible, the model of war offers important advantages over the model of law.

There are disadvantages as well. Most obviously, in war but not in law, fighting back is a *legitimate* response of the enemy. Second, because fighting back is legitimate, in war the enemy soldier deserves special regard once he is rendered harmless through injury or surrender. It is impermissible to punish him for his role in fighting the war. Nor can he be "unpleasant[ly]" interrogated after he is captured. The Third Geneva Convention follows the Hague Convention in requiring POWs to tell their captors their name, rank, and serial number. Beyond that, it provides: "Prisoners of war who refuse to answer [questions] may not be threatened, insulted, or exposed to unpleasant or disadvantageous treatment of any kind."[16] And, when the war concludes, the enemy soldier must be repatriated. Third, when nations fight a war, other nations may legitimately opt for neutrality.

Here, however, Washington has different ideas, designed to eliminate these tactical disadvantages in the traditional war model. Washington regards international terrorism not only as a military adversary but also as a criminal activity and criminal conspiracy. In the law model, criminals do not get to shoot back, and their acts of violence subject them to legitimate punishment. That is what we see in Washington's prosecution of the war on terrorism. Captured terrorists may be tried before military or civilian tribunals, and shooting back at Americans, including American troops, is a federal crime (for the statute under which John Walker Lindh was indicted punishes anyone who "outside the United States attempts to kill, or engages in a conspiracy to kill, a national of the United States" or "engages in physical violence with

---

[15] John Ward Anderson, "Afghans Falsely Held by U.S. Tried to Explain; Fighters Recount Unanswered Pleas, Beatings – and an Apology on Their Release," *Washington Post*, Mar. 26, 2002, p. A14. See also Susan B. Glasser, "Afghans Live and Die with U.S. Mistakes; Villagers Tell of Over 100 Casualties," *Washington Post*, Feb. 20, 2002, p. A1.

[16] Geneva Convention (III) Relative to the Treatment of Prisoners of War, 6 U.S.T. 3317, signed on Aug. 12, 1949, at Geneva, Article 17.

intent to cause serious bodily injury to a national of the United States; or with the result that serious bodily injury is caused to a national of the United States.").[17] Furthermore, the United States may rightly demand that other countries not be neutral about murder and terrorism. Unlike the war model, a nation may insist that those who are not with us in fighting murder and terror are against us, because by not joining our operations they are providing a safe haven for terrorists or their bank accounts. By selectively combining elements of the war model and elements of the law model, Washington is able to maximize its own ability to mobilize lethal force against terrorists while eliminating most traditional rights of a military adversary, as well as the rights of innocent bystanders caught in the crossfire.

A limbo of rightlessness

The legal status of Al Qaeda suspects imprisoned at the Guantánamo Bay Naval Base in Cuba is emblematic of this hybrid war–law approach to the threat of terrorism. In line with the war model, they lack the usual rights of criminal suspects – the presumption of innocence, the right to a hearing to determine guilt, the opportunity to prove that the authorities have grabbed the wrong man. But, in line with the law model, they are considered unlawful combatants, because they are not uniformed forces, and therefore they lack the rights of prisoners of war.[18] Initially, the American government declared that the Guantánamo Bay prisoners have no rights under the Geneva Conventions. In the face of international protests, Washington quickly backpedaled and announced that the Guantánamo Bay prisoners would indeed be treated in most respects as decently as POWs – but it also made clear that the prisoners have no right to such treatment. One conspicuous way in which they will *not*

---

[17] Count One of the Lindh indictment charges him with violating 18 U.S.C. §2332(b)(2), "Whoever outside the United States attempts to kill, or engages in a conspiracy to kill, a national of the United States shall in the case of a conspiracy by two or more persons to commit a killing that is murder as defined in section 1111(a) of this title, if one or more of such persons do any overt act to effect the object of the conspiracy, be fined under this title or imprisoned for any term of years or for life, or both so fined and so imprisoned." See *U.S.* v. *Lindh*, 212 F.Supp. 541, 547 (E.D. Va. 2002). Subsection (b)(1) imposes a sentence of 20 years (for attempts). Subsection (c) likewise criminalizes "engag[ing] in physical violence with intent to cause serious bodily injury to a national of the United States; or with the result that serious bodily injury is caused to a national of the United States."

[18] Lawful combatants are defined in the Hague Convention (IV) Respecting the Laws and Customs of War on Land, Annex to the Convention, 1 Bevans 631, signed on Oct. 18, 1907, at The Hague, Article 1. The definition requires that combatants "have a fixed distinctive emblem recognizable at a distance." Protocol I Additional to the Geneva Conventions of 1949, 1125 U.N.T.S. 3, adopted on June 8, 1977, at Geneva, Article 44(3), makes an important change in the Hague Convention, expanding the definition of combatants to include nonuniformed irregulars. However, the United States has not agreed to Protocol I.

be treated as decently as POWs is that they will not be given hearings to determine whether they are actually Al Qaeda or Taliban fighters or simply innocent bystanders swept up by mistake. Neither criminal suspects nor POWs, neither fish nor fowl, they inhabit a limbo of rightlessness. Secretary of Defense Rumsfeld's statement that the US may continue to detain them even if they are acquitted by a military tribunal dramatizes the point.

To see how extraordinary their status is, consider an analogy. Suppose that Washington declares a war on organized crime. Troops are dispatched to Sicily, and a number of Mafiosi are seized, brought to Guantánamo Bay, and imprisoned without a hearing for the indefinite future, maybe the rest of their lives. They are accused of no crimes, because their capture is based not on what they have done but on what they might do. After all, to become "made guys" they took oaths of obedience to commit criminal acts, if so ordered. Seizing them accords with the war model: they are enemy foot soldiers. But they are foot soldiers out of uniform; they lack a "fixed distinctive emblem," in the words of the Hague Convention (unless wrap-around sunglasses count as a fixed distinctive emblem). That makes them unlawful combatants, so they lack the rights of POWs. They may object that it is only a unilateral declaration by the American president that has turned them into combatants in the first place – he called it a war, they did not – and that, since they do not regard themselves as literal foot soldiers, it never occurred to them to wear a fixed, distinctive emblem. They have a point. It seems too easy for the president to divest anyone in the world of rights and liberty simply by announcing that the United States is at war with them and then declaring them unlawful combatants if they resist. But, in the hybrid war–law model, they protest in vain.

Consider another example. In January 2002, US forces in Bosnia seized five Algerians and a Yemeni suspected of Al Qaeda connections and took them to Guantánamo Bay. The six had been jailed in Bosnia, but a Bosnian court released them for lack of evidence, and the Bosnian Human Rights Chamber issued an injunction that four of them be allowed to remain in the country pending further legal proceedings. The Human Rights Chamber, ironically, was created under US auspices in the Dayton peace accords, and it was designed specifically to protect against treatment like this. Ruth Wedgwood, a well-known international law scholar and a member of the Council on Foreign Relations, defended the Bosnian seizure in war-model terms. "I think we would simply argue this was a matter of self-defense. One of the fundamental rules of military law is that you have a right ultimately to act in self-defense. And if these folks were actively plotting to blow up the U.S. embassy, they should be considered combatants and captured as combatants in a war."[19] Notice

---

[19] Interview with Melissa Block, National Public Radio (NPR), *All Things Considered*, Jan. 18, 2002.

that Professor Wedgwood argues in terms of what the men seized in Bosnia were *planning to do*, not what they *did*; notice as well that the decision of the Bosnian court that there was insufficient evidence does not matter. These are characteristics of the war model.

In addition, two American citizens alleged to be Al Qaeda operatives (Jose Padilla, a.k.a. Abdullah al Muhajir, and Yaser Esam Hamdi) have been held in American military prisons, with no crimes charged and no hearing. The president described Padilla as "a bad man" who aimed to build a nuclear "dirty" bomb and use it against America; and the Justice Department has classified both men as "enemy combatants" who may be held indefinitely.[20] Yet, as military law expert Gary Solis points out, "Until now, as used by the attorney general, the term 'enemy combatant' appeared nowhere in U.S. criminal law, international law or in the law of war."[21] The phrase comes from the 1942 Supreme Court case *Ex parte Quirin*, but all the court says there is that "an enemy combatant who without uniform comes secretly through the lines for the purpose of waging war by destruction of life or property" would "not . . . be entitled to the status of prisoner of war, but . . . be offenders against the law of war subject to trial and punishment by military tribunals."[22] For the court, in other words, the status of a person as a non-uniformed enemy combatant makes him a criminal rather than a warrior, and determines *where* he is tried (in a military, rather than a civilian, tribunal) but not *whether* he is tried. *Ex parte Quirin* presupposes that criminals are entitled to hearings: without a hearing how can suspects prove that the government made a mistake? *Quirin* embeds the concept of "enemy combatant" firmly in the law model. In the war model, by contrast, POWs may be detained without a hearing until hostilities are over. But POWs were captured either in uniform or in battle, and only their undoubted identity as enemy soldiers justifies such open-ended custody. Apparently, Hamdi and Padilla will get the worst of both models – open-ended custody with no trial, like POWs, but no certainty beyond the US government's say-so that they really are "bad men." This is the hybrid war–law model. It combines the *Quirin* category of "enemy combatant without uniform," used in the law model to justify a military trial, with the war model's practice of indefinite confinement with no trial at all.

The case for the hybrid approach

Is there any justification for the hybrid war–law model, which so drastically diminishes the rights of the enemy? An argument can be offered along the

---

[20] Both have challenged their detention in federal court, and both have lost. *Padilla* v. *Rumsfeld*, 256 F.Supp. 218 (S.D.N.Y. 2003); *Hamdi* v. *Rumsfeld*, 337 F.3d 335 (4th Cir. 2003).

[21] Gary Solis, "Even a 'Bad Man' Has Rights," *Washington Post*, June 25, 2002, p. A19.

[22] *Ex parte Quirin*, 317 U.S. 1, 31 (1942).

following lines. In ordinary cases of war among states, enemy soldiers may well be morally and politically innocent. Many of them are conscripts, and those who are not do not necessarily endorse the state policies they are fighting to defend. But enemy soldiers in the war on terrorism are, by definition, those who have embarked on a path of terrorism. They are neither morally nor politically innocent. Their sworn aim – "Death to America!" – is to create more 9/11s. In this respect, they are much more akin to criminal conspirators than to conscript soldiers. Terrorists will fight as soldiers when they must, and metamorphose into mass murderers when they can.

Furthermore, suicide terrorists pose a special, unique danger. Ordinary criminals do not target innocent bystanders. They may be willing to kill them if necessary, but bystanders enjoy at least some measure of security because they are not primary targets. Not so with terrorists, who aim to kill as many innocent people as possible. Likewise, innocent bystanders are protected from ordinary criminals by whatever deterrent force the threat of punishment and the risk of getting killed in the act of committing a crime offer. For a suicide bomber, neither of these threats is a deterrent at all – after all, for the suicide bomber one of the hallmarks of a *successful* operation is that he winds up dead at day's end. Given the unique and heightened danger that suicide terrorists pose, a stronger response that grants potential terrorists fewer rights may be justified. Add to this the danger that terrorists may come to possess weapons of mass destruction, including nuclear devices in suitcases. Under circumstances of such dire menace, it is appropriate to treat them as though they embody the most dangerous aspects of both warriors and criminals. That is the basis of the hybrid war–law model.

The case against expediency

The argument against the hybrid war–law model is equally clear. The United States has simply chosen the bits of the law model and the bits of the war model that are most convenient for American interests, and ignored the rest. The model abolishes the rights of potential enemies (and their innocent shields) by fiat – not for reasons of moral or legal principle, but solely because the United States does not want them to have rights. The more rights they have, the more risk they pose. But Americans' urgent desire to minimize our risks does not make other people's rights disappear. Calling our policy a war on terrorism obscures this point.

The theoretical basis of the objection is that the law model and the war model each come as a package, with a kind of intellectual integrity. The law model grows out of relationships within states, while the war model arises from relationships between states. The law model imputes a ground-level community of values to those subject to the law – paradigmatically, citizens of a state, but also visitors and foreigners who choose to engage in conduct that affects a state. Only because law imputes shared basic values to the community can a state condemn the conduct of criminals and inflict punishment on them. Criminals deserve condemnation and punishment because their conduct violates norms that we are entitled to count on their sharing. But, for the same reason – the imputed community of values – those subject to the law ordinarily enjoy a presumption of innocence and an expectation of safety. The government cannot simply grab them and confine them without making sure they have broken the law, nor can it condemn them without due process for ensuring that it has the right person, nor can it knowingly place bystanders in mortal peril in the course of fighting crime. They are our fellows, and the community should protect them just as it protects us. The same imputed community of values that justifies condemnation and punishment creates rights to due care and due process.

War is different. War is the ultimate acknowledgment that human beings do not live in a single community with shared norms. If their norms conflict enough, communities pose a physical danger to each other, and nothing can safeguard a community against its enemies except force of arms. That makes enemy soldiers legitimate targets; but it makes our soldiers legitimate targets as well, and, once the enemy no longer poses a danger, he should be immune from punishment, because if he has fought cleanly he has violated no norms that we are entitled to presume he honors. Our norms are, after all, *our* norms, not his.

Because the law model and war model come as conceptual packages, it is unprincipled to wrench them apart and recombine them simply because it is in America's interest to do so. To declare that Americans can fight enemies with the latitude of warriors, but if the enemies fight back they are not warriors but criminals, amounts to a kind of heads-I-win-tails-you-lose international morality in which whatever it takes to reduce American risk, no matter what the cost to others, turns out to be justified. This, in brief, is the criticism of the hybrid war–law model.

To be sure, the law model could be made to incorporate the war model merely by rewriting a handful of statutes. Congress could enact laws permitting imprisonment or execution of persons who pose a significant threat of terrorism whether or not they have already done anything wrong. The standard of evidence could be set low and the requirement of a hearing eliminated. Finally, Congress could authorize the use of lethal force against terrorists regardless of the danger to innocent bystanders, and it could immunize officials from lawsuits or prosecution by victims of collateral damage. Such statutes would violate the Constitution, but the Constitution could be amended to incorporate antiterrorist exceptions to the Fourth, Fifth, and Sixth Amendments. In the end, we would have a system of law that captures all the essential features of the war model.

It would, however, be a system that imprisons people for their intentions rather than their actions, and that offers the innocent few protections against mistaken detention or inadvertent death through collateral damage. Gone are the principles that people should never be punished for their thoughts, only for their deeds, and that innocent people must be protected rather than injured by their own government. In that sense, at any rate, repackaging war as law seems merely cosmetic, because it replaces the ideal of law as a protector of human rights with the more problematic goal of protecting some innocent people by sacrificing others. The hypothetical legislation incorporates war into law only by making law look more like war. It no longer resembles law as Americans generally understand it.

The threat to international human rights

In the war on terrorism, what becomes of international human rights? It seems beyond dispute that the war model poses a threat to international human rights, because honoring human rights to the same extent as in peacetime is neither practically possible nor theoretically required during war. Combatants are legitimate targets; noncombatants maimed by accident or mistake are regarded as collateral damage rather than victims of atrocities; cases of mistaken identity get killed or confined without a hearing because combat conditions preclude due process. To be sure, the laws of war specify minimum human rights, but these are far less robust than rights in peacetime – and the hybrid war–law model reduces this schedule of rights even further by classifying the enemy as unlawful combatants.

One striking example of the erosion of human rights in the fight against terror is tolerance of torture. It should be recalled that a 1995 Al Qaeda plot to bomb eleven US airliners was thwarted by information tortured out of a Pakistani suspect by the Philippine police – an eerie, real-life version of the familiar philosophical thought-experiment.[23] The *Washington Post* reports that since 9/11 the United States has engaged in the summary transfer of dozens of terrorism suspects to countries where they will be interrogated under torture.[24] In the words of one American official, "We don't kick the [expletive] out of them. We send them to other countries so they can kick the [expletive] out of them."[25] But it is not just the United States that has proven

[23] Doug Struck *et al.*, "Borderless Network of Terror; Bin Laden Followers Reach Across Globe," *Washington Post*, Sept. 23, 2001, p. A1 ("'For weeks, agents hit him with a chair and a long piece of wood, forced water into his mouth, and crushed lighted cigarettes into his private parts,' wrote journalists Marites Vitug and Glenda Gloria in 'Under the Crescent Moon,' an acclaimed book on Abu Sayyaf. 'His ribs were almost totally broken and his captors were surprised he survived.'").

[24] Rajiv Chandrasakaran and Peter Finn, "U.S. Behind Secret Transfer of Terror Suspects," *Washington Post*, Mar. 11, 2002, pp. A1, A15.

[25] Dana Priest and Barton Gelman, "U.S. Decries Abuse But Defends Interrogations; 'Stress and Duress' Tactics Used on Terrorism Suspects Held in Secret Overseas Facilities," *Washington Post*, Dec. 26, 2002, p. A1. The same article, however, details American

willing to tolerate torture for security reasons. In December 2002, the Swedish government snatched a suspected Islamic extremist to whom it had previously granted political asylum, and the same day had him transferred to Egypt, where Amnesty International reported that he had been tortured to the point where he walks only with difficulty. Returning him to Egypt violates European human rights law; apparently, the reason for returning him the same day as his arrest was simply to prevent his wife from taking timely legal action.[26] Sweden is not, to say the least, a traditionally hard-line nation on human rights issues. None of this international transportation is lawful – indeed, it violates international treaty obligations under the Torture Convention that in the United States have constitutional status as "supreme Law of the Land" – but that may not matter under the war model, in which even constitutional rights may be abrogated.[27] As one American official put it, "There was a before 9/11, and there was an after 9/11. After 9/11 the gloves come off."[28] In the words of another official, "If you don't violate someone's human rights some of the time, you probably aren't doing your job."[29]

It is natural to suggest that this suspension of human rights is an exceptional emergency measure to deal with an unprecedented threat. This naturally raises the question of how long human rights will remain suspended. When will the war be over?

Here, the chief problem is that the war on terrorism is not like any other kind of war. The enemy, terrorism, is not a territorial state or nation or government. There is no opposite number to negotiate with. There is no one on the other side to call a truce or declare a cease-fire, no one among the enemy authorized to surrender. In traditional wars among states, the war aim is,

interrogation techniques that are very harsh: prisoners "are held in awkward, painful positions and deprived of sleep with a 24-hour bombardment of lights."

[26] Peter Finn, "Europeans Tossing Terror Suspects Out the Door," *Washington Post*, Jan. 29, 2002, p. A1; Anthony Shadid, "Fighting Terror / Atmosphere in Europe, Military Campaign / Asylum Bids; in Shift, Sweden Extradites Militants to Egypt," *Boston Globe*, Dec. 31, 2001. On the violation of European human rights law, see *Chahal* v. *United Kingdom* (1997), 23 E.H.R.R. 413.

[27] Article 3(1) of the Torture Convention provides that "No State Party shall expel, return ('*refouler*') or extradite a person to another State where there are substantial grounds for believing that he would be in danger of being subjected to torture." Article 2(2) cautions that "No exceptional circumstances whatsoever, whether a state of war or a threat of war, internal political instability or any other public emergency, may be invoked as a justification of torture." But no parallel caution is incorporated into Article 3(1)'s non-*refoulement* rule, and a lawyer might well argue that its absence implies that the rule may be abrogated during war or similar public emergency. Convention against Torture and Other Cruel, Inhuman or Degrading Treatment or Punishment, 1465 U.N.T.S. 85. Ratified by the United States, Oct. 2, 1994. Entered into force for the United States, Nov. 20, 1994. Article VI of the US Constitution provides that treaties are the "supreme Law of the Land."

[28] Priest and Gellman, "U.S. Decries Abuse," note 25 above.   [29] *Ibid.*

as Clausewitz argued, to impose one state's political will on another's. The *aim* of the war is not to kill the enemy – killing the enemy is the *means* used to achieve the real end, which is to force capitulation. In the war on terrorism, no capitulation is possible. That means that the real aim of the war is, quite simply, to kill or capture all of the terrorists – to keep on killing and killing, capturing and capturing, until they are all gone.

Of course, no one expects that terrorism will ever disappear completely. Everyone understands that new anti-American extremists, new terrorists, will always arise and always be available for recruitment and deployment. Everyone understands that even if Al Qaeda is destroyed or decapitated, other groups, with other leaders, will arise in its place. It follows, then, that the war on terrorism will be a permanent war, at least until the United States decides to abandon it. The war has no natural resting point, no moment of victory or finality. It requires a mission of killing and capturing, in territories all over the globe, that will go on in perpetuity. It follows as well that the suspension of human rights implicit in the hybrid war–law model is not temporary but permanent.

Perhaps with this fear in mind, Congressional authorization of President Bush's military campaign limits its scope to those responsible for 9/11. But the war on terrorism has taken on a life of its own that makes the Congressional authorization little more than a pointless formality. (In any case, the White House position is that while the Congressional resolution was welcome, the president did not need it to act.) Because of the threat of nuclear or biological terror, the American leadership launched a war on Iraq regardless of whether Iraq was implicated in 9/11; and the president's yoking of Iraq, Iran, and North Korea into a single "axis of evil" because they back terror suggests that the war on terrorism might eventually encompass these nations as well. Russia invokes the American war on terrorism to justify its attacks on Chechin rebels, and China uses it to deflect criticisms of its campaign against Uighur separatists. So too, Israeli Prime Minister Sharon repeatedly links military actions against Palestinian insurgents to the American war on terrorism. "War on terrorism" is not the code name of a discrete, neatly boxed American operation – it has become a model of politics, a worldview with its own premises and consequences. As I have argued, it includes a new model of state action, the hybrid war–law model, which depresses human rights from their peacetime standard to the wartime standard, and indeed even further. So long as it continues, the war on terrorism means the end of human rights, at least for those near enough to be touched by the fire of battle.

Eight fallacies about liberty and security

Preface

This chapter originated as a speech given at the Thomas J. Dodd Center at the University of Connecticut on the third anniversary of 9/11. It emphasizes civil liberties within the United States, but also argues against the disastrous moral fallacy of supposing that trade-offs of liberty and security are acceptable when it is a matter of one's own security and someone else's rights; that is no trade-off. The chapter requires only a few minor updates, plus one larger elaboration of a short argument advanced in the chapter.

The updates

This chapter warns about how easy it is for relatively trivial conduct to result in lengthy prison sentences under the draconian statutes defining material support for terrorism (see footnote 4). This has been amply born out in numerous cases of young men with jihadist ambitions but no evident skills or concrete plans who were nonetheless convicted of material support or conspiracy. For example, two youthful cousins from Chicago hoped to become jihadis. They traveled to Egypt, hoping to receive training – what kind of training, or from whom, was never clear. After returning to the United States a month later, they planned to learn the use of firearms, discussed the possibility of taking an online course in gunsmithing, and researched the purchase of weapons. They never made any concrete terrorist plans, however, and according to their indictment, one of them told an unnamed person that they needed five more years to complete their preparations for violent jihad.[1] The indictment does not allege that they ever met with any terrorist group anywhere. They nevertheless pled guilty to conspiring to provide material support for terrorism.[2]

The main text of this chapter was first published in 2005 – see Acknowledgments.

[1] *United States* v. *Ahmed*, Indictment, at 9 (www.investigativeproject.org/documents/case_docs/760.pdf).

[2] Press Release, US Department of Justice, "Chicago Cousins Plead Guilty to Conspiracy to Provide Material Support for Terrorism," Jan. 15, 2009 (www.justice.gov/opa/pr/2009/January/09-nsd-041.html).

In another prominent case, a group of young men drew long sentences for playing paintball in Virginia to prepare for jihad in Afghanistan.[3]

The chapter also expresses concerns about extensive electronic surveillance and data mining, the use of which subsequently became a heated issue in US politics. As long ago as 2005 it emerged that the US government had engaged in extensive warrantless and illegal electronic surveillance (justified on the theory that Congress's authorization in 2001 to use military force against Al Qaeda superseded the prior law against electronic surveillance). Telecommunications companies had cooperated with the government; lawsuits against the companies failed because the government invoked the state secrets defense to stop them. Eventually, the US Congress legalized the surveillance program. The issue made headlines again in 2013 after the whistleblower Edward Snowden revealed the vast extent of data mining and cooperation between the National Security Agency (NSA) and major internet companies including Google, Apple, YouTube, Facebook, Apple, and Skype. It appears that if anything, the chapter greatly underestimated the growth of the surveillance state. The chapter warns about the possibility that rogue government employees might misuse the surveillance apparatus – and in real life, the NSA's Inspector General has documented a dozen cases of employees abusing the surveillance system to spy on present and former lovers – cases that led the NSA to open a file labeled "LOVEINT" for such cases.[4] To be sure, this is a trivially small number of cases out of a vast number of NSA operations, and the NSA reportedly takes great care to identify and purge from its systems information that it is legally prohibited from acquiring – namely, e-mail messages and telephone calls from US nationals within the United States. By definition, though, even a conscientious agency cannot know how many undetected mistakes it has made. More importantly, its governing law is designed to protect only Americans from intrusive surveillance, and the consequences of mistaken identification of foreign terrorist threats can be fatal.

The chapter warns against a "fallacy of small numbers" – the fallacy of overestimating both the likelihood of terrorist threats and the efficacy of rights restrictions in preventing them. An interesting quantitative study has confirmed this point. John Mueller and Mark Stewart estimate, based on "extensive datasets on terrorism that have been generated over the last decades," that the annual risk of an American dying in a terrorist attack is about one in 3.5 million. By way of comparison, the risk of becoming a homicide victim is one in 8,000,

---

[3] *United States* v. *Khan*, 309 F. Supp. 2d 789 (E.D. Va. 2004).

[4] Letter from Dr. George Ellard, NSA Inspector General, to Sen. Charles E. Grassley, Sept. 11, 2013 (www.nsa.gov/public_info/press_room/2013/grassley_letter.pdf). LOVEINT was first reported in the media in Siobhan Gorman, "NSA Officers Spy on Love Interests," *Washington Wire*, Aug. 23, 2013 (http://blogs.wsj.com/washwire/2013/08/23/nsa-officers-sometimes-spy-on-love-interests/). "LOVEINT" is, of course, a little joke, modeled on SIGINT (signals intelligence) and HUMINT (human intelligence).

and the risk of dying from cancer is one in 500.[5] The authors estimate that current US antiterrorism measures would be cost-effective only if they thwarted a large-scale terrorist attack nearly every day.[6]

The chapter discusses the case of Zacarias Moussaoui, accused of participating in the 9/11 plot. At the time of writing, Moussaoui had not yet been tried, and the chapter does not take a position on his guilt. In 2006, Moussaoui was convicted of conspiracy charges and sentenced to life in prison without parole.

ELABORATING THE "MILITARIZATION OF CIVILIAN LIFE" FALLACY

One argument in this chapter requires more extensive treatment. The chapter warns briefly against what I label "the fallacy of the militarization of civilian life." This is the view that the legislature and the judiciary must, as a matter of institutional competence, defer to the superior military competence of the executive acting as military commander in chief. According to this view, even if the president is not exercising a distinctively military function, anything the president claims is necessary for fighting terrorism falls under his war powers, and other branches of government must defer to the commander in chief's decision. For example, deciding on the basis of evidence whether someone arrested within the United States is or is not a detainable enemy combatant seems more like a judicial function than a military function; but President Bush argued that his classification of Jose Padilla (arrested in Chicago) as an enemy combatant deserved near-total deference. That is because of the commander in chief's superior institutional competence to make military decisions.

The fallacy, of course, is that a civilian commander in chief has no obvious military competence. Constitutionally, the reason for making a civilian the commander in chief of the armed forces seems plainly to be securing civilian control of the military, not creating a "fighting president" on the model of Napoleon or Frederick the Great. When I wrote this chapter, I was aware that this sketchy argument needed more historical support than I was able to provide. Over the next several years, I set out to examine the military and constitutional history of the commander-in-chief power in detail; the results were published in a lengthy law review article.[7] I have omitted the article from this book because much of it deals with details of military history, US constitutional history, and the theory of civilian–military relations that venture away from my main themes. But the argument turns out to have great importance

---

[5] John Mueller and Mark G. Stewart, "The Terrorism Delusion: America's Overwrought Response to September 11," *International Security*, 37 (2012), 81–110, at 95–6.
[6] *Ibid.*, p. 107.
[7] David Luban, "On the Commander-in-Chief Power," *Southern California Law Review*, 477 (2008), 81.

for the torture debate – indeed, far greater importance than I realized when I wrote it – and I will therefore provide an overview here.

The connection with the torture debate is that – unbeknownst to the public at the time I wrote this chapter – the Bybee–Yoo torture memo invokes the commander-in-chief power to argue that laws against torture cannot bind the president. The argument came to be called the *commander-in-chief override*. According to the override argument, the separation of powers among executive, legislative, and judicial branches entails that when the president acts as military commander in chief, his decisions override statutes, including the statute prohibiting torture. That is because statutes are made and elaborated by the other branches. If those statutes could limit the commander in chief, the other branches would in effect be impinging on war powers that, by constitutional design and tradition, are solely and wholly the president's. An earlier secret memo had also asserted the commander in chief's "plenary constitutional power to take such military actions as he deems necessary and appropriate."[8]

In other words, the general arguments for a broad commander-in-chief power that the Bush administration had been raising for more than two years in connection with Guantánamo and detention were used to authorize torture. To be sure, the Bybee–Yoo memo argued that the US interrogation methods are not torture, but they also argued in the alternative that the torture statute could not bind the president.

My historical investigations confirmed the basic claims about the commander-in-chief power advanced in capsule form in the present chapter. The article made a constitutional claim and a theoretical claim. The constitutional claim is that the commander-in-chief power is far more limited than the override argument suggests. The president's commander-in-chief authority is narrowly military, and furthermore it is limited by law – just the opposite of the override theory's principal assertion. The argument required two steps, one based on the Constitution's original meaning and the other demonstrating that the framers' concerns remain alive today. In the founding era, federalists and antifederalists alike wished to limit the president's military powers. They worried that a president commanding a standing army might launch an anti-republican coup and become a Caesar or a Cromwell (as writers of that period, even defenders of a strong presidency like Alexander Hamilton, liked to put it). Furthermore, the president might be tempted to launch military adventures for the sake of his own personal glory, as both John Adams and James Madison warned. The history, text, and structure of the Constitution point to a strong

---

[8] Memorandum from John C. Yoo to Timothy Flanigan, Deputy Counsel to the President (Sept. 25, 2001 (www.justice.gov/olc/2001/milit-ops-terrorists.pdf)). The memo added that neither the War Powers Act nor Congress' authorization to use military force can "place any limits on the President's determinations as to any terrorist threat, the amount of military force to be used in response, or the method, timing, and nature of the response. These decisions, under our Constitution, are for the President alone to make."

impulse to limit the commander in chief's power, and they offer no support for the claim that the framers meant the commander-in-chief power to override the very laws that presidents are constitutionally required to execute faithfully.

One might fear that originalist fears about a standing army are a poor way to understand the powers of the commander in chief of a vast modern military. As Samuel Huntington warned in *The Soldier and the State*, the great modern treatise on civilian–military relations, "The activities of the Praetorian Guard offer few useful lessons for civilian control: the problem in the modern state is not armed revolt but the relation of the expert to the politician."[9] Remarkably, though, Huntington's own conclusion was not far from the framers': on grounds of institutional competence, genuinely military decisions should be left to the experts, not the politicians. US civilian–military relations are governed by a moral compact dating back to the Revolutionary War, under which the military abstains from politics and leaves political decision-making to the political leaders, while for its part the civilian leadership generally defers to the military on military matters, refrains from politicizing the military, and exercises great prudence and caution in authorizing the use of force. The commander-in-chief override threatens this moral compact, and in that way the framers' concerns about commander-in-chief overreach remain our concerns today. Nor, of course, is the problem of military adventurism anachronistic, as the Iraq War dramatically illustrated.

Indeed, to fully understand the context of the Bush administration's aggressive assertion of the commander-in-chief authority, it is important to note the astounding military hubris among the civilian leadership in the immediate aftermath of the 2003 invasion of Iraq. That "mission accomplished" moment marked the apogee of military bravado in the White House and the Pentagon. Nothing can convey the civilians' sense of military omnipotence better than a short memo written by Secretary of Defense Donald Rumsfeld to Douglas Feith, his Undersecretary of Defense for Policy, a few days after the capture of Baghdad and Basra. I quote it in its entirety:

> We need more coercive diplomacy with respect to Syria and Libya, and we need it fast. If they mess up Iraq, it will delay bringing our troops home.
>
> We also need to solve the Pakistan problem.
>
> And Korea doesn't seem to be going well.
>
> Are you coming up with proposals for me to send around?
>
> Thanks.[10]

[9] Samuel P. Huntington, *The Soldier and the State: The Theory and Politics of Civil–Military Relations* (Cambridge, MA: Harvard University Press: 1957), p. 20.

[10] Memo from Donald Rumsfeld to Doug Feith, "Issues w/Various Countries," Apr. 7, 2003, Rumsfeld Library (http://library.rumsfeld.com/doclib/sp/1686/2003-04-07%20to%20Doug%20Feith%20re%20Issues%20with%20Various%20Countries.pdf#search=%22Libya%22).

Soon enough, the US occupation turned into an Iraqi nightmare, in large part because the civilian leadership was in over its head. My article drew repeatedly on the tragedy of Iraq to illustrate the fallacy of supposing that civilian command of the military rests on institutional competence rather than checks and balances.

I set this constitutional history in a larger context of military history to show that the model of a fighting president of unbounded powers, modeled on the warrior kings of heroic and medieval times, was already nearly obsolete by the eighteenth century. By that time, generals commanded from the rear, not the front, and monarchs almost never played the role of generals; Frederick the Great and Napoleon were the last of the monarch-generals, and no American president (including George Washington) has ever commanded troops in battle during his term of office. Modern democratic nation states place different demands on their leaders.

Along with these constitutional and historical arguments, I offered a political theory of the commander-in-chief power. It is that limiting the commander-in-chief power is the way a modern constitutional democracy like the United States uses separation-of-powers devices to address an age-old problem of politics: domesticating the warrior. The point of vesting commander-in-chief authority in a civilian president is to ensure civilian control of the military, not to create a warrior-president. In a scheme of checks and balances, the commander-in-chief power generates the countervailing need to control the civilian president, and getting this balance right preoccupied the framers.

The problem of domesticating warriors in a civilian society has always been with us. It was a theme of ancient writers going back to Plato, Homer, and the Hebrew Bible, and indeed it was a central theme of one of the oldest surviving works of literature, the *Gilgamesh* epic (and therefore I label it the "Gilgamesh problem"); it was a problem the Roman republic wrestled with, and eventually failed to solve after Caesar crossed the Rubicon.

The Gilgamesh problem arises wherever we find the age-old institution of *fused dominion*: the fusion of supreme military authority with supreme political authority. Much of human history has been dominated by warrior-kings, the paradigm form of fused dominion; its modern perversion is the military dictatorship. History has seen two very different models of fused dominion. One is a *consolidationist* model, which aimed to fuse military and political supremacy because martial prowess was what societies wanted and needed from their kings. The other is a *separationist* model, in which supreme military command is delegated to a civilian as a separation-of-powers device to rein in militaries and prevent them from seizing control of civil society.

In the eyes of some veteran members of the Bush administration, asserting strong executive power was an essential corrective to a dangerous weakening of the presidency that went back to the 1970s. For them, the crisis of 9/11 provided an opportunity to rectify the structure of government, and bring the executive agencies under the strong arm of the "unitary executive." This program did not succeed; indeed, in the last days of the Bush administration the Justice Department retracted some of its most aggressive assertions of executive power.[11]

The Obama administration does not champion the unitary executive theory. But that does not mean the Obama administration has ceded executive power, and some say that Obama has thrown the weight of the presidency around at least as much as his predecessor.

To complete the update, however, it is important to realize that Obama has been very reluctant to invoke the commander-in-chief power. Even when Obama brought the United States into the 2011 Libyan intervention, over legal objections from many members of Congress, his administration did not base its refusal to comply with the terms of the War Powers Act on the commander-in-chief authority. It went on record accepting the power of Congress to limit military activities (even while rejecting Congressional objections to the Libyan intervention with dubious arguments).[12] The closest Obama has come to a broad assertion of his commander-in-chief authority happened during the 2013 Syria crisis, when he declared that as commander in chief, he believed that a military strike against Syria was advisable. In the face of political opposition, he turned to Congress for authorization; however, in doing so, Obama said, "I believe I have the authority to carry out this military action without specific congressional authorization."[13] Even this statement comes nowhere near asserting a commander-in-chief override, and it may have reflected only an interpretation of the War Powers Act, not the commander-in-chief power.[14]

To cite another contrast, Obama has made very little use of signing statements attached to legislation objecting to parts of it – one of President Bush's favorite devices to press his commander-in-chief prerogatives, by asserting that the legislation would infringe on his constitutional authority as commander in chief. In his first term in office, Obama issued only twenty signing

---

[11] Steven G. Bradbury, "Memorandum for the Files: Re: Status of Certain OLC Opinions Issued in the Aftermath of the Terrorist Attacks of September 11, 2001 (www.justice.gov/olc/docs/memostatusolcopinions01152009.pdf).

[12] The Obama administration argued that the Libya intervention was not an armed conflict because no American forces would be in danger. Libya and War Powers, Hearing Before the Senate Foreign Relations Committee, S. Hrg. 112–89, 112th Congress, 1st session (June 28, 2011), at pp. 8–9, 12, 18, 22 (testimony of Harold Hongju Koh, State Department Legal Adviser) (www.fas.org/irp/congress/2011_hr/libya.pdf).

[13] Statement of the president on Syria, Aug. 31, 2013 (www.whitehouse.gov/the-press-office/2013/08/31/statement-president-syria).

[14] For the best discussion of approaches to the unilateral presidential decision to use force, see Marty Lederman, "The Constitution, the Charter, and Their Intersection," part i, Opinio Juris blog, Sept. 1, 2013 (http://opiniojuris.org/2013/09/01/syria-insta-symposium-marty-lederman-part-constitution-charter-intersection/).

statements, as compared with Bush's 110 in the same amount of time.[15] Only once has Obama objected that Congress was interfering with his commander-in-chief powers, and that was on a minor issue.[16]

That does not mean the issue is gone. There is a difference between not relying on the commander-in-chief power and explicitly limiting it. The Obama administration has not done the latter, but it came close. In a 2013 speech, Obama said, "Our laws constrain the power of the President, even during wartime, and I have taken an oath to defend the Constitution of the United States."[17] This unremarkable sentence requires a bit of decoding to show how radically it repudiates the theories of the Bush administration. The US Constitution specifies that the president must "take care that the laws be faithfully executed"; it also specifies that the president must swear an oath to "preserve, protect and defend the Constitution of the United States."[18] On their surface, the Take Care Clause and the Oath Clause reinforce and harmonize with each other. However, during the Bush years, some conservative scholars argued that the Oath Clause means that the president must do whatever it takes to protect the country, whether or not it is legal. They pointed out that great US presidents, including Jackson and Lincoln, had appealed to the Oath Clause for just such purposes – in Jackson's case, by not enforcing a statute, and in Lincoln's, by suspending habeas corpus.[19] Lincoln famously asked the rhetorical question, "[A]re all the laws *but one*, to go unexecuted, and the government itself go to pieces, lest that one be violated?"[20] He was responding to the criticism "that one who is sworn to 'take care that the laws be faithfully executed,' should not himself violate them."[21] Obama's brief sentence, declaring that it is precisely his oath that places him under legal constraints even in wartime when he is exercising his

---

[15] Signing statements for both are listed on the website Presidential Signing Statements 2001–Present (www.coherentbabble.com/listBHOall.htm).

[16] Barack Obama, "Statement on Signing the National Defense Authorization Act for Fiscal Year 2013," Jan. 2, 2013, at p. 1 (www.whitehouse.gov/the-press-office/2013/01/03/statement-president-hr-4310). The issue was the president's authority to transfer some third-country detainees from Parwan, Afghanistan. Notably, Obama did not invoke the commander-in-chief authority on the weightier issues of his authority to deal with Guantánamo.

[17] Barack Obama, "The Future of Our Fight Against Terrorism," speech at the National Defense University, May 23, 2013 (www.whitehouse.gov/the-press-office/2013/05/23/remarks-president-barack-obama).

[18] The Take Care Clause is in Article ii, section 3 of the Constitution, and the Oath Clause is in Article II, section 8.

[19] James D. Richardson, Ed., *A Compilation of the Messages and Papers of the Presidents*, vol. ii, p. 576 (Washington, DC: Government Printing Office, 1897); vol. vi, p. 25.

[20] President Abraham Lincoln, July 4th Message to Congress (July 4, 1861) (http://millercenter.org/scripps/archive/speeches).

[21] *Ibid.*

commander-in-chief powers, seems clearly to reject the "Lincolnian" argument
for presidential emergency powers unconstrained by law.

EIGHT FALLACIES ABOUT LIBERTY AND SECURITY

We often hear it said that in times of danger we confront difficult trade-offs
between national security and civil liberties, or between national security and
human rights. We nod our heads, and reflect that tough times call for tough
measures. An American official, commenting on the harsh and even brutal
techniques that US interrogators use on suspected terrorists, put it bluntly.
"If you don't violate someone's human rights some of the time, you probably
aren't doing your job."[22] While some people might find such talk appalling,
others find it realistic, tough-minded, and oddly reassuring. We face terrible
threats posed by ruthless international terrorists who have already proven
themselves eager for mass murder – and who may well gain access to weapons
of apocalyptic power. Confronted with these threats, excessive concern with
human rights and civil liberties seems legalistic and, however well-meaning it
is, misguided. Trade-offs are inevitable, and the only important question then
becomes where to draw the line. How much liberty should be sacrificed in the
name of security? How many human rights can we afford to respect?

The constitutional scholar John Hart Ely once remarked that no answer is
what the wrong question begets.[23] In this chapter, I argue that the questions in the
last paragraph are the wrong ones to ask; unfortunately, it is not non-answers
they beget, but wrong answers. The whole conversation about "trade-offs"
conceals persistent fallacies, and once we take care to eliminate the fallacies, the
questions themselves become far less obvious, and in certain ways less urgent.

Fallacy one: the Mel Brooks fallacy

First, the supposed "trade-off" between security and rights is too easy as long as
it's a trade-off of your rights for my security.[24] Mel Brooks once said that
tragedy is when I break a fingernail, and comedy is when you fall down a
manhole and die. Proponents of the so-called trade-off win specious support by
building in an implicit Mel Brooks theory of rights: do unto the rights of others

---

[22] Dana Priest and Barton Gellman, "U.S. Decries Abuse But Defends Interrogations; 'Stress and Duress' Tactics Used on Terrorism Suspects Held in Secret Overseas Facilities," *Washington Post*, p. A1. Another official explained, "There was a before 9/11, and there was an after 9/11. After 9/11 the gloves come off."

[23] John Hart Ely, *Democracy and Distrust: A Theory of Judicial Review* (Cambridge, MA: Harvard University Press, 1980), p. 72.

[24] This is one of the main themes of David Cole's important book, *Enemy Aliens: Double Standards and Constitutional Freedoms in the War on Terrorism* (New York: New Press, 2003).

whatever it takes to make me feel more secure. This is no real trade-off. The trade-off question becomes genuine only when we pose it in its legitimate form: how many of *your own* rights are you willing to sacrifice for added security?

Even in this form, the question is deceptively sloppy. As a respectable, middle-aged, native-born, white, tenured professor who leads a dull life, I know the odds are slender that I will ever need to invoke the right against self-incrimination or the right to a speedy, public trial, let alone the right not to be shipped off to the Jordanian police for interrogation. (Knock on wood.) So I am likely to undervalue these rights. In my own mind, I unconsciously classify them as OPR – other people's rights. Illicitly, I have returned to the Mel Brooks theory. So long as the government targets only Muslims and foreigners, young men, and aging charismatic clerics, paring back on the rights of the accused is no tragedy, in the Mel Brooks sense of tragedy.

Perhaps the question becomes more vivid if we respectable folks imagine that our own children might someday flirt with a radical group that runs afoul of the law.[25] Even then, however, it is easy to dismiss the hypotheticals because they sound too far-fetched to hit home. Psychologically, it is very difficult to weigh the importance of rights and civil liberties without assuming, consciously or not, the Mel Brooks theory that rights I and my loved ones are unlikely to need are less important than my physical security. But avoiding the Mel Brooks theory is what we must do. Conceptually, we should pose the question using John Rawls' device of an imaginary "veil of ignorance" that at the moment of choice cloaks us from all knowledge of who we are. Suppose that at the moment of choosing your security/rights package, you have no knowledge of whether, when the veil of ignorance falls away, you will find yourself a young man of Middle Eastern birth, detained indefinitely without access to counsel or a hearing of any kind, even though you are not a terrorist and are guilty of nothing but minor visa violations. In that case, you are likely to want certain rock-bottom protections to hedge

---

[25] If your college student offspring is careless enough to donate money or even a cellphone to a radical Palestinian group that the government has designated as a foreign terrorist organization, he or she faces many years in prison for providing material support to terrorists. The statutes are startlingly broad. The Secretary of State is authorized to designate as "terrorist organizations" any group of two or more individuals who use or even threaten to use firearms in any country in a way that directly or indirectly endangers life or property (8 U.S.C. § 1182(a)(3)(B)). Anyone who provides material support to a designated organization can receive up to fifteen years in prison (if no one dies at the hands of organization) or life imprisonment (if someone dies) (18 U.S.C. § 2339B). And what is material support? It includes any amount of money, communications equipment, facilities, or transportation (18 U.S.C. § 2339A(b)). More than that: it includes training, personnel, and expert advice and assistance, startlingly broad categories that can include writing an editorial in support of the group. See *Humanitarian Law Project* v. *Holder*, 561 U.S. 1 (2010), which upheld the material support statutes against a constitutional challenge.

against the possibility of losing your liberty for years because you are the wrong nationality in the wrong place at the wrong time.

Some might reply that it is government's job to protect the interests of its own citizens over those of foreigners. But the human rights of foreigners constitute a moral limit to nationalistic self-preference, and discounting the interests of others can lead to results fairly described as grotesque. When the United States began planning for an American presence in post-genocide Rwanda, Pentagon planners informed the commander of the UN force that they needed a body count of the genocide because their superiors considered one American casualty to be the equivalent of 85,000 dead Rwandans.[26] This kind of faux-objective corpse calculus may sound refreshingly hard-nosed to some, a cost-benefit trade-off reminiscent in spirit of Jeremy Bentham, the founder of modern utilitarianism, who regarded human rights as nonsense and inalienable human rights as "nonsense on stilts."[27] But even hard-nosed utilitarians believe that "each counts for one and none for more than one." Fortunately, the Mel Brooks-like theories of the Rwanda planners are not the official view of the US government, which endorses universal human rights. Indeed, one of President George W. Bush's policy advisers has described the president's view as the "fairly radical belief that a child in an African village whose parents are dying of AIDS has the same importance before God as the president of the United States."[28] This is a strong and welcome dose of human-rights thinking, and it is a useful corrective to the Mel Brooks fallacy.

Fallacy two: thinking that liberties and rights are different from security

The veil of ignorance thought experiment highlights a feature about civil liberties and human rights that the security-versus-liberty question conceals: rights are themselves forms of security. They are, specifically, security against abuses of the government's police power. The framers of the Constitution were unsentimental men who knew that government officials will inevitably be tempted to abuse the law to get rich, intimidate their opponents, persecute their enemies, or entrench their own power. They also understood that law

---

[26] Samantha Power, "A Problem from Hell": America and the Age of Genocide (New York: Basic Books, 2002), p. 381 (citing Roméo Dallaire, the commander of UNAMIR, the UN's peacekeeping force in Rwanda).

[27] Jeremy Bentham, "Anarchical Fallacies; An Examination of the Declaration of Rights of the Man and the Citizen Declared by the Constituent Assembly in France During the French Revolution," in The Works of Jeremy Bentham (Edinburgh: William Tate, 1843/ 1824), p. 501 (http://files.libertyfund.org/files/1921/0872.02_Bk.pdf).

[28] Elizabeth Bumiller, "Evangelicals Sway White House on Human Rights Issues Abroad," New York Times, Oct. 26, 2003, p. 1. The quotation is from Michael Gerson, who subsequently became a syndicated newspaper columnist.

enforcement is impatient with the niceties of process; enforcement officials will seek the shortest distance between two points. Furthermore, they understood the arrogance of power – the inevitable tendency of those on top to trust their own judgment and assume their own infallibility. For that reason, our Constitution not only protects our rights; it overprotects them. Even if the best source of evidence against a criminal is his own testimony, the framers insisted that he has the right against self-incrimination. Innocent or guilty, he has the right to counsel. Furthermore, as Robert Bork observes, "Courts often give protection to a constitutional freedom by creating a buffer zone, by prohibiting a government from doing something not in itself forbidden but likely to lead to an invasion of a right specified in the Constitution" – a practice that Bork, hardly a flaming liberal, agrees with.[29] To diminish civil liberties means to diminish our security against abuses and errors of government officials.

Understood in these terms, the trade-off between security and civil liberties might represent a judgment that we fear our own government less than we fear terrorists. Only a paranoid conspiracy theorist thinks that the government is planning to send in the black helicopters, or is operating with the kind of bad faith and malice that suggests we should fear paring back on Bork's buffer zones.

But one need not be a paranoid or a conspiracy theorist to believe that government can be error-prone, inefficient, and unwilling to admit mistakes. Indeed, most conservatives who favor paring back civil liberties in the name of security believe all these things. If the question is, for example, empowering the government to engage in cybersearches to compile profiles of Americans and detect suspicious-looking patterns of behavior, consider the possibility of error and the harm it might do.

Several times in the last few years, I tried to use my credit card and discovered that my bank had frozen it because their theft-detection software found a suspicious pattern of purchases. Twice, it was because I was traveling far from my home. Several times, I had made three or four back-to-back purchases of the kind of goodies thieves buy (gasoline, clothing, electronics). The errors were entirely understandable. That did not make them less inconvenient – and once, stranded abroad, the lack of the credit card put me in a genuine jam.

Is the government's terrorist-detection software likely to be less error-prone than my bank's theft-detection software? If anything, the opposite is likely to be true, because the stakes of a false negative are so much higher that analysts will likely err on the side of suspicion. Now imagine that the software error labeled me a potential terrorist, instead of merely blocking my credit card. This

---

[29] Robert H. Bork, *The Tempting of America* (New York: Free Press, 1990). Bork is discussing the case *NAACP* v. *Alabama*, 357 U.S. 449 (1958), where the Supreme Court upheld the right of the NAACP not to turn its membership lists over to the state of Alabama, on the ground that the state's subpoena of the lists would have a chilling effect on membership and thus impinge on the First Amendment right of political association.

might lead to embarrassing interrogations of my employers and friends, an "invitation" to go visit the FBI, or perhaps even an arrest. It might cost me my job. If I happen to have a Muslim name, or to have traveled recently to Pakistan, the odds are worse. If I am an alien who overstayed my visa, I face indefinite detention in an immigration gulag.

Even if this is not a genuine worry (but how, except on the Mel Brooks theory, could it not be?), the government cannot possibly guarantee that information it collects will never be released improperly – for example, sold by a rogue bureaucrat (or a hacker) to my insurance company.[30] The rights-security trade-off – actually, I am arguing, a security-security trade-off – is less hypothetical than may at first appear. "Better safe than sorry!" is not just a pro-security argument, it is a pro-civil-liberties argument as well.

Fallacy three: the fallacy of tendentious labeling

We often have a tendency to think that civil libertarians are idealists, while advocates of strong security measures, even at the expense of civil liberties, are tough-minded realists. In fact, however, the argument is equally strong for saying that it is the other way around: pro-security people have a naive faith in the probity of government (see fallacy two), while civil libertarians, who think that government will abuse its power, are the tough-minded realists.

Of course, this too is a one-sided and exaggerated worldview. Better than either is to appreciate that thinking in terms of realists and idealists, the tough-minded and the tender-minded, and other dichotomies of this character, gets us nowhere. It should simply be dropped from the repertoire of respectable argumentation. Labeling those who wish to restrict civil liberties "pragmatists" and denying the label to those who wish to protect them strongly is not helpful.

Fallacy four: the fallacy of small numbers

The question, "How many of your rights are you willing to sacrifice for added security?" is too sloppy because it does not specify how much added security you are likely to gain. The probability of my falling victim to a terrorist attack is, in absolute numerical terms, very slight – how slight is obviously unquantifiable – and so the subjective sense of danger many of us feel bears little

---

[30] See *U.S.* v. *Czubinski*, 106 F.3d 1069 (1st Cir. 1997), upholding the conviction of an Internal Revenue Service employee who gathered unauthorized confidential tax information about a number of people, including a woman he had dated a few times, a man who had defeated Czubinski in a city council election, and a district attorney who had once prosecuted Czubinski's father. Czubinski apparently did nothing with the information, but that should not make us feel more relieved. None of us have the slightest idea how many other Czubinskis are out there reading our tax forms for their own amusement, and not getting caught.

relation to any objective measure of likelihood. Psychologists have long known that people overestimate small risks once the risks become psychologically salient, and none of us are immune from this tendency. We are beyond the realm of rational comparison.

It is even more difficult to calculate what increment of added security any given increment in governmental power at the expense of rights can create. But that is the real question. Critics of American intelligence have charged that 9/11 should have been detected and stopped before it happened; but defenders of the intelligence community, including the authors of the *9/11 Commission Report* – an official inquiry into intelligence failures that failed to stop the attacks – argue persuasively that what seems plain in hindsight is often impossible to grasp *ex ante*. When you do not know clearly what you are looking for, isolated scraps of information often appear meaningless.

Let us suppose that the intelligence community's defenders are right about this. The clear implication is that added intelligence-gathering capacity may not provide a big boost in security. Many of us are prone to an understandable mistake: first we picture a terrorist attack that is a sure thing – for example, we picture 9/11, which is a sure thing in our own minds because it actually happened. Then we ask ourselves what sacrifice in our liberty we would be willing to undergo in order to prevent it. The answer is obvious: we would be willing to sacrifice a lot of liberty to prevent 9/11. But posed that way the question is nonsensical. It is simply a disguised version of a fairy-tale hypothetical: what sacrifice in our rights would we be willing to undergo to undo 9/11? 9/11 is a low-probability event; the government possesses formidable intelligence and law-enforcement capacity even without new restrictions on civil liberties; and giving the government added powers to investigate and detain people may itself lower that probability only by a little. As a matter of fact, it might actually raise the probability of missing the next terrorist attack, if the new powers inundate the government with useless information, or provoke negative reactions that cause potential informants to withhold information out of fright or anger.

If the trade-off question were posed accurately – that is, without the faulty assumption that loss of liberty makes us significantly safer – it would be this: what sacrifice in our rights would we be willing to undergo to reduce the already-small probability of another 9/11 by a factor of, say, one in ten? From, let us say, 1 percent annually to 0.9 percent – an annual saving of less than half a statistical life? And by how much would you be willing to raise the probability of yourself undergoing a false arrest in order to achieve an increment in security that registers only in the third decimal place? That question no longer has an obvious answer. Obviously, my numbers are entirely hypothetical. They are not even guesstimates. But small probabilities, whatever their actual magnitude, are far more realistic than large ones.

Fallacy five: the fallacy of the perpetual emergency

The US Constitution contains a few provisions for times of emergency – for example, by empowering Congress to call forth the national militia to execute the laws, suppress insurrections, and repel invasions (Article I, section 8), or to suspend habeas corpus "when in cases of rebellion or invasion the public safety may require it" (Article I, section 9). Famously, President Lincoln suspended the writ of habeas corpus in the Civil War without Congressional permission. He did so out of fear that unless border-state Confederate sympathizers could be quickly detained they might sabotage essential rail lines: Maryland was too close for comfort to the nation's capital. Suspending habeas corpus was a controversial measure at the time – Lincoln was probably violating the Constitution – but the emergency condition the United States found itself in arguably justified Lincoln's decision.

9/11 likewise marked a true emergency. In the immediate aftermath, when no one knew how wide the conspiracy was, or who was involved, or whether a follow-up attack was already in motion, the FBI detained thousands of Middle Eastern men and interviewed many more. Did the emergency justify a massive short-term dragnet? I think it did. The embarrassment and fright of the interviewees was a small price to pay for an absolutely essential investigation. Even those who were wrongly arrested and detained should have been able to understand that in such a situation investigators had little alternative to sweeping very broadly (although it would have been far better if, afterward, the government had at least apologized publicly).

But many of them were detained for months, not just hours or days. During the first ten days they were allowed no access to counsel, and subsequently permitted only one outside phone call per week. The Justice Department refused to release their names or even a count of how many there were. To justify its night-and-fog policy, the department explained that it did not want to tip off Al Qaeda about which of their operatives were in custody. But this rationale made sense only for the first few days after 9/11, when Al Qaeda was presumably scrambling to find out which of its operatives with sensitive information had been arrested. Weeks and months later, the idea that Al Qaeda might still be in the dark about who has gone AWOL is absurd. Nor is this simply harmless error: it turned out that none of those secretly detained were Al Qaeda operatives; and, of the estimated 5,000 detained in the initial dragnet, only five have been charged with terrorism-related crimes, and only one has been convicted.[31]

---

[31] David Cole, *Enemy Aliens: Double Standards and Constitutional Freedoms in the War on Terrorism* (New York: New Press, 2003), pp. 25–6. Two others were acquitted, and one was convicted of nonterrorist-related charges. In the first seven weeks after 9/11, 12,000 individuals were detained. Nearly 4,000 more have been detained since then.

At this point, the plea of emergency no longer makes sense: calling long-term conditions (like the standing danger of terrorism) an "emergency" is a confusion. Emergencies are temporary departures from normal conditions. 9/11 was an emergency. Daily life under long-term risk is not. Any abrogation of rights due to long-term "emergency" conditions should be regarded as permanent, not temporary.

Fallacy six: the fallacy of confusing substantive liberties with their safeguards

To speak of loss of civil liberties (or rights) actually blends together two distinct issues, because civil liberties encompass both powers and protections. A power is a substantive liberty: an ability to do something. A protection is a guarantee against official abuses. Freedom of religion is a power: it is the right to practice your religion without government persecution. By contrast, the Sixth Amendment rights "to a speedy and public trial, by an impartial jury of the State and district wherein the crime shall have been committed . . . and to be informed of the nature and cause of the accusation; to be confronted with the witnesses against him [the defendant]; to have compulsory process for obtaining witnesses in his favor, and to have the assistance of counsel" are all protections against the possibility of criminal punishment by mistake or malice.

The distinction between powers and protections is not clear-cut: the right to hire the defense lawyer of my choice is a power as well as a protection (or, more precisely, it is a power contained within a protection). Furthermore, protections can be formally rephrased as powers – thus, the right to a trial by jury can be rephrased as the right to retain my liberty of movement unless convicted by a jury. But less formalistically, the distinction is straightforward common sense. Protections are primarily rights to certain kinds of due process, designed to ward off government error and abuse. They are only derivatively rights to exercise substantive liberties, and the rights they establish are valuable only when the government is after us. Powers, on the other hand, mark out substantive areas of activity that deserve protection so that people can engage in them; they are only derivatively rights to due process if government wants to prevent us from engaging in protected activities. The emphasis is entirely different. Powers, like the rights to free speech, free exercise of religion, freedom of the press, and freedom to associate protect goods that are desirable in and of themselves. Protections, like the rights of criminal defendants, are valuable only if we get into trouble with the law; a trial by jury, unlike a religious service, is not anyone's idea of a morning well spent.

It might be supposed that powers are more important than protections, so that it would be morally worse to constrict powers in the name of security. Actually, the loss of protections is more dangerous. Consider the most familiar of emergency restrictions on our powers: a curfew, for example, during urban riots, or a blackout, or a terrorist attack. Imposing a curfew diminishes people's powers, but it does not enormously increase the risk of government abuse. Furthermore, restricting powers is likely to be done cautiously, because it typically affects everyone, which means that there are real political consequences attached to government being too harsh. I do not suggest this is inevitably true: many dictatorships have brutally clamped down on powers for years or even decades. But in the contemporary United States, which is not exactly teetering on the brink of fascism, government is very wary of imposing major inconveniences on Americans across the board. It has become conventional wisdom that if government tried to institute time-consuming, invasive airport security arrangements it would pay a political price. When the government proposed its Total Information Awareness (TIA) and Terrorism Information and Protection System (TIPS), public outrage over privacy invasions and a culture of informants quickly doomed both programs.

Those who argue that perhaps we have too many liberties for the insecure world we live in may have a point when they are referring to powers. Perhaps, for example, none of us can ever again afford the liberty of being able to board airliners without having our shoes X-rayed and our luggage searched. The loss of protections is a different matter. If the right of habeas corpus is suspended, or people are detained incommunicado, or arrested secretly, or assassinated, part of the firewall that protects us from government-inflicted evils has gone. Without the firewall, innocent people may be arrested or killed by mistake (or, what is even worse, *not* by mistake). If they truly are innocent people, then, by hypothesis, detaining them does nothing to enhance security. It makes them worse off without making anyone better off – the very definition of an unmitigated evil.

The reply is that over-inclusive arrests or killings are a necessary evil, because it is simply too difficult or costly to use the procedures that get it right. Better that a hundred innocent people be imprisoned than that one terrorist escape the dragnet, if that terrorist might be carrying a suitcase full of smallpox. Eliminating false positives might let through too many false negatives.

Maybe; but that proposition should never be taken on faith. Its proponents must prove that public safety requires wider latitude for officials to shortcut procedures designed to protect people from being imprisoned or killed by mistake. They must prove that public safety would be threatened unless it is possible to keep the names of detainees secret or hold them incommunicado. The blanket argument that even one false negative might be a terrorist with a suitcase nuke or a crop duster filled with anthrax proves far too much, because the only way to eliminate literally *all* false negatives would be to kill or imprison millions. Or, if the argument is that our ordinary constitutional protections were designed for less perilous times, the response is that all times are perilous. The Civil War, World War II, and the Cold War were all perilous times. In the Civil War-era case *Ex parte Milligan*, the Supreme Court confronted and rejected the argument that ours is a fair-weather Constitution. The court wrote that the constitutional framers

> foresaw that troublous times would arise, when rules and people would become restive under restraint, and seek by sharp and decisive measures to accomplish ends deemed just and proper... The history of the world had taught them that what was done in the past might be attempted in the future. The Constitution of the United States is a law for rulers and people, equally in war and in peace, and covers with the shield of its protection all classes of men, at all times, and under all circumstances. No doctrine, involving more pernicious consequences, was ever invented by the wit of man than that any of its provisions can be suspended during any of the great exigencies of government.[32]

Fallacy seven: presuming guilt

We sometimes hear official spokesmen argue that terrorists do not deserve the protection of our rights. Sometimes, the argument adds a rhetorical flourish: "Why should terrorists benefit from the very rights they are trying to destroy?" Such arguments were often used, for example, to justify denying legal process to the Guantánamo detainees. But it assumes that they *are* terrorists, which is the very thing that due process is supposed to settle. Asking, "Why should terrorists benefit from the very rights they are trying to destroy?" is like asking, "Why should a guilty criminal get a fair trial?" The answer is obvious: the fair trial is the way we have devised to determine who is and who is not a guilty criminal. Without the trial, all we have is the authorities' say-so that it is indeed a *guilty* criminal we are talking about. The very posing of the rhetorical question already assumes guilt, or assumes that it is indeed terrorists we are talking about (rather than innocent people wrongly presumed to be terrorists).

Sometimes the fallacy is transparent, as, for example, when we are told for years that the reason Guantánamo internees should not get their Geneva Convention right to a hearing to determine if they really are enemy combatants is that they are Al Qaeda fighters and therefore not entitled to Geneva Convention rights. Of course, the question is whether they are indeed Al Qaeda fighters rather than innocent bystanders swept up by mistake. (During the 1991 Gulf War, two-thirds of those initially detained as possible enemy fighters were released after their hearings.) Our government has admitted that some of the Guantánamo detentions were mistakes, and has repatriated more than eighty detainees – after more than a year of imprisonment, apparently false imprisonment. Many remaining prisoners in Camp X-Ray reportedly have fallen into clinical depression, and suicide attempts have occurred at alarmingly high rates; one suspects that the American public tolerates this out of a lethal mix of the

[32] *Ex parte Milligan*, 71 U.S. 2, 120-1 (1866).

Mel Brooks fallacy and the repeated assertion that Camp X-Ray contains terrorists – the fallacy of presuming guilt, which readily translates into the thought that the inmates deserve the treatment they are getting. In June 2004, the Supreme Court held that the Guantánamo detainees are entitled to hearings on whether they are actually enemy combatants, but, as of November 2004, the government was still fighting against their right to appeal, and has dragged its feet in providing the requisite process.[33]

Another transparent example of the fallacy of presuming guilt is the government's threat to move Zacharias Moussaoui out of the civilian courts and into a military tribunal because it might be too difficult to convict him in civil court (because of that pesky Sixth Amendment right "to have compulsory process for obtaining witnesses in his favor"). Moussaoui is a particularly unappealing case, because he gloats about his Al Qaeda membership and admits that he is America's enemy. But he also claims to have played no role in the 9/11 attacks, and that could be true. To offer the need for convicting him as a reason for moving his case to a military tribunal presumes that he is guilty.

These, I have said, are transparent fallacies. But the fallacy of presuming guilt can creep into public discourse in a subtler way. Consider Judge Michael Mukasey's otherwise capable opinion in *Padilla* v. *Bush*, which concerns the government's right to hold US citizen Jose Padilla without charges or trial because he is an alleged Al Qaeda fighter who hoped to make a "dirty bomb" to detonate in an American city.[34] The government claims that, as an unlawful enemy combatant, Padilla can be detained until the war on terrorism is over – that is, detained indefinitely. Upholding the government's position, Judge Mukasey cited a 1942 case, *Ex parte Quirin*, which concerned a group of German saboteurs (including one US citizen) captured in the United States.[35] The Supreme Court's opinion in *Quirin* upheld the government's right to detain and punish the saboteurs, and Judge Mukasey argued that the government's right to detain Padilla logically follows from the right to detain and punish: the greater power includes the lesser.

This argument sounds entirely plausible – but only until we realize that it *assumes* that if he were tried Padilla would be convicted rather than acquitted, and indeed that after conviction he would be sentenced either to life imprisonment or death, rather than a fixed term of years. If either of these assumptions is false – that is, if he would be acquitted or sentenced to a fixed term of years – then the power to detain Padilla indefinitely without a trial is a greater power, not a lesser one, than the power to detain and punish him after a trial.

---

[33] *Rasul* v. *Bush*, 542 U.S. 466 (2004); *Hamdi* v. *Rumsfeld*, 542 U.S. 507 (2004).

[34] *Padilla* v. *Bush*, 233 F. Supp. 2d 564 (S.D.N.Y. 2002). The decision was overturned on appeal, but on grounds unrelated to the arguments considered here. Eventually, Padilla was tried and convicted in federal court.

[35] *Ex parte Quirin*, 317 U.S. 1 (1942).

The judge's argument assumes guilt in order to deny the right to a trial designed to ascertain guilt. That is a fallacy, and a particularly insidious one.

Fallacy eight: the militarization of civilian life

In *Padilla*, as in other war on terrorism cases, the government appeals to the president's war powers to argue that the judiciary should defer to the executive on military matters such as whom to designate an enemy combatant.[36] In June 2004, the Supreme Court partially rebuffed this argument, holding that Yaser Hamdi (an American citizen captured allegedly fighting for the Taliban in Afghanistan, and held as an enemy combatant) must receive a hearing on whether he actually is an enemy combatant.[37] Even here, though, the court did not grant Hamdi the same level of review offered to habeas corpus petitioners in the criminal process: instead of placing the burden of proof on the government, the court created a rebuttable presumption that the government is right.[38] So even *Hamdi* accepts the argument that judges should defer to the executive on military matters – an argument to which our judiciary has usually been very receptive. The proposition that judges should not second-guess generals on military matters seems self-evident, and it has been firmly established in our jurisprudence since the *Korematsu* case upheld the military necessity of interning Japanese-Americans in concentration camps during World War II.[39] The Japanese internment has subsequently come to be regarded as a national disgrace by nearly everyone, although right-wing revisionists have predictably begun to defend it once again.[40] But, national disgrace or not, *Korematsu*'s basic argument for judicial deference has lost none of its luster. Judges need to keep their hubris in check and leave war to the professionals.

---

[36] Originally, the executive branch claimed that the president's war powers prevent federal judges from scrutinizing such decisions at all, but it was rebuffed by the Fourth Circuit Court of Appeals. Apparently, the executive power grab was too much for the Fourth Circuit, arguably the most conservative in the nation. The argument suggests that worries about executive abuse of the police power to enhance its own power – see fallacy two – are not merely hypothetical.

[37] *Hamdi v. Rumsfeld*, 542 U.S. 507 (2004).

[38] In the fall of 2004, the United States released Hamdi and returned him to Afghanistan, thereby mooting the question of how much due process he would ultimately receive.

[39] *Korematsu v. United States*, 323 U.S. 414 (1944).

[40] See David D. Lowman, *MAGIC: The Untold Story of U.S. Intelligence and the Evacuation of Japanese Residents from the West Coast During WW II* (Provo, UT: Athena Press, 2000); Michelle Malkin, *In Defense of Internment: The Case for "Racial Profiling" in World War II and the War on Terror* (Washington, DC: Regnery, 2004). For a modest defense of *Korematsu*, see Richard A. Posner, "The Truth About Our Liberties," *Responsive Community* (Summer 2002), 4–5. Mark Tushnet has "defended" *Korematsu* in what he describes as an "ironic sense." Mark Tushnet, "Defending *Korematsu*?: Reflections on Civil Liberties in Wartime," *Wisconsin Law Review* (2003), 273–307, at 274.

But the argument rests on a fallacy, because the president of the United States is a civilian, not a general. We pride ourselves on the principle of civilian control of the military, which (thankfully) differentiates us from the large part of the world governed by military juntas. The president's war power is, fundamentally, a power of civilian control over the uses of the military. It is not grounded in the executive branch's military expertise or prowess, and it is not an argument about who is best suited to make technical military judgments. Thus, it is not hubris for other branches of government to review executive claims that military necessity overrides civil liberties. Both Hamdi and Padilla were classified as enemy combatants by civilians in the executive branch, and the evidence offered to back that classification consisted of affidavits by a civilian employee of the Defense Department. The case had nothing to do with military expertise, and there was really no need for courts to defer to the executive, because the basic task – determining how the law should classify a set of facts – is a pre-eminently judicial function, as Judge Mukasey himself acknowledged.

Why is this important? One of the peculiarities of the war on terrorism is that it may need to be waged invisibly in American cities, and the "battlefield" could turn out to be the entire country, or indeed anywhere in the world. (Indeed, less than two weeks after 9/11, lawyers in the Justice Department's Office of Legal Counsel produced an opinion justifying presidential use of military force against terrorists within US territory, even if it cost civilian casualties as collateral damage.[41]) If

(1) the executive is exercising his war powers in short-cutting peacetime civil liberties, and
(2) other branches of government must defer to the executive on war-powers issues, and
(3) the battlefield is coextensive with the United States, or the world,

a dangerous consequence follows: civil liberties and human rights exist only at the sufferance of the American president, who can unilaterally reduce or suspend them based on factual declarations of military exigency that demand deferential review by the rest of government. All that stands between us and the militarization of civilian life is the president's say-so.

---

[41] Memorandum for Alberto R. Gonzales, Counsel to the President; William J. Haynes II, General Counsel Department of Defense from John C. Yoo, Deputy Assistant Attorney General and Robert J. Delahunty, Special Counsel, Re: Authority for the Use of Military Force to Combat Terrorist Activities Within the United States, Oct. 23, 2001 (www. justice.gov/opa/documents/memomilitaryforcecombatus10232001.pdf). Withdrawn, Oct. 6, 2008, by Steven G. Bradbury, Principal Deputy Assistant Attorney General, Memorandum for the Files Re: Oct. 23, 2001 OLC Opinion Addressing the Domestic Use of Military Force to Combat Terrorist Activities (www.fas.org/irp/agency/doj/olc/caution.pdf).

The fallacy lies in confusing the president's formal war powers with military expertise, and deferring to the former because we are thinking of the latter.[42] This is a particularly dangerous error in fearful times like ours, when our instincts may well make us receptive to arguments of military necessity – even when they come from the lips of civilians who never saw a day of combat in their lives. Military necessity always seems to trump concern for civil liberties, and that should make us especially vigilant against specious claims of military necessity in everyday life.

Conclusion

Let me return to my original question. How much liberty should be sacrificed for security? I began by saying that this is the wrong question, because it rests on mistaken assumptions. Once we take care *not* to suppose that it is somebody else's liberty that will be sacrificed, nor to suppose that only the rights of the guilty and the terrorists are in jeopardy, nor that pro-security is the tough-minded, pragmatic answer, nor that these are military issues best left to the executive, nor that they are merely short-term emergency measures, the question takes a different form. It becomes something like this: *How much of your own protection against bureaucratic errors or malice by the govern-ment – errors or malice that could land you in jail – are you willing to sacrifice in return for minute increments in security?* This, it seems to me, is not an easy question to answer, but the most plausible answer is "not much"; and "none" seems like a reasonable place to start.

---

[42] Even the *Hamdi* opinion conflates the president's status as (civilian) commander in chief with military expertise. The Supreme Court states that "our Constitution recognizes that core strategic matters of warmaking belong in the hands of those who are best positioned and most politically accountable for them," apparently not recognizing that "those who are best positioned" – military commanders – and those who are "most politically accountable" for making them – elected officials – are not the same people (*Hamdi* v. *Rumsfeld*, 542 U.S. 507, 531 (2004)). Furthermore, to support this assertion, the Court cites two earlier decisions – one for the proposition that courts should not "intrude upon the authority of the Executive in military and national security affairs," and the other recognizing "broad powers in military commanders engaged in day-to-day fighting in a theater of war" (at 531, quoting *Department of Navy* v. *Egan*, 484 U.S. 518, 530 (1988) and *Youngstown Sheet & Tube* v. *Sawyer*, 343 U.S. 579, 587 (1952)). Plainly, the executive is not a military commander engaged in day-to-day fighting in a theater of war.

II

The ticking bomb as moral fantasy and moral fraud

3

Liberalism, torture, and the ticking bomb

Preface

This chapter was published concurrently in its present form and in a more extended version that appeared in Karen Greenberg's collection *The Torture Debate in America* (Cambridge University Press, 2005). The latter version included a longer and fuller analysis of the torture memos; I have used the shorter version here because other chapters of this book go into the torture memos in greater detail. The chapter received wide circulation: in March 2006 it was excerpted in *Harper's Magazine* and published in translation in the German cultural magazine *Die Zeit Kursbuch*. Together with the following two chapters, it represents the philosophical core of this book's analysis of torture and its critique of discussing torture through ticking-bomb hypotheticals.

I began writing the chapter when the Bybee–Yoo torture memo became public in the summer of 2004, shortly after the sensational Abu Ghraib revelations. It needs only slight factual updating. At the time I finished it, only two of the torture memos were public. It was not until April 2009 that the Obama administration released the remaining torture memos, all but one of which were shortly republished by David Cole in *The Torture Memos: Rationalizing the Unthinkable* (New York Review of Books, 2009). The existence of CIA "black sites" – secret prisons in Poland, Romania, and Thailand – had not yet emerged, nor was it clear what interrogation techniques the Justice Department had approved for CIA use. I also wrote before the issue of nonaccountability for torture became salient. By the time the smoke had cleared, only a handful of low-level enlisted personnel had been punished for Abu Ghraib, and, ultimately, none of the 101 potential torture cases investigated by a special prosecutor resulted in criminal referrals. I discuss the issue of nonaccountability in this book's final chapter.

One important update concerns my discussion of the Levin memorandum's analysis of "severe physical suffering" (as distinct from severe physical pain). I missed the significance of Levin's insistence that suffering must be prolonged to count as severe – a requirement that is not in the torture statute. At the

The main text of this chapter was first published in 2005 – see Acknowledgments.

time I wrote the chapter, the technique of "waterboarding" had not yet been exposed to the public. Waterboarding episodes last only a few seconds, at most a minute or two, and Levin's requirement was used to approve waterboarding, as became clear in subsequent torture memos. (For discussion, see Chapters 7 and 8) This is a remarkable example of the legal contortions that the memo authors were compelled to resort to in order to ensure that the CIA's techniques could not be prosecuted as torture.

LIBERALISM, TORTURE, AND THE TICKING BOMB

Introduction

Torture used to be incompatible with American values. Our Bill of Rights forbids cruel and unusual punishment, and that has come to include all forms of corporal punishment except prison and death by methods purported to be painless. Americans and our government have historically condemned states that torture; we have granted asylum or refuge to those who fear it. The Senate ratified the Convention Against Torture, Congress enacted antitorture legislation, and judicial opinions spoke of "the dastardly and totally inhuman act of torture."[1]

Then came 9/11. Less than one week later, a feature story reported that a quiz in a university ethics class "gave four choices for the proper US response to the terrorist attacks: A.) execute the perpetrators on sight; B.) bring them back for trial in the United States; C.) subject the perpetrators to an international tribunal; or D.) torture and interrogate those involved."[2] Most students chose A and D – execute them on sight and torture them. Six weeks after 9/11, the press reported that frustrated FBI interrogators were considering harsh interrogation tactics;[3] a few weeks after that, the *New York Times* reported that torture had become a topic of conversation "in bars, on commuter trains, and at dinner tables."[4] By mid November 2001, the *Christian Science Monitor* found that 32 percent of surveyed Americans favored torturing terror suspects.[5] Alan Dershowitz reported in 2002 that "during numerous public appearances since September 11, 2001, I have asked audiences for a show of hands as to how many would support the use of nonlethal torture

---

[1] See, e.g., *Filartiga* v. *Pena-Irala*, 630 F.2d 876, 883 (2nd Cir. 1980).

[2] Amy Argetsinger, "At Colleges, Students Are Facing a Big Test," *Washington Post*, Sept. 17, 2001, p. B1.

[3] See, e.g., Walter Pincus, "Silence of 4 Terror Probe Suspects Poses Dilemma for FBI," *Washington Post*, Oct. 21, 2001, p. A6.

[4] Jim Rutenberg, "Torture Seeps into Discussion by News Media," *New York Times*, Nov. 5, 2001, p. C1.

[5] Abraham McLaughlin, "How Far Americans Would Go to Fight Terror," *Christian Science Monitor*, Nov. 14, 2001, p. 1.

in a ticking-bomb case. Virtually every hand is raised."[6] American abhorrence of torture now appears to have extraordinarily shallow roots.

To an important extent, one's stance on torture is independent of progressive or conservative ideology. Dershowitz suggests that torture should be regulated by a judicial warrant requirement.[7] Liberal Senator Charles Schumer has publicly rejected the idea "that torture should never, ever be used."[8] He argues that most US senators would back torture to find out where a ticking time bomb is planted. By contrast, William Safire, a self-described "conservative ... and card-carrying hard-liner," expresses revulsion at "phony-tough" pro-torture arguments, and forthrightly labels torture "barbarism."[9] Examples like these illustrate how vital it is to avoid a simple left–right reductionism. For the most part, American conservatives belong no less than progressives to liberal culture, broadly understood. Henceforth, when I speak of "liberalism," I mean it in the broad sense used by political philosophers from John Stuart Mill on, a sense that includes conservatives as well as progressives, so long as they believe in limited government and the importance of human dignity and individual rights.

My aim in this chapter is threefold. First, in sections I and II, I will examine the place of torture within liberalism. I hope to demonstrate that there are reasons that liberals find torture peculiarly abhorrent to their political outlook – but also reasons why liberal revulsion towards torture may be only skin-deep. On its surface, liberal reverence for individual rights makes torture morally unacceptable; at a deeper level, the same liberal ideas seemingly can justify interrogational torture in the face of danger. These ideas allow us to construct a liberal ideology of torture, by which liberals reassure themselves that essential interrogational torture is detached from its illiberal roots. The liberal ideology of torture is expressed perfectly in "ticking-bomb hypotheticals" designed to show that even perfectly compassionate liberals (like Senator Schumer) might justify torture to find the ticking bomb.

Second, I will criticize the liberal ideology of torture and suggest that ticking-bomb stories are built on a set of assumptions that amount to intellectual fraud (sections III and IV). Ticking-bomb stories depict torture as an

---

[6] Alan M. Dershowitz, *Why Terrorism Works* (New Haven, CT: Yale University Press, 2002), p. 150. Dershowitz, a Harvard Law School professor, achieved a certain notoriety in the torture debate by arguing that because governments will use torture whether it is forbidden or not, it should be regulated by instituting torture warrants that the president would be required to sign. Dershowitz has claimed that he is an opponent of torture, despite his torture-warrant proposal and his regular recourse to ticking-bomb hypotheticals.

[7] *Ibid.*, pp. 158–61.

[8] Federal Government's Counterterrorism Efforts: Hearing Before the Senate Judiciary Subcommittee, 108th Congress (2004) (statement of Sen. Charles Schumer, Member, Senate Judiciary Committee).

[9] William Safire, "Seizing Dictatorial Power," *New York Times*, Nov. 15, 2001, p. A31.

emergency exception, but use intuitions based on the exceptional case to justify institutionalized practices and procedures of torture. In short, the ticking bomb begins by denying that torture belongs to liberal culture, and ends by constructing a torture culture.

My third aim in the chapter is to illustrate these dialectical adventures of the liberal ideology of torture through a case study of the executive-branch lawyers who solicited or wrote memoranda justifying some cases of official brutality (section V).[10] The result, I believe, will be a perfect example of how a secretive torture culture emerges from the liberal ideology of torture – a disquieting illustration of how liberalism deals with the unpleasant question of torture.

I Putting cruelty first

Unhappily, torture is as old as human history. Montaigne once wrote, "nature herself, I fear, attaches to man some instinct for inhumanity."[11] That sounds right. Most children at some point entertain sadistic fantasies, and many act them out. Infantile sadism may actually be an essential stage in the process of differentiating self from the other and acquiring physical agency in the external world: "I can pinch and I feel nothing, but you or she or the cat yelps in pain; I am not you or her or the cat; and it's fun making you or her or the cat notice me." Causing pain in others allows the child to learn that some of the objects around him are subjects with feelings of their own, and, in this way, bouts of infantile sadism may be essential to developing adult empathy. But, while infantile sadism may be essential for human development, eventually

---

[10] Most of the memoranda, Abu Ghraib-related reports, and other essential documents dealing with US interrogation policy, torture, and treatment of detainees have been assembled by Karen J. Greenberg and Joshua L. Dratel, Eds., *The Torture Papers: The Road to Abu Ghraib* (Cambridge University Press, 2005) [hereinafter *Torture Papers*]. A smaller collection of torture papers, including many of the Abu Ghraib photographs and an astute analysis, has also appeared: Mark Danner, *Torture and Truth: America, Abu Ghraib, and the War on Terror* (New York Review of Books, 2004). Both collections include the memorandum dated August 1, 2002, which I shall refer to as the "Bybee memo" (because it went out over the signature of Jay S. Bybee, although its principal author was apparently John C. Yoo). Memorandum from Jay S. Bybee, Assistant Attorney General, US Department of Justice, to Alberto R. Gonzales, Counsel to the President (Aug. 1, 2002), reprinted in *Torture Papers*, p. 172, and in Danner, *Torture and Truth*, p. 115. In fact, the 1,249-page *Torture Papers* was out of date before it was printed in January 2005. The Bybee memo was replaced on December 30, 2004, and new information and memoranda have leaked out intermittently ever since. A second volume of torture papers is currently under preparation. Many arguments in the debate about torture appear in a superb anthology: Sanford Levinson, Ed., *Torture: A Collection* (Oxford University Press, 2004).

[11] Michel de Montaigne, "Of Cruelty" [first published in 1580], in *The Complete Essays of Montaigne* (Donald M. Frame, Trans.) (Stanford University Press, 1958), pp. 306, 316.

torture fantasies must be repressed. To be sure, sadism persists in some people's erotic lives. But apart from consensual bedroom behavior, liberal societies condemn torture as a serious and depraved form of battery.

Yet the modern liberal's revulsion towards torture is unusual. As Nietzsche and Foucault remind us, through most of human history there was no taboo on torture in military and juridical contexts, and so no need to repress the infantile sadism that nature has bequeathed us.[12] Indeed, Judith Shklar notes a remarkable fact – namely, that cruelty did not seem to figure in classical moral thought as an important vice: "One looks in vain for a Platonic dialogue on cruelty. Aristotle discusses only pathological bestiality, not cruelty. Cruelty is not one of the seven deadly sins... The many manifestations of cupidity seem, to Saint Augustine, more important than cruelty."[13] It is only in relatively modern times, Shklar thinks, that we have come to "put cruelty first" – that is, regard it as the most vicious of all vices.[14] She thinks that Montaigne and Montesquieu, both of them proto-liberals, were the first political philosophers to think this way; and, more generally, she holds that "hating cruelty, and putting it first [among vices], remain a powerful part of the liberal consciousness."[15] Shklar also observes that putting cruelty first, as liberals do, incurs genuine moral costs: "It makes political action difficult beyond endurance, may cloud our judgment, and may reduce us to a debilitating misanthropy."[16]

Perhaps these difficulties account for the ease with which we abandoned our reluctance to torture in the aftermath of 9/11. But I believe there are indeed reasons why torture and cruelty are particularly incompatible with liberalism. And, as I hope to show, one way this incompatibility manifests itself is through arguments designed to show that torturing terrorists for information is not done out of cruelty.

II   The five aims of torture

What makes torture, the deliberate infliction of suffering and pain, especially abhorrent to liberals? This may seem like a bizarre question, because the answer seems self-evident: making people suffer is a horrible thing. Pain hurts and bad pain hurts badly. But let me pose the question in different terms. Realistically, the abuses of detainees at Abu Ghraib, Baghram, and Guantá-namo pale by comparison with the death, maiming, and suffering in collateral

---

[12] Both Nietzsche and Foucault describe torture as a festive occasion. See Friedrich Nietzsche, *On the Genealogy of Morals* [first published in 1887], in Walter Kaufmann, Ed. and Trans., *Basic Writings of Nietzsche* (New York: Random House, 1968), pp. 439, 501–3 ("Without cruelty there is no festival"); Michel Foucault, *Discipline and Punish: The Birth of the Prison* (Alan Sheridan, Trans.) (New York: Vintage Books, 1979), p. 8 (describing "the gloomy festival of punishment").

[13] Judith N. Shklar, *Ordinary Vices* (Cambridge, MA: Harvard University Press, 1984), p. 7.

[14] *Ibid.*, p. 8.   [15] *Ibid.*, p. 43.   [16] *Ibid.*

damage during the Afghan and Iraq wars. Bombs crush limbs and burn people's faces off; nothing even remotely as horrifying has been reported in American prisoner abuse cases. Yet, as much as we may regret or in some cases decry the wartime suffering of innocents, we do not seem to regard it with the special abhorrence that we do torture. This seems hypocritical and irrational, almost fetishistic, and it raises the question of what makes torture more illiberal than bombing and killing.[17] The answer lies in the relationship between torturer and victim. The self-conscious aim of torture is to turn its victim into someone who is isolated, overwhelmed, terrorized, and humiliated. Torture aims to strip away from its victim all the qualities of human dignity that liberalism prizes. The torturer inflicts pain one-on-one, deliberately, up close, and personal, in order to break the spirit of the victim – in other words, to tyrannize and dominate the victim. The relationship between them becomes a perverse parody of friendship and intimacy: intimacy transformed into its inverse image, where the torturer focuses on the victim's body with the intensity of a lover, except that every bit of that focus is bent to causing pain and tyrannizing the victim's spirit.[18]

I am arguing that torture is a microcosm, raised to the highest level of intensity, of the tyrannical political relationships that liberalism hates the most. I have said that torture isolates and privatizes. Pain forcibly severs our concentration on anything outside of us; it collapses our horizon to our own body and the damage we feel in it. Even much milder sensations of prolonged discomfort can distract us so much that it becomes impossible to pay attention to anything else, as anyone knows who has had to go to the bathroom in a situation where it cannot be done. Ludwig Wittgenstein wrote that the world of the happy is different from the world of the unhappy,[19] and this is not

---

[17] I have heard this argument from several people, but Paul Kahn and Mike Seidman have pressed it on me most compellingly in conversation.

[18] My point here is somewhat different from that of Henry Shue, who examines the argument that since killing is worse than torture, and killing is permitted in warfare, torture might be as well. Shue argues that in warfare there is a kind of reciprocity between combatants, who place each other mutually at risk, whereas torture is more like killing the defenseless. Henry Shue, "Torture," *Philosophy and Public Affairs*, 7(2), (1978), 124–43, at 124, 125, 129–30. I am arguing that torture is like tyrannizing the defenseless rather than killing them. David Sussman argues that the special evil in torture consists in "forcing its victim into the position of colluding against himself through his own affects and emotions, so that he experiences himself as simultaneously powerless and yet actively complicit in his own violation." David Sussman, "What's Wrong with Torture?", *Philosophy and Public Affairs*, 1(4) (2005), 1–33, at 33. The idea seems to be "that the only thing that matters to [the torture victim] is pleasing this other person who appears infinitely distant, important, inscrutable, powerful, and free." Sussman, "What's Wrong with Torture?", 25–6. For a further examination of the evils of torture, see Chapter 5 of this book; there I take up Sussman's idea further.

[19] Ludwig Wittgenstein, *Tractatus Logico-Philosophicus* [first published in 1921](D. F. Pears and B. F. McGuinness, Trans.) (London: Routledge Classics, 2001), p 87.

simply a figure of speech when we suffer severe pain. The world of the man or woman in great pain is a world without relationships or engagements, a world without an exterior. It is a world reduced to a point, a world that makes no sense and in which the human soul finds no home and no repose.[20]

And torture terrorizes. The body in pain winces; it trembles. The muscles themselves register fear. This is rooted in pain's biological function of impelling us in the most urgent way possible to escape from the source of pain – for that impulse is indistinguishable from panic. US interrogators have reportedly used the technique of "waterboarding" to break the will of detainees.[21] Waterboarding involves immersing the victim's face in water or wrapping it in a wet towel to induce drowning sensations. As anyone who has ever come close to drowning or suffocating knows, the oxygen-starved brain sends panic signals that overwhelm everything else. You can experience suffocation-panic for yourself right now by fully exhaling and then holding your breath for 60 seconds.

And torture humiliates. It makes the victim scream and beg; the terror makes him lose control of his bowels and bladder.[22] The essence of cruelty is inflicting pain for the purpose of lording it over someone – we sometimes say "breaking" them – and the mechanism of cruelty is making the victim the audience of your own mastery. Cruelty always aims at humiliation. One curious feature of legal procedure in both ancient Greece and Rome was a rule "that slaves were permitted to [testify in a court of law] only under torture."[23] Sir Moses Finley's plausible explanation is that the rule served to mark off the

---

[20] This is one of Elaine Scarry's chief points in *The Body in Pain: The Making and Unmaking of the World* (Oxford University Press, 1985), p. 33 ("As in dying and death, so in serious pain the claims of the body utterly nullify the claims of the world."). Scarry offers perhaps the most famous phenomenology of torture. However, as will soon become apparent, I differ from Scarry because she thinks that torture exists only in the context of interrogation. ("Torture consists of a primary physical act, the infliction of pain, and a primary verbal act, the interrogation," p. 28); ("Pain and interrogation inevitably occur together," p. 29). I subsequently argue that coupling torture with interrogation is only one historically significant motivation for torture.

[21] See, e.g., Responses of Alberto R. Gonzales, Nominee to be Attorney General of the United States, to Written Questions of Senator Richard J. Durbin, 3–5 (2005) [hereinafter Gonzales' Responses to Durbin] (posing questions about waterboarding, with evasive answers); Douglas Jehl, "Questions Left by C.I.A. Chief on Torture Use," *New York Times*, Mar. 18, 2005, p. A1 (describing a question about waterboarding posed by Sen. John McCain to CIA head Porter Goss and his evasive answer); Editorial, "Torture Showdown," *Wall Street Journal*, Jan. 6, 2005, p. A16 (describing waterboarding as "the most coercive technique that was ever actually authorized" by US officials).

[22] The Fay–Jones Report on Abu Ghraib mentions "an alleged contest between the two Army dog handlers to see who could make the internees urinate or defecate in the presence of the dogs." Lieutenant General Anthony R. Jones and Major General George R. Fay, "The Fay–Jones Report" (Aug. 2004), in *Torture Papers*, note 10 above, pp. 987, 1070 (hereinafter Fay–Jones Report).

[23] Moses I. Finley, *Ancient Slavery and Modern Ideology* (Princeton, NJ: Markus Wiener, 1998), p. 162.

absolute difference in status between slaves and even the lowliest freemen.[24] The torture rule reinforces the message that slaves are absolutely subjugated. Humiliation occurs when I am low and you are high and you insist on it.

Victor's pleasure

The predominant setting for torture has always been military victory. The victor captures the enemy and tortures him. I recently saw some spectacular Mayan murals depicting defeated enemies from a rival city-state having their fingernails torn out before being executed in a ritual re-enactment of the battle.

Underneath whatever religious significance attaches to torturing the vanquished, the victor tortures captives for the simplest of motives: to relive the victory, to demonstrate the absoluteness of his mastery, to rub the loser's face in it, and to humiliate the loser by making him scream and beg. For the victorious warrior, it is fun; it is entertainment.[25] It prolongs the rush of victory. Montaigne denounced what he called "the uttermost point that cruelty can attain" – namely, torture "for the sole purpose of enjoying the pleasing spectacle of the pitiful gestures and movements, the lamentable groans and cries, of a man dying in anguish."[26] Even if the torturer's motives do not reach that level of cruelty, the victim's humiliation and subjugation are undeniable.

Already we can see why liberals abhor torture. Liberalism incorporates a vision of engaged, active human beings possessing an inherent dignity regardless of their social station. The victim of torture is in every respect the opposite of this vision. The torture victim is isolated and reduced instead of engaged and enlarged, terrified instead of active, humiliated instead of dignified. And, in the paradigm case of torture, the victor's torment of defeated captives, liberals perceive the living embodiment of their worst nightmare: tyrannical rulers who take their pleasure from the degradation of those unfortunate enough to be subject to their will.

There are at least four other historically significant reasons for torture besides victor's cruelty (the paradigm case), and, as we shall see, all but one of them is fundamentally inimical to liberalism.

---

[24] *Ibid.*, p. 163. I suppose that the rationale was that if a slave were permitted to testify against his own master freely, then the society would be admitting that property can freely betray its owner, a dangerous thought in slaveholding societies. Hence, the slave can only be permitted to testify under compulsion. Hannah Arendt claimed it was because the ancients believed that "nobody can invent a lie under torture," but this speculation does nothing to explain why slaves and only slaves had to be tortured. Hannah Arendt, *The Human Condition*, 2nd edn. (University of Chicago Press, 1998), p. 129, n.78.

[25] Nietzsche, *Genealogy of Morals*, p. 501 (describing "the pleasure of being allowed to vent his power freely upon one who is powerless, the voluptuous pleasure 'de faire le mal pour le plaisir de le faire', the enjoyment of violation").

[26] Montaigne, "Of Cruelty," p. 316.

Terror

First, there is torture for the purpose of terrorizing people into submission. Dictators from Hitler to Pinochet to Saddam Hussein tortured their political prisoners so that their enemies, knowing that they might face a fate far worse than death, would be afraid to oppose them. Genghis Khan's conquests were made easier because his reputation for cruelty against those who opposed him led cities to surrender without a fight. Terror is a force-magnifier that permits a relatively small number of police to subdue a far larger population than they could if would-be rebels were confident that they would be treated humanely upon capture. But of course, a practice that exists to make it easier to subdue and tyrannize people is fundamentally hostile to liberals' political philosophy.

Punishment

Second, until the last two centuries, torture was used as a form of criminal punishment. It was torture as a form of punishment that drew Montaigne's condemnation, and it is noteworthy that the Eighth Amendment to the US Constitution prohibits cruel and unusual punishments, rather than cruelty more generally. Beccaria condemns punishments that are more cruel than is absolutely necessary to deter crime, arguing on classical-liberal grounds that people in the state of nature will surrender only the smallest quantum of liberty necessary to secure society: "The aggregate of these smallest possible portions of individual liberty constitutes the right to punish; everything beyond that is an abuse and not justice, a fact but scarcely a right."[27] Beccaria makes it clear that torture would turn society into "a herd of slaves who constantly exchange timid cruelties with one another."[28] Such punishments, he adds, "would also be contrary to justice and to the nature of the social contract itself,"[29] presumably because turning society into a herd of slaves undermines the liberal understanding of the ends of society. Beccaria was widely read in America during the founding era.[30]

Foucault argues that the abolition of punitive torture had little to do with increased humanitarianism. Instead, it had to do with a change in the distribution of crime in Western Europe. As the West grew more prosperous, property crimes eclipsed crimes of passion as a social problem. This led to calls for a milder but

---

[27] Cesare Beccaria, *On Crimes and Punishments* [first published in 1764](David Young, Trans.) (Cambridge, MA: Hackett, 1986), pp. 8–9.

[28] *Ibid.*, p. 10.   [29] *Ibid.*

[30] Irene Quenzler Brown and Richard D. Brown, *The Hanging of Ephraim Wheeler: A Story of Rape, Incest, and Justice in Early America* (Cambridge, MA: Harvard University Press, 2003), pp. 192–4, 260–1, 264, 278 (discussing prominent Revolutionary-era figures influenced by Beccaria); Adam Jay Hirsch, *The Rise of the Penitentiary: Prisons and Punishment in Early America* (New Haven, CT: Yale University Press, 1992), p. 26 (noting Beccaria's influence in early America).

more certain system of punishments. The trouble with torture is that when the punishment is so awful, the temptation to mercy becomes too great. Imprisonment, out of sight and out of mind, replaced the public spectacle of torment.[31]

Be that as it may, it seems equally clear that punitive torture had no place in liberal polities. Torture, as Foucault explains, was a symbolic assertion of the absolute sovereign whose personal prerogatives had been affronted by crime. It was a ritual of royal dominance and royal revenge, acted out in public spectacle to shock and awe the multitude.[32] With the growth of liberal democracy, the ideology of popular sovereignty deflated the purpose of punitive torture: if the people rule, then the responsibility of torture would fall on the people, and the need for a spectacle of suffering by which the people could impress themselves seemed pointless.[33]

Extracting confessions

Curiously, when Beccaria writes explicitly about the subject of torture, he does not mention torture as punishment. Rather, he polemicizes against judicial torture in order to extract confessions from criminal suspects.[34] This is the third historically significant use of torture, distinct from punishment, even though judges administer both. The French language has different words for them: le supplice, torture as punishment, and la question, torture to extract confessions. As John Langbein observes, premodern legal rules required either multiple eyewitnesses or confessions for criminal convictions. At first glance, these were important rights of the accused, but they had the perverse effect of legitimating judicial torture in order to make convictions possible. But once it was accepted that the criminal justice system could base guilty verdicts on various types of evidence that rationally establish facts, rather than insisting on the ritual of confession, then the need for torture to secure convictions vanished.[35] Furthermore, the only crimes for which the primary evidence is the perpetrator's own words are crimes of heretical or seditious belief – and liberalism rejects the criminalization of belief.[36]

---

[31] Foucault, *Discipline and Punish*, pp. 82–9.

[32] *Ibid.*, pp. 48–9 ("It is a ceremonial by which a momentarily injured sovereignty is reconstituted. It restores that sovereignty by manifesting it at its most spectacular... This practice of torture was ... a policy of terror: to make everyone aware, through the body of the criminal, of the unrestrained presence of the sovereign.").

[33] Granted, the public spectacle of suffering certainly persisted in the American practice of lynching.

[34] Beccaria, *On Crimes and Punishments*, pp. 29–33.

[35] John H. Langbein, *Torture and the Law of Proof: Europe and England in the Ancien Regime* (University of Chicago Press, 1977), pp. 4–5, 45–69; John H. Langbein, "Torture and Plea Bargaining," *University of Chicago Law Review*, 46 (1978), 3–22, at 4–5.

[36] See Alan Donagan, "The Right Not to Incriminate Oneself," *Social Philosophy and Policy*, 1(02) (1984), 137–48, at 143–4.

Intelligence gathering

These, then, are the four illiberal motives for torture: victor's pleasure, terror, punishment, and extracting confessions. That leaves only one rationale for torture that might conceivably be acceptable to a liberal: torture as a technique of intelligence gathering from captives who will not talk. This may seem indistinguishable from torture to extract confessions, because both practices couple torture with interrogation. The crucial difference lies in the fact that the confession is backward-looking, in that it aims to document and ratify the past for purposes of retribution, while intelligence gathering is forward-looking because it aims to gain information to forestall future evils like terrorist attacks.

It is striking, and in obvious ways reassuring, that this is the only rationale for torture that liberal political culture admits could even possibly be legitimate. To speak in a somewhat perverse and paradoxical way, liberalism's insistence on limited governments that exercise their power only for instrumental and pragmatic purposes creates the possibility of seeing torture as a civilized, not an atavistic, practice, provided that its sole purpose is preventing future harms. Rejecting torture as victor's spoils, as terror, as punishment, and as a device to force confession drastically limits the amount of torture that a liberal society might conceivably accept. But more importantly, the liberal rationale for torture as intelligence gathering in gravely dangerous situations transforms and rationalizes the motivation for torture. Now, for the first time, it becomes possible to think of torture as a last resort of men and women who are profoundly reluctant to torture. And in that way, liberals can for the first time think of torture dissociated from cruelty – torture authorized and administered by decent human beings who abhor what circumstances force them to do. Torture to gather intelligence and save lives seems almost heroic. For the first time, we can think of kindly torturers rather than tyrants.

I shall be arguing shortly that this way of thinking represents a dangerous delusion. But before abandoning the subject of how torture "became civilized," it is important to note one other dimension in which torture has become less cruel.

Readers of Foucault's *Discipline and Punish* will probably never forget its nauseating opening pages, in which Foucault describes in loving detail the gruesome death by torture of the man who assaulted Louis XV.[37] Foucault aims to shock, of course, and he certainly succeeded with me: I closed the book and would not open it again for twenty years. There is a vast difference, however, between the ancient world of torture, with its appalling mutilations, its roastings and flayings, and the tortures that liberals might accept: sleep deprivation, prolonged standing in stress positions, extremes of heat and cold, bright lights and loud music – what some refer to as "torture lite."

---

[37] Foucault, *Discipline and Punish*, pp. 3–6.

I do not mean to diminish how horrible these experiences are, nor do I mean to suggest that American interrogators never go further than torture lite. Waterboarding, withholding of pain medication from wounded captives, putting lit cigarettes in their ears, rape, and beatings all go much further.[38] At least five, and maybe more than twenty captives have been beaten to death by American interrogators.[39] My point is rather that liberals generally draw the line at forms of torture that maim the victim's body. This, like the limitation of torture to intelligence gathering, marks an undeniable moderation in torture,

[38] The Fay–Jones Report mentions alleged sodomy of a detainee with a police stick. Fay–Jones Report, *Torture Papers*, p. 1076. A memorandum to FBI officials reported the placing of lit cigarettes in detainees' ears at Guantánamo. See Neil A. Lewis and David Johnston, "New F.B.I. Files Describe Abuse of Iraq Inmates," *New York Times*, Dec. 21, 2004, p. A1. For that matter, there need be nothing "lite" about "torture lite." According to Lewis and Johnston, in the words of an FBI agent, "On another occasion, the A/C had been turned off, making the temperature in the unventilated room probably well over 100 degrees. The detainee was almost unconscious on the floor, with a pile of hair next to him. He had apparently been literally pulling his own hair out throughout the night." The withholding of pain medication and waterboarding or other faux-suffocation techniques reportedly have been admitted by US officials in the interrogation of Abu Zubaidah and Khalid Sheik Mohammed. See, e.g., Douglas Jehl and David Johnston, "C.I.A. Expands Its Inquiry into Interrogation Tactics," *New York Times*, Aug. 29, 2004, p. A10; Dana Priest, "CIA Puts Harsh Tactics on Hold," *Washington Post*, June 27, 2004, p. A1; Susan Schmidt, "Disclosure of Authorized Interrogation Tactics Urged," *Washington Post*, July 3, 2004, p. A3.

[39] In one case of a detainee death, several soldiers have been charged with abuse rather than homicide due to insufficient evidence. In another case, two soldiers were charged with premeditated murder. Eric Schmitt, "Navy Charges 3 Commandos with Beating of Prisoners," *New York Times*, Sept. 25, 2004, p. A7. Army investigators have recommended that at least three Army Reserve soldiers be charged with negligent homicide for their role in the beating to death of two prisoners in the Bagram detention facility outside Kabul. Tom Bowman, "Charges Urged in Deaths of Detainees," *Baltimore Sun*, Sept. 16, 2004, p. A1. Two marines were charged with negligent homicide in relation to the death of Nagem Sadoon Hatab in the Camp Whitehorse detention center outside Nasiriyah. The charges against one of the marines were eventually dropped. Deborah Hastings, "Iraq POW Death Remains a Mystery," *Times Union* (Albany, NY), Aug. 1, 2004, p. A2. And a Navy SEAL, whose identity has not been released, is being court-martialed in connection with the beating of Manadel Jamadi, who was later killed, allegedly by CIA interrogators, in Abu Ghraib (and whose body was photographed there, packed in ice). Schmitt, "Navy Charges 3 Commandos," p. A7; "Court-Martial of Navy SEAL in Abuse of Iraqi Postponed," *Washington Post*, Mar. 22, 2005, p. A18. According to an independent panel's report on Abu Ghraib, there have been "five cases of detainee deaths as a result of abuse by U.S. personnel during interrogations" already substantiated. "Final Report of the Independent Panel to Review DOD [Department of Defense] Detention Operations (Aug. 2004)," in *Torture Papers*, pp. 908, 914 (hereinafter Schlesinger Report). Yet a more recent account reports that "at least 26 prisoners have died in American custody in Iraq and Afghanistan since 2002 in what Army and Navy investigators have concluded or suspect were acts of criminal homicide, according to military officials." Douglas Jehl and Eric Schmitt, "U.S. Military Says 26 Inmate Deaths May Be Homicide," *New York Times*, Mar. 16, 2005, p. A1.

the world's most immoderate practice. It is almost enough to persuade us that torture lite is not torture at all, or at least that it is not cruel enough to make liberals wince, at least not when the stakes are sufficiently high. Indeed, they may even deny that it is torture.

Let me summarize this part of my argument. Liberals, I have said, rank cruelty first among vices – not because liberals are more compassionate than anyone else, but because of the close connection between cruelty and tyranny. Torture is the living manifestation of cruelty, and the peculiar horror of torture within liberalism arises from the fact that torture is tyranny in micro-cosm, at its highest level of intensity. The history of torture reinforces this horror because torture has always been bound up with military conquest, regal punishment, dictatorial terror, forced confessions, and the repression of dissi-dent belief – a veritable catalog of the evils of absolutist government that liberalism abhors. For all these reasons, it should hardly surprise us that liberals wish to ban torture absolutely – a wish that became legislative reality in the Torture Convention's insistence that nothing can justify torture.[40]

But what about torture as intelligence gathering, torture to forestall greater evils? I suspect that throughout history this has been the least common motivation for torture, and thus the one most readily overlooked. And yet it alone bears no essential connection with tyranny. This is not to say that the torture victim experiences it as any less terrifying, humiliating, or tyrannical. The victim, after all, undergoes abject domination by the torturer. But it will dawn on reluctant liberals that the torturer's goal of forestalling greater evils is one that liberals share. It seems like a rational motivation, far removed from cruelty and power lust. In fact, the liberal may for the first time find it possible to view torture from the torturer's point of view rather than the victim's.

Thus, even though absolute prohibition remains liberalism's primary teach-ing about torture, and the basic liberal stance is empathy for the torture victim, a more permissive stance remains an unspoken possibility, the Achilles' heel of absolute prohibitions. As long as the intelligence needs of a liberal society are slight, this possibility within liberalism remains dormant, perhaps even unnoticed. But when a catastrophe like 9/11 happens, liberals may cautiously conclude that, in the words of a well-known *Newsweek* article, it is "Time to Think About Torture."[41]

But the pressure of liberalism will compel them to think about it in a highly stylized and artificial way, what I will call the "liberal ideology of torture." The liberal ideology insists that the sole purpose of torture must be intelligence

---

[40] "No exceptional circumstances whatsoever, whether a state of war or a threat of war, internal political instability or any other public emergency, may be invoked as a justifica-tion of torture." Convention Against Torture and Other Cruel, Inhuman or Degrading Treatment or Punishment, Article 2, Mar. 4, 1984, S. Treaty Doc. No. 100-20, 1465 U.N.T.S. 85, 114 (hereinafter Convention Against Torture).

[41] Jonathan Alter, "Time to Think About Torture," *Newsweek*, Nov. 5, 2001, p. 45.

gathering to prevent a catastrophe; that torture is necessary to prevent the catastrophe; that torturing is the exception, not the rule, so that it has nothing to do with state tyranny; that those who inflict the torture are motivated solely by the looming catastrophe, with no tincture of cruelty; that torture in such circumstances is, in fact, little more than self-defense; and that, because of the associations of torture with the horrors of yesteryear, perhaps one should not even call harsh interrogation "torture."

And the liberal ideology will crystallize all of these ideas in a single, mesmerizing example: the ticking time bomb.

III   The ticking bomb

Suppose the bomb is planted somewhere in the crowded heart of an American city, and you have custody of the man who planted it. He will not talk. Surely, the hypothetical suggests, we should not be too squeamish to torture the information out of him and save hundreds of lives. Consequences count, and abstract moral prohibitions must yield to the calculus of consequences.

Everyone argues the pros and cons of torture through the ticking time bomb. Senator Schumer and Professor Dershowitz, the Israeli Supreme Court, and indeed every journalist devoting a think-piece to the unpleasant question of torture, begins with the ticking time bomb and ends there as well. The Schlesinger Report on Abu Ghraib notes that "for the U.S., most cases for permitting harsh treatment of detainees on moral grounds begin with variants of the 'ticking time-bomb' scenario."[42] At this point in my argument, I mean to disarm the ticking time bomb and argue that it is the wrong thing to think about. If so, the liberal ideology of torture begins to unravel.

But before beginning these arguments, I want to pause and ask why this jejune example has become the alpha and omega of our thinking about torture. I believe the answer is this: the ticking time bomb is proffered against liberals who believe in an absolute prohibition against torture. The idea is to force the liberal prohibitionist to admit that yes, even he or she would agree to torture in at least this one situation. Once the prohibitionist admits that, then she has conceded that her opposition to torture is not based on principle. Now that the prohibitionist has admitted that her moral principles can be breached, all that is left is haggling about the price. No longer can the prohibitionist claim the moral high ground; no longer can she put the burden of proof on her opponent. She is down in the mud with them, and the only question left is how much further down she will go. Dialectically, getting the prohibitionist to address the ticking time bomb is like getting the vegetarian to eat just one little oyster because it has no nervous system. Once she does that – gotcha!

---

[42] Schlesinger Report, note 39 above, pp. 908, 974.

The ticking-time-bomb scenario serves a second rhetorical goal, one that is equally important to the proponent of torture. It makes us see the torturer in a different light – one of the essential points in the liberal ideology of torture because it is the way that liberals can reconcile themselves to torture even while continuing to "put cruelty first." Now, he is not a cruel man or a sadistic man or a coarse, insensitive, brutish man. The torturer is instead a conscientious public servant, heroic the way that New York firefighters were heroic, willing to do desperate things only because the plight is so desperate and so many innocent lives are weighing on the public servant's conscience. The time bomb clinches the great divorce between torture and cruelty; it placates liberals, who put cruelty first.

Wittgenstein once wrote that confusion arises when we become bewitched by a picture.[43] He meant that it is easy to get seduced by simplistic examples that look compelling but actually misrepresent the world in which we live. If the subject is the morality of torture, philosophical confusions can have life-or-death consequences. I believe the ticking time bomb is the picture that bewitches us.

I do not mean that the time-bomb scenario is completely unreal. To take a real-life counterpart: in 1995, an Al Qaeda plot to bomb eleven US airliners and assassinate the Pope was thwarted by information tortured out of a Pakistani bomb-maker by the Philippine police.[44] According to journalists Marites Dañguilan Vitug and Glenda M. Gloria, the police had received word of possible threats against the Pope. They went to work. "For weeks, agents hit him with a chair and a long piece of wood, forced water into his mouth, and crushed lighted cigarettes into his private parts... His ribs were almost totally broken that [sic] his captors were surprised that he survived..."[45] Grisly, to be sure – but if they had not done it, thousands of innocent travelers might have died horrible deaths.

But look at the example one more time. The Philippine agents were surprised he survived – in other words, they came close to torturing him to death before he talked. And they tortured him for weeks, during which time they did not know about any specific Al Qaeda plot. What if he too did not know? Or what if there had been no Al Qaeda plot? Then they would have tortured him for weeks, possibly tortured him to death, for nothing. For all they knew at the time, that is exactly what they were doing. You cannot use the argument that preventing the Al Qaeda attack justified the decision to torture, because at the moment the decision was made no one knew about the Al Qaeda attack.

[43] Ludwig Wittgenstein, *Philosophical Investigations* (G. E. M. Anscombe, Trans.) (3rd edn., Oxford: Blackwell, 1958), pp. 47e–48e.

[44] Doug Struck *et al.*, "Borderless Network of Terror: Bin Laden Followers Reach Across Globe," *Washington Post*, Sept. 23, 2001, p. A1.

[45] Marites Dañguilan Vitug and Glenda M. Gloria, *Under the Crescent Moon: Rebellion in Mindanao* (Manila: Ateneo Center for Social Policy and Public Affairs, 2000), p. 223.

The ticking-bomb scenario cheats its way around these difficulties by stipulating that the bomb is there, ticking away, and that officials know it and know they have the man who planted it. Those conditions will seldom be met.[46] Let us try some more realistic hypotheticals and the questions they raise:

(1) The authorities know there may be a bomb plot in the offing, and they have captured a man who may know something about it, but may not. Torture him? How much? For weeks? For months? The chances are considerable that you are torturing a man with nothing to tell you. If he does not talk, does that mean it is time to stop, or time to ramp up the level of torture? How likely does it have to be that he knows something important? Fifty-fifty? Thirty-seventy? Will one out of a hundred suffice to land him on the waterboard?

(2) Do you really want to make the torture decision by running the numbers? A 1 percent chance of saving a thousand lives yields ten statistical lives. Does that mean that you can torture up to nine people on a 1 percent chance of finding crucial information?

(3) The authorities think that one out of a group of fifty captives in Guantánamo might know where Osama bin Laden is hiding, but they do not know which captive. Torture them all? That is, do you torture forty-nine captives with nothing to tell you on the uncertain chance of capturing bin Laden?

(4) For that matter, would capturing Osama bin Laden demonstrably save a single human life? The Bush administration has downplayed the importance of capturing bin Laden because American strategy has succeeded in marginalizing him. Maybe capturing him would save lives, but how certain do you have to be? Or does it not matter whether torture is intended to save human lives from a specific threat, as long as it furthers some goal in the war on terrorism? This last question is especially important once we realize that the interrogation of Al Qaeda suspects will almost never be employed to find out where the ticking bomb is hidden. Instead, interrogation is a more general fishing expedition for any intelligence that might be used to help "unwind" the terrorist organization. Now, one

---

[46] See Oren Gross, "Are Torture Warrants Warranted? Pragmatic Absolutism and Official Disobedience," *Minnesota Law Review*, 88 (2004), 1481–51, at 1501–3. Gross reminds us, however, that the catastrophic case can actually occur (pp. 1503–4). The ticking-bomb case might occur if a government has extremely good intelligence about a terrorist group – good enough to know that it has dispatched operatives to carry out an operation, and good enough to identify and capture someone in the group who knows the details – but not good enough to know the details without getting them from the captive. Israel seems like a setting in which cases like this might arise, and, indeed, Mark Bowden reports on just such a case. Mark Bowden, "The Dark Art of Interrogation," *Atlantic Monthly*, Oct. 2003, pp. 51, 65–8. Importantly, however, the Israeli interrogator obtained the information through trickery, not torture.

might reply that Al Qaeda is itself the ticking time bomb, so that unwinding the organization meets the formal conditions of the ticking-bomb hypothetical. This is equivalent to asserting that any intelligence that promotes victory in the war on terrorism justifies torture, precisely because we understand that the enemy in the war on terrorism aims to kill American civilians. Presumably, on this argument, Japan would have been justified in torturing American captives in World War II on the chance of finding intelligence that would help them shoot down the *Enola Gay*, the airplane that dropped the atomic bomb on Hiroshima. I assume that a ticking-bomb hard-liner will not flinch from this conclusion. But, at this point, we verge on declaring all military threats and adversaries that menace American civilians to be ticking bombs whose defeat justifies torture. The limitation of torture to emergency exceptions, implicit in the ticking-bomb story, now threatens to unravel, making torture a legitimate instrument of military policy. And then the question becomes inevitable: why not torture in pursuit of any worthwhile goal?

(5) Indeed, if you are willing to torture forty-nine innocent people to get information from the one who has it, why stop there? If suspects will not break under torture, why not torture their loved ones in front of them? They are no more innocent than the forty-nine you have already shown you are prepared to torture. In fact, if only the numbers matter, torturing loved ones is almost a no-brainer if you think it will work. Of course, you will not know until you try whether torturing his child will break the suspect. But that just changes the odds; it does not alter the argument.

The point of the examples is that in a world of uncertainty and imperfect knowledge, the ticking-bomb scenario should not form the point of reference. The ticking bomb is the picture that bewitches us. The real debate is not between one guilty man's pain and hundreds of innocent lives. It is the debate between the certainty of anguish and the mere possibility of learning something vital and saving lives. And, above all, it is the question about whether a responsible citizen must unblinkingly think the unthinkable and accept that the morality of torture should be decided purely by totaling up costs and benefits.[47] Once you accept that only the numbers count, then anything, no matter how gruesome, becomes possible. "Consequentialist rationality," as Bernard Williams notes sardonically, "will have something to say even on the difference between massacring seven million, and massacring seven million and one."[48]

[47] For a powerful version of the consequentialist argument, which acknowledges these consequences and accepts them (at least for dialectical purposes), see Louis Michael Seidman, "Torture's Truth," *University of Chicago Law Review*, 72 (2005), 881–918.
[48] Bernard Williams, "A Critique of Utilitarianism," in J. J. C. Smart and Bernard Williams, *Utilitarianism: For and Against* (Cambridge University Press, 1973), pp. 77–150, at pp. 75, 93.

I am inclined to think that the path of wisdom instead lies in Holocaust survivor David Rousset's famous caution that normal human beings do not know that everything is possible.[49] As Williams says, "there are certain situations so monstrous that the idea that the processes of moral rationality could yield an answer in them is insane" and "to spend time thinking what one would decide if one were in such a situation is also insane, if not merely frivolous."[50]

IV   Torture as a practice

There is a second, insidious, error built into the ticking-bomb hypothetical. It assumes a single, *ad hoc* decision about whether to torture, by officials who ordinarily would do no such thing except in a desperate emergency. But in the real world of interrogations, decisions are not made one-off. The real world is a world of policies, guidelines, and directives. It is a world of practices, not of *ad hoc* emergency measures. Therefore, any responsible discussion of torture must address the practice of torture, not the ticking-bomb hypothetical. I am not saying anything original here; other writers have made exactly this point.[51] But somehow, we always manage to forget this and circle back to the ticking time bomb. Its rhetorical power has made it indispensable to the sensitive liberal soul, and we would much rather talk about the ticking bomb than about torture as an organized social practice.

Treating torture as a practice rather than as a desperate improvisation in an emergency means changing the subject from the ticking bomb to other issues like these: should we create a professional cadre of trained torturers? That means a group of interrogators who know the techniques, who learn to overcome their instinctive revulsion against causing physical pain, and who acquire the legendary surgeon's arrogance about their own infallibility. It has happened before. Medieval executioners were schooled in the arts of agony as part of the trade: how to break men on the wheel, how to rack them, and even how to surreptitiously strangle them as an act of mercy without the blood-thirsty crowd catching on.[52] In Louis XVI's Paris, torture was a hereditary family trade whose tricks were passed on from father to son.[53] Who will teach

---

[49] David Rousset, *The Other Kingdom* (Ramon Guthrie, Trans.) (New York: Howard Fertig, 1982), p. 168.

[50] Williams, "A Critique of Utilitarianism," p. 92, suggests "that the unthinkable was itself a moral category."

[51] See, e.g., Bowden, "Dark Art of Interrogation," pp. 74, 76; Michael Ignatieff, "The Torture Wars," *New Republic*, Apr. 22, 2002, p. 40; Marcy Strauss, "Torture," *New York Law School Review*, 48 (2003), 201–74, at 270–1.

[52] Arthur Isak Applbaum, "Professional Detachment: The Executioner of Paris," *Harvard Law Review*, 109 (1995), 458–86, at 459–60, 475.

[53] *Ibid.*, p. 459.

torture techniques now? Should universities create an undergraduate course in torture? Or should the subject be offered only in police and military academies?[54] Do we want federal grants for research to devise new and better techniques? Patents issued on high-tech torture devices? Companies competing to manufacture them? Trade conventions in Las Vegas? Should there be a medical subspecialty of torture doctors, who ensure that captives do not die before they talk?[55] The questions amount to this: do we really want to create a torture culture and the kind of people who inhabit it? The ticking time bomb distracts us from the real issue, which is not about emergencies, but about the normalization of torture.

Perhaps the solution is to keep the practice of torture secret in order to avoid the moral corruption that comes from creating a public culture of torture. But this "solution" does not reject the normalization of torture. It accepts it, but layers on top of it the normalization of state secrecy. The result would be a shadow culture of torturers and those who train and support them, operating outside the public eye and accountable only to other insiders of the torture culture.

Just as importantly, who guarantees that case-hardened torturers, inured to levels of violence and pain that would make ordinary people vomit at the sight, will know where to draw the line on when torture should be used? They rarely have in the past. They did not in Algeria.[56] They did not in Israel, where, in 1999, the Israeli Supreme Court backpedaled from an earlier consent to torture lite because the interrogators were torturing two-thirds of their Palestinian captives.[57] In the Argentinian Dirty War, the tortures began because terrorist cells had a policy of fleeing when one of their members had disappeared for forty-eight hours, leaving authorities two days to wring the information out of the captive.[58] Mark Osiel, who has studied the Argentinean military in the Dirty War, reports that many of the torturers initially had qualms

---

[54] We should recall that for years American instructors taught torture to Latin American military officers at the School of the Americas in Fort Benning, Georgia. See Dana Priest, "U.S. Instructed Latins on Executions, Torture," *Washington Post*, Sept. 21, 1996, p. A1.

[55] Summarizing extensive studies by researchers, Jean Maria Arrigo notes medical participation in 20–40% of torture cases. One study, a random survey of 4,000 members of the Indian Medical Association (of whom 743 responded), revealed that "58% believed torture interrogation permissible; 71% had come across a case of probable torture; 18% knew of health professionals who had participated in torture; 16% had witnessed torture themselves; and 10% agreed that false medical and autopsy reports were sometimes justified." Jean Maria Arrigo, "A Utilitarian Argument Against Torture Interrogation of Terrorists," *Science and Engineering Ethics*, 10 (2004), 543, 548.

[56] This is the conclusion Michael Ignatieff draws from the memoirs of French torturer Paul Aussaresses, who remains completely unapologetic for torturing and killing numerous Algerian terrorists. Ignatieff, "Torture Wars," p. 42.

[57] Bowden, "Dark Art of Interrogation," pp. 74–6.

[58] Mark J. Osiel, *Mass Atrocity, Ordinary Evil, and Hannah Arendt: Criminal Consciousness in Argentina's Dirty War* (New Haven, CT: Yale University Press, 2002), p. 40.

about what they were doing, until their priests reassured them that they were fighting God's fight.[59] By the end of the Dirty War, the qualms were gone, and, as John Simpson and Jana Bennett report, hardened young officers were placing bets on who could kidnap the prettiest girl to rape and torture.[60] Escalation is the rule, not the aberration.[61]

There are two fundamental reasons for this: one rooted in the nature of bureaucracy and the other in social psychology. The liberal ideology of torture presupposes a torturer impelled by the desire to stop a looming catastrophe, not by cruelty. Implicitly, this image presumes that the interrogator and the decision-maker are the same person. But the defining fact about real organizations is the division of labor. The person who decides whether this prisoner presents a genuine ticking-bomb case is not the interrogator. The decision about what counts as a ticking-bomb case – one where torture is the lesser evil – depends on complex value judgments, and these are made further up the chain of command. The interrogator simply executes decisions made elsewhere.

Interrogators do not inhabit a world of loving kindness, or of equal concern and respect for all human beings. Interrogating resistant prisoners nonviolently and nonabusively still requires a relationship that in any other context would be morally abhorrent. It requires tricking information out of the subject, and the interrogator does this by setting up elaborate scenarios to disorient the subject and propel him into an alternative reality. The subject must be deceived into thinking that his high-value intelligence has already been revealed by someone else, so that it is no longer of any value. He must be fooled into thinking that his friends have betrayed him or that the interrogator is his friend. The interrogator disrupts his sense of time and place, disorients him with sessions that never take place at predictable times or intervals, and manipulates his emotions. The very names of interrogation techniques show this: "emotional love," "emotional hate," "fear up harsh," "fear up mild," "reduced fear," "pride and ego up," "pride and ego down," "futility."[62] The interrogator may set up a scenario to make the subject think he is in the clutches of a much-feared secret police organization from a different country ("false flag"). Every bit of the subject's environment is fair game for manipulation and deception, as the interrogator aims to create the total lie that gets the subject talking.[63]

---

[59] Ibid., pp. 120–1.
[60] John Simpson and Jana Bennett, The Disappeared and the Mothers of the Plaza: The Story of the 11,000 Argentinians Who Vanished (New York, St. Martin's Press, 1985), p. 109.
[61] Ignatieff, "Torture Wars," p. 42.
[62] Schlesinger Report, note 39 above, pp. 908, 966–7; see also Chris Mackey and Greg Miller, The Interrogator's War: Inside the Secret War Against Al Qaeda (London: John Murray, 2004), pp. 479–83.
[63] See Bowden, "Dark Art of Interrogation," pp. 64–5.

Let me be clear that I am not objecting to these deceptions. None of these practices rises to the level of abuse or torture lite, let alone torture heavy, and surely tricking the subject into talking is legitimate if the goals of the interrogation are legitimate. But what I have described is a relationship of totalitarian mind-control more profound than the world of Orwell's *Nineteen Eighty-Four*. The interrogator is like Descartes' "evil deceiver," and the subject lives in a false reality reminiscent of *The Matrix*. The liberal fiction that interrogation can be done by people who are neither cruel nor tyrannical runs aground on the fact that regardless of the interrogator's character off the job, on the job, every fiber of his concentration is devoted to dominating the mind of the subject.

Only one thing prevents this from turning into abuse and torture, and that is a clear set of bright-line rules, drummed into the interrogator with the intensity of a religious indoctrination, complete with warnings of fire and brimstone. American interrogator Chris Mackey reports that warnings about the dire consequences of violating the Geneva Conventions "were repeated so often that by the end of our time at [training school] the three syllables 'Lea-ven-worth' [the US maximum-security military prison] were ringing in our ears."[64]

But what happens when the line is breached? When, as in Afghanistan, the interrogator gets mixed messages about whether Geneva applies, or hears rumors of ghost detainees, of high-value captives held for years of interrogation in the top-secret facility known as "Hotel California," located in some nation somewhere?[65] Or when the interrogator observes around him the move from deception to abuse, from abuse to torture lite, from torture lite to beatings and waterboarding? Without clear lines, the tyranny innate in the interrogator's job has nothing to hold it in check.[66] Perhaps someone, somewhere in the chain of command, is wringing hands over whether this interrogation

---

[64] Mackey and Miller, *The Interrogator's War*, p. 31.

[65] Toby Harnden, "Welcome to the CIA's Hotel California," *Daily Telegraph* (London), Mar. 4, 2003, p. 11 (describing a secret interrogation center named for an Eagles song because "you can check in any time, but you can never leave").

[66] This point is made in the Fay–Jones Report, note 22 above, on Abu Ghraib. After noting that conflicting directives about stripping prisoners and using dogs were floating around simultaneously (p. 987), the report adds (p. 1004): "Furthermore, some military intelligence personnel executing their interrogation duties at Abu Ghraib had previously served as interrogators in other theaters of operation, primarily Afghanistan and GTMO [Guantánamo]. These prior interrogation experiences complicated understanding at the interrogator level. The extent of 'word of mouth' techniques that were passed to the interrogators in Abu Ghraib by assistance teams from Guantánamo, Fort Huachuca, or amongst themselves due to prior assignments is unclear and likely impossible to definitively determine. The clear thread in the CJTF-7 policy memos and published doctrine is the humane treatment of detainees and the applicability of the Geneva Conventions. Experienced interrogators will confirm that interrogation is an art, not a science, and knowing the limits of authority is crucial. Therefore, the existence of confusing and inconsistent interrogation technique policies contributed to the belief that additional interrogation techniques were condoned in order to gain intelligence."

qualifies as a ticking-bomb case; but the interrogator knows only that the rules of the road have changed and the posted speed limits no longer apply. The liberal fiction of the conscientious interrogator overlooks a division of moral labor in which the person with the fastidious conscience and the person doing the interrogation are not the same.

The fiction must presume, therefore, that the interrogator operates only under the strictest supervision, in a chain of command where his every move gets vetted and controlled by the superiors who are actually doing the deliberating. The trouble is that this assumption flies in the face of everything that we know about how organizations work. The basic rule in every bureaucratic organization is that operational details and the guilty knowledge that goes with them get pushed down the chain of command as far as possible. As sociologist Robert Jackall explains,

> it is characteristic ... that details are pushed down and credit is pulled up. Superiors do not like to give detailed instructions to subordinates... One of the privileges of authority is the divestment of humdrum intricacies... Perhaps more important, pushing details down protects the privilege of authority to declare that a mistake has been made... Moreover, pushing down details relieves superiors of the burden of too much knowledge, particularly guilty knowledge.[67]

We saw this phenomenon at Abu Ghraib, where military intelligence officers gave military police vague orders like: "'Loosen this guy up for us.' 'Make sure he has a bad night.' 'Make sure he gets the treatment.'"[68] Suppose that the 18-year-old guard interprets "make sure he has a bad night" to mean, simply, "keep him awake all night." How do you do that without physical abuse?[69] Furthermore, personnel at Abu Ghraib witnessed far harsher treatment of prisoners by "other governmental agencies" (OGA),[70] a euphemism for the CIA. They saw OGA spirit away the dead body of an interrogation subject, and allegedly witnessed a contract employee rape a youthful prisoner.[71] When that

[67] Robert Jackall, *Moral Mazes: The World of Corporate Managers* (Oxford University Press, 1988), p. 20.

[68] Seymour M. Hersh, *Chain of Command: The Road from 9/11 to Abu Ghraib* (New York: HarperCollins, 2004), p. 30.

[69] As a military police captain told Hersh, "when you ask an eighteen-year-old kid to keep someone awake, and he doesn't know how to do it, he's going to get creative." Hersh, *Chain of Command*, p. 34.

[70] See Fay–Jones Report, note 22 above, pp. 987, 990: "Working alongside non-DOD [Department of Defense] organizations/agencies in detention facilities proved complex and demanding. The perception that non-DOD agencies had different rules regarding interrogation and detention operations was evident [p. 987].... The appointing authority and investigating officers made a specific finding regarding the issue of 'ghost detainees' within Abu Ghraib. It is clear that the interrogation practices of other government agencies led to a loss of accountability at Abu Ghraib [p. 990]."

[71] Hersh, *Chain of Command*, pp. 44–5.

is what you see, abuses like those in the Abu Ghraib photos will not look outrageous. Outrageous compared with what?

This brings me to the point of social psychology. Simply stated, it is this: we judge right and wrong against the baseline of whatever we have come to consider "normal" behavior, and if the norm shifts in the direction of violence, we will come to tolerate and accept violence as a normal response. The psychological mechanisms for this renormalization have been studied for more than half a century, and by now they are reasonably well understood.[72] Rather than detour into psychological theory, however, I will illustrate the point with the most salient example – one that seems so obviously applicable to Abu Ghraib that the Schlesinger Commission discussed it at length in an appendix to its report.[73] This is the famous Stanford prison experiment. Male volunteers were divided randomly into two groups who would simulate the guards and inmates in a mock prison. Within a matter of days, the inmates began acting like actual prison inmates – depressed, enraged, and anxious. And the guards began to abuse the inmates to such an alarming degree that the researchers had to halt the two-week experiment after just seven days. In the words of the experimenters:

> The use of power was self-aggrandising and self-perpetuating. The guard power, derived initially from an arbitrary label, was intensified whenever there was any perceived threat by the prisoners and this new level subsequently became the baseline from which further hostility and harassment would begin... The absolute level of aggression as well as the more subtle and "creative" forms of aggression manifested, increased in a spiralling function.[74]

It took only five days before a guard, who prior to the experiment described himself as a pacifist, was forcing greasy sausages down the throat of a prisoner who refused to eat; and in less than a week, the guards were placing bags over prisoners' heads, making them strip, and sexually humiliating them in ways reminiscent of Abu Ghraib.[75]

---

[72] For details, see David Luban, "The Ethics of Wrongful Obedience," in Deborah L. Rhode, Ed., *Ethics in Practice: Lawyers' Roles, Responsibilities, and Regulation* (Oxford University Press, 2000), pp. 94–120, at pp. 101–3; David Luban, "Integrity: Its Causes and Cures," *Fordham Law Review*, 72 (2003), 279–310, at 293–8. Both these papers are republished in my book *Legal Ethics and Human Dignity* (Cambridge University Press, 2007).

[73] Schlesinger Report, note 39 above, pp. 908, 970–1.

[74] Craig Haney et al., "Interpersonal Dynamics of a Simulated Prison," *International Journal of Criminology and Penology*, 1 (1973), 69–97, at 94; see also Philip G. Zimbardo et al., "The Mind Is a Formidable Jailer: A Pirandellian Prison," *New York Times Magazine*, Apr. 8, 1973, pp. 40–2, and the remarkable internet slide-show of the experiment, Philip G. Zimbardo, "Stanford Prison Experiment: A Simulation Study of the Psychology of Imprisonment Conducted at Stanford University" (1999) (www.prisonexp.org).

[75] John Schwartz, "Simulated Prison in '71 Showed a Fine Line Between 'Normal' and 'Monster,'" *New York Times*, May 6, 2004, p. A20; Zimbardo, "Stanford Prison

My conclusion is very simple. Abu Ghraib is the fully predictable image of what a torture culture looks like. Abu Ghraib is not a few bad apples – it is the apple tree. And you cannot reasonably expect that interrogators in a torture culture will be the fastidious and well-meaning torturers that the liberal ideology fantasizes.

This is why Alan Dershowitz has argued that judges, not torturers, should oversee the permission to torture, which in his view must be regulated by warrants. The irony is that Jay S. Bybee, who signed the Justice Department's highly permissive torture memo, is now a federal judge. Politicians pick judges, and if the politicians accept torture, the judges will as well. Once we create a torture culture, only the naive would suppose that judges will provide a safeguard. Judges do not fight their culture – they reflect it.

For all these reasons, the ticking-bomb scenario is an intellectual fraud. In its place, we must address the real questions about torture – questions about uncertainty, questions about the morality of consequences, and questions about what it does to a culture and the torturers themselves to introduce the practice. Once we do so, I suspect that few Americans will be willing to accept that everything is possible.

V   The construction of a torture culture: the torture lawyers of Washington

A skeptic might respond that my dire warnings about a torture culture are exaggerated, overwrought, and (above all) hypothetical. Would that it were so. As a coda to the argument I have presented, I wish to offer a case study of a torture culture constructed under our noses in Washington. I am referring to the group of lawyers in President George W. Bush's administration who wrote the highly permissive secret memoranda that came close to legitimizing torture for interrogation purposes. These lawyers illustrate as graphically as any group how quickly and easily a secret culture of torture supporters can emerge even in the heart of a liberal culture. They illustrate as well how readily the liberal ideology of torture transforms into something far removed from liberalism.

By now, the background is well known, but it may be worthwhile to recapitulate briefly. There were, in reality, over a dozen memoranda pertaining to the status and treatment of detainees circulated between the White House, the Department of Defense, the State Department, and the Justice

Experiment," slides 8, 18, 21, 28, 33. The sausage incident is described in Craig Haney and Philip G. Zimbardo, "The Socialization into Criminality: On Becoming a Prisoner and a Guard," in June Louin Tapp and Felice J. Levine, Eds., *Law, Justice, and the Individual in Society: Psychological and Legal Issues* (New York: Holt, Rinehart, and Winston, 1977), pp. 198–223, at p. 209.

Department.[76] The most controversial, though, emerged from the Office of Legal Counsel in the Justice Department ("OLC"). Two OLC memos, written in early 2002, concluded that the Geneva Conventions do not cover Al Qaeda or Taliban captives.[77] These set the stage for President Bush's memo of February 7, 2002, affirming that conclusion, and asserting that prisoners would be treated consistently with Geneva "to the extent appropriate and consistent with military necessity" – a large loophole for intelligence-gathering.[78] In effect, the president, relying on the OLC, proclaimed that if military necessity requires it, Geneva is gone.

Six months later, OLC tendered another memo, this one on the question of whether harsh interrogation tactics violate US obligations under the Torture Convention and its implementing statutes. This memo, drafted in part by Professor John Yoo and signed by OLC head Jay S. Bybee, reached a series of startling conclusions: that the infliction of pain rises to the level of torture only if the pain is as severe as that accompanying "death, organ failure, or serious impairment of body functions";[79] that the infliction of psychological pain rises to the level of torture only if the interrogator specifically intended it to cause "lasting ... damage" such as post-traumatic stress disorder;[80] that it would be unconstitutional to apply antitorture laws to interrogations authorized by the president in the war on terrorism;[81] and that, "under the current

---

[76] Many are included in *Torture Papers*, note 10 above. All the OIC torture memos, including five that were not released at the time *The Torture Papers* was published, are reproduced in David Cole, Ed., *The Torture Memos: Rationalizing the Unthinkable* (New York Review of Books, 2009).

[77] Draft Memorandum from John Yoo, Deputy Assistant Attorney General, US Department of Justice, Office of Legal Counsel, and Robert J. Delahunty, Special Counsel, US Department of Justice, Office of Legal Counsel, to William J. Haynes II, General Counsel, Department of Defense (Jan. 9, 2002), in *Torture Papers*, note 10 above, p. 38; Memorandum from Jay S. Bybee, Assistant Attorney General, US Department of Justice, Office of Legal Counsel, to Alberto R. Gonzales, Counsel to the President, and William J. Haynes II, General Counsel, Department of Defense (Jan. 22, 2002), in *Torture Papers*, note 10 above, p. 81. In July 2005, the District of Columbia Court of Appeals endorsed this view in *Hamdan* v. *Rumsfeld*, 415 F.3d 33, 40–2 (D.C. Cir. 2005), concluding that Article 3 of the Geneva Conventions does not apply to Al Qaeda captives. Article 3, which is identical in the four Geneva Conventions, provides basic human rights, including the right not to be subjected to cruel, humiliating, or degrading treatment, to prisoners who do not qualify for full Geneva protection. (Subsequent to the original publication of this chapter, that decision was overturned.)

[78] Memorandum from President George W. Bush to the Vice President *et al.* (Feb. 7, 2002), in *Torture Papers*, note 10 above, pp. 134–5. A second loophole is that President Bush declared only that "the United States Armed Forces shall continue to treat detainees humanely." The president's declaration does not cover the CIA.

[79] Memorandum from John C. Yoo, Deputy Assistant Attorney General, US Department of Justice, Office of Legal Counsel, to Alberto R. Gonzales, Counsel to the President (Aug. 1, 2002), in *Torture Papers*, note 10 above, pp. 172, 176 (hereinafter Bybee memo); also in Cole, *Torture Memos*.

[80] *Torture Papers*, p. 177.   [81] *Ibid.*, p. 173.

circumstances, necessity or self-defense may justify interrogation methods that might violate" the criminal prohibition on torture.[82]

The Bybee memo proved to be enormously influential. In January 2003, Defense Secretary Donald Rumsfeld formed a working group on interrogation techniques, which produced its own report in April.[83] Significantly, the working-group report was based substantially on the Bybee memo, and in fact, incorporated portions of it verbatim. The working-group report, in turn, influenced policy on interrogation tactics. Two months after the Bybee memo, a military lawyer, Lieutenant Colonel Diane Beaver, produced a memo of her own that legitimized harsh interrogational tactics, including "the use of a wet towel to induce the misperception of suffocation," provided that there is a legitimate national security objective.[84]

None of these memoranda and reports were produced in a vacuum. The Bybee memo "was vetted by a larger number of officials, including lawyers at the National Security Council, the White House counsel's office, and Vice President Cheney's office."[85] Apparently, the then White House counsel Alberto Gonzales requested the memorandum.[86] And the Department of Defense working group was formed after the head of an Army interrogation team requested permission to escalate to harsher tactics.[87]

Once they were leaked, the OLC memoranda proved to be incredibly controversial, not only because of their conclusions, but also because of a near consensus that the legal analysis in the Bybee memo was bizarre. The memo argued that because a healthcare statute lists severe pain as a possible symptom of a medical emergency, only pain equivalent to that accompanying medical emergencies is severe.[88] It attempted to show that while the necessity defense applies to torture, it need not apply to life-saving abortions. It also argued that Congress had defined torture so as to permit its use when necessary, even though Congress categorically forbade torture regardless of its purpose.[89] And it argued that the president has authority to order torture regardless of the

---

[82] *Ibid.*

[83] US Department of Defense, Working Group Report on Detainee Interrogations in the Global War on Terrorism: Assessment of Legal, Historical, Policy and Operational Considerations (Apr. 4, 2003), in *Torture Papers*, note 10 above, p. 286.

[84] Memorandum from Diane E. Beaver, Staff Judge Advocate, to Department of Defense Joint Task Force (Oct. 11, 2002), in *Torture Papers*, note 10 above, pp. 229, 235.

[85] Priest, "CIA Puts Harsh Tactics on Hold," p. A1.

[86] See David Johnston and Neil A. Lewis, "Bush's Counsel Sought Ruling About Torture," *New York Times*, Jan. 5, 2005, p. A1; R. Jeffrey Smith and Dan Eggen, "Gonzales Helped Set the Course for Detainees," *Washington Post*, Jan. 5, 2005, p. A1.

[87] Press Briefing by White House Counsel Judge Alberto Gonzales, Department of Defense General Counsel William Haynes, Department of Defense Deputy General Counsel Daniel Dell'Orto, and Army Deputy Chief of Staff for Intelligence General Keith Alexander (June 22, 2004) (www.whitehouse.gov/news/releases/2004/06/20040611-14.html).

[88] Bybee memo, note 79 above, pp. 172, 176.   [89] *Ibid.*, p. 209 and n.23.

statutory prohibition, without bothering so much as to raise the question whether this runs contrary to the Take Care Clause of the Constitution.[90] It is hard not to agree with Peter Brooks' blunt assessment: the Bybee memo "offers a remarkable example of textual interpretation run amok – less 'lawyering as usual' than the work of some bizarre literary deconstructionist."[91] Unsurprisingly, in the wake of the Abu Ghraib scandal, the Justice Department repudiated the Bybee memo. Indeed, former OLC lawyers from past Republican administrations criticized the memo, and Ruth Wedgwood, perhaps the most prominent academic defender of Bush administration legal positions in the war on terrorism, denounced the Bybee memo in a blistering *Wall Street Journal* editorial, which she co-authored with the former CIA director R. James Woolsey.[92] Shortly before Alberto Gonzales faced confirmation hearings as attorney general, the OLC issued a new torture memorandum (the "Levin memorandum"), repudiating and replacing the Bybee memo. It was posted unannounced on the Department of Justice's website, on December 30, 2004.[93]

What should we make of this? Not much, some might say. The Justice Department has disowned the Bybee memo, Mr. Bybee has been promoted out of the OLC to the federal appellate bench, and Professor Yoo, the principal author of the Bybee memo, has left government service. One way to understand the Bybee memo is that it represents an odd moment when several stars and planets fell into an unusual alignment and the moonshine threw the OLC into a peculiarly aggressive mood. Now, however, the OLC has officially rescinded the Bybee memo and replaced it with a document that begins with a ringing affirmation of US opposition to torture.[94]

But the lawyers' torture culture is not just the OLC in an isolated period of time, now past. It would be a dramatic mistake to suppose that the Justice Department has abandoned its views merely because it has disowned the Bybee memo. Although the Levin memo condemns torture and repudiates the Bybee memo's narrow definition of "severe pain," a careful reading shows that it does not broaden it substantially. Stunningly, all its illustrative examples of "the nature of the extreme conduct that falls within the statutory definition" of torture are on the upper end of the scale of barbarism.[95] They include, for

[90] The Take Care Clause requires that the president "shall take Care that the Laws be faithfully executed." U.S. Const. art. II, 3.

[91] Peter Brooks, "The Plain Meaning of Torture?", *Slate*, Feb. 9, 2005 (www.slate.com/id/2113314).

[92] Ruth Wedgwood and R. James Woolsey, "Law and Torture," *Wall Street Journal*, June 28, 2004, p. A10.

[93] Memorandum from Daniel Levin, Acting Assistant Attorney General, US Department of Justice, Office of Legal Counsel, to James B. Comey, Deputy Attorney General (Dec. 30, 2004), in Cole, *Torture Memos*, p. 128.

[94] The Levin memo begins: "Torture is abhorrent both to American law and values and to international norms." Cole, *Torture Memos*, p. 128.

[95] *Ibid.*, p. 140.

example, "severe beatings to the genitals, head, and other parts of the body with metal pipes, brass knuckles, batons, a baseball bat, and various other items; removal of teeth with pliers ... cutting off ... fingers, pulling out ... finger-nails" and similar atrocities.[96] Levin includes no hint that torture lite, or even torture medium, is prohibited by the statute. The Levin memo's analysis of "severe mental pain" differs from that of the Bybee memo in that it no longer suggests that the term encompasses only psychological damage that lasts for months or even years. Again, however, its illustrative examples all involve damage that lasted for years.[97] Nor does Levin criticize the Bybee memo's analyses of self-defense or necessity; it simply declines to discuss defenses. Similarly, it leaves open the question of whether the president can authorize torture, declaring evasively that because this president opposes torture, any discussion of the limits of his authority is unnecessary.[98] The Levin memo does acknowledge that techniques causing "severe physical suffering" count as torture even if they do not cause "severe physical pain" – and that may rule out some stress positions that the Bybee memo permits.[99] But apart from this one change, the Levin memo represents the minimum possible cosmetic emendation of the Bybee memo. It retracts only the arguments that journalists had jumped on (the "organ failure" definition of torture and the excessive emphasis Bybee placed on the specific intent requirement), retains a concep-tion of torture as atrocity fully in line with the liberal ideology, and evades the questions of criminal defenses and presidential authority to authorize torture.

Indeed, the OLC prepared other opinions, never released or leaked, which addressed specific interrogation techniques – and the Levin memo leaves these untouched.[100] In December 2004, the Bush administration fought off restric-tions (passed by a 96 to 2 Senate vote) which "would have explicitly extended to intelligence officers a prohibition against torture or inhumane treatment, and would have required the C.I.A. as well as the Pentagon to report to

---

[96] Ibid.
[97] Ibid., p. 146. Compare the Levin memo (arguing that mental pain "must extend for some period of time"), with the Bybee memo, note 79 above, p. 172 (arguing that mental pain must be "of significant duration, e.g., lasting for months or even years").
[98] Levin memo, note 93 above, p. 130.   [99] Ibid., p. 143.
[100] The Levin memo alludes to earlier opinions about the treatment of detainees and states that "we ... do not believe that any of their conclusions would be different under the standards set forth in this memorandum." Cole, Torture Memos, p. 130, n.8. Although this passage refers to the "treatment of detainees" in general, rather than interrogation techniques in particular, we may infer that the earlier opinions concerned interrogation techniques because the subject of the opinions was whether the treatment in question violates the prohibition on torture. These approved techniques include waterboarding. Toni Locy and John Diamond, "Memo Lists Acceptable 'Aggressive' Interrogation Methods," USA Today, June 28, 2004, p. A5. [2013 addition: this surmise was confirmed with the release of the Bybee–Yoo "techniques memo" in 2009. It is reprinted in Cole, Torture Memos.]

Congress about the methods they were using."[101] When asked why the administration resisted these restrictions, both Alberto Gonzales and Condoleezza Rice replied that it was to deny protection to people who are not entitled to it.[102] Neither finished the sentence: "not entitled to protection from torture or inhumane treatment."

One major loophole that the torture lawyers exploit is the distinction drawn in the Torture Convention between torture and "cruel, inhuman, or degrading" treatment ("CIDT").[103] The convention bans both, but U.S. implementing legislation criminalized only torture, not CIDT.[104] Mr. Gonzales told the US Senate in his written answers to questions that cruel, inhuman, and degrading treatment of detainees is forbidden to interrogators only within US territory.[105] The legal basis for this opinion was another piece of loophole lawyering on a par with the Bybee memo. When the United States ratified the Torture Convention, it attached a reservation interpreting "cruel, inhuman, and degrading" treatment to mean treatment violative of the Fifth, Eighth, or Fourteenth Amendments to the US Constitution.[106] Because these amendments do not apply extraterritorially, Mr. Gonzales argued, the prohibition on CIDT does not bind US interrogators abroad. Clearly, however, the Senate's reservation was referring to the substantive standards in the three amendments, not their jurisdictional scope.[107] To read it as Mr. Gonzales does would attribute to the Senate the remarkably absurd proposition that by definition, nothing US interrogators do abroad could ever be cruel, inhuman, or degrading.

[101] Douglas Jehl and David Johnston, "White House Fought New Curbs on Interrogations, Officials Say," *New York Times*, Jan. 13, 2005, p. A1.

[102] Gonzales' Responses to Durbin, note 21 above, pp. 7–8; Letter from Joshua B. Bolten, Director, Office of Management and Budget, and Condoleezza Rice, Assistant to the President for National Security Affairs, to Representative Peter Hoekstra and Senator Susan Collins, pp. 8–9 (Oct. 18, 2004) (www.fas.org/irp/news/2004/10/wh101804.pdf).

[103] Convention Against Torture, note 40 above, S. Treaty Doc. at 19, U.N.T.S at 113.

[104] Convention Against Torture and Other Cruel, Inhuman, or Degrading Treatment or Punishment, S. Exec. Rep. No. 101-30, at 8, 25 (1990).

[105] Gonzales' Responses to Durbin, note 21 above, pp. 1–2; see also Letter from Senators Patrick Leahy, Dianne Feinstein, and Russell D. Feingold, to then-Attorney General John Ashcroft (Jan. 25, 2005) (referring to Alberto Gonzales' written response to a Senate query on the extraterritorial permissibility of cruel, inhuman, or degrading treatment) (on file with the Virginia Law Review Association), and the detailed response, Letter from William E. Moschella, Assistant Attorney General, to Sen. Patrick J. Leahy (Apr. 4, 2005) (spelling out in detail the legal basis for Mr. Gonzales' answer) (on file with the Virginia Law Review Association).

[106] Convention Against Torture, note 104 above, S. Exec. Rep. No. 101-30, at 29.

[107] The Senate has a long-standing practice of adding reservations to human rights treaties stipulating that the rights they grant are no broader than those the US Constitution grants. The purpose of such reservations is to ensure that the treaties do not interfere with our domestic jurisprudence. Read in this normal way, the reservation simply ensures that the Convention Against Torture's meaning of "cruel" is the same as the Eighth Amendment's meaning.

It goes on. In March 2004, the OLC prepared a draft memorandum loopholing the Geneva Convention's prohibition on removing captives from the country of their capture and authorizing brief transfers of Iraqi captives out of Iraq for interrogation.[108] In early 2005, there were new revelations that the United States engages in "extraordinary renditions" – sending suspects for interrogation to states that engage in torture.[109] Reportedly, secret legal opinions justify extraordinary renditions, which may violate the Torture Convention.[110] In one well-known case, Maher Arar, a Canadian citizen of Syrian birth, was detained while transferring from one flight to another in New York City and sent to Syria, where he was tortured for a year. He is currently suing the US government, which has moved to dismiss his suit on remarkable grounds, asserting that the facts needed to litigate his case are US state secrets, and therefore he has no case.[111] In another well-known case, Omar Abu Ali, a US citizen of Saudi descent, was allegedly snatched by Saudi agents from his university classroom in Saudi Arabia, tortured, and detained for a year and a half at US request. When his parents filed for habeas corpus, the government offered no rebuttal of their allegations, instead arguing that the court lacks jurisdiction, and grounding the government's action in the president's foreign-affairs power (not even his commander-in-chief power).[112]

In April 2005, the circle beginning with the Abu Ghraib scandal closed, as a military investigation of alleged abuses at Guantánamo concluded that several of the humiliating techniques that drew shocked responses at Abu Ghraib – techniques such as sexually humiliating detainees, forcing them to wear women's underwear on their heads, leading them around on leashes, and forcing them to do dog tricks – are not illegal, and indeed have been authorized all along by Army Field Manual 34–52, the standard US Army doctrine regarding interrogation.[113] Along with this creative and unprecedented

---

[108]   Draft Memorandum from Jack I. Goldsmith III, Assistant Attorney General, US Department of Justice, Office of Legal Counsel, to Alberto R. Gonzales, Counsel to the President (Mar. 19, 2004), in *Torture Papers*, note 10 above, pp. 366, 367–8. Discussed in detail in Chapter 8 below, pp. 221–6.

[109]   Jane Mayer, "Outsourcing Torture," *New Yorker*, Feb. 14 and 21, 2005, p. 106.

[110]   Article 3 of the Torture Convention forbids the return of a person to "another State where there are substantial grounds for believing that he would be in danger of being subjected to torture." Convention Against Torture, note 40 above, S. Treaty Doc. No. 100-20, at 6, 1465 U.N.T.S. at 114.

[111]   Memorandum in Support of the United States' Assertion of State Secrets Privilege at 2–3, *Arar v. Ashcroft*, No. 04-CV-249-DGT-VVP (E.D.N.Y. Jan. 18, 2005) (on file with the Virginia Law Review Association). After lengthy litigation Arar lost.

[112]   *Abu Ali v. Ashcroft*, 350 F. Supp. 2d 28, 31 (D.D.C. 2004). Judge Bates, an appointee of President George W. Bush, rejected the government's arguments with outrage (pp. 40–1).

[113]   Army Regulation 15-6: Final Report: Investigation of FBI Allegations of Detainee Abuse at Guantánamo Bay, Cuba Detention Facility, pp. 8, 15–16, 19 (Apr. 1, 2005) (www.defense.gov/news/jul2005/d20050714report.pdf). This report, based on investigations by Lieutenant General Mark Schmidt and Brigadier General John Furlow, remains classified; the document cited here is an unclassified summary released on June 9, 2005.

interpretation of Army doctrine, the report "found no evidence of torture or inhumane treatment at [Guantánamo]."[114] Apparently, the Army no longer regards many of the Abu Ghraib techniques as "inhumane."

Conclusion

The only reasonable inference to draw from these recent efforts by the government to defend its actions is that the torture culture is still firmly in place, notwithstanding official condemnation of torture. Indeed, given that lawyers at the highest levels of government continue to loophole the laws against torture as energetically as ever, more than half a year after the Abu Ghraib revelations, the only reasonable inference to draw is that the US government is currently engaging in brutal and humiliating interrogations. At most, torture has given way to CIDT. The persistence of interrogational brutality should surprise no one, because the liberal ideology of torture fully legitimizes it. The memos illustrate the ease with which arguments that pretend that torture can exist in liberal society, but only as an exception, quickly lead to erecting a torture culture, a network of institutions and practices that regularize the exception and make it standard operating procedure.

For this reason, the liberal ideology of torture, which assumes that torture can be neatly confined to exceptional ticking-bomb cases and surgically severed from cruelty and tyranny, represents a dangerous delusion. It becomes more dangerous still coupled with an endless war on terrorism, a permanent emergency in which the White House eagerly insists that its emergency powers rise above the limiting power of statutes and treaties. Claims to long-term emergency powers that entail the power to torture should send chills through liberals of the right as well as the left, and no one should still think that liberal torture has nothing to do with tyranny.

[114] *Ibid.*, p. 1.

4

Unthinking the ticking bomb

Preface

This chapter was originally written for an essay collection discussing and honoring Henry Shue's classic book *Basic Rights: Subsistence, Affluence, and U.S. Foreign Policy*. *Basic Rights* is best known for its argument that rights to subsistence – a species of economic rights – are as basic as security rights. My chapter focused instead on a security right, the right against torture, which is another topic central to Shue's concerns. For Shue, both security and subsistence rights are *basic*, by which Shue means they are rights that must be satisfied if the enjoyment of other rights is to be possible at all.

There are a few small factual points where the chapter needs to be updated. When I wrote it, the US government had not admitted that it engaged in torture; since then, President Barack Obama has conceded on the record in his official speeches that the United States had tortured captives. The chapter points out that the US public at the time was remarkably indifferent to its government's torture, and cites public-opinion polls; since then, the same polls have shown a slow but steady increase in pro-torture sentiment (a topic that I take up in more detail in Chapter 10). We now have a better account of the interrogation of Abu Zubaydah, which is discussed briefly in this chapter, through the testimony and memoirs of Ali Soufan, the FBI interrogator who, without resorting to torture or abuse, obtained the most important information that Zubaydah had to give. Soufan's account supports what I say in the chapter.[1]

The most important update is conceptual, not factual. The chapter offers an analysis of the evils of torture that is more rudimentary and less exact than the theory offered in the following chapter. The two are consistent, but I now think

The main text of this chapter was first published in 2009 – see Acknowledgments.
[1] For Soufan's testimony, see "What Went Wrong: Torture and the Office of Legal Counsel in the Bush Administration": Hearing Before the Subcommittee on Administrative Oversight and the Courts of the Senate Committee on the Judiciary, 111th Congress (2009), pp. 22–5 (testimony of Ali Soufan); his full written statement is available at www. judiciary.senate.gov/hearings/testimony.cfm?id=e655f9e2809e5476862f735da14945e6&wit_id=e655f9e2809e5476862f735da14945e6-1-2. Ali H. Soufan, *The Black Banners: The Inside Story of 9/11 and the War Against Al Qaeda* (New York: Norton, 2011).

that the next chapter's version is more illuminating. Both focus on the point that the context of fear and humiliation in which torture occurs change the experienced character of the pain and suffering. In Chapter 5, I argue that that is because the aim of torture is to use pain and suffering as a medium to send the victim a message of total subjugation to the torturer. When I wrote the present chapter, I had not yet arrived at that understanding.

The main point of this chapter is the critique of ticking-bomb hypotheticals as a plausible way to discuss torture; it follows up and elaborates on Chapter 3. The argument is both philosophical and political. Philosophically, it criticizes one of contemporary philosophy's favorite analytical strategies: using extreme cases to test points of principle. Here I argue that it is a mistake to suppose that moral rationality can deliver a univocal verdict on every conceivable case, and that extreme cases are often exactly the ones in which moral rationality runs out. Although I do not draw the distinction in the chapter, the argument applies to two different ways of arguing from hypotheticals. One involves weird or impossible hypotheticals (saving five lives by throwing a very fat man in front of a runaway trolley, or similar exercises in the philosophical cottage industry of "trolley-ology"). The other is posing very stripped-down, schematic cases with clear intuitive answers, and reasoning from them by analogy to hard cases. The problem with the former is that we have no reason to suppose that moral rationality can deliver a reliable verdict on all logically possible sets of facts; the problem with the latter is that moral rationality may not be capable of confidently analogizing hard cases to easy ones. Depending on how they are framed, ticking-bomb cases can take either of these two forms, or both (when the case is so schematic that it could only happen in a weirdly improbable situation). Finally, I argue that the attempt to "think the unthinkable" runs the risk of losing a very important moral category of practices that we reject precisely because they have become unthinkable. Examples of such practices include slavery, massacre, and rape. The first two of these at least have been accepted for much of human history. I take up this point about unthinkability again in Chapter 5, where I argue that the reason these practices have become unthinkable is that opening them for reconsideration would compel us to put too many other central values on the table.

The political critique of ticking-bomb hypotheticals is that they deflect public attention from torture as it takes place in the real world to torture as it appears in fantasy cases (in Shue's words, "torture in dreamland") with cartoon villains and heroes and the uncertainties airbrushed out. I point out that *in fact* there are no authenticated US cases of the ticking-bomb scenario, and that the best-known cases are more like urban legends. Of course, this does not mean ticking-bomb cases could not happen or that they have not happened, but it does support the argument that talking about them is a distraction from discussing the actual practice of torture with no ticking bombs in the background. Insofar as public attentiveness to any issue is in short supply, displacing important questions with fantasy questions stifles thinking about the important questions.

In this update, it seems important to discuss two additional cases that often appear in ticking-bomb discussions: a lurid 2002 German murder case, and the location (and destruction) of Osama bin Laden.

The case of Daschner and Gäfgen

The German case involved a young man, Markus Gäfgen, who was convicted by a court in Frankfurt, Germany, of kidnapping and murdering Jakob von Metzler, the 11-year-old son of a banker. According to the trial judgment, after luring Jakob into his apartment, Gäfgen smothered him and hid his body in a pond. He then sent a note demanding ransom. The Frankfurt police trailed Gäfgen as he picked up the ransom money, deposited it into his bank account, and prepared to flee Frankfurt; they arrested him at the airport. Under interrogation, Gäfgen claimed that Jakob was being held by (imaginary) accomplices, but would not say where. Wolfgang Daschner, the deputy chief of the Frankfurt police, feared the boy might be dying from cold or thirst, so there was no time to lose. According to the court, Daschner urged the interrogators to torture Gäfgen (for example, by bending back his thumb and wrist) – but this they refused to do.[2]

The next morning, before Gäfgen's interrogator arrived at work, Daschner allegedly ordered a policeman named Ennigkeit to threaten Gäfgen with torture, and, if necessary, to inflict it. Acting on Daschner's instructions, Ennigkeit told Gäfgen that he would be subjected to "intolerable pain" by a specialist who was already en route to Frankfurt by helicopter; then he would be placed in a cell "with two big 'Negroes' who would anally assault him."[3]

---

[2] Landgericht Frankfurt am Main [Frankfurt Regional Court], Presseinformation, Schriftliche Urteilsgründe in der Strafsache gegen Wolfgang Daschner [written basis of judgment][hereinafter: Schriftliche Urteilsgründe], May 15 2005 (www.anstageslicht. de/dateien/LG_PM150205_DASCHNER.pdf), p. 13. All of the details described are drawn from this judgment and the judgment of the European Court of Human Rights cited in the following footnote.

[3] *Gäfgen v. Germany*, ECHR No. 22978/05, June 1, 2010, ¶ 26, available at http://hudoc.echr. coe.int/sites/eng/pages/search.aspx?i=001-99015#{"itemid":["001-99015"]}. The character of Ennigkeit's imagination scarcely needs comment. See, e.g., ¶¶ 15, 29, 80, 94 for details about the threats. It appears that there was no "torture specialist" being helicoptered in. Rather, when Daschner's subordinates refused to follow his orders, they mentioned another officer who was on vacation who might do it, and Daschner ordered him brought back by helicopter. Nothing in the trial court judgment indicates that this other officer was a torture specialist; at most, the implication is that his colleagues thought he might be willing to follow Daschner's orders. In any case, the other officers decided not to do what Daschner told them. Schriftliche Urteilsgründe, p. 13.

After ten minutes of threats, Gäfgen broke and led police to the boy's body. Gäfgen was convicted of murder, but Daschner and Ennigkeit were convicted of aggravated coercion, and ultimately – to the outrage of many Germans – a court awarded Gäfgen €3,000 damages for the violation of his human dignity involved in the torture threat.

Intuitively, the Gäfgen case seems like a real-life ticking bomb. Leave to one side the difference between threatening torture and actually inflicting it, because Daschner intended to carry out the threat if necessary.[4] Didn't Daschner do just the right thing in his effort to save Jakob's life?

One of the conditions in a genuine ticking-bomb case is that torture is the last resort to get the life-saving information. As the Bush administration adviser (and torture opponent), Philip Zelikow, put it, "[T]he elementary question would not be: Did you get information that proved useful? Instead it would be: Did you get information that could have been usefully gained only from these methods?"[5] Elementary or not, Zelikow's question is not often asked. What if we ask it about Daschner?

Daschner's colleagues testified that they rejected his plan to threaten torture because "an entire spectrum of measures was still available," including confronting Gäfgen with Jakob's sister.[6] One possibility jumps out. In hindsight, it is obvious why Magnus Gäfgen would not talk: Jakob was already dead. If he led the police to the body he would face charges of murder as well as kidnapping. Any competent investigator would have understood that this was a possible or even likely explanation of Gäfgen's stubborn silence – namely, that the boy was already dead and Gäfgen was hoping to beat a murder rap. Indeed, Gäfgen's first interrogator had asked him whether the boy was dead.[7] Before resorting to torture, Daschner could have tried promising Gäfgen immunity from prosecution for murder. Perhaps the promise would be a lie, or even impossible to keep under German law, but Daschner was bound to try. In fact, it appears that Daschner had not personally interrogated Gäfgen at all before ordering Ennigkeit to threaten torture.[8]

Lying promises are not nice; but compared to torture they are plainly the lesser evil. But what if an immunity promise would genuinely have made it impossible to prosecute Gäfgen for murder? In that case, Gäfgen would go free, or else be convicted only of lesser charges – a galling failure of criminal justice to punish a heinous crime. But it seems that a galling failure to punish a crime is still a lesser evil than torture. Or, if one wishes to argue that it is not,

[4] Ibid., ¶ 15.
[5] Philip Zelikow, "Legal Policy in a Twilight War," Houston Journal of International Law, 30 (2007–8), 89, 105.
[6] "Die Legende vom Helden Daschner," ZeitOnline, Nov. 25, 2004 (www.zeit.de/2004/49/ Daschner). See also Schriftliche Urteilsgründe, p. 6.
[7] Schriftliche Urteilsgründe, p. 5.   [8] Ibid., p. 6; Gäfgen v. Germany, ¶¶ 14–15.

notice the implication: we are now saying that torture is justified not only in ticking-bomb cases but also in cases where it is necessary to obtain a criminal conviction. Welcome back to the sixteenth century.

Of course, it is possible that nothing except the torture threat (or actual torture) would have succeeded.[9] That might have happened; the Gäfgen case is not a science-fiction hypothetical. But it seems vitally important to notice that neither is it an *actual* case in which no technique except torture or threatened torture would have produced information that might save a life. We will never know, because Daschner did not try lesser techniques, and apparently did not want to try them.[10]

The hunt for Osama bin Laden

In 2011, the question of torture bubbled to the surface again, when US special forces killed Osama bin Laden in Pakistan. Almost immediately, former Attorney General Michael Mukasey proclaimed in the pages of the *Wall Street Journal* that the trail to Bin Laden "began with a disclosure from Khalid Sheikh Mohammed (KSM), who broke like a dam under the pressure of harsh interrogation techniques that included waterboarding. He loosed a torrent of information – including eventually the nickname of a trusted courier of bin Laden."[11]

Now, Osama bin Laden was not a ticking bomb; his capacity to loose imminent threats on the United States had dwindled over the years of pursuit and flight. So this would be a case of torture to accomplish a less pressing goal than saving lives.

But even setting this point to one side, it is important to notice that Mr. Mukasey's claim was untrue. As the Constitution Project recounts, drawing on readily available public sources, the courier's name (Ahmed al-Kuwaiti) did not come from KSM. It was one of many given by torture victim Mohammed al Qahtani in 2002, but without any sense that al-Kuwaiti was important: Qahtani named him only as a man who had once given him computer training. The first real hint that al-Kuwaiti was a significant Al Qaeda figure came in 2004 from

---

[9] Gäfgen's interrogator had earlier offered Gäfgen reduced charges for the kidnapping, which proved ineffective because the child was already dead. Schriftliche Urteilsgründe, p. 17. This strongly suggests that nobody tried offering Gäfgen immunity from murder charges, or even a charge reduction to manslaughter, if Jakob was dead.

[10] *Gäfgen* v. *Germany*, ¶ 47; "Die Legende vom Helden Daschner." Daschner's subordinates had refused his orders to torture Gäfgen and explained that they had not exhausted the lawful methods of persuading Gäfgen to talk.

[11] Michael B. Mukasey, "The Waterboarding Trail to bin Laden," *Wall Street Journal*, May 6, 2011 (http://online.wsj.com/article/SB10001424052748703859304576305023876506348.html).

detainee Hassan Ghul – but, according to two US senators familiar with the record, Ghul gave up that information *before* his "enhanced" interrogation began.

As for KSM, he *denied* al-Kuwaiti's role, and it was his denial that aroused the interrogators' suspicions.[12] Of course, KSM would surely have denied al-Kuwaiti's role if he had not been tortured, arousing the same interrogator suspicions. So the right answer to Zelikow's "elementary" question should have been that torture was unnecessary to discover or confirm that al-Kuwaiti was the courier. The then CIA director Leon Panetta stated in a private letter to Senator John McCain, written shortly after bin Laden's death, that no detainee in the CIA's custody gave up the name of the courier.[13]

A second conclusion is that KSM's torture did not "work." As we will see in Chapter 7, the theory behind the torture program was to induce "learned helplessness" in its victims, so that afterward they would become docile, compliant, and cooperative. The point was not to induce them to give up information under torture, but to use torture to break them, so they would give up the information cooperatively in the aftermath. Here, however, KSM did not cooperate. Even in his supposedly helpless, broken, and docile state, he lied about al-Kuwaiti.

Thus, this supposed success story of the "enhanced interrogation" program actually amounts to an embarrassing counterexample to the success and necessity claims on torture's behalf. For we have just seen that torture was neither necessary nor sufficient to get Ghul and KSM to confirm the identity of al-Kuwaiti. Torture was not needed in Ghul's interrogation, and it did not produce candor in KSM's.

Of course, the dearth of genuine ticking-bomb cases is not germane to the philosophical methodology of testing principles by posing hypothetical cases; but it reinforces the political argument that focus on ticking-bomb cases diverts public debate from institutionalized torture when ticking bomb cases are not the issue. By diverting attention to cases in which torture is supposedly justified, the ticking-bomb discourse invites us to view the entire policy through the lens of the ticking bomb. In that way, ticking-bomb discourse not only diverts but also distorts political thinking.

By now there is a large literature on ticking-bomb cases; in keeping with my overall approach in this book, I shall not address this literature. However, I want to make one exception, briefly discussing Fritz Allhoff's recent book *Terrorism, Ticking Time-Bombs, and Torture*, which offers the most worked-out

---

[12] The Report of the Constitution Project's Task Force on Detainee Treatment, pp. 245–7.

[13] Greg Sargent, "Exclusive: Private Letter from CIA Chief Undercuts Claim Torture Was Key to Killing Bin Laden," *Washington Post*, May 16, 2011 (www.washingtonpost.com/blogs/plum-line/post/exclusive-private-letter-from-cia-chief-undercuts-claim-torture-was-key-to-killing-bin-laden/2011/03/03/AFLFF04G_blog.html).

and responsible defense of torture I have seen.[14] Allhoff offers a robust and unapologetic defense of torture in exceptional cases when it is the lesser evil, and an equally robust defense of using hypothetical ticking bombs as a philosophical tool for defending lesser-evil torture. Allhoff's basic motivation for defending interrogational torture is straightforward: where torture opponents focus relentlessly on the evils inflicted on the victim, he focuses on the evil of terrorist violence that torture is meant to prevent. Fully acknowledging the evils of torture, he nevertheless insists on viewing evil comparatively rather than absolutely – an approach I criticize in this chapter, but that I certainly accept as a reasonable one. This is not the place to offer an elaborate response to a long book, but I do want to highlight three major flaws I see in Allhoff's approach.

(1) Allhoff takes great care to emphasize that he is not defending "pervasive, institutionalized torture" but is focusing "on exceptional cases rather than normalized ones."[15] That is why he wants to study ticking-bomb hypotheticals: he insists that "ticking-time-bomb cases are not about torture policy; they are about one-off applications of torture."[16] He complains that criticism focusing on the evils of torture policy "misses the point of the dialectic since the realm of discourse at this stage is nonempirical; rather, it is about the hypothetical cases."[17] To this, one might respond that it is Allhoff who misses the point – in Shue's words, that hypothetical cases of one-off torture in ticking-bomb cases are "torture in dreamland." If the plausible ticking-bomb cases inevitably presuppose policies and not one-off decisions, then dealing with the hypothetical one-off cases nonempirically is a serious methodological error.

(2) What makes Allhoff's argument noteworthy is that he tackles the empirical arguments as well. In his view, critics who worry about a burgeoning torture bureaucracy are simply overrating the dangers. An effective torture program might need no more than "ten torture sites set up around the world and ... only thirty medical personnel *worldwide*. Not much of an institution."[18] Scientific research that contributes to torture "need not originally be undertaken for that reason," and the same goes for technology.[19] As for the corruption of police and military establishments, that would be necessary only if practices of torture become business as usual, not when torture is reserved for exceptional cases. Allhoff is confident that it will be possible to confine torture to the exceptional cases.

---

[14] Fritz Allhoff, *Terrorism, Ticking Time-Bombs, and Torture: A Philosophical Analysis* (University of Chicago Press, 2012). I would also like to mention Yuval Ginbar, *Why Not Torture Terrorists? Moral, Practical, and Legal Aspects of the "Ticking Bomb" Justification for Torture* (Oxford University Press, 2008); Ginbar, unlike Allhoff, is a torture critic whose argument is consonant with the approach I take in this book.
[15] Allhoff, *Terrorism, Ticking Time-Bombs, and Torture*, pp. 143–4.
[16] *Ibid.*, p. 117.   [17] *Ibid.*   [18] *Ibid.*, p. 148.   [19] *Ibid.*

Allhoff's preferred legal mechanism for confining torture to exceptional cases without routinizing it is strict accountability coupled with a necessity defense in criminal prohibitions against torture. As Allhoff notices, the US Supreme Court has expressed skepticism about whether a necessity defense exists in federal criminal law (see Chapter 8 of this book); but at least one legal system – that of Israel – does have a necessity defense against accusations of torture. Given Allhoff's confidence that permission to torture in ticking-bomb cases poses no real danger of metastasizing into full-blown practice of torture, it is worth looking closely at the case of Israel. I wish to underline that the reason for focusing on Israel is that, overall, it has a strong commitment to rule-of-law institutions, including a supreme court that does not hesitate to tackle national security cases, a robust human-rights nongovernmental organization community, and sophisticated public-interest litigation. If banning torture in all but exceptional ticking-bomb cases fails in Israel, it seems to me good reason to suspect that it will fail elsewhere as well.

In 1987, Israel's Landau Commission approved the use of what it labeled "a moderate measure of physical pressure" by security services against terrorism suspects in extreme cases.[20] This included violent shaking, stress positions, painfully tightened handcuffs, and sleep deprivation.[21] Ten years later, reports surfaced that the security forces were now abusing 85 percent of Palestinians arrested in national security cases.[22] This is a familiar dynamic: what begins as special treatment in special cases soon overflows the boundaries and becomes the rule. Legal complaints led to the 1999 Israeli Supreme Court decision discussed in the present chapter, which outlawed all the General Security Service's harsh interrogation practices, because they are "degrading and infringe upon an individual's human dignity."[23]

As this chapter explains, the court allowed only one exception: it acknowledged that in a genuine ticking-bomb case, an interrogator who used the forbidden techniques out of desperation could defend himself against criminal charges by pleading necessity. In Israel, the necessity defense is statutorily available for all crimes. But the court wisely rejected the security service's

[20] State of Israel, Commission of Inquiry into the Methods of Investigation of the General Security Service Regarding Hostile Terrorist Activity (1987) (www.hamoked.org/files/2012/115020_eng.pdf), § 4.7, p. 80.

[21] The techniques were enumerated by the Israeli Supreme Court in *Public Committee Against Torture in Israel (PCATI)* v. *State of Israel*, HCJ 5100/94 (1999) (www.law.yale.edu/documents/pdf/Public_Committee_Against_Torture.pdf, ¶¶ 8–13.

[22] B'Tselem, *Routine Interrogation Methods of the General Security Service* (1998) (www.btselem.org/publications/summaries/199802_routine_torture), p. 5; B'Tselem, Legislation Allowing the Use of Physical Force and Mental Coercion in Interrogations by the General Security Service (2000) (www.btselem.org/download/200001_torture_position_paper_eng.doc), pp. 31–2.

[23] *PCATI* v. *Israel*, ¶ 25. The quoted words are in connection with one of the stress positions, but the court reaches the same conclusion about the other techniques.

request for *ex ante* permission to use physical pressure in ticking-bomb cases, because that would turn the necessity exception into a rule. If the security services wanted to use their banned techniques, they would have to do it case by case and run the risk that their actions would not be judged necessary.

Unfortunately, even that narrow exception turned out badly. After the court's decision, abusive interrogators simply described their coercive interrogations as ticking-bomb cases, and the security service's inspector went along. Out of 550 complaints of torture between 2000 and 2007, only four resulted in discipline, and none were referred for criminal prosecution.[24] Martin Scheinin, the UN's Special Rapporteur on human rights in the fight against terrorism, explained that the security service drastically expanded the notion of a ticking-bomb case.[25] Scheinin also reported that the security service began to give advance approval for harsh interrogation in ticking-bomb cases. Scheinin politely noted that "this appears to render the use of special interrogation techniques a matter of policy rather than a case-by-case ex post facto defence in respect of wrongful conduct."[26]

In other words, the security services evaded the Supreme Court's decision. A 2007 survey by the Israeli human rights groups HaMoked and B'Tselem found that 29 percent of Palestinian detainees reported naked body searches, three-fourths reported insults and humiliations, and a startling 96 percent reported prolonged handcuffing in one of the forbidden stress positions, the *shabach*.[27]

Furthermore, there was no accountability to hold torture in check; Allhoff emphasizes the need for accountability. As lawyers representing torture complainants explained to me in 2011, the security service's inspectors demanded that complainants show up in person at the security service's facility, unaccompanied by anyone else, to give evidence about what befell them. Unsurprisingly, released prisoners who may have been tortured were unwilling to march voluntarily back into the lion's den; therefore, the investigations died. The Public Committee Against Torture in Israel (PCATI) complained that out of more than 700 torture complaints (through 2012), none led to a criminal investigation. A blue-ribbon government commission agreed with the complaint, and in 2013 the government agreed to establish an independent investigator of torture allegations, one who is not part of the security service.[28]

---

[24] Report of the Special Rapporteur on the promotion and protection of human rights and fundamental freedoms while countering terrorism, Martin Scheinin, Addendum: Mission to Israel, Including Visit to Occupied Palestinian Territory, A/HRC/6/17/Add.4, 16 Nov. 2007, ¶ 19.

[25] *Ibid.*, ¶ 20.   [26] *Ibid.*, ¶ 21.

[27] B'Tselem, *Absolute Prohibition: The Torture and Ill-Treatment of Palestinian Detainees*, May 2007, pp. 59–60 (www.btselem.org/publications/summaries/200705_utterly_forbidden).

[28] Yonah Jeremy Bob, "Rule of Law: Transforming the Shin Bet," *Jerusalem Post*, June 13, 2013 (www.jpost.com/Features/Front-Lines/Rule-of-Law-Transforming-the-Shin-Bet-316488). For incisive analysis, see Itamar Mann and Omer Shatz, "The Necessity Procedure: Laws of Torture in Israel and Beyond, 1987–2009," *Unbound*, 6 (2010), 59.

Allhoff, I should note, is suspicious about PCATI's factual claims "given the group's obvious political design" and the likelihood that "a significant percentage" of the torture complaints could be frivolous.[29] His skepticism is unwarranted: the government commission that recommended independent investigators confirmed PCATI's accusation.[30] Allhoff wrote before this was known, but even so I find it telling that he reserves his skepticism entirely for PCATI because of its advocacy mission, apparently without any corresponding suspicion that the security service might have their own political reasons for not prosecuting their own investigators.

The lesson seems obvious. Like water seeking a crack, security services *will* find the loopholes in any prohibition against torture except an absolute one. They *will* enlarge it: torture and abuse may start small, but they metastasize. And they will do so under the guise of the ticking-bomb case – the vastly improbable hypothetical that has turned into the most effective propaganda device ever devised on behalf of torture in the modern world.

Allhoff concedes that "torture has almost assuredly been underprosecuted in Israel," but adds that "there is no reason to think that Israel's failure to prosecute would transfer to other law enforcement or judicial jurisdictions."[31] I could hardly disagree more. As we shall see in Chapter 10, the United States prosecuted *none* of the 101 torture cases referred to an independent prosecutor, including four in which the detainee died. No officers were tried much less convicted for Abu Ghraib; and David Passaro, a contract interrogator who beat a detainee to death with a flashlight, was convicted only of assault. In the United States, just as much as in Israel, nonaccountability for torture is the rule, not the exception. Allhoff's sanguine conviction that torture can be confined to the exceptional cases, and that governments can be relied upon to hold their intelligence services accountable, seems rather like wishful thinking.

[29] Allhoff, *Terrorism, Ticking Time-Bombs, and Torture*, p. 238, n. 29.
[30] The Public Commission to Examine the Maritime Incident of 31 May 2010, Second Report—The Turkel Commission: Israel's Mechanisms for Examining and Investigating Complaints and Claims of Violations of the Laws of Armed Conflict According to International Law (Feb. 2013), ¶ 88, p. 414 (www.turkel-committee.gov.il/files/new-Doc3/The%20Turkel%20Report%20for%20website.pdf). "Representatives of the Public Committee against Torture in Israel claimed before the Commission that since the establishment of the Mavtan in 1992, 'over 700 complaints [were submitted to the Mavtan] and not a single criminal investigation was opened'. And indeed, from the material submitted to the Commission, it appears that the Mavtan and the Mavtan's Supervisor have never recommended that a criminal investigation be initiated on the basis of a complaint, and the Attorney-General has never instructed that such a criminal investigation be opened." For additional evidence of "necessity interrogations," see Ginbar, *Why Not Torture Terrorists?*, pp. 207–19; Miriam Gur-Arye and Florian Jessberger, "The Protection of Human Dignity in Interrogations: May Interrogative Torture Ever Be Tolerated? Reflections in Light of Recent German and Israeli Experiences," *Israel Law Review*, 44 (2011), 256–60.
[31] Allhoff, *Terrorism, Ticking Time-Bombs, and Torture*, p. 238.

(3) Allhoff also has a response to the objection that ticking-bomb cases require a vanishingly unlikely confluence of conditions: they do not all have to be met for a case to provide robust moral intuitions.

For example, consider the condition that one must know that the torture will be efficacious. Allhoff surveyed more than 800 of his students on their intuitions concerning ticking-bomb cases, and discovered that there was no statistically significant difference in their responses between cases in which torture would certainly reveal the bomb's location and cases in which there is only a 1 percent chance of success. By contrast, he *did* find a statistically significant difference if the torture victim was guilty or innocent (in one of his thought experiments, the terrorist would break only if interrogators tortured his innocent daughter). For Allhoff, the former finding shows that moral intuitions about ticking-bomb cases can be robust even if not all the ideal conditions are met; the latter finding shows that subjects' responses are subtler than straightforward cost-benefit analysis or utilitarianism.[32]

Perhaps he is right, but another interpretation is possible: that the students' reactions to these hypotheticals are grounded in the desire to punish terrorists as much as in the desire to save lives. After all, the second hypothetical demonstrates reluctance to torture the innocent to save lives, while the first shows that the very small chance that torture will save lives does not much matter if the torture victim is a guilty terrorist.[33] We should never take at face value the intuition that our eagerness to inflict pain on a person we loathe comes from altruistic reasons rather than hate.

UNTHINKING THE TICKING BOMB

I

Henry Shue has had a long-standing interest in basic rights to physical security. That is of course a central theme of his book *Basic Rights*. Shue elaborates the case for basic rights against torture, more specifically, in an important pair of papers spanning a quarter century.[34] When Shue wrote his now-classic

---

[32] *Ibid.*, pp. 103–10. Allhoff also found that men are significantly more protorture than women on most of these cases.

[33] Allhoff constructed the hypotheticals so that the number of expected lives saved would be the same in both the high- and low-probability cases: a 100 percent chance of saving 100 lives versus a 1 percent chance of saving 10,000. So the similarity in responses is open to multiple interpretations: that the subjects are rational calculators who view the cases as essentially similar, or that the subjects have equal desire to torture a terrorist regardless of the likelihood that it will do any good.

[34] Henry Shue, "Torture," *Philosophy and Public Affairs*, 7 (1978), 124–43, and "Torture in Dreamland: Disposing of the Ticking Bomb," *Case Western Reserve Journal of International Law*, 37 (2006), 231–9.

paper on torture in the late 1970s, he had important real-world examples in mind – mostly, Latin American dictatorships such as the Pinochet regime, which used torture as a device for terrorizing citizens into submission. The United States bore some responsibility for supporting and propping up several anticommunist authoritarianisms that indulged in terroristic torture; and, as we learned in 1996, the School of the Americas in Fort Benning, Georgia, had actually helped train Latin American security forces, using instruction manuals that advocated torture.[35] But the United States was not itself a state that tortured. By the 1990s, in fact, the United States had joined the international Convention Against Torture (CAT), which declares that torture is always illegal even in times of war or national emergency; and, in compliance with the CAT, the United States has enacted stringent antitorture laws.

By the time Shue wrote his second torture paper in 2005, the dictatorships that formed his primary illustrations had disappeared. The chief example was now quite different, and it was probably one that Shue did not anticipate in 1978. Now, the issue was torture by the United States. The chief motivation is intelligence-gathering rather than terrorizing populations into obedience. The US government has not admitted that it has tortured detainees, and, in fact, indignantly insists that the United States does not torture. But, as is well known, this statement turns out to mean only that, under strained legal interpretations of the antitorture laws, the government's harsh interrogation tactics do not technically qualify as torture.[36] This is a result that few analysts outside the US government accept.

The United States has also enacted a law prohibiting 'CIDT' – cruel, inhuman, or degrading treatment that falls short of torture. This law was enacted over the objections of the Bush administration. After it was enacted, President Bush appended a signing statement suggesting that he considered it an unconstitutional encroachment on his authority, so that he was not bound by it. In any event, however, the Department of Justice contrived an interpretation of the law under which conduct does not count as cruel, inhuman, or degrading if it advances a legitimate governmental interest such as intelligence gathering.[37] Apparently,

[35] Dana Priest, "U.S. Instructed Latins on Executions, Torture," *Washington Post*, Sept. 21, 1996.
[36] See Chapters 4, 6, and 9.
[37] The interpretation appears in a letter of April 4, 2005 from Assistant Attorney General William E. Moschella to Senator Patrick Leahy (www.scotusblog.com/movabletype/arch-ives/CAT%20Article%2016.Leahy-Feinstein-Feingold%20Letters.pdf). Although I did not know it at the time I wrote this chapter, the interpretation was endorsed in a lengthy memorandum by the Justice Department's Office of Legal Counsel. See US Department of Justice, Office of Legal Counsel, Memorandum from Steven G. Bradbury to John Rizzo, May 30, 2005, Re: Application of United States Obligations Under Article 16 of the Convention Against Torture to Certain Techniques That May Be Used in the Interrogation of High Value al Qaeda Detainees, in David Cole, Ed., *The Torture Memos: Rationalizing the Unthinkable* (New York Review of Books, 2009), pp. 225–75, at pp. 226, 247.

the US government has a strong commitment to its freedom to use cruel techniques in interrogations, strong enough that it will use every legal argument its lawyers can think of to preserve that freedom. The top officials of the Bush administration met dozens of times to approve "enhanced" interrogation plans for detainees, and President Bush admitted that he was aware of the meetings.[38]

Parallel with US government enthusiasm for harsh interrogation practices, the American public has become increasingly tolerant of torture, provided that the subjects are described as terrorists.[39] When President Bush admitted in summer 2006 that the CIA was indeed using "enhanced interrogation techniques," little public outrage was heard, and the US Congress – a reliable weather vane of public opinion – responded by augmenting the president's authority to interpret the Geneva Conventions' protections against cruel treatment as he sees fit. Similarly, when confessed 9/11 planner Khalid Sheikh Mohammed (KSM) declared – as part of his March 2007 confession – that he had been tortured, American media expressed no interest, except when commentators fretted that it might make it hard to try KSM because of pesky evidentiary rules against admitting tortured testimony.

Of course, one can only speculate why poll-respondents answer as they do. It may indicate a kind of collective callousness, or reveal that brutality has always had a much larger following than elites like to deceive themselves into thinking. But one guess about why Americans are so well disposed to torture is the steady and (in my view) astonishing popularity of the "ticking-bomb scenario" (or, as I shall abbreviate it, TBS). In the TBS, you have captured someone involved in a bomb plot. He is your only source of information about where the bomb is located, and you have only a few hours before the bomb goes off, killing hundreds of innocent people. (On some versions of the TBS, it is a nuclear bomb in a large city.) He won't talk. Do you torture him or not?

The TBS is, among other things, a remarkably effective propaganda device. For one thing, it is nearly ubiquitous in discussions of torture. More importantly,

---

[38] George W. Bush, *Decision Points* (London: Virgin Books, 2011), p. 170: "[CIA Director] George Tenet asked if he had permission to use enhanced interrogation techniques, including waterboarding, on Khalid Sheikh Mohammed... 'Damn right,' I said." See also Jan Crawford Greenburg, Harold L. Rosenberg, and Ariane de Vogue, "Sources: Top Bush Advisors Approved 'Enhanced Interrogations,'" *ABC News*, Apr. 9, 2008 (http://abcnews.go.com/TheLaw/LawPolitics/Story?id=4583256&page=1); Greenburg, Rosenberg, and de Vogue, "Bush Aware of Advisors' Interrogation Talks," *ABC News*, Apr. 11, 2008(http://abcnews.go.com/TheLaw/LawPolitics/story?id=4635175&page=1).

[39] A June 2008 poll found 44 percent of Americans agreeing that "Terrorists now pose such an extreme threat that governments should now be allowed to use some degree of torture if it may gain information that saves innocent lives" – up from 36 percent two years earlier (www.worldpublicopinion.org/pipa/pdf/jun08/WPO_Torture_Jun08_packet.pdf), p. 3. The latter survey was conducted in nineteen countries. The United States was in the top third for protorture sentiment and in the bottom third for sentiment favoring an absolute prohibition on torture (p. 2).

it is simple, easy to grasp, emotionally powerful, and – above all – it seems to have only one right answer, the pro-torture answer. Thus, the journalist and political commentator Charles Krauthammer writes:

> Let's take the textbook case. Ethics 101: A terrorist has planted a nuclear bomb in New York City. It will go off in one hour. A million people will die. You capture the terrorist. He knows where it is. He's not talking.

> Question: If you have the slightest belief that hanging this man by his thumbs will get you the information to save a million people, are you permitted to do it? Now, on most issues regarding torture, I confess tentativeness and uncertainty. But on this issue, there can be no uncertainty: Not only is it permissible to hang this miscreant by his thumbs. It is a moral duty.[40]

I note in passing that there are actually two different argumentative routes to reach this conclusion in the TBS. One is that *anyone* would be permitted (or obligated?) to torture under these circumstances. The other, more subtle and circumspect, version of the argument is that only government officials have a special public obligation to dirty their hands if the public welfare demands it. Some philosophers have suggested that public officials must be guided by a largely consequentialist public morality that would be unacceptable as private morality.[41] At several points Krauthammer suggests that he holds the latter interpretation, that regardless of whether everyone must take a rigorously consequentialist point of view, public officials who fail to do so are irresponsible and feckless. In the same vein, the moral philosopher Jean Bethke Elshtain writes, "Far greater moral guilt falls on a person in authority who permits the deaths of hundreds of innocents rather than choosing to 'torture' one guilty or complicit person."[42]

Promiscuous invocation of the TBS has real-life consequences. According to a piece by Jane Mayer in *The New Yorker*, in November 2006, General William Finnegan, the dean of the US Military Academy, flew to Hollywood to meet with the producers and writers of the popular television series *24*, in which heroic agent Jack Bauer routinely tortures terrorists in various incarnations of the TBS. General Finnegan's mission was to persuade *24*'s makers to stop

---

[40] Charles Krauthammer, "The Truth About Torture: It's Time to Be Honest About Doing Terrible Things," *Weekly Standard*, Dec. 5, 2006 (www.weeklystandard.com/Content/Public/Articles/000/000/006/400rhqav.asp).

[41] See, e.g., Stuart Hampshire's two papers in his collection *Public and Private Morality* (Cambridge University Press, 1978); or Thomas Nagel's "The Fragmentation of Value," in Nagel, *Mortal Questions* (Cambridge University Press, 1991), pp. 128–41.

[42] Jean Bethke Elshtain, "Reflections on the Problem of 'Dirty Hands,'" in Sanford Levinson, Ed., *Torture: A Collection* (Oxford University Press, 2004), pp. 77–92, at p. 87. It is not clear why Elshtain puts scare-quotes around the word "torture"; perhaps it is because she doubts that the kind of techniques used by the US government really are torture? Perhaps because "torture" is such a disagreeable word?

dramatizing the TBS, because the show – wildly popular among US military forces – was leading to abuse and mistreatment of detainees, as the TBS overrode the careful training that the soldiers had in how to treat captives.[43] He brought along experienced interrogators to explain why the scripts are preposterous. Such is the power and the peril of the TBS: it can even override military training backed by threats of court-martial and prison. The meeting was to no avail: Mayer described the show's producer as a friend and ideological soul mate of pro-torture politicians. The next season of 24 included at least as much torture.

In 2007, I attended a conference of antitorture nongovernmental organizations (NGOs) who had come to the unhappy conclusion that they were losing the fight against torture, because their arguments about torture's illegality, its worldwide condemnation, and its horrors simply have no traction in the face of the TBS; the purpose of the conference was to produce a response. All participants agreed that doing so is devilishly hard. Not that anyone among the antitorture organizations thought the TBS actually does establish the justifiability of torture. Responding to it is hard in the same way, and for some of the same reasons, that epistemologists find it hard to respond to brain-in-the-vat Cartesian hypotheses that seem to establish the truth of radical skepticism. The question-begging assumptions built into Cartesian hypotheses are built in in subtle ways, and it takes patient, delicate, argumentation to show this.[44] The Cartesian hypotheses, on the other hand, seem simple, powerful, and irrefutable on their surface. A child can understand them; many children have discovered them on their own. The power of the example seems more direct, more visceral, and (therefore) more convincing than hyper-intellectualized responses. The same is true with the TBS.

The disanalogy between Cartesian hypotheses and the TBS is that nobody takes Cartesian examples as practical threats to common sense; it is not even clear what taking them seriously would amount to. Opponents of torture, unfortunately, need to respond in the public forum to the friends of torture; they need to meet the TBS sound bite with something equally short and equally pithy. That is nearly impossible to do.

---

[43] Jane Mayer, "Letter from Hollywood: Whatever It Takes," New Yorker, Feb. 19, 2007 (www.newyorker.com/fact/content/articles/070219fa_fact_mayer). A Pentagon survey reveals that one-third of US troops deployed in Iraq believe that torture should be allowed if it reveals information about insurgents; 40 percent approve of it if it would save the life of a fellow soldier; and 10 percent admitted to abusing detainees themselves. Thomas E. Ricks and Ann Scott Tyson, "Troops at Odds with Ethical Standards," Washington Post, May 5, 2007, p. A1.

[44] See, e.g., Michael Williams, Unnatural Doubts (Princeton University Press, 1995) and The Problems of Knowledge: A Critical Introduction to Epistemology (Oxford University Press, 2001).

II

The first thing to notice about the TBS is that it rests on a number of assumptions, each of which is improbable, and which taken together are vanishingly unlikely. It assumes that an attack is about to take place, and that "the authorities" somehow know this; that the attack is imminent; that it will kill a large number of innocent people; that the authorities have captured a perpetrator of the attack who knows where the time bomb is planted; that the authorities know that they have the right man, and know that he knows; that means other than torture will not suffice to make him talk; that torture will make him talk – he will be unable to resist or mislead long enough for the attack to succeed, even though it is mere hours away; that alternative sources of information are unavailable; that no other means (such as evacuation) will work to save lives; that the sole motive for the torture is intelligence-gathering (as opposed to revenge, punishment, extracting confessions, or the sheer victor's pleasure in torturing the defeated enemy); and that the torture is an exceptional expedient rather than a routinized practice.[45] Some of these assumptions can be dropped or modified, of course. But in its pure form, the TBS assumes them all.

That makes the TBS highly unlikely. For the authorities to know that an attack is going to take place, and that their captive knows where the bomb has been planted, will normally require substantial human intelligence ("Humint") – informants or infiltrators of the enemy organization. That is rare; Israel's is most likely the only national intelligence service that has first-rate Humint on its adversaries. Rarer still are cases where the Humint exists but is unable to provide independent information on the ticking bomb's location. Furthermore, torture is notoriously unreliable, not least because its victims sometimes die under torture or fall unconscious. So, to assume that torture will work while other methods of interrogation will not is to assume something doubtful. The reader will have little difficulty in seeing the improbability of many of the other assumptions in the TBS. It stipulates that the interrogator knows things that interrogators will seldom know.

Thus, for example, Krauthammer writes, "The principle would be that the level of inhumanity of the measures used ... would be proportional to the need and value of the information. Interrogators would be constrained to use the least inhumane treatment necessary relative to the magnitude and imminence of the evil being prevented and the importance of the knowledge being obtained." The incoherence of this "principle" should be clear: you cannot know the need and value of the information unless you already know what it is.

---

[45] This is a version of a list drawn from the Association for the Prevention of Torture's report, "Defusing the Ticking Bomb Scenario" (www.apt.ch/), combined with some of the factors I discuss in Chapter 3.

Moreover, it is important to notice that some of the methods of "torture lite" used by American agents – prolonged isolation, sleep deprivation, sexual humiliation – are time-consuming, and incompatible with the imminence requirement of the TBS. Ergo, the TBS implies that "torture heavy," not "torture lite," is the true subject of discussion.

The second point to notice about the TBS, closely related to its unlikelihood, is the lack of documented cases of it. Authentic cases, not myths; I say this, because the subject is drenched in myths. A few examples will illustrate.

(1) In 1995, the Philippine authorities captured Abdul Hakim Murad, a Pakistani bomb-maker who accidentally detonated chemicals in his Manila apartment and then was foolish enough to come back to try to retrieve his laptop. They tortured him for 67 days with great brutality, and, in the end, Murad revealed details of a plot to blow up eleven US airliners, and another to assassinate the pope. Murad is sometimes cited as the poster-child of the TBS, a real-life argument for the efficacy of torture.[46]

In fact, however, Murad was tortured without his interrogators knowing what his plots were, or even whether there were any imminent plots – all they knew was that he was a bomb-maker. They simply had no idea that there was a genuine, time-sensitive, ticking bomb. They were on a fishing expedition, and torture was their first resort, not their last. Furthermore, they themselves expressed surprise that Murad did not die under their torture, in which case the interrogation would have failed; apparently, they did not care enough about finding ticking bombs to stop beating him with chairs. Third, Murad did not in fact reveal information under torture, despite beatings that broke most of his ribs, cigarettes ground out on his genitals, and near-drowning by being pumped full of water. He finally talked only when the interrogators threatened to turn him over to the Israelis, who, as one journalist put it, he feared as much as he hated.[47] Last, but far from least: all the information about the plots was in Murad's laptop computer. Darius Rejali, in his magisterial book *Torture and Democracy*, describes the Murad interrogation as a textbook case of "how a police force is progressively deskilled by torture."[48] In other words: when torture is the first resort, decrypting computers becomes only

---

[46] The factual description of Murad's treatment comes from Marites Dañguilan Vitug and Glenda M. Gloria, *Under the Crescent Moon: Rebellion in Mindanao* (Manila: Ateneo Center for Social Policy and Public Affairs, 2000), p. 223.

[47] Peter Maass, "Torture, Tough or Lite; If a Terror Suspect Won't Talk, Should He Be Made To?", *New York Times*, Mar. 9, 2003; see also Vitug and Gloria, *Under the Crescent Moon*, p. 223. Darius Rejali observes that Murad cannot have been merely afraid of Israeli torture, given what he had already been through, and speculates plausibly that his fear was long-term imprisonment in Israel – both because he hated Jews, and because he may have calculated that his prospects for release were greater in the Philippines. Darius Rejali, *Torture and Democracy* (Princeton University Press, 2007), p. 507.

[48] Rejali, *Torture and Democracy*, p. 507.

a secondary skill. In that case, torture becomes the A-option; torture breeds more torture. Murad's torture turned out to be unnecessary, as well as insufficient, to discover the life-saving information.

(2) Two years ago, I gave a talk about torture and the TBS to a large audience of cadets at West Point, the US Army military academy. Talking to the cadets and their instructors, I learned that they were preoccupied with the case of an Army officer in Iraq who discovered that his troops were going to be ambushed. He had a captive who knew the details. When the captive would not talk, the officer fired his pistol into the ground next to the captive's head – which frightened him into revealing all. Having saved his men, the officer then did the honorable thing and turned himself in. He was punished for it. The cadets were understandably upset by the outcome. Is this not a version of the TBS? And did the officer not do the right thing? And wasn't it wrong to punish him for doing the right thing?

But the cadets had the facts wrong. According to journalist Tom Ricks, the officer – Lieutenant Colonel Allen West – had heard about an assassination plot against himself (not an ambush of his unit), and captured a policeman who may or may not have been a conspirator. West watched while his troops beat the man for an hour, shouting, "Who the fuck is trying to kill him?" – to no avail. That was when West told the man, "Either you answer the questions, or die tonight," and fired one or two shots next to his head. The man stiffened in terror, but still revealed nothing. According to Ricks, "At that point, the senior sergeant present decided he had seen enough. 'Sir, I don't think he knows,' he said to West. ('It was something I had never experienced before and don't care to again,' the sergeant first class added in his statement.) 'Put him back in the cell,' West responded."[49] After self-reporting his actions, West was charged with assault, fined, and relieved of his command. The rumor mill did the rest. There was no ticking bomb, and West apparently had the wrong man.[50]

(3) In 2006, President Bush revealed the existence of secret CIA prisons, along with "alternative" interrogation procedures which turned out to include stress positions, waterboarding, and other forms of torture.[51] Bush defended these procedures by discussing the case of Abu Zubaydah, a detainee who was interrogated through the alternative procedures. According to the

---

[49] Tom Ricks, *Fiasco: The American Military Adventure in Iraq* (Penguin, 2006), pp. 280–1. Ricks footnotes his version of the story to a document titled "CID Report of Investigation—Final" (Feb. 6, 2004), with exhibits and sworn statements.

[50] West, however, maintains that the more flattering version of the story is true. Gina Cavallaro, "Tarnished Soldier Runs for Congress," *Army Times*, Jan. 5, 2008 (www.armytimes.com/article/20080103/NEWS/801030318/O-5-sacked-over-detainee-treatment-runs-for-Congress).

[51] "President Discusses Creation of Military Commissions to Try Suspected Terrorists," Sept. 6, 2006 (www.whitehouse.gov/news/releases/2006/09/20060906-3.html).

president, Zubaydah was a major Al Qaeda planner, and his "alternative" interrogation revealed important information: the identity of accused terrorist Ramzi bin al Shibh, information leading to al Shibh's capture as well as that of 9/11 mastermind KSM, and the plans of an unnamed "terrorist" who turned out to be Jose Padilla.[52]

However, all the president's assertions are either contested or provably false. Al Shibh's identity was well known even before Zubaydah's capture.[53] Al Shibh's capture, according to journalist Ron Suskind, resulted from information provided by the Emir of Qatar, not Zubaydah; the Emir also provided information that helped locate KSM. For that matter, Zubaydah was not an important Al Qaeda figure; he was the equivalent of Al Qaeda's travel agent, and furthermore he was insane. Finally, he did not break under torture, but rather began to talk when a new interrogator discontinued torture and persuaded Zubaydah that revealing information was his religious obligation.[54] At that point Zubaydah did reveal Padilla's identity, but Padilla was not exactly the purveyor of a ticking bomb. He supposedly hoped to manufacture a radioactive "dirty bomb," but explained that he would centrifuge the radioactive material (which he did not possess) by spinning it in a bucket over his head. (In the interest of fairness, I should note that the value of Zubaydah's interrogation remains a matter of dispute. In December 2007, former CIA agent John Kiriakou made headlines by conceding that Zubaydah was tortured, but called it torture that "probably saved lives." In the wake of Kiriakou's statements, FBI and CIA sources sharply disagreed with each other, with the FBI backing Suskind's account, and the CIA backing President Bush's.[55])

In other words, there have been no undisputed TBSs in American experience. Perhaps some are unreported. But, given the enormous public-relations advantage that would accrue to the Bush administration by leaking details of an authentic TBS, the fact that the dog has not barked in seven years seems like a significant basis for doubt. The ready public acceptance of TBS myths may reflect the desire of torture supporters for factual validation of their fantasies.

[52] George W. Bush speech, "President Discusses Creation of Military Commissions to Try Suspected Terrorists," Sept. 6, 2006 (http://georgewbush-whitehouse.archives.gov/news/releases/2006/09/20060906-3.html).

[53] My own Lexis/Nexis search on al Shibh's name turned up 87 hits in major newspapers from before the date of Zubaydah's capture.

[54] Ron Suskind, The One Percent Doctrine: Deep Inside America's Pursuit of Its Enemies Since 9/11 (New York: Simon & Schuster, 2006), pp. 99–100 (on Bush's mischaracterizations of Abu Zubaydah); pp. 111, 115–18 (on the interrogation of Abu Zubaydah); pp. 136–40 (on the role of the Emir of Qatar in the capture of KSM and Ramzi bin al Shibh).

[55] Dan Eggen and Walter Pincus, "FBI, CIA Debate Significance of Terror Suspect; Agencies Also Disagree on Interrogation Methods," Washington Post, Dec. 18, 2007.

III

Once we set out the conditions assumed in the TBS, we are in a position to notice one of the most important ways it cheats in evoking pro-torture moral intuitions. It assumes that it is the terrorist himself, or someone complicit with the terrorist, who will be tortured for information. But that assumption runs the risk that the real source of the pro-torture intuitions in the TBS is not the "rational moral calculus" Krauthammer speaks of – one person's pain weighed against many people's lives (and pain) – but rather rage at a guilty terrorist and the desire to punish him harshly. It seems quite likely that many people consciously or unconsciously approve of the torture of terrorists for punitive reasons, which they may deceive themselves into repackaging under a conse-quentialist, intelligence-gathering rationale. (Krauthammer, for example, warns against punitive motives but seems to enjoy writing sentences like this: "Anyone who blows up a car bomb in a market deserves to spend the rest of his life roasting on a spit over an open fire.") One might even speculate that the popularity of the TBS grows out of frustrated hatred of terrorists, with many citizens relishing the thought of torturing this monster and there-fore gravitating to hypotheticals in which it would happen and seem right.

This concern about rage masquerading as rationality is critically important, because a great many detainees claim that they are cases of mistaken identity (and this has been proven to be true in the highly publicized case of Moham-med El-Masri, a German cabdriver who was kidnapped and rendered by US agents). A former US contract interrogator explained to me that, in Iraq, detainees were brought in whose arrest report stated nothing beyond "sus-pected of anti-Coalition activity" – and that this often meant only that they were young men in the vicinity of roadside bombs. When interrogators have no facts to go on (he elaborated), they find it harder to use noncoercive means such as persuading the detainee that "we already know everything about you, so you might as well talk." Under these circumstances, interrogators turn to abuse. The upshot is that innocent men have been wrongly abused by US interrogators. Anyone who uses the TBS to defend torture must, if he is intellectually honest, defend it in cases where it is quite possible that the captive is innocent. Otherwise, the TBS-monger is cheating.

In order to control for this way of cheating, we must make sure that in describing the TBS we build in that the person being tortured for information is completely innocent. Perhaps it is the terrorist's 7-year-old child, who will not reveal her daddy's location out of love and loyalty. Or, to remove even this childish level of complicity, perhaps it will turn out that the only way Jack Bauer can break the terrorist is to torture his child, who knows nothing of intelligence value, in front of him.[56] Or torture someone else's innocent children?

[56] This is Samuel Scheffler's hypothetical, in the introduction to his *Consequentialism and Its Critics* (Oxford University Press, 1988), p. 3.

(Two can play at the game of hypothetical-mongering.) Will Krauthammer or Elshtain insist that, as a public official, the president lies under a moral obligation to order it? Krauthammer, at any rate, tries to position himself as a hard-headed consequentialist, by using the phrase "rational moral calculus" to explain why torture is morally required in the TBS. But, if he or Elshtain would flinch at answering "yes" in the grotesque hypotheticals I have just posed, they will reveal that it is loathing of the terrorist, not rational moral calculation, that drives their response to the original TBS, where it is the guilty terrorist who is being tortured. Krauthammer might reply that I am doing the same thing by surreptitiously appealing to our protective instincts towards children. Very well. Would Krauthammer or Elshtain proclaim a moral obligation to torture a completely innocent adult to locate the ticking bomb?

Perhaps they will bite the bullet and answer "yes." That would be a consist-ent consequentialist answer, but it would not be an answer that preserves the persuasive force of the TBS. It would be interesting to hear the audience response if the TBS enthusiast – let us suppose it is Alan Dershowitz giving a speech[57] – poses the problem thus: "If the only way to get a terrorist to reveal the location of the ticking bomb is to torture *you* – that's right, you, the audience member, personally, for days on end – do you think the government should do it? You'll be kidnapped, hooded, have your clothes cut off; you'll be diapered and dressed in an orange jumpsuit, blindfolded, shot up with sedative, flown to Cuba, beaten, stripped naked and mocked by members of the opposite sex, hogtied, blasted with ear-splitting rap music and strobe lights for hours, hosed down and thrown into a frigid cell overnight, then shackled to an eye-bolt in the floor and made to stand up until your ankles double in size and your kidneys start to fail. Then you'll be chained to the ceiling with your arms behind your back, and lastly have sterilized needles thrust under your finger-nails. For some reason or other, that's the only thing that will make the terrorist talk. Should we do it?"[58] It seems likely that the audience member would either dismiss the hypothetical as preposterous or answer with a resounding "no."

But instead Krauthammer or Elshtain might distinguish the torture of the innocent and the torture of the guilty and respond that interrogational torture can be justified only against someone who has forfeited rights against torture by planting the time bomb. That would be a coherent deontological response to my hypothetical questions, one that might explain why torturing the terrorist is acceptable but torturing the innocent person is not.[59] In that

[57] Dershowitz has said that he often raises the TBS to audiences.
[58] All but the last technique have been used by US authorities. The sterile needles idea is Dershowitz's own: *Why Terrorism Works* (Yale University Press, 2002), p. 144 ("a sterilized needle inserted under the fingernails to produce unbearable pain without any threat to health or life").
[59] So Jeff McMahan argues in "Torture, Morality, and Law," *Case Western Reserve Journal of International Law*, 37 (2005), 241–8, at 244–5. In McMahan's view, if an agent has

case, however, the notion that public officials must obey a consequentialist, dirty-hands public morality has been abandoned. Now the morality turns out to be consequentialism limited by a deontological restriction inexplicable on consequentialist grounds. And, having allowed one restriction to consequentialist calculation, Krauthammer and other advocates of torture must explain why it is the only one. In particular, they must answer the question of whether it really is true that our wrongful actions can waive all rights, even the right against torture. Many of us – including all the governments that joined the CAT – disagree. We think that wrongful action can waive some rights but not others, and that the right against torture, like the right against rape, is bedrock – torture is evil enough that, in the words of CAT, "no exceptional circumstances whatsoever, whether a state of war or a threat of war, internal political instability or any other public emergency, may be invoked as a justification of torture."[60]

IV

Why the special revulsion for torture? Why is it worse than killing? What, specifically, characterizes the evil of torture?

One might find this a silly question, and answer in the simplest way: it's the pain, stupid! No experience is more horrible than severe pain; and, one might think, nothing more needs to be said. Many people would prefer death to prolonged severe pain. Those who devised Christian doctrines of Hell imagine it as a place of endless torture, not of endless oblivion; for that reason, Bayle argued that a God who tortures eternally is an unjust monster, since the punishment is disproportionate to any imaginable sin.[61] One might melo-dramatize the point: Find the living being who is enduring the worst pain (physical or mental) at any given moment and you have found, quite literally, the point of greatest horror in the universe at that moment. As you read these words, the locus of greatest horror on Earth may be a hospital bed in Kingston, Jamaica; tomorrow, in a collapsed mineshaft in Szechuan Province; next week, in the house of a man in San Francisco who has accidentally killed his own beloved child; an hour later, in your own house, as your herniated disc leaves you panting in agony on the bathroom floor. Disproportionately often, the point of greatest horror will be in a torture chamber somewhere. Torture is not just one bad thing among many; while it is occurring, it may be, depending on its severity, quite literally the most horrible thing in the world.

There is indeed more to be said than "it's the pain," however. The awfulness of pain, including physical pain, is deeply connected with its context. The pain

made it inevitable that somebody is going to be harmed, either the terrorist or the potential victims, fairness requires that it be the terrorist.

[60] Convention Against Torture, Article 2(2).

[61] See Susan Neiman, *Evil in Modern Thought* (Princeton University Press, 2002), p. 19.

of childbirth is undoubtedly comparable to or even worse than many tortures, including severe ones. Men, I am told, could not bear the pain that birthing mothers endure. Yet millions of women whom no one would call irrational have preferred natural childbirth to anesthesia; the connection of birth pangs to a joyful or even ecstatic event transforms the sensations' character without diminishing their painfulness.

In the case of torture, the connection is with fearful, degrading, soul-destroying events. Fear is perhaps the most important evil-maker connected with the pain of torture. The torture victim never knows whether his torturer will do even worse things; the uncertainty is perpetual. Today it may be "torture lite" – sleep deprivation or bombardment with loud, cacophonous music; tomorrow, the torturer may beat me or mutilate me or kill me. As the example of Murad (who did not reveal information under torture, but did under the threat of the Israelis) illustrates, fear may be worse than the torture itself.

The difference fear makes should be obvious, but I have discovered that it is not. Surprisingly often, especially discussing these issues with soldiers or veterans, I have heard the sneering response, "If that's torture, I got tortured in basic training," as if this were a triumphant *reductio* of claims that forced prolonged standing, extremes of hot and cold, or sleeplessness amount to torture. Sometimes, the friends of torture point out that these interrogation tactics were devised by the architects of the US military's SERE program, which consists of training in how to resist enemy mistreatment. It cannot be torture, they argue, because we do it to our own guys and they do not call it torture.

These arguments are silly, because they focus only on physical sensations and neglect the crucial difference: SERE participants and soldiers in basic training know that those inflicting the treatment on them have no intention of killing or maiming them; they also know that within a short, fixed period of time the treatment will stop. They have none of the fear of a torture victim who knows neither of these things, and whose captors tell him that unless he talks he may be in Guantánamo forever. Torture inevitably intensifies pain with terror.

Many writers have focused as well on the connection between torture and humiliation or degradation. I do not mean only that torturers like to humiliate their victims – they mock their naked bodies, they force them to masturbate or drink their own piss or do dog tricks or beg for mercy. I am referring to two additional facts. First, the experience of acute pain is itself degrading because it reduces us to mere prisoners of our bodies.[62] Second, the relation between the

---

[62] This diagnosis of the evil of torture comes from Louis Michael Seidman, "Torture's Truth," *University of Chicago Law Review*, 72 (2005), 881–918, at 905, and Elaine Scarry's famous analysis in *The Body in Pain: The Making and Unmaking of the World* (Oxford University Press, 1985), p. 29. See also Jean Améry, "Torture," in *At the Mind's Limits: Contemplations by a Survivor on Auschwitz and Its Realities* (Sidney Rosenfeld and Stella P. Rosenfeld, Trans.) (Bloomington, IN: Indiana University Press, 1980), p. 33: "[T]he tortured person is only a body, and nothing else beside that."

torturer and the victim is one of absolute domination and absolute subordination. The torturer, as Jean Améry remarks, "has control of the other's scream of pain and death; he is master over flesh and spirit, life and death."[63] Améry (a torture victim himself) elaborates:

> But in the world of torture man exists only by ruining the other person who stands before him. A slight pressure by the tool-wielding hand is enough to turn the other – along with his head, in which are perhaps stored Kant and Hegel, and all nine symphonies, and the World as Will and Representation – into a shrilly squealing piglet at slaughter. When it has happened and the torturer has expanded into the body of his fellow man and extinguished what was his spirit, he himself can then smoke a cigarette or sit down to breakfast or, if he has the desire, have a look in at the World as Will and Representation.[64]

Like fear, humiliation and degradation are horror-multipliers to the physical sensations of cruel treatment.

In the previous chapter, I argued that liberals "put cruelty first" among the vices – Judith Shklar's famous phrase – precisely because torture is a microcosm of the totalitarian political relationships that liberalism fears the most.[65] David Sussman locates the evil of torture in the fact "that the only thing that matters to [the torture victim] is pleasing this other person who appears infinitely distant, important, inscrutable, powerful, and free."[66] In his 1978 paper, Henry Shue focuses on the defenselessness of the torture victim. Although these diagnoses of torture's evil have significant points of difference, they all call attention to the degrading relational character of torture, in addition to the pain and the fear. Améry's remarks highlight as well the corruption and deformation of the torturer. Seidman and Sussman both point to the destruction of the torture victim's will.[67] And Améry identifies one more evil folded into torture:

> [W]ith the very first blow that descends on him he loses something we will perhaps temporarily call 'trust in the world'. . .
>
> The expectation of help, the certainty of help, is indeed one of the fundamental experiences of human beings, and probably also of animals. . . The expectation of help is as much a constitutional psychic element as is the struggle for existence. Just a moment, the mother says to her child who is moaning with pain, a hot-water bottle, a cup of tea is coming right away, we won't let you suffer so! I'll prescribe you a medicine, the doctor assures,

---

[63] Améry, "Torture," p. 35.   [64] *Ibid.*

[65] See Chapter 3, pp. 48–56; see also Améry, "Torture," p. 39.

[66] David Sussman, "What's Wrong with Torture?", *Philosophy and Public Affairs*, 33 (2005), 1–33, at 25–6. Sussman offers a slightly different explanation in "Defining Torture," *Case Western Reserve Journal of International Law*, 37 (2005), 225–30, at 227–30, where he describes the distinctive evil of torture as forced passivity.

[67] Sussman, "Defining Torture," p. 4; Seidman, "Torture's Truth," p. 907.

it will help you. Even on the battlefield, the Red Cross ambulances find their way to the wounded man. In almost all situations in life where there is bodily injury there is also the expectation of help; the former is compensated by the latter. But with the first blow from a policeman's fist, against which there can be no defense and which no helping hand will ward off, a part of our life ends and it can never again be revived.[68]

Those who have spent time in the company of torture victims will have little difficulty understanding how terrible a loss this is.

We need not choose among these explanations of the evil of torture; they augment each other (and all of them are found in Améry's famous essay, the most analytical memoir of a torture survivor I have read). Torture is the union of relational and nonrelational evils, which function as horror-multipliers of the raw physical sensations. The pain, the fear, the degradation, the domination combine to make torture the greatest human evil. If there are any limits to what people can do in pursuit of legitimate ends, the prohibition on torture seems like an obvious candidate.

V

The ticking bomb is the subject of Shue's 2005 paper on torture. Like other writers on the TBS, he focuses on its improbability. In his earlier paper, Shue raised a methodological objection to fanciful hypotheticals in moral philosophy: "[T]here is a saying in jurisprudence that hard cases make bad law, and there might well be one in philosophy that artificial cases make bad ethics."[69] If the improbable features are the ones that secure the desired conclusion, then nothing of significance follows: "[O]ne cannot easily draw conclusions for ordinary cases from extraordinary ones."[70] Shue raises the same objection to artificial torture examples in *Basic Rights*.[71]

Before turning to Shue's re-evaluation of this caution in the 2005 paper, let us pause to consider the adage that artificial cases make bad ethics. It might mean one or more of several things; and, in the remainder of the chapter I unfold the argument by elaborating on the things it might mean. Here are two:

(1) By focusing on improbable artificial cases, theorists misdirect readers' attention from genuine issues in the real world to specious issues. They

---

[68] Améry, "Torture," pp. 28–9.   [69] Shue, "Torture," p. 141.   [70] *Ibid.*
[71] Henry Shue, *Basic Rights: Subsistence, Affluence, and U.S. Foreign Policy*, 2nd edn. (Princeton University Press, 1996), pp. 196–7, n. 25. Shue's objection to artificial cases in philosophy turns out to be central to his argument that duties to avoid harming others and duties to protect others are far less different than many philosophers suppose (p. 59). See also pp. 184–7, n. 13, where Shue rejects a supposed counterexample to one of his theses by demonstrating that the counterexample can be saved only at the cost of making it "contorted and exotic," and "treating this eccentric example as a clear case would be question-begging against my view, I think" (p. 187).

illicitly change the subject from important and authentic questions about the limits of legitimate interrogation in non-TBS cases to intuition-mongering about a tendentious hypothetical.

Or it might mean (emphasizing the "hard cases make bad law" trope):

(2) Policies have to do with rules, procedures, protocols, and laws. Lawmakers should build policies and rules around typical cases and ignore the rare hard cases; and moralists should ignore the weird ones. Thus, even if there were rare cases of morally justifiable torture, procedures and laws should not accommodate them by making exceptions for them.

Shue and I both have criticized the TBS on ground (1).[72] Politically, I continue to think this is the crucial point: the TBS has displaced genuine issues in the public forum and substituted a fictitious example stacked in favor of torture-permissiveness. That is a good reason for changing the subject away from the TBS, rather than trying to respond to it.

However, changing the subject will seem to many like mere evasiveness, and someone whose mind is not made up about the torture issue may insist that the torture opponent respond to the hypothetical rather than dodging it. Interpretation (1) will not help; it says nothing about whether torture would in fact be justifiable in the TBS, assuming that the improbable happened and it actually occurred. In his 1978 paper, Shue concedes that torture would be permissible in a genuine TBS.[73] He recants that view in the 2005 paper; but before examining the recantation, we must ask what follows from the 1978 concession.

In the 1978 paper, Shue argues that very little follows from it, because all he has conceded is "the permissibility of torture in a case *just like this*"[74] – that is, a case in which all the conditions in the TBS are satisfied.

I am not so sure. The problem is that once one has conceded the permissibility of torture in a TBS case, one has apparently admitted that the prohibition on torture is not moral bedrock. As Krauthammer puts it,

> However rare the cases, there are circumstances in which, by any rational moral calculus, torture not only would be permissible but would be required (to acquire life-saving information). And once you've established the principle, to paraphrase George Bernard Shaw, all that's left to haggle about is the price. In the case of torture, that means that the argument is not whether torture is ever permissible, but when—i.e., under what obviously stringent circumstances: how big, how imminent, how preventable the ticking time bomb.[75]

---

[72] See Chapter 3; Luban, "Torture, American-Style," *Washington Post*, Nov. 27, 2005, p. B1 (www.washingtonpost.com/wp-dyn/content/article/2005/11/25/AR2005112501552.html).

[73] Shue, "Torture," p. 141.   [74] *Ibid.*

[75] Krauthammer. I made the same point in roughly the same words in Chapter 3, in order to explain why torture proponents are so fond of the TBS.

"Haggling about the price" means haggling about which of the assumptions in the TBS can be relaxed and still suffice to justify torture. What if one knows only that the captive is a high-ranking terrorist who might know something useful, but maybe nothing that prevents any particular ticking bomb – but, on the other hand, the mistreatment is "only" sleep deprivation? This, after all, is very likely the reality of US torture. After making the initial concession, any prohibition on torture faces significant dialectical pressure towards balancing tests and the consequentialist conclusion that interrogational torture can be justified whenever the expected benefits outweigh the expected costs.

This is where (2) becomes important. Interpretation (2) also concedes the logical possibility of cases of justifiable torture but insists, on roughly rule-consequentialist grounds, that the law (or policies, or protocols) should not carve out exceptions for them. The reason is that by carving out an exception, the prohibition on torture is weakened, or becomes less enforceable, and the result will be too many cases of unjustified torture. The argument on the other side, of course, is that rigorously enforcing antitorture laws in all cases without exception will deter officials from engaging in torture even in the rare TBS cases where, by hypothesis, it is the right thing to do. And the counterargument to this objection is, simply, that the ticking-bomb cases are so improbable that the genuine worry about underdeterrence (the result of building exceptions into the antitorture rule) is far more compelling than the worry about overdeterrence (in a genuine TBS).

Some who agree that the ban on torture must stand may still object to the idea of punishing someone who has, in the rare case of a TBS, done the right thing by violating the ban. That is why most proponents of (2) advocate leaving the antitorture rule in place but permitting accused torturers to plead necessity in the rare authentic TBS, or, alternatively, to receive a sentencing discount or even a pardon if they are convicted of the crime of torture. The first of these was the strategy adopted by the Israeli Supreme Court in its momentous 1999 decision banning torture. The court allowed that under Israeli law an accused torturer could plead necessity; but when the Israeli security service argued that in that case the court should create an *ex ante* permission to torture in ticking-bomb cases, the court refused. An *ex ante* permission is a "general administrative power" – a rule, not an exception – whereas the necessity defense concerns "an individual reacting to a given set of facts; it is an ad hoc endeavour, in reaction to an event. It is the result of an improvisation given the unpredictable character of the events" and is not to be turned into a rule.[76] The court perceived the trap it would fall into if

---

[76] *Public Committee Against Torture in Israel (PCATI)* v. *Israel* [1999], HCJ 5100/94, IsrSC 43(4) 817, reprinted in 38 I.L.M. 1471 (1999), ¶ 36. Oren Gross has offered a similar argument.

it turned the possibility of an *ex post* defense into an *ex ante* permission: the *ex ante* permission would be a rule, not an exception. With or without the necessity defense, interpretation (2) allows us to acknowledge the justifiability of torture in the TBS while maintaining rigid prohibitions against torture and CIDT.

In his 2005 paper, Shue goes beyond (1) and (2) and renounces his earlier concession that torture would be justifiable even in a genuine TBS case. He now maintains that the true TBS is not merely improbable, it is actually impossible. That is because, among the key conditions defining the TBS, are the requirements that it be an exceptional emergency measure and not an institutionalized practice, and the related point that the torturer be a conscientious, reluctant interrogator who uses torture only in the rare cases where all the TBS conditions are met. But a torturer must be competent; he must have training and the opportunity to practice; his training requires teachers, and his equipment must have been acquired in advance. There will be a doctor present, to ensure that the subject of interrogation does not die. The torturer is not Jack Bauer but an apparatchik in a torture bureaucracy. A TBS without a torture bureaucracy is impossible. Shue writes:

> To try to leave a constrained loophole for the competent "conscientious offender" is in fact to leave an expanding loophole for a bureaucracy of routinized torture, as I misguidedly did in the 1978 article.[77]

The "moderate" position on torture represented by (2) is, in Shue's words, torture in dreamland. "So I now take the most moderate position on torture, the position nearest to the middle of the road, feasible in the real world: never again. Never, ever, exactly as international law indisputably requires."[78]

VI

The trouble is that to those who, like Krauthammer, believe in a "rational moral calculus" of costs and benefits, constructing a bureaucracy of routinized torture may be a price worth paying if the bureaucracy stays small enough and the stakes are large enough. The consequentialist may concede to Shue that you will not be able to succeed in the ticking-bomb case without a bureaucracy of torture, and will surely count this as a negative in the cost-benefit analysis. But the consequentialist will not necessarily concede that the costs outweigh the benefits even accounting for this large negative. The consequentialist does not concede that the requirement that torture be an exception and not a practice is an indispensable feature of the TBS.

---

[77] Shue, "Torture in Dreamland," p. 238. I offer similar arguments in Chapter 3.
[78] Shue, "Torture in Dreamland."

Shue's response is this: "You cannot be a little bit pregnant, you cannot – if you are an alcoholic – have a drink only on special occasions, and you cannot – if your politicians are not angels – employ torture only on special occasions."[79] Once torture becomes a governmental practice, it inevitably metastasizes, as the evidence of torture-states like France in Algeria, Argentina under the junta, and Israel before the Supreme Court banned "physical pressure," illustrates. There are good reasons based in organizational psychology to explain why torture bureaucracies cannot cabin their work to the exceptional cases.

This argument may not persuade, however, because so far the US torture bureaucracy has managed to stay fairly small. The number of people the CIA has subjected to "enhanced interrogation techniques" has been fewer than thirty, while the notorious special interrogation plans of Guantánamo were apparently used on only two detainees. It is unclear how much brutality there has been in Iraq and Afghanistan – certainly it includes hundreds of victims – but much of it (or so I am told by former interrogators) is unauthorized kicking and beating at the time of arrest rather than authorized interrogational torture. Now, it may be that the unauthorized torture is the causal consequence of officially weakening the prohibitions on detainee abuse, and therefore should be laid at the feet of the torture bureaucracy. And it may also be that only the opposition of antitorture forces has kept the torture bureaucracy from metastasizing more rapidly than it already has. But whatever the cause, the slow rate of metastasis will be something that emboldens hard-nosed consequentialists to embrace torture, including its bureaucracy, if it wards off greater evils. The general point is simple: any finite costs to torture can be outweighed by sufficient expected benefits. The worse the anticipated evil, the more horrible are the things we can do to ward it off.

VII

This is, indeed, a familiar drawback to consequentialism: it always makes morality hostage to evil. "Would you torture to stop the ticking bomb from detonating?" is no different in form from "Would you set up a torture bureaucracy in order to make sure you could torture effectively in a TBS?"; nor is it different in form from "Would you commit genocide to stop a larger genocide?" or "Would you rape one child to prevent ten children from being raped?" Consequentialism has easy answers to all these questions – Bernard Williams thought that fact is itself a fatal objection to consequentialism – and its answer is that enormous evils can nevertheless be lesser evils, and lesser evils can be morally obligatory even though they are enormously evil. The worse the world is, the worse the behavior that morality countenances to combat evil, with no limit to how low we can sink.

[79] *Ibid.* I argued in similar fashion in Chapter 3.

For many of us, however, a system that imposes no intrinsic limits on how low we can sink lacks the essential character of morality – call it the moral attractiveness of acting morally. What would be the point of morality if moral action no longer has any connection with elemental decency?

Here I mean to be making a different point from Williams' well-known argument that consequentialists' insistence that we do something awful to stop something even more awful fails to account for the agent's integrity. My argument here is not about personal integrity – that is, the special first-personal character of one's own values – but about whether a system in which any atrocity, no matter how vile, can be permitted (or, worse, required) can count as a morality. Consequentialists will not downplay the evils of torture, as I have described them above. They cannot, because their system demands that they assign accurate weights to consequences. But, without knowing what the alternatives are, consequentialists will likewise not believe that any moral conclusions whatever follow from identifying the evils of torture. While their position is not a logical contradiction, it severs the ground of morality – the goodness and evil of states of affairs – from the ground of action.

There may simply be an unbridgeable gulf between the theoretical sensibilities of nonconsequentialists, who regard compulsory choice among monstrous evils as morally pointless, the equivalent of rearranging deck chairs on the *Titanic*, and those of consequentialists, who patiently point out that the rearranged chairs actually would make the doomed passengers a tad more comfortable in their final minutes, and is that not a good thing?

Another indicator of the unbridgeable gulf is this. To the nonconsequentialist, recognizing the surpassing horror of torture provides an iron-clad reason not to engage in it. To the consequentialist, recognizing the surpassing horror of torture provides an iron-clad reason to do anything to prevent it – including committing it in lesser degree. Thus, in a variant of the TBS in which torturing one captive is the only way to learn the location where ten hostages are being held and tortured – not completely fanciful during the Iraqi insurgency – the same revulsion towards torture that underwrites an absolute prohibition on torture also urges us to engage in it.

VIII

These reflections on the unbridgeable gulf between consequentialist and nonconsequentialist thinking about torture, manifested in the fact that the identical revulsion towards torture can pull in conflicting directions given a suitably contrived hypothetical, suggest a third interpretation of Shue's dictum that "artificial cases make bad ethics."

In the previous chapter, I quoted in connection with the TBS a saying of Williams, that "there are certain situations so monstrous that the idea that the processes of moral rationality could yield an answer in them is insane," and "to spend time thinking about what one would decide if one were in such a situation is also insane, if not merely frivolous."[80]

(3) Ordinary practices of moral rationality fail in cases where all courses of action are monstrous. The artificial cases ethicists cook up to control for monstrosity by isolating the right- and wrong-making characteristics of action are misleading. That is precisely because they cover over the monstrousness with a veneer of rationality.

The thought here is that a genuine TBS, like the hypothetical in which the torture of one is weighed against the torture of ten, or in which committing genocide can avert a slightly larger genocide, represents moral singularities analogous to mathematical singularities: points where otherwise well-behaved functions misbehave, as $y = 1/x$ has a singularity at $x = 0$.

To explicate this idea, I suggest the following meta-ethical and justificatory picture. Moral systems, including consequentialism and its various alternatives, arise by generalizing and abstracting from prototypical cases in which they make intuitive sense and yield intuitively satisfying answers. By this I mean not only that the answers seem obviously correct but also that they seem correct for just the reason that the system offers. (One might suggest, as a slightly more complex picture, that the systems are not mere generalizations from intuitions about prototypes, but rather the result of a process of achieving reflective equilibrium with those intuitions. For present purposes, the details of the justificatory picture are unimportant.) Moral systems are on this view heuristics, complex rules of thumb, based on a bet that the prototypical cases are sufficiently representative that the moral systems they generate contain principles commitment to which will yield a satisfactory moral life. The three principal secular moral systems that attract allegiance from contemporary philosophers – aretaic, deontological, and consequentialist, focusing respectively on actors, acts, and outcomes – will yield largely identical resolutions of a broad range of cases; and each seems powerfully and intuitively appealing in their prototypical cases. Each, therefore, might lay claim to offering a total system of morality, and adherents will be tempted to roll up their sleeves and get to work showing how the system can accommodate even the apparent counterexamples that are prototypical cases of the rival systems.

But completeness claims are illusory, and the temptation to smooth out the bumps should be resisted. Even the best heuristics can fail in trick cases; and the heuristics represented by the chief moral systems can yield inconsistent results in unusual cases. This should not surprise us: the origin of moral systems suggests that they are good only over certain domains, those in

[80] Bernard Williams, "A Critique of Utilitarianism," in J. J. C. Smart and Bernard Williams, *Utilitarianism: For and Against* (Cambridge University Press, 1973), p. 92.

the neighborhoods of their prototypical cases. Hopefully, those are large neighborhoods; but there is no reason to suppose the absence of singularities.

On the picture I have just sketched, moral rationality is entitled to be blithely pluralistic, or even theoretically indifferent, over the wide range of cases in which the major systems converge, and monistic in the prototypical cases where the systems are at their strongest. You know them when you see them; what I am describing is intuitionism at the meta-level. When faced with a clear-cut rights violation and no countervailing rights, think in deontological terms; when faced with a clear-cut cost-benefit trade-off, think in consequentialist terms. When the cases are not so clear-cut, take your best shot at it. But there will be cases, like the genuine TBS, in which the systems, regarded as total systems, yield flatly inconsistent outcomes, with no higher-level principle available to remove the contradiction. On logical grounds, such inconsistency is intolerable. But on pragmatic grounds, one may do better as a blithe pluralist who has no rational answers in some cases than as a principled monist who purchases consistency at the cost of fanaticism in hard cases.

Put in other words, the real mistake may be in assuming that any moral system is universal, rather than simply a good way of systematizing a large class of cases. It may simply be better to shrug our shoulders in intolerable dilemmas and admit that whatever decision we make will be taken on grounds unrelated to moral rationality rather than to insist on using a system that was not built for cases like this.

IX

Shue began his 1978 paper with a striking observation:

> Whatever there is to say about torture, there appear to be moral reasons for not saying it... Mostly, they add up to a sort of Pandora's Box objection: if practically everyone is opposed to all torture, why bring it up, start people thinking about it, and risk weakening the inhibitions against what is clearly a terrible business?[81]

Unfortunately, he adds, it is too late for silence: Pandora's box is already open, because the torturers are torturing away.

But are the only alternatives silence and dispassionate debate? Williams suggests that "the *unthinkable* was itself a moral category."[82] Although he does not elaborate, we can spell out this observation along roughly the following lines: there are some abominations that, as a society, we do not have moral debates about because they fall so far below the threshold of the acceptable that we do not need to argue about them. These make up "the unthinkable." Slavoj Zizek illustrates with an example:

---

[81] Shue, "Torture," p. 124.   [82] Williams, "A Critique of Utilitarianism," p. 92.

> A clear sign of progress in Western society is that one does not need to argue against rape: it is "dogmatically" clear to everyone that rape is wrong. If someone were to advocate the legitimacy of rape, he would appear so ridiculous as to disqualify himself from any further consideration.[83]

The prohibition on rape, Zizek suggests, belongs to "the set of unwritten rules that form the background of every individual's activity, telling us what is acceptable and what is unacceptable."[84]

Obviously, we *can* think the unthinkable, and even debate it. But the debate will not be a dispassionate weighing of options. Staying with Zizek's example, suppose we raise a version of the TBS in which the only way to break the terrorist is to rape him. Or suppose that the only way Jack Bauer can prevent ten women from being raped is to rape one woman. You will never see that plotline on television, for obvious reasons: the audience, which is meant to root for Jack Bauer, would find Jack the rapist viscerally revolting. That is the mark of the unthinkable.

Conversely, if we insist on arguing the costs and benefits of rape with an unblinking accountant's eye, as if it is just one option among others, we run the risk of normalizing it, moving it out of the category of the unthinkable. That is the Pandora's box argument, which, as Shue says, risks weakening inhibitions.

How else can we think about it? Zizek writes that "most of us can imagine a singular situation in which we might resort to torture – to save a loved one from immediate, unspeakable harm perhaps. I can." In what Zizek calls "the unavoidable brutal urgency of the moment," it is unclear what I would do. But if I would torture, that is not a fact about rationality, or justifiability, or, ultimately, about morality. It is a fact about me. The essential thing is that "it cannot become an acceptable standard; I must retain the proper sense of the horror of what I did."[85] Put in other words, torture must remain unthinkable, and that means conversations about it must retain the proper sense of horror.

This is a final reason that artificial cases make bad ethics. They are deeply cartoonish; this is true not only of the TBS, but also of a great many cases populating philosophy journals, with fat men thrown in front of runaway trolleys, blown out of mine shafts with bazookas, or impaled on pitchforks as they fall from windows. (Fat men fare badly in moral philosophy.) The cartoonishness makes it easy to treat them as brain-teasers, in which case the option-sets they present assume an air of unreality that makes them all equally thinkable. So the fourth interpretation of Shue's dictum might be put thus:

(4) Artificial cases make bad ethics because their very artificiality makes the unthinkable thinkable.

---

[83] Slavoj Zizek, "Knight of the Living Dead," *New York Times*, Mar. 24, 2007.
[84] *Ibid.*   [85] *Ibid.*

X

Throughout this chapter, I have been struck by an air of paradox involved in the very act of writing it. By analyzing the specific evil of torture, and examining the senses of Shue's dicta that artificial cases make bad ethics and "whatever there is to say about torture, there appear to be moral reasons for not saying it," I have aimed to explain why we should stop talking about the ticking bomb. In saying that, I have talked about it incessantly. This is a reluctant decision, based on the fact that ducking the hypothetical simply seems evasive. But enough is enough.

Whereof one should not speak, thereof one must be silent.

III

The evils of torture

5

A communicative conception of torture

One of the most basic questions a book on torture must answer is what exactly torture is.

One could dispute this claim. Why does a word we understand all too well need to be defined? When the US Department of Justice's secret torture memos were released in 2009, the journalist Kathleen Parker wrote this:

> Several years ago, I asked a veteran journalist for advice.
>
> "I'm trying to figure out if I have an ethical conflict," I began.
>
> "If you have to ask, you do," he said...
>
> Apply the same construct to torture. If we have to ask, it probably is.[1]

Pursuing the same line of thought, Jeremy Waldron observes that the prohibition on torture is not like a tax regulation, which needs precision because we expect even blameless taxpayers to push to the limits of the law. It is more like the prohibitions on domestic violence and sexual harassment, where you have no business demanding precise guidance on exactly how far you can go.[2]

For Waldron, the prohibition on torture represents a legal archetype – "a particular provision in a system of norms which has a significance going beyond its immediate normative content, a significance stemming from the fact that it sums up or makes vivid to us the point, purpose, principle, or policy of a whole area of law."[3] The prohibition of torture is archetypal of the fundamental commitment of law not to rule through brutality or savagery.[4] To paw through the law against torture looking for loopholes undermines that fundamental commitment of the law itself.

I agree with Waldron's analysis and Parker's rule of thumb. Indeed, part of my argument in this book is that the fundamental dishonesty in the

I am grateful to Gabriella Blum, Kim Ferzan, Mark Graber, Deborah Hellman, Leslie Kendrick, Seth Lazar, Judith Lichtenberg, Rachel Luban, Micah Schwartzman, and Henry Shue for their comments on an earlier draft of this chapter.

[1] Kathleen Parker, "Is It Torture?", *Washington Post*, Apr. 26, 2009.

[2] Jeremy Waldron, "Torture and Positive Law: Jurisprudence for the White House," *Columbia Law Review*, 105 (2005), 1681–1750, at 1701, reprinted in Waldron, *Torture, Terror, and Trade-offs: Philosophy for the White House* (Oxford University Press, 2012).

[3] *Ibid.*, p. 1723.   [4] *Ibid.*, p. 1726.

torture memos came from pretending that "torture," "severe pain," and "cruel, inhuman, and degrading treatment" are purely technical concepts that demand minute legal line-drawing. Later in this chapter, I label this pretense the *fundamental trick*. It was the fundamental trick that allowed the torture lawyers, quoting Parker again, to "torture the English language trying to justify the unjustifiable."[5] Pursuing this line of thought, one might suspect that to demand a definition of torture is merely the opening gambit in a game of loophole lawyering. Why muddy the waters with definitions that invite pettifoggery?

One reason is that "torture" is, in fact, a term of law as well as a term of ordinary language. Invoking it carries legal consequences, and that means judges and juries need a legal definition, even if primary actors should settle for Parker's "if you have to ask, don't do it" rule of thumb. Just as importantly, a definition of torture can help us identify what the most important evils associated with torture are. There are, after all, other reasons to define a concept besides sorting which items do or do not fall under it. We define concepts to learn something about them by seeing how they hang together with our other concepts. That philosophical aim, which has nothing to do with law, will occupy the second part of this chapter.

I begin the chapter by discussing legal definitions of torture – a topic taken up from several angles in later chapters. But after that discussion I want to propose a very different definition of torture, not necessarily usable for legal purposes and not meant to replace the legal definition, which will help us better understand why torture is an archetype of evil. The defining feature of torture, I will argue, is the use of pain or suffering as a communicative medium for displaying the absolute mastery of the torturer and the absolute helplessness of the victim. This nonlegal definition, focusing not only on the painfulness of torture but on its inextricable link with subjugation and humiliation, aims to identify the essential features that place torture among the greatest affronts to human dignity. It shows why torture violates a *moral* archetype.

Legal definitions of torture

Let us start with the legal definition of torture, in article 1, section 1 of the 1984 Convention Against Torture and Other Forms of Cruel, Inhuman or Degrading Treatment and Punishment (CAT). CAT, an international treaty with more than 150 parties including the United States, is the most important legal document concerning torture. Its prohibition of torture by now belongs to customary international law, and many think it is part of the *jus cogens* – the small circle of unwaivable rules of international law. CAT makes torture an international crime, and defines it as follows:

[5] Parker, "Is It Torture?"

> For the purposes of this Convention, torture means any act by which severe pain or suffering, whether physical or mental, is intentionally inflicted on a person for such purposes as obtaining from him or a third person information or a confession, punishing him for an act he or a third person has committed or is suspected of having committed, or intimidating or coercing him or a third person, or for any reason based on discrimination of any kind, when such pain or suffering is inflicted by or at the instigation of or with the consent or acquiescence of a public official or other person acting in an official capacity. It does not include pain or suffering arising only from, inherent in or incidental to lawful sanctions.[6]

There is a lot of language in this definition, and it will help to take it apart clause by clause. In the course of unpacking it, I will also explain some of the ways the authors of the US Department of Justice's torture memos – the "torture lawyers" for short – tortured its language to (in Parker's words) justify the unjustifiable.

The core understanding of torture

> *[T]orture means any act by which severe pain or suffering, whether physical or mental, is intentionally inflicted on a person...*

CAT's core understanding of the experience of torture (*torture* as a noun) is severe mental or physical pain or suffering, and its core understanding of the act of torture (*torture* as a verb) is intentionally inflicting that experience on someone.

The two go together. Of course, in ordinary language, we sometimes describe an awful experience as "torture," hyperbolically referring to the experience alone, without supposing that anyone has intentionally inflicted it. And we can imagine severe pain or suffering being inflicted by another person unintentionally, in two ways:

(1) unknowingly – imagine a cattle rancher who turns on her electric fence without realizing that a passerby down the road is leaning on it and will receive an excruciating electrical shock;
(2) knowingly but unintentionally – think of a surgeon performing a necessary life-saving procedure in full knowledge that the patient will experience severe postoperative pain.

In (2), the crucial difference between the surgeon and a torturer is that if a new technology enabled the surgeon to operate without any postoperative pain, she would gratefully use it. The torturer aims at pain. "Would you still do

---

[6] UN General Assembly, *Convention Against Torture and Other Cruel, Inhuman or Degrading Treatment or Punishment*, 10 Dec. 1984, United Nations, Treaty Series, vol. 1465, p. 85, article 1(1).

it if it didn't cause pain?" is a useful question for discerning intention. If the answer is yes, the pain is not your intention. If the answer is no, the pain is your intention. Even if the torturer's purpose for inflicting pain is not sheer sadism but intelligence gathering, the pain-infliction is not merely an unwanted byproduct of the torturer's action. There are no accidental waterboarders.

In these examples, the passerby and the patient might exclaim "That was torture!", referring to the painful experience regardless of the intention. But CAT is, by its terms, defining *acts* of torture, and in fact *criminal* acts of torture, and that entails the intention to make the victim hurt or suffer.

Mental and physical pain or suffering

The definition speaks of mental and physical pain or suffering. There are forms of physical suffering other than pain, so the distinction captures a genuine difference. Think of extreme heat, extreme cold, or being unable to breathe – all among the forms of suffering (not pain) that US interrogators inflicted on their prisoners. Treating "pain or suffering" as a single thing (pain-and-suffering) was one of the sophisms the torture lawyers used to argue that techniques that create suffering but not pain cannot be torture.[7] So the distinction is not only genuine but also important in practice.

As for mental pain or suffering, Chapter 7 examines it in detail, so I will say no more here than the obvious: there is such a thing as mental pain or suffering, and CAT treats it on a par with physical pain or suffering. Rightly so: clinical research on torture victims finds no difference in the severity of after effects between those who suffered physical pain and those who suffered only mental pain. Interviewers of torture victims report that often their victims' worst memories are of the mental tortures.

The meaning of "severe" and the fundamental trick

What about the concept of "severe" pain or suffering? How severe is severe? As other chapters of this book explain in detail, the torture lawyers' fundamental trick was to treat severity as an arcane technical concept of law or medicine that only experts can grasp. That allowed them to assert that the CIA's brutal methods of "enhanced" interrogation never crossed the line set by the criteria the experts established.

The first torture memo was the 2002 Bybee memo, written by John Yoo but signed by Jay Bybee. Notoriously, the Bybee memo argued that "severe pain"

---

[7] US Department of Justice, Office of Legal Counsel, Memorandum from Jay S. Bybee to Alberto R. Gonzales, Aug. 1, 2002, Re: Standards of Conduct for Interrogation Under 18 U.S.C. §§ 2340–2340A ("Bybee memo"), reprinted in David Cole, Ed., *The Torture Memos: Rationalizing the Unthinkable* (New York Review of Books, 2009), p. 47, n.3.

is a technical concept in US healthcare law referring to the pain level of acute medical emergencies, and therefore equivalent only to the pain "accompanying serious physical injury, such as organ failure, impairment of bodily function, or even death."[8] Even on its own terms the argument was specious, because the healthcare laws do not treat "severe pain" as a legal term of art. In fact the memo used the fundamental trick twice, first in interpreting healthcare statutes that mention "severe pain" as a sometimes symptom of a medical emergency to make them sound like limiting legal *definitions* of severe pain, and second in pretending that the torture statute intended the same limiting definition.

Three years later, Bybee's successor Steven Bradbury assured the CIA's general counsel that the "enhanced" techniques did not inflict severe pain or suffering because the CIA had informed him that "medical personnel watch for signs of physical distress or mental harm so significant as possibly to amount to the 'severe physical or mental pain or suffering' that is prohibited."[9] The argument amounts to a vicious circle, and seldom is the word "vicious" more appropriate: we, the lawyers, assure you that your techniques will not inflict severe pain because you, the CIA, assured us that they will not. But Bradbury concealed the absurdity of the argument behind the reassuring mask of medical expertise: apparently, "severity" of pain is for the CIA's torture doctors to diagnose. This too is the fundamental trick of pretending that "severe pain" is a technical concept.

The fundamental trick continued to work mischief years after the torture memos were written.[10] In an official report exonerating the torture lawyers from charges of unethical conduct, the Justice Department official David Margolis speculated "that Congress might have adopted a definition of torture that differed from the colloquial use of the term."[11] In that case it was not

---

[8] *Ibid.*, p. 41. I discuss this in detail later in this book.

[9] US Department of Justice, Office of Legal Counsel, Memorandum from Steven G. Bradbury to John Rizzo, May 10, 2005, Re: Application of 18 U.S.C. §§ 2340–2340A to Certain Techniques That May Be Used in the Interrogation of a High Value al Qaeda Detainee ("Bradbury techniques memo"), in Cole, *Torture Memos*, p. 158; see also pp. 156–7, 162–8. Yoo and Bybee argued similarly five years earlier. US Department of Justice, Office of Legal Counsel, Memorandum from Jay S. Bybee to John Rizzo, Aug. 1, 2002, Interrogation of al Qaeda Operative ("Bybee techniques memo"), reprinted in Cole, *Torture Memos*, pp. 110, 117, and especially clearly at p. 118: "You have also indicated that, should it appear at any time that Zubaydah is experiencing severe pain or suffering, the medical personnel on hand will stop the use of any technique."

[10] The following paragraphs draw on my blog post "The Fundamental Trick: Pretending that 'Torture' is a Technical Term," Balkinization blog, Feb. 26, 2010 (http://balkin. blogspot.co.uk/2010/02/fundamental-trick-pretending-that.html). This post was part of a debate with journalist Stuart Taylor, which Taylor and I continued through two more rounds. See also "Stuart Taylor Responds," Balkinization blog, Feb. 26, 2010 (http:// balkin.blogspot.co.uk/2010/02/stuart-taylor-responds.html).

[11] David Margolis, *Memorandum of Decision Regarding the Objections to the Findings of Professional Misconduct in the Office of Professional Responsibility's Report of*

wrong that the torture memos ignored a federal court decision that repeatedly described waterboarding as torture, or a Supreme Court case that called sleep deprivation torture. Both these judicial opinions predated Congress's definition, and therefore they were, necessarily, using the word "torture" colloquially – that is, *merely* colloquially.

Margolis' argument plainly turns on what I have called the fundamental trick: pretending that the legal definition of "torture" is something technical rather than colloquial. Because Congress defined it as a legal term of art, only lawyers can figure out what it means, using the Powerful Methods of Legal Analysis.

This is all nonsense. If we suppose that dictionaries are reliable guides to the colloquial meanings of words, then let us see how they define torture:

> The *Oxford English Dictionary (OED)* (1971): "severe or excruciating pain or suffering (of body or mind)"
>
> *Webster's Third International* (1971): "intense pain"
>
> *Webster's Second International* (1953): "severe pain" and "extreme pain"
>
> *American Heritage Dictionary* (1976): "severe physical pain."

I have picked widely used dictionaries that predate the legal definitions, to avoid the possible objection that today's dictionary definitions (which are more or less the same) look like the law because they borrowed from the law. Also, these dictionaries do not predate the law by much, so there is little chance that the colloquial meaning shifted between the time the dictionaries were published and the time the laws were written.

In other words, the colloquial meaning of "torture" is virtually the same as the legal definition. The *OED*'s definition, in particular, is so similar to CAT's definition that it seems likely that whoever drafted article 1 of CAT consulted the *OED*.

Of course, "severe pain" is a vague concept, because there is no sharp boundary between pain that is severe and pain that is merely bothersome. But there is a difference between vague and obscure.[12] "Severe pain" is not an

---

Investigation into the Office of Legal Counsel's Memoranda Concerning Issues Relating to the Central Intelligence Agency's Use of "Enhanced Interrogation Techniques" on Suspected Terrorists, Jan. 5, 2010 (http://judiciary.house.gov/hearings/pdf/DAGMargolis-Memo100105.pdf), p. 61.

[12] It might be objected that vague is bad enough. US law contains a "void for vagueness" doctrine that declares excessively vague criminal statutes unconstitutional. But the torture statute is no vaguer than other criminal laws whose constitutionality is clearly established – for example, federal statutes prohibiting any "scheme or artifice to defraud" (18 U.S.C. § 1343), or any gifts given "corruptly" to public officials in return for favors (18 U.S.C. § 201(b)). Recklessness in criminal law is defined (vaguely!) as consciously disregarding a "substantial and unjustifiable risk." Innumerable legal doctrines, including that of self-defense in criminal law, demand judgments about what kind of behavior is "reasonable," a term that is certainly no less vague than "severe pain." For discussion of

obscure term, because everyone who has ever given birth to a baby, been kicked in the wrong place playing sports, broken a bone, suffered a migraine, or slipped a disc knows what it is.

What about the pain of organ failure or death – the criteria that the Bybee memo used, supposedly to give some guidance to interrogators by removing the vagueness? The answer is almost too obvious to bear mention. Almost none among us have experienced the pain of organ failure (in any case, are the failures of all organs equally painful?), and none of the living can report on the pain of death. Insofar as we are able to speculate about what death will feel like, as I suppose all of us do, we believe that there are more and less painful ways to die. Under the guise of providing interrogators with a workable test of the vague term "severe," Yoo and Bybee substituted a definition that only the dead or dying could apply, and not very confidently. One can guess that the lawyers' real goal was to pick criteria that sound so extreme that almost nothing would seem to fulfill them.

I am not denying that there are technical words in the law that also have colloquial meaning. When I started studying law I was confused by the word "consideration." In legalese it means "the inducement to a contract." I mistook it for a colloquial word meaning "something to think about." Oops. But there is no comparably specialized legal definition of "severe pain." What you see on the surface of the statute is truly all there is. Anyone who tells you otherwise is playing the fundamental trick on you.

The fundamental trick is an authority grab disguised as interpretation. It mystifies the law and pretends that legal language is so complicated, and so different from common-sense language, that we outsiders should not worry our pretty little heads about it. We should leave it to the experts. In other words: if you sprain your ankle and someone asks you, "Is the pain severe?" your answer would have to be, "What are you asking me for? Go ask Bybee and Yoo!"

Custodial torture

One final comment on the opening clause of CAT's definition of torture. CAT does not make explicit one of its essential assumptions – namely, that the perpetrator has the victim in his or her clutches. That is an important assumption, because otherwise we could imagine lawful acts of warfare at a distance – the use of incendiary weapons comes to mind – that would count as torture.[13] Some might argue that acts of warfare using pain-inflicting

---

the vagueness issue, see the exchanges between Bart DePalma and me in *The OLC Memos, Federalist Society On-Line Debate Series*, Apr. 24, 2009 (www.fed-soc.org/debates/dbtid.27/default.asp).

[13] While the laws of war forbid the infliction of unnecessary suffering, they nowhere include in that prohibition weapons that necessarily inflict severe pain in the course of disabling

weapons *should* count as torture, but doing so would muddy the waters. It would miss the distinctive target of CAT – namely, *custodial* torture – and we would eventually have to reintroduce the same distinction using different words in order to specify the evil that CAT aims to outlaw.

In this respect the US statutory definition does better: it specifies that the perpetrator's victim is a person "within his custody or physical control," making explicit the assumption that CAT leaves unstated.[14]

State-sponsored torture

when such pain or suffering is inflicted by or at the instigation of or with the consent or acquiescence of a public official or other person acting in an official capacity...

Why does CAT restrict its definition to government-inflicted torture? Plainly, it does not mean to imply that torture inflicted by private, non-governmental thugs is different from state-sponsored torture, either in the experience of the victim or the intention of the perpetrator. There might be an argument that state-sponsored torture is worse because the state is supposed to be our *recourse* against violence, and the despair of the victim will be greater from the knowledge that the rescuer has become the perpetrator. Hopelessness will then reach its maximum, in just the way that hopelessness must reach its maximum in Dante's Hell, where "God save me!" is unavailable because God himself commanded the torture.[15]

I think this is a significant argument, but it is surely not what the drafters of CAT had in mind. After all, even if state-inflicted torture is worse than private torture, by definition both pass the threshold of severe pain or suffering. Once that threshold is past, fine-grained comparisons of tortures seem beside the point.

The straightforward reason for CAT's restriction to state-sponsored torture is that state behavior is the problem that needed to be addressed on an international level. Law enforcement against private wrongdoers is a domestic

---

or killing the enemy. Some specific weapons, like blinding lasers, have been prohibited by international treaties, but incendiary weapons are not among them.

[14] 18 U.S.C. § 2340(1).

[15] This suggestive argument comes from Roy Eidelson (private communication to Stephen Soldz, forwarded to me), Jan. 18, 2013. It is Eidelson's extrapolation of work on "shattered assumptions" by the psychologist Ronnie Janoff-Bulman, *Shattered Assumptions: Towards a New Psychology of Trauma* (New York: Simon & Schuster, 1992). Eidelson mentions three ways that government-sponsored torture shatters our assumptions. First, by removing a recourse, it shatters an assumption that the world is a benevolent place, where torture is an outlier. Second, government torture carries "some peculiar claim to legitimacy ...[s]o government torture perhaps puts the lie to justice in the world more powerfully." Third, because our sense of self-worth is linked to our place in society, being tortured by our own government assaults the sense of self-worth.

responsibility of states, and states have little or no reason to neglect the problem of private torture. The uniquely international problem is torture by states themselves, and CAT represents states' efforts to bind themselves to abstinence and prevention.

Other international legal instruments do not restrict their criminalization of torture to state-sponsored torture. Notably, the Rome Statute of the International Criminal Court includes torture among the crimes against humanity and war crimes, and in neither case is there a limitation to state torture.[16]

The purposes of torture

inflicted on a person for such purposes as obtaining from him or a third person information or a confession, punishing him for an act he or a third person has committed or is suspected of having committed, or intimidating or coercing him or a third person, or for any reason based on discrimination of any kind...

CAT should be criticized for insinuating that the purpose for which states torture people is relevant to whether the acts are torture. The list of proscribed purposes raises a familiar lawyer's question: is the list exhaustive, so that pain-infliction for any other purpose does not count as torture? Or is the list open-ended? Here, the treaty language itself says "for such purposes as [items on the list]," a signal that the list is nonexhaustive. Presumably, CAT's drafters listed specific purposes to underline that these could never justify torture, just in case states might be tempted to imagine otherwise. If that is the reason for the list, however, the drafters would have done better by explicitly ending it with the phrase "or any other purpose whatsoever." That would drive home the correct conclusion: torture is torture, regardless of its purpose.[17]

This is not a merely hypothetical issue. An example of the confusion the list of purposes creates appears in the *Elements of Crimes* of the International Criminal Court, a document that itemizes the specific elements that must be proven for each crime in the court's statute. The statute itself includes war crimes labeled "cruel treatment" and "torture."[18] The *Elements* itemizes five elements of these two crimes that are identical, one of which is the infliction of "severe physical or mental pain or suffering upon one or more persons." Substantively, therefore, the crimes are identical, and both amount to torture. The difference between them is that the one labeled "torture" adds a sixth element, absent from the crime of cruel treatment: that "the perpetrator

---

[16] The Rome Statute contains an antitorture provision for noninternational armed conflicts (which are conflicts between states and nonstate groups). There is also a crime against humanity of torture, and crimes against humanity can be committed by torturers associated with nonstate groups as well as states.

[17] The US antitorture statute leaves out the list entirely, which is preferable.

[18] Rome Statute of the International Criminal Court, articles 8(2)(c)(i)(3)-(4).

inflicted the pain or suffering for such purposes as: obtaining information or a confession, punishment, intimidation or coercion or for any reason based on discrimination of any kind." In other words, the *Elements* copies CAT's list of purposes and treats them as an additional item that must be proven to charge torture rather than cruel treatment. That is exactly the mistake the list of purposes in CAT invites: thinking that the purpose of torture matters as to whether it is torture.[19]

Pain and punishment

It does not include pain or suffering arising only from, inherent in or incidental to lawful sanctions...

Lawful punishment by imprisonment surely inflicts severe mental suffering on many people serving long sentences. For that matter, jailers sometimes have to physically subdue and restrain violent inmates, which might inflict severe pain on them. As long as the institution of imprisonment exists, these intentional inflictions of pain or suffering are real possibilities and even inevitabilities. The final clause of CAT's definition makes it clear that pain and suffering of these sorts do not count as torture, even if they are severe. However, the clause must not be interpreted to permit punishment by torture. The "purposes" clause of the CAT definition makes clear that punishment by torture is forbidden.

A hierarchy of abuses and obligations?

CAT's definition of torture is a legal and historical milestone, even if it can be mined for loopholes or interpreted perversely. As the definition of an international crime, it advances the ball by specifying the *mens rea* (intending), *actus reus* (inflicting severe mental or physical pain or suffering), and circumstances (the rest of the definition) – all the textbook elements of a crime. Its definitional core, intentional infliction of severe mental or physical pain or suffering, makes straightforward sense. And CAT establishes important state obligations: to criminalize torture, to investigate torture and prosecute or

---

[19] This is not the only thing wrong with the way that the ICC *Elements* defines the crimes. By defining cruel treatment and torture identically, as the infliction of severe pain or suffering, it overlooks that, under CAT, cruel treatment is supposed to include treatment less severe than torture. One of the US torture memos picked this subtle error up to argue that certain CIA tactics that in OLC's view did not amount to torture were therefore also not "cruel" under international law. Steven G. Bradbury, Memorandum for John A. Rizzo, Acting General Counsel, Central Intelligence Agency, Re: Application of the War Crimes Act, the Detainee Treatment Act, and Common Article Three of the Geneva Conventions to Certain Techniques that May Be Used by the CIA in the Interrogation of High Value al Qaeda Detainees [hereinafter: Bradbury war crimes memo], July 20, 2007, pp. 62–3 (www.justice.gov/olc/docs/memo-warcrimesact.pdf).

extradite torturers, to train law enforcement personnel in the prohibition against torture, to provide torture victims a civil remedy, to refrain from returning people to countries where they will be tortured, and others.

Confusion starts to enter when we turn from the article 1 definition to the final substantive article of CAT, article 16. Article 16 concerns "other acts of cruel, inhuman or degrading treatment or punishment which do not amount to torture as defined in article 1," and it instructs each state-party to "undertake to prevent [it] in any territory under its jurisdiction." The problem is that undertaking to prevent so-called "CIDT" (Cruel, Inhuman, or Degrading Treatment) is a weaker obligation than the many obligations CAT imposes on states to prohibit torture. Notably, CAT obligates states to make torture a crime; it does not obligate them to make CIDT a crime.

The US torture lawyers seized on this unfortunate split-level structure of obligations, with strong obligations against torture and only a weak obligation against CIDT. They did so in three distinct ways. The first, and most significant, was that most of the principal torture memos simply ignored CIDT and analyzed only the prohibition on torture. For them, whether abuse was CIDT was an uninteresting question. When the Senate ratified CAT, it added a proviso (a "declaration" in international law lingo) stating that CAT's substantive articles are not self-executing. That means their obligations lack the force of law in the United States until Congress implements them. Congress criminalized torture but said nothing about CIDT. Because Congress had not implemented article 16, it followed that CIDT was not prohibited – so why think about it, even if preventing CIDT remains an international law obligation? In 2005, Congress rectified this omission and passed legislation prohibiting – but still not criminalizing – CIDT.[20]

Second, the torture lawyers seized on the stipulation in article 16 that states must undertake to prevent CIDT in territory under their jurisdiction, and argued that the sites of detainee abuse lay outside US jurisdiction.[21] In its 2005 legislation, Congress closed that loophole as well.

The Senate worked additional mischief when it ratified CAT. It added an understanding according to which the phrase "cruel, inhuman or degrading" treatment means in US law only the kind of treatment forbidden by constitutional prohibitions on cruel and unusual punishment and on violations of due process of law. The Supreme Court's case law has held that government conduct violates due process when it "shocks the conscience."[22] This less than

---

[20] This is the Detainee Treatment Act, 42 U.S.C. § 2000dd.

[21] US Department of Justice, Office of Legal Counsel, Memorandum from Steven G. Bradbury to John Rizzo, May 30, 2005, Re: Application of United States Obligations Under Article 16 of the Convention Against Torture to Certain Techniques That May Be Used in the Interrogation of High Value al Qaeda Detainees ("Bradbury CIDT memo"), in Cole, *Torture Memos*, pp. 226, 247.

[22] *Rochin v. California*, 342 U.S. 165 (1952).

helpful formula has been refined in subsequent decisions, and the torture lawyers seized on cases in which the court discerned a "sliding scale" in what shocks the conscience. Conduct that would shock the conscience if done gratuitously – for example, a high-speed police chase that forces a motorcycle off the road and kills the rider – may not shock the conscience if the rider was a dangerous fleeing fugitive and the police cruiser could stop the motorcycle in no other way.[23]

Once they discovered the sliding scale, the torture lawyers were in a position to argue that "enhanced" interrogation to defend America against terrorists would not shock the conscience.[24] After all, the interrogations were tightly controlled, and the governmental interest in national security is maximally important. Then they ran the reasoning in reverse: no conscience-shocking, no due process violation; no due process violation, no CIDT.

There is a gigantic *non sequitur* in this argument. Read carefully, its conclusion is that nothing short of torture is cruel, inhuman, or degrading if it is done in a controlled manner to defend against terrorists.[25] But of course it is the *kind of treatment* inflicted on someone that is cruel, inhuman, or degrading, not the *purpose* for which the treatment is inflicted. Intentionally inflicting cruel treatment or humiliation for a supposedly good purpose does not make the cruelty less cruel or the humiliation less humiliating. That would be like saying that a justifiable killing is not a killing at all. If a legal argument of this sort follows logically from US legal doctrines – and it is by no means an illogical argument – it shows that US constitutional language like "due process" has become unhinged from reality.[26]

It has become unhinged, furthermore, in an especially repugnant way. It wires untruthfulness into the very meanings of words. Evidently, our good purpose not only justifies an otherwise bad act, but it also cleanses and beautifies it, and thus the law no longer permits us to call the act by an ugly

---

[23] *City of Sacramento* v. *Lewis*, 523 U.S. 833, 846 (1998).

[24] Bradbury CIDT memo, note 21 above, p. 227.

[25] It might be objected that Bradbury explicitly disavowed this conclusion: "We do not conclude that any conduct, no matter how extreme, could be justified by a sufficiently weighty government interest coupled with appropriate tailoring." Bradbury CIDT memo, p. 261. But the reason for the disavowal is only that "our inquiry is limited to the program under consideration, in which the techniques do not amount to torture." Read carefully, then, Bradbury is arguing that because the CIA program is less severe than torture, the weighty government interest in national security indeed means it cannot be cruel, inhuman, or degrading. Using similar reasoning, Bradbury argued in a subsequent opinion that intensive sleep deprivation does not count as degrading treatment or an outrage on personal dignity if it is done for an important national security purpose. Bradbury war crimes memo, note 19 above, pp. 64–9.

[26] I do not mean to suggest that Bradbury's argument is sound. David Cole trenchantly criticizes his reasoning in his introduction to *The Torture Memos*, pp. 31–4, as well as in "The Sacrificial Yoo: Accounting for Torture in the OPR Report," *Journal of National Security Law and Policy*, 4 (2010), 455–64.

name. Cruel, inhuman, and degrading treatment is a bad thing. Therefore, if we do it, it cannot be cruel, inhuman, or degrading. This is Ministry of Truth stuff.

My purpose here is not to delve into the minutiae of US legal arguments, or even their degradation of language, but to emphasize that it was CAT's split-level structure that opened the space for these arguments to be made. In one way, the split-level choice makes sense: no doubt there are ways of humiliating or degrading people that do not amount to torturing them, and torture seems worse. Probably CAT's drafters thought they were doing the world a service by including an article that condemns CIDT even if it is less than torture.

But deriving a hierarchy of obligations from a hierarchy of evils is not an inevitable choice, and other international instruments do not differentiate in this way. At the opposite end from CAT, consider the 1949 Geneva Conventions. All four Conventions contain a provision that forbids certain forms of mistreatment, including:

(a) violence to life and person, in particular murder of all kinds, mutilation, cruel treatment and torture. . .
(c) outrages upon personal dignity, in particular humiliating and degrading treatment.[27]

Here we find no differential obligations: all these forms of abuse are prohibited, period. Here, furthermore, there is no hint of a hierarchy of evils. Cruel treatment and torture are bundled together with murder and mutilation under the rubric of violence, and humiliating and degrading treatment is bundled under the rubric of outrages on personal dignity. Nothing in the text indicates that some members of either bundle are worse than others, nor that one bundle represents a worse evil than the other.

Lying between CAT's double hierarchy (of evils and of obligations) and the Geneva Conventions' absence of hierarchy in either respect, we find the European Convention on Human Rights, the most stringently enforced human-rights treaty in the world. As interpreted by the European Court of Human Rights, it creates a hierarchy of evils but no hierarchy of obligations. The European Convention's article 3 reads: "No one shall be subjected to torture or to inhuman or degrading treatment or punishment." Like the Geneva Conventions, the text identifies no differential obligations. In its case law, however, the European Court has constructed a hierarchy of evils, with torture at the apex, "deliberate inhuman treatment causing very serious and cruel suffering" in the middle, and inhuman or degrading treatment at the bottom.[28]

---

[27] Geneva Conventions of 1949, art. 3. Article 3 applies to noninternational armed conflicts.
[28] *Askoy* v. *Turkey*, 23 Eur. H.R. Rep. 553, ¶ 63 (1996).

The hierarchy of evils doctrine originated in Ireland's suit against the UK for interrogation of IRA suspects using stress positions, hooding, sleep deprivation, noise, and deprivation of food and drink. The European Commission on Human Rights declared that the five techniques were torture, but, in 1978, the court downgraded the commission's finding to inhuman and degrading treatment, sparing the UK the stigma of being labeled a torture state.[29] The court nevertheless found the UK in breach of article 3; without a hierarchy of obligations, a violation is a violation. In any event, the hierarchy of evils is not a major point of doctrine. Many of the court's cases involve multiple forms of cruelty committed against the plaintiff, and the court seldom finds a need to sort them into torture and lesser forms of abuse.[30] In a 1999 decision, it even cautioned that "certain acts which were classified in the past as 'inhuman and degrading' as opposed to 'torture' could be classified differently in the future," because the convention is a living document.[31]

"No exceptional circumstances whatsoever..."

To round out this part of the discussion, I want to add one more point about CAT. In many ways CAT's most illuminating feature is not its definition of torture, nor the various obligations it creates to fight against torture. It is this powerful declaration in article 2(2):

> No exceptional circumstances whatsoever, whether a state of war or a threat or war, internal political instability or any other public emergency, may be invoked as a justification of torture.

By including this language in CAT, states went on record that in their view torture is special. It is in a class by itself. Perhaps that signals that states do accept a hierarchical view of evils, one that places torture in the lowest circle of the *Inferno*.

Article 2(2) makes it clear that the prohibition on torture does not fall under the "power of the exception," which dispenses with it in emergencies. The right against torture is an all-weather friend, not a fair-weather friend. The prohibition may never be balanced away in a cost-benefit analysis or proportionality test. Nor may any of CAT's clauses be interpreted, as lawyers might be tempted

---

[29] *Ireland v. United Kingdom*, App. No. 5310/71, [1978] ECHR 1 (1978), ¶ 167.

[30] Once in a while it does. *Aydin v. Turkey*, App. No. 23178/94, 25 Eur. H.R. Rep. 251 (1997) concerned a young woman who was blindfolded for three days, stripped, beaten, "paraded naked in humiliating circumstances," and bombarded with cold water from a high-pressure hose. Then she was raped. The court said that her treatment would have been torture even without the rape, and that the rape would have been torture without the other abuses. ¶¶ 84, 86. Without the rape, the abuse she suffered for three days bears striking resemblance to that suffered by some US detainees for months. By the yardstick of *Aydin*, their treatment was torture.

[31] *Selmouni v. France*, App. No. 25803/94, 29 Eur. H.R. Rep. 403, ¶ 101 (1999).

to interpret them, as tacitly incorporating balancing tests or defenses of necessity, military or otherwise. CAT's ban on torture is an absolute ban.

Some may respond that CAT simply gets all this wrong; and nothing I have said so far entitles me to declare that CAT gets it right. For that argument, we will need a fuller understanding of torture than the legal definition can provide – a task I undertake in the remainder of this chapter. Based on that understanding, I will suggest that the prohibition of torture amounts to a moral archetype, a concept inspired by Waldron's parallel notion of a legal archetype. By calling it a moral archetype, I mean that the prohibition closely connects with other values that the world has come to regard as fundamental – fundamental concepts of human dignity, human equality, and the rejection of total domination of some people by others. To weaken the prohibition on torture, I will argue, would call those other values into question as well, at least potentially unraveling the moral advances of the past two centuries.

If I am right, it may explain why three-fourths of the world's governments have accepted article 2(2) and the bright line that it draws. Obviously, the law can get things wrong, but such a widespread consensus should at least give pause to those who advocate torture in (supposed) emergency situations. Strangely, publicists and philosophers who defend torture as a last resort seldom find the legal prohibition of torture an interesting fact that deserves reflection. One seldom finds anything as forthright as the following "truth in labeling" authorial caution:

> My proposal runs contrary to the official commitments of three-fourths of the world's governments. To accept my proposal, the world's governments must withdraw from those commitments, or, failing to withdraw, they and their interrogators must be prepared to commit serious crimes that violate their own laws and international law.

Perhaps this caution should become a standardized first footnote in any reputable publication purporting to defend torture, like the standardized health warnings printed on packets of cigarettes.

Summary of the legal definition

Before pursuing these arguments, it is time to sum up our discussion of the legal definition of torture. In short, CAT's definition gave us a useful formula – torture as severe mental or physical pain or suffering – and an indispensable template for states drafting their own laws against torture to fulfill their treaty obligations. CAT's definition of torture is nevertheless imperfect. It ought to specify that it pertains to custodial torture, and it ought to clarify that its list of purposes that make acts into torture is merely illustrative, and that torture for other purposes is still torture and still prohibited. That would ward off misreading the list as a limitation that wrongly links the designation of intentional acts as torture to the aims of the torturer. CAT's limitation to government-sponsored torture has a rationale, but it is inessential to the definitions of both torture as an experience and the act of torture. Lastly, CAT's split-level structure of obligations to fight vigorously against torture but merely to "undertake to prevent" CIDT is an invitation to mischief that is conceptually unnecessary, even if one accepts the hierarchical view that torture is worse than CIDT.

Even apart from these concerns, the CAT definition does not offer a full understanding of torture and its evils. That is not the purpose of a legal definition. Law is meant to be usable, not deep. Its rules are aimed at all kinds of people, deep and shallow, reflective and no-nonsense, moralists and cynics, refined and brutish, educated and ignorant. Legal prohibitions are not meant to make you think; they are meant to make you behave. Furthermore, they must employ only concepts susceptible to the kinds of evidence that practical men and women can recognize and offer to judges and juries who are looking for proof, not subtleties.

We should therefore not expect that CAT's legal definition of torture says all that should be said about the character of torture, or its evils, or the opprobrium attached to it. For that reason, I want to think these issues through afresh, taking guidance from CAT's definition, but not limiting the effort to the terms CAT sets out.

Defining torture: a new start

We have seen that CAT places torture in an infernal class by itself. States have never said about killing anything remotely as categorical as CAT's declaration that no exceptional circumstances whatsoever justify torture. After all, more than half the world's people live in countries that have the death penalty. Killing in war is lawful, and even peacetime human-rights treaties prohibit only "arbitrary" killings by the state, not all killings. As long as a century and a half ago, the Lieber Code (the first modern legal code for war) prohibited torture categorically, even though Lieber permitted "direct destruction of life," "all withholding of sustenance or the means of life from the enemy," and even the starvation of civilians.[32]

CAT's definition of torture sheds no light on what makes torture unique among the misfortunes we visit on each other. For legal purposes, explaining that intuition is unnecessary, and too much theorizing would actually weaken the force of the prohibition by inviting controversy. Thus, my observation that the legal definition sheds no light on why the ban is uniquely categorical is not

[32] US Army, General Orders No. 100, Adjutant General's Office, 1863 (http://avalon.law.yale.edu/19th_century/lieber.asp#sec1), arts. 15–17.

a criticism of that definition. It does mean that to understand the evils of torture, we need to move past CAT's definition.

The main point I shall argue is this: CAT's definition centers on pain and suffering, but the evil of torture cannot be reduced to sensations alone. To see this, recall an example that I used in Chapter 4: women whom no one would deem irrational often choose natural childbirth despite the pain. Its association with a joyful event transforms excruciating pain into an experience they do not regard as evil.

The example suggests that the evil of physical torture lies in the linkage between suffering and its context. Natural childbirth links pain with creation, love, and the miracle of human life. Torture links pain with fear, uncertainty, and the horror of being wholly in the power of a maleficent enemy. The fact that it is *custodial* torture matters crucially. Being in the clutches of the enemy and at his mercy – and understanding through the suffering he inflicts that he has no mercy – is an essential part of torture's evil.

The Stoics recognized this special character of torture. Seneca observed that even the Stoic sage quails when he sees the instruments of torture displayed, and "the spectacle overcomes those who would have patiently withstood the suffering."[33] This last observation should be read carefully. Seneca means, quite literally, that the terror is more unbearable than the suffering itself.[34] That is why displaying the instruments is actually the commencement of the torture. Seneca admits that diseases can be as painful as torture, but

> that which shakes us most is the dread which hangs over us from our neighbour's ascendancy [lit. 'another's power', *aliena potentia*]; for it is accompanied by great outcry and uproar... Picture to yourself under this head the prison, the cross, the rack, the hook, and ... all the other contrivances devised by cruelty... It is not surprising that our greatest terror is of such a fate.[35]

Ruefully, Seneca admits, "it is our Stoic fashion to speak of all those things, which provoke cries and groans, as unimportant and beneath notice; but you and I must drop such great-sounding words, although Heaven knows, they are true enough."[36]

Notably, Seneca emphasizes suffering amplified by imagination, and he associates the horrors of torture with being in another's power and having that power

---

[33] Seneca, *Epistles 1–65* (Richard M. Gummere, Trans.) (Cambridge, MA: Harvard University Press, 1917), Epistle 14, p. 87. I am grateful to Nancy Sherman for first calling this epistle to my attention.

[34] Of course, Seneca is speculating. Without experiencing the suffering, how could he know? But let us not forget that Seneca was writing at a time when torture was public and frequent, and he writes with the confidence of someone who has observed unfortunates before, during, and after their torture.

[35] *Ibid.*, Epistle 14, p. 85.   [36] *Ibid.*, Epistle 13, p. 75.

put on spectacular display. But imagination does not merely amplify suffering; it transforms its content – that is, the way we experience pain or suffering – in this case, as absolute subordination to another person who uses pain to announce that subordination. Pain now becomes a medium of communication. Bearing these observations in mind, I shall define torture as follows:

Communicative definition of torture

> Torture of someone in the torturer's custody or physical control is the assertion of unlimited power over absolute helplessness, communicated through the infliction of severe pain or suffering on the victim that the victim is meant to understand as the display of the torturer's limitless power and the victim's absolute helplessness.

I label this definition "communicative" because it focuses on the infliction of pain or suffering to announce, or communicate, the total subordination of the victim to the torturer. The communicative definition encompasses mental as well as physical torture. So long as the mental suffering is severe, and it is inflicted in a context that communicates the absolute dominance of the torturer and helplessness of the victim, it qualifies as torture.

The communicative definition is different from, and more complicated than, the legal definition we have examined. I wish to reiterate that it is not intended to replace the legal definition, which serves its own purposes. Indeed, the communicative definition would be useless for legal purposes, if for no other reason than the near impossibility of proving in a court of law through ordinary evidence that an act is a communication of unlimited power over absolute helplessness, using pain as a medium, and intended to be such.

The definition offered here means to capture a distinctive feature of torture, which lies in the connection of pain and suffering with subordination and helplessness as two sides of the same experience. The pain of torture is not only an experience in itself but also a medium of communication; it is *contentful* pain – in this respect wholly unlike pain resulting from natural causes like illness or injury, whose noteworthy experienced characteristic is its senselessness, its lack of meaningful content.[37] By contrast, what the pain of torture communicates is the absolute subordination of the victim to the enemy's sovereign cruelty.

---

[37] The philosopher Wilfrid Sellars notices a "notorious 'ing-ed' ambiguity" in certain concepts. "Communication" is one of them: it can refer to the act of communicat*ing* or to the content communicat*ed*. The point that I am making here – that the pain and suffering inflicted by the torturer are contentful – helps resolve the ambiguity in the present case. Pain and suffering are the medium through which the message of mastery and subjugation is communicated, but by virtue of communicating that message, the pain and suffering are themselves contentful. Here, the form of communicat*ing* changes the content communicat*ed*. Sellars' phrase appears in his "Empiricism and the Philosophy of Mind," in *Science, Perception, and Reality* (Austin, TX: Ridgeview,

The contemporary philosopher David Sussman sheds light on how pain and suffering convey this message of the absolute abjectness of the victim before the torturer. Sussman observes that torture puts the victim "into the position of colluding against himself through his own affects and emotions, so that he experiences himself as simultaneously powerless and yet actively complicit in his own violation."[38] Why "actively complicit"? Because, after all, pain and suffering are deep within the victim. The victim may not want to talk, or beg, or scream, or weep, but now her own body and mind gang up with the torturer to make her do it. Sensations and emotions, the most intimate parts of the victim, transfer their allegiance to a new sovereign, the torturer.

Sussman's focus on this interior aspect of torture perhaps underplays the other side, the directionality of the pain and suffering – the fact that they come from outside, from the torturer, who announces his sovereignty with a fanfare of suffering that the body and mind of the victim cannot ignore.[39] From the torturer's point of view, pain or suffering is the medium by which he conveys the message that he is now the master and the victim is now nothing. The torturer's intentions automatically become the most passionately interesting thing in the universe to the victim. The reading of the victim's own pain as a medium of the torturer's intentions marks torture as a meaning-conveying act.

Some possible objections

In order to further explain the communicative definition, I would like to consider some potential objections to it, based on the concern that it may leave out acts that ought to count as torture.

For example, what if the torturer has no subjective intention to communicate a message of total domination over the victim? What if the torturer is an anguished official, who – with exquisite politeness and deepest regret – explains to the victim that much as he respects the victim and hates what he is about to do, duty and necessity require him to torture the victim? And suppose it is true that the "polite torturer" feels respect for the victim and has no intention to assert dominance. Would that make the pain-infliction any the

1963), § 24, p. 154; reprinted as *Empiricism and the Philosophy of Mind*, with an Introduction by Richard Rorty and a Study Guide by Robert Brandom (Cambridge, MA: Harvard University Press, 1997).

[38] David Sussman, "What's Wrong with Torture?", *Philosophy and Public Affairs*, 33(1), (2005), 1–33, at 4.

[39] *Ibid.*, p. 32. Sussman here adopts the communicative conception of torture I am emphasizing, when he writes that "the victim experiences his body in all its intimacy as the *expressive medium* of another will" (emphasis added). For some reason, Sussman associates this with punitive torture, not interrogational torture, and thinks it is a less central case than interrogational torture ("torture 'proper,'" p. 31). I do not see an important difference between the two.

less torture? Clearly not. But then is it not a mistake to define torture as communication through pain of absolute dominance? The simplest response to this challenge is that the communicative definition states a sufficient condition of torture, not a necessary condition – or, put in less philosophical terms, the definition is not designed to capture every imaginable form of intentional pain-infliction that could rightly be named "torture." Rather, the definition is meant to capture the typical dynamics of torture as we actually find it in current and historical practices – torture where the point of the practice is to break the will and spirit of the victim and assert the torturer's mastery. For that surely *is* the point, whether the aim is victor's pleasure, terror, extracting confessions, punishing crime, or obtaining information – the five historical practices of torture I cataloged in Chapter 3. Even if the communicative definition does not state a general theorem about all possible torture, it clearly does capture something essential to the typical practices of torture we find in our world.

Furthermore, I doubt that the "polite torturer" really is an exception or counterexample to the communicative definition. In torture the adage that actions speak louder than words applies in a very literal way. The polite torturer may fervently insist that he respects the victim as he respects himself, and that asserting dominance is the furthest thing from his intention; and when he says this he may be subjectively sincere (or at least think he is). But the torture itself sends a different message, for precisely the reason Sussman identifies: the victim's senses and emotions are now wholly at the torturer's command, and the torturer is commanding them to do that which the victim finds most unbearable. The message torture sends is independent of the torturer's subjective intentions or verbal disclaimers, because its communicative content as a message of dominance over helplessness comes from the nonconventional fact that torturing someone is an exertion of dominance over helplessness. The performance enacts the message, in a way analogous to the linguistic phenomenon of onomatopoeia.

The fundamental point here is that even though torturers normally intend to send the message of absolute dominance over absolute helplessness, the content and assertion of the message are independent of the torturer's subjective intentions – just as the content of the sentences I utter is independent of my subjective intentions. In an anomalous case where the torturer's subjective intentions have nothing to do with communicating the absolute abjectness of the victim, the content of the message will be controlled by its normal meaning, not by the torturer's anomalous intentions.

Does the victim's subjective state matter? For example, what if the victim is not helpless, and knows it? In some cases, the victim may know that the torture will end the moment his lawyer arrives at the jailhouse.[40] Or the victim

----

[40] I am indebted to Mark Graber for this example.

may know the legal limits on what the torturer can do (perhaps he studied the torture memos). Crucially, in many instances the victim can choose to end the torture by giving up the information the torturer wants. Would these cases not fall outside the communicative definition of torture?

Again the answer is no. In the former two cases, the proper conclusion is simply that the victim has been tortured during the time limits allotted and within the legal limits. Knowing that the torturer's power is not limitless in relation to the outside world does not negate the message that the torturer's power to inflict severe pain and suffering on the victim is absolute in relation to the victim. In the case where the victim gives up the information he or she is trying to hide, the torturer has succeeded in breaking the victim's will. In all these cases, the fear that the torturer will, out of whim or out of rage, go beyond any limits is always there; it is a fear hard-wired into the very circumstances of custodial torture, and that fact is precisely what defines the message of absolute dominance and absolute helplessness conveyed by the pain.

Making, taking, breaking

Does that mean that if the victim resists successfully, perhaps even laughing defiantly in the torturer's face, the act is not torture, because the torturer has not absolutely dominated the victim? Of course not. An assertion of absolute dominance can fail to induce absolute dominance, just as a factual assertion can be disbelieved and rejected.

That observation highlights one important piece of this communicative model of torture. The torturer uses pain and suffering to send a message, but the aim is not merely to send the message. The torturer uses pain and suffering to communicate total domination in order to make it happen that he totally dominates the victim. The communication succeeds only when the victim takes up the message by believing it. What completes the *making true* is the *taking as true*.

The victim, we may assume, will fight desperately to defy the message of total subjugation, using all the limited resources a helpless captive has available: will, courage, and spirit (which are importantly different from each other); indignation and rage; and religious faith, if the victim has it.

These psychic resources may succeed for a while in resisting the torturer's message, and therefore falsifying it and keeping the victim intact. But eventually they will almost certainly fail. Physical and mental pain exhaust the will, as everyone who has ever suffered prolonged pain or depression knows all too well. They discourage and dispirit the sufferer; they undermine the faith of the faithful. In the Gospels, the cross causes even Jesus to ask in anguish why God has forsaken him.[41]

---

[41] Matthew 27:46; Mark 15:34.

The torturer's control over the victim's pain and suffering automatically make the torturer the most passionately interesting person in the universe to the victim, the one whose opinions are of greatest immediate significance. It matters crucially that the torturer has custody of the victim, cutting him off from any social contact that might contradict the message of radical hierarchy and radical worthlessness that torture sends. We take our cues from other people, and few of our beliefs, even perceptual beliefs, could survive perpetual contradiction by those around us. That holds especially of our belief in our own worth, which to an incalculable extent rests on the esteem in which we are held by others. By cutting the victim off from any society other than the torturer's, the torturer undermines the victim's confidence in his own worth, which relies on the reinforcement of those around us. It is a form of death.[42] Losing confidence in their own worth, torture victims stand at risk of losing their final resource of resistance: anger and indignation at their treatment.

When the torturer succeeds, the victim takes on board the message of radical humiliation, and we then say that the victim is *broken*. Psychologists talk about it as "learned helplessness" and Stockholm syndrome, when the victim becomes docile and cooperative.[43] It is the golden moment that interrogators aim at. Orwell brilliantly represents that moment in *Nineteen Eighty-Four*, when Winston Smith betrays his lover Julia and in her place genuinely loves Big Brother. The broken Smith is, in an important sense, no longer fully human.

First corollary: the experienced content of pain and suffering

One essential corollary of this definition is that the pain of torture cannot be separated, even conceptually, from the communication of absolute dominance over absolute helplessness. The victim experiences the pain not only as physical or mental sensations but also as a humiliation of the self at the hands of an infinitely cruel other.

The philosopher Robert Brandom explains the difference between pain as humans experience it and brute physical sensation by distinguishing *sapience* (conceptual awareness) from *sentience* (sensuous awareness).[44] "Our sapience

---

[42] Hannah Arendt noted that "the language of the Romans ... used the words 'to live' and 'to be among men' (*inter homines esse*) or 'to die' and 'to cease to be among men' (*inter homines esse desinere*) as synonyms." Hannah Arendt, *The Human Condition* (University of Chicago Press, 1958), pp. 7–8.

[43] Martin E. Seligman, "Learned Helplessness," *Annual Review of Medicine*, 23 (1972), 407–12. Seligman, whose research heavily influenced the psychologists who designed the CIA's torture program, conducted experiments in which dogs, subjected to random electrical shocks unconnected with their behavior, soon became so passive that they no longer even tried to avoid the shocks.

[44] Robert B. Brandom, *Reason in Philosophy* (Cambridge, MA: Harvard University Press, 2009), p. 135.

is not just something added to our sentience, leaving that base undisturbed. Sapience fundamentally transforms our sentience, turning mere inchoate *sensation* into articulated *perception*. Our sentience is not that of the beasts."[45] I have said that pain is the medium and absolute domination is the message; but it would be more accurate to say that for a sapient being, the medium *is* the message.[46]

It follows that the pain and suffering of torture cannot be understood reductively or "medically" as neural events of a specified intensity ("severe," or merely "serious," as one US statute confusingly puts it, or not even serious), apart from the contents of the message they convey.[47] Severity must be understood not as a quantitative measure of negative neural stimulation, but as an index of how hard it is to ignore or deny the message the pain or suffering communicates. That is why the torture memos' assurance that the CIA would stop short of torture by having torture doctors on hand to examine the victims for symptoms of severity rests on a sinister mistake.

But focusing on the communicative context of the pain or suffering also explains why one of the most common arguments in the US torture debate fails. That argument notices that the CIA's "enhanced" techniques were drawn from a program of resistance training administered to candidates for US Special Forces in a mock prisoner-of-war camp –"SERE" (Survival Evasion Resistance Escape) training. Thousands of US personnel have taken the SERE course, and the common argument is that if we do it to our own volunteers, it cannot be torture.

The argument misses the all-important difference in contexts. A SERE volunteer knows things the prisoner cannot know. He knows that the resistance training will end in a fixed and short amount of time, that the trainers do not want to kill him or destroy him, that they care about his health, and, most fundamentally, that they are on his side. Crucially, the SERE volunteer can make it stop at any time by quitting the program. He will not get into the Special Forces then – but ultimately it is in his control. SERE veterans report that the training seems entirely real at the time – scary and awful – but the difference in context makes it different in kind from torture.[48] The pain and suffering convey different content in these very different contexts.

Second corollary: the evils of torture

A second corollary is a set of consequences that yield a fuller understanding of the evils of torture. The definition centers on the communicative or

---

[45] *Ibid.*, p. 137.   [46] See in this connection note 37, above.

[47] 18 U.S.C. § 2339(d)(2)(distinguishing "severe" from "serious" pain and suffering).

[48] In the legal terms of the US torture statute, the volunteer nature of SERE training, and the ability to opt out, very likely negate a crucial element of the definition of torture: that the victim be within the torturer's "custody or physical control." 18 U.S.C. § 2340(1).

message-sending function of custodial torture. We can elaborate seven specific evils (seven deadly sins?) that follow from the definition:

(1) the *form* of the message: inflicting mental or physical pain or suffering;
(2) the *content* of the message: "I, the torturer, am everything; you, the victim, are nothing; I am the master, you are the dog";
(3) the *means* or *manner* by which torture sends the message: compelling the victim's own senses and emotions to turn against her (Sussman's point);
(4) the *intended effect* of the message: breaking the will, courage, and spirit of the victim;
(5) the *moral falsehood* of the message of radical inequality and subordination, coupled with:
(6) the self-fulfilling (or, in philosophical language, "performative" and "truth-making") character of the message: by using pain and suffering to convey the message that the victim is broken, torture wears the victim down and makes it so;
(7) the totalitarian relationship torture establishes between the torturer and the victim, in which the torturer becomes sovereign over the most intimate sensations and emotions of the victim.

Notice that the legal definition of torture focuses only on the first item on this list – the infliction of pain or suffering. It rightly belongs first; obviously, the pain and suffering are the fundamental evil of torture. And, as I suggested above, there are good reasons for focusing the legal definition on the most tangible and provable of the evils. But noticing the multiple dimensions of evil curled up in the concept of torture is essential if we wish to understand why the world condemns torture so categorically.

The evils on this list are not the only basis for regarding torture as an affront to morality. For example, I have omitted from this list the crucial evil of torture that most concerns health professionals who treat torture survivors:

(8) the lasting aftereffects of the torture, including depression, post-traumatic stress disorder (PTSD), fearfulness, and fundamental loss of trust in the world.

In tandem with these aftereffects, we can add – as an evil associated with the act of torture rather than the experience of torture:

(9) the torturer's indifference to those lasting aftereffects.

Both surely belong on the list of torture's evils, but they do not follow specifically from the definition of torture offered here. They are collateral consequences of torture. The same is true of

(10) the corruption of the torturer, as well as the physicians, psychologists, lawyers, and other professionals connected with the torture enterprise, including military and law-enforcement personnel and political leaders;

(11) the further corruption induced by the inevitable coverups; and

(12) the tendency of institutionalized torture to metastasize from cases in which it is supposedly "justified" to borderline cases, and then across the border – as the border itself gets redrawn because, as a consequence of torture's corrupting effects, the baseline sense of what is normal and what is not changes in the minds and practices of those on the torture team.

Cataloging these evils does not by itself prove that under no circumstances could torture ever be justified. It is always possible to invent imaginary cases in which all the evils summed together still turn out to be the lesser evil. But the character of evil associated with torture places it in a category similar to slavery: the category of practices about which the question, "do the benefits outweigh the costs?" seems out of order – even if earlier civilizations saw nothing odd about the question and even assumed the answer was yes.[49] As I put it in Chapter 4, torture (like slavery) belongs in the category of the unthinkable. This obviously does not mean it cannot be thought, but only that such thoughts are radically at odds with central parts of our moral framework – most basically, assumptions about human worth and human equality. Returning to Waldron's conception of a legal archetype, with which I began this chapter, we might say that just as the prohibition on torture is a legal archetype, the abolition of torture is a moral archetype, with significance beyond its immediate normative content. That is because to put the question of torture back into play compels us to put other central values into play as well: not only the rejection of cruelty, but also of totalitarian domination, along with belief in the indecency of humiliating and degrading other people, rejection of radical human hierarchy with broken men and women at the bottom, and the perverseness of creating a class of corrupt professionals whose job is to assist in all the other evils and then to cover it all up. To reject the ban on torture would cast doubt on even minimum modern conceptions of human equality, human dignity, liberal government, and even simple decency.

Third corollary: torture and CIDT

A final corollary concerns the relationship between torture and CIDT. The legal definitions are ambivalent about whether these are different in degree alone or in kind. On the one hand, they ground the difference in how severe the pain or suffering is, which sounds like a difference in degree. On the other, they suggest a sharp break, when mistreatment crosses the line to torture, and state obligations under CAT balloon.

Defined communicatively, the act of torture *is* an act of humiliation. The humiliation of the victim is not an incidental consequence of pain or

---

[49] This is the theme explored in more detail in Chapter 4.

suffering – it is the fundamental message that the pain and suffering of torture aim to convey. Torture always and necessarily humiliates the victim.

It is not necessarily true the other way around. Not all humiliations are torture. But strategies of piling one small insult and humiliation on top of another, in a disorienting custodial environment, clearly aim to break the victim in precisely the way that the communicative definition proposes as the hallmark of torture. If the message is the same and the medium is generically identical (mental or physical pain or suffering), we might conclude that accumulated humiliation and degradation crosses the line into torture; or, as I prefer to think about it, we might conclude that the distinction between CIDT and torture simply does not matter. If you have to ask whether it is torture, it is.

6

Human dignity, humiliation, and torture

This chapter originated as a lecture on Jewish ethics, in a series honoring the late philosopher Isaac Franck. My own writing has been almost entirely secular, and I am not a scholar of Jewish philosophy. Nevertheless, I have come to realize from the smatterings of Jewish law I have studied that my approach to many issues is very close in spirit to some central themes in Jewish ethics. This is specifically true of one of my themes in the present chapter, the central ethical importance of respecting human dignity by not humiliating people – a theme, as I hope to show, that similarly occupies pride of place in rabbinic ethics. The particular context for my argument is a subject of surpassing current importance: the torture and degradation of detainees by the US government in the "war on terrorism."

Eleanor Roosevelt's tea party

I begin with a famous story, almost a parable, about the drafting of the Universal Declaration of Human Rights (UDHR) – the first and most influential document for the contemporary human-rights movement worldwide.

Eleanor Roosevelt chaired the UN committee charged with producing the UDHR, but the intellectual heavy lifting came from four other remarkable committee members: René Cassin, a French Jew; John Humphrey, a Canadian lawyer; and two philosophy professors, P. C. Chang from China and Charles Malik, a Lebanese Christian.

Shortly after the process began, Eleanor Roosevelt hosted a tea party in her New York apartment, attended by Chang, Malik, and Humphrey. As she reports in her diary, Chang and Malik launched into a vigorous debate about the philosophical foundations of human rights. Chang favored a pluralist approach, while Malik took a more absolutist stance. Soon, the debate turned into a deep discussion of Aquinas and Confucius – and Roosevelt admits that by that point she was completely lost, and contented herself with refilling the teacups.

The main text of this chapter was first published in 2009 – see Acknowledgments. It has been substantively revised to eliminate redundancies with other chapters. It is based on my Isaac Franck Memorial Lecture at Georgetown University in that year.

What Roosevelt discreetly left unsaid was how vividly the tea party demonstrated to her the importance of *not* getting bogged down in philosophical debates about human rights. As a politically wise humanitarian, Roosevelt understood that all would be lost if the delegates had to figure out who actually gets it right, Aquinas or Confucius – or Kant, or Dewey, or Marx.

Interestingly, a special UNESCO commission charged with canvassing philosophical ideas about human rights from all over the world reached a similar conclusion. Jacques Maritain, who belonged to this commission, wrote that everyone agreed about the most important human rights – provided that nobody asked them why.[1]

The legal scholar Cass Sunstein has coined the phrase "incompletely theorized agreements" to describe the kind of agreement that Roosevelt thought the UDHR had to be.[2] As Larry Solum puts the conception, "When you cannot reach agreement at the deep end of the pool of ideas, head for the shallow end!"[3] And, above all, head *off* the deep thinkers at the pass before they insist on actually getting to the bottom of things.

The issue arose one more time in the UDHR negotiations, when several Latin American delegates proposed inserting a reference to God in the declaration's preamble. The majority of delegates quickly scuttled the proposal, which they were certain would simply divide nations against each other on religious grounds and make agreement impossible. Instead, the UDHR rests the idea of human rights on a different foundation: *human dignity*. Other human-rights documents, like the UN Charter and the Charter of Human Rights of the European Union, also invoke human dignity as the core value human rights are supposed to protect. And the Helsinki Accords makes an even stronger claim: human rights "derive from the inherent dignity of the human person."[4]

However, it should be clear from this sketchy history that in the UDHR and its successor instruments, the term "human dignity" is really a kind of placeholder – an uncontroversial, neutral-sounding term for the unknown X that anchors human rights. Of course, "human dignity" is not entirely a culturally neutral term that speaks in the same way to every tradition.

[1] The story of Roosevelt's tea party, and of the UNESCO commission and Maritain's comment, are both told in Mary Ann Glendon, *A World Made New: Eleanor Roosevelt and the Universal Declaration of Human Rights* (New York: Random House, 2001).

[2] Cass R. Sunstein, "Incompletely Theorized Agreements," *Harvard Law Review*, 108 (1995), 1733–72.

[3] Lawrence Solum, "Legal Theory Lexicon: Overlapping Consensus and Incompletely Theorized Agreements," Legal Theory Blog, Aug. 17, 2008 (http://lsolum.typepad.com/legal_theory_lexicon/2004/05/legal_theory_le_1.html).

[4] Helsinki Accords, Final Act of the Conference on Security and Cooperation in Europe, adopted at Helsinki, Aug. 1, 1975, reprinted in 14 I.L.M. 1292 (1975), Principle 7; Charter of Human Rights of the European Union (2000), Article 1 (www.europarl.europa.eu/charter/default_en.htm).

The phrase "human dignity" has Stoic origins (in Cicero's *De Officiis*, I.30), and the concept plays a prominent role in Christianity. Philosophically, the notion that human beings have a dignity, not merely a price, is central to Kant's conception of rational beings as ends in themselves. It is a pre-eminently European term.

European or not, it did the job that Eleanor Roosevelt hoped it would: the UDHR passed the UN General Assembly with no negative votes. And it may well be that this happened in part because "human dignity" means whatever you want it to mean, which is another way of saying that it does not mean very much.

To borrow a phrase from John Rawls, the world's nations have reached an overlapping consensus on the central importance of human dignity, in which each culture and subculture may tell its own story about what human dignity is and where it comes from. In Rawls' terminology, each has a "comprehensive doctrine" that explains human dignity.[5] In a situation of overlapping consensus, the comprehensive doctrines disappear from view, and only the shared concept remains in the intersection of all those doctrines.

The advantage of incomplete theorization and overlapping consensus are obvious – they make agreement possible. But the disadvantage is equally obvious: once a concept has been whittled down to a mere placeholder, it does no work in helping you resolve contested questions about human rights.

One approach to this difficulty is to say, "Damn the incomplete theorization, full speed ahead!" As philosophers, we should ignore politicians' worries about getting everyone to sign on the dotted line, and forge ahead towards the intellectual showdown that Roosevelt was so eager to avoid. Let us work out an analysis of human dignity from first principles, and jettison any comprehensive doctrines that get the wrong answer.

I am skeptical of this bold metaphysical approach, because I suspect that any first principles strong enough to yield a rich concept of human dignity will turn out to carry a lot of cultural freight that undermines their claim to universality. But there is another approach, and that is to return to the particular traditions and hear what they have to say about human dignity. Once we do that, it may turn out that even people outside the tradition will find its ideas attractive enough to adopt. That is the approach I propose in this chapter. I want to develop a characteristically Jewish notion of human dignity.

I pull two main points from the texts I consider. The first is that human dignity is not a metaphysical property of individual human beings, but rather a property of relations between human beings – between, so to speak, the dignifier and the dignified. The second point is that, for the most part,

---

[5] John Rawls, "The Domain of the Political and Overlapping Consensus," in Samuel Freeman, Ed., *Collected Papers* (Cambridge, MA: Harvard University Press, 1999), pp. 480–1.

respecting human dignity means something quite down to earth: it means not humiliating people. So the theme of this part of my discussion is to insist on the central ethical importance of nonhumiliation. My claim is that this is a lesson close to the heart of Jewish ethics.

I then turn from these general and somewhat abstract ideas to something very concrete, very sordid, and very upsetting: the issue of torture and so-called cruel, inhuman, and degrading treatment that falls short of torture – what lawyers abbreviate as "CIDT."

It will be important to my argument that the United States, like every other country that tortures, accompanies torture with humiliation; indeed, that one of the defining evils of torture is the humiliation it visits on its victims. If so, then perhaps the notion of human dignity as nonhumiliation, so central to Jewish ethics, can help us understand why these practices are so deeply wrong.

In our image, after our likeness

For Jews, as for Christians, the central sacred text explaining human dignity is Chapter 1, verses 26 and 27 of the Book of Genesis: "And God said, 'Let us make man in our image, after our likeness'... And God created man in his image, in the image of God He created him; male and female He created them." Humans have dignity because we are created in the image of God, the *imago Dei*.

To a certain kind of biblical literalist, these two verses show that God has something like a human body; and, of course, the Torah contains many references to God walking, to God's back, and finger, and face. This kind of literalism is Maimonides' target in the first chapter of the *Guide of the Perplexed*, where he explains that the image and likeness are intellectual, not physical. It is childish to think that God has a literal physical body that ours resembles; in any case, our defining property is not our physical shape but our intellect.

But later in the *Guide*, Maimonides offers an even more austere argument than the rejection of God's corporeality. God is wholly unlike anything else, and Maimonides follows the logic of that proposition to several surprising and perhaps unwelcome conclusions. First, the radical dissimilarity of God and created things means that any property we ascribe to God and to ourselves – any shared property that might form the basis of likeness – is falsely or equivocally ascribed.[6] So the idea that our minds resemble God's mind turns out to be just as anthropomorphic and false as the crude belief that God has broad shoulders and washboard abs.[7]

---

[6] Moses Maimonides, *The Guide of the Perplexed* (Shlomo Pines, Trans.) (University of Chicago Press, 1963), vol. i, ch. 56 , 130–1.

[7] *Ibid.*, ch. 53, pp. 119–20. "The reasons that led those who believe in the existence of attributes belonging to the Creator to this belief are akin to those that led those who

In fact, for Maimonides, no assertion about God can be literally and unequivocally true: the very subject–predicate form of the assertion falsely splits off God's essence from His properties.[8] Eventually, Maimonides will push this argument to a drastic conclusion and insist on a kind of ineffabilism: our talk about God can have meaning only as allegory or parable, designed to enable the only true form of response to God, which, he dramatically insists, is total silence.[9]

One corollary of this view, it seems to me, is a powerful epistemological humility about God – so powerful that it thins the distinction between religious belief and agnosticism almost to the vanishing point. After all, if all propositions about God are false, and human knowledge comes in propositional form, then we can *know* nothing about God's properties.[10] As a second corollary, Maimonides rejects any form of biblical literalism. The method of interpretation must be nonliteral interpretation, *drash*. Taken together, epistemological modesty and antiliteralism powerfully open up a space for rationalist reflection on sacred texts. It is a space where Jewish ethics and secular ethics can meet and debate in a fruitful way.

What, then, should our *drash* be about human beings created in God's image and likeness? If Maimonides is right, the question "In what respect are we like God?" is simply the wrong question to ask. Searching for some metaphysical property of humans called "human dignity" is a dead end, because it requires us to know God's unknowable properties. All that we really can infer from the biblical text is that a certain relationship exists between God and man – the relationship of "creating in one's own image" – and that human dignity lies in the fact of this relationship.

A more subtle point is this: if God creates us in his image, perhaps our being created in God's image entails the human ability to engage each other in a parallel kind of relationship – a relationship of honoring and

believe in the doctrine of His corporeality to that belief... The people in question have, as it were, divested God of corporeality but not of the modes of corporeality, namely, the accidents—I mean the aptitudes of the soul, all of which are qualities." Isaac Franck, in whose honor this lecture was composed, wrote illuminatingly about Maimonides' "negative theology," and its relation to Aquinas. See Isaac Franck, "Maimonides and Aquinas on Man's Knowledge of God: A Twentieth-Century Perspective," in *A Philosopher's Harvest: The Philosophical Papers of Isaac Franck*, Ed. William Gerber (Washington, DC: Georgetown University Press, 1988), pp. 3–24.

[8] Maimonides, *The Guide of the Perplexed*, vol. 1, ch. 57, pp. 132–3.

[9] *Ibid.*, ch. 59, p. 139.

[10] *Ibid.*, ch. 57, p. 132. Distinguishing negative theology from agnosticism becomes especially thorny given one other implication that Maimonides draws from his argument: that the literal falsehood of propositions about God includes the proposition "God exists." For philosophers who believe, with Kant, that existence is not a predicate (i.e., a property), Maimonides would not be entitled to this conclusion, and in any case his argument about the ineffability of God pragmatically presupposes the existence of a God about whom the premises of the argument are true.

acknowledging the other by treating him or her as a being in my own image. A well-known *midrash* implicitly takes this point of view:

> R. Akiva says: "Love your fellow as yourself" (Lev. 19:18), this is the greatest principle of the Torah... R. Tanhuma explained: "He made him in the likeness of God" (Gen. 5:1). (*Genesis Rabba* 24)

Rabbi Tanhuma explicitly connects the *imago Dei*, the creation of man in God's own image, with "Love your fellow as yourself," the classic expression of honor for the human dignity of the other. As God creates man in his likeness, men and women live up to that image by acknowledging others as likenesses of themselves.

I am suggesting that instead of thinking about "human dignity" as a metaphysical property of human beings, we should take as our basic notion the relational property of "respecting human dignity." In Jewish ethics, that basic relation gets spelled out in this way: "Person X treats Person Y as if Y is X's likeness," which is a pedantic way of saying, "Love your fellow as yourself."[11]

Think of this as the relation between the dignifier and the dignified: "the dignifier treats the dignified as if the dignified is the dignifier's likeness." Once we elaborate what this relation entails, we will have, in effect, an implicit definition of human dignity.

This elaboration can very likely be accomplished in more than one way. The catalog of rights in the UDHR offers one specification of the kinds of behaviors that acknowledge other people's likeness to myself and how I would wish to be treated. But the various comprehensive doctrines may have alternative elaborations. So the next task is to discover what practices the Jewish tradition recognizes as respecting human dignity.

The wrong of humiliation in rabbinic ethics

In the biblical story of Tamar, the widow Tamar sleeps with her own father-in-law, Judah, as a prostitute, and conceives a child. Because her face was covered, Judah has no idea that the prostitute he coupled with was Tamar. When he learns that Tamar, the widow of his son, has become pregnant, he orders her burned to death in a fiery furnace. But as she is being led to her execution, she asks that certain tokens Judah had given to her when she was playing

---

[11] I will make no effort here to reconcile this way of thinking with Emanuel Levinas' ethics, in which our infinite responsibility to the other is connected not with the other's likeness to us, but rather to the other's radical otherness. For a clear discussion of this point, see Hilary Putnam, "Levinas on What Is Demanded of Us," in Putnam, *Jewish Philosophy as a Guide to Life: Rosenzweig, Buber, Levinas, Wittgenstein* (Bloomington, IN: Indiana University Press, 2008), pp. 68–99, at pp. 70–1, 80–3.

the prostitute be sent to him. Seeing the tokens, he realizes that he is the father of her child, and spares Tamar (Gen. 38: 6–26).

The Talmud focuses on one detail of this revolting story: the fact that Tamar discreetly sent the tokens to Judah instead of announcing in public that he was the father of her child. What impressed the rabbis was the colossal risk she took. What if the tokens never arrived? What if Judah did not recognize them? Or what if, recognizing them, Judah decided to do nothing? Then Tamar would have died a horrible death. Tamar was willing to run that risk rather than shaming Judah in public. Rabbi Shimon ben Yochai treats Tamar's courage as an exemplar, and derives a moral from the story:

> It is better that a person should cast himself into a fiery furnace than that he should shame his fellow in public. (Babylonian Talmud [BT], *Bava Metzia* 59a)

This particular *sugya* belongs to an extended discussion of forms of harming others by shaming them. Drawing on various biblical proof-texts, the rabbis come up with several equally melodramatic formulas, like this:

> If anyone makes his friend's face turn white [from shame] in public, it is as if he had spilled his blood.

To which one rabbi replies, "What you are saying is right, because I have seen how the red coloring leaves and his face turns white" (BT, *Bava Metzia* 59a). Or this: a man who sleeps with another man's wife must be punished, but he still has a share in the "world to come"; but "one who shames his fellow person in public has no share in the World to Come!" (BT, *Bava Metzia* 59a). For Maimonides as well, shaming another person by calling him by an insulting nickname in public is one of the small set of sins grave enough to deny you a place in the "world to come."[12]

Passages like these should persuade us that the nonhumiliation of others occupies a central place in Jewish ethics. Once we appreciate this, we can find the theme in many contexts unrelated to shaming someone with words.

Consider, for example, Maimonides' discussion of *tzedakah*, almsgiving, which is among the most famous passages in all rabbinics. Maimonides is overwhelmingly concerned that *tzedakah* not shame the recipient. In fact, he says straightforwardly that "whoever gives *tzedakah* to a poor man ill-manneredly ... has lost all the merit of his action even though he should give him a thousand gold pieces."[13] Maimonides prefers giving too little money, but graciously, to giving an adequate amount with ill grace. He ranks giving

[12] Moses Maimonides, *Mishneh Torah*, Laws of Repentance, ch. III.14.
[13] Moses Maimonides, *Mishneh Torah*, "Gifts to the Poor," in Isadore Twersky, Ed., *A Maimonides Reader* (West Orange, NJ: Behrman House, 1972), Book 7, ch. 10, § 7, p. 136.

before you are asked higher than giving after you are asked. And he praises anonymous giving because it will not shame the recipient.[14] Every value judgment in his discussion of the forms of giving manifests the central concern for sparing the poor person who receives *tzedakah* from humiliation.

The same concerns govern a series of Talmudic strictures requiring the rich to avoid ostentation during communal mourning in order to avoid shaming the poor who are also present. Wealthy people bringing gifts of food to the house of a mourner should not bring the food on fancy platters, or serve beverages in elegant glasses, because then the poor who are also bringing food to the house of mourning will be shamed. Because the poor often cover the deceased's face, which has been discolored through hard work, the rich must cover the faces of their dead as well. And the rich, like the poor, must be transported to their graves in plain coffins (BT, *Mo'Ed Katan* 27a–b).

All these examples, it appears, have to do with the ethical centrality of not humiliating or shaming people. The same ethical tradition reappears in contemporary form in Avishai Margalit's definition of a decent society as one whose institutions do not humiliate people.[15]

One question is whether not humiliating people is really the same as honoring human dignity. Is human dignity not something more grandiose, more significant, than merely not being embarrassed?

Of course, it may be – and in any case, some violations of human dignity have nothing directly to do with humiliation. But humiliating people is certainly a central case of violating human dignity, and the rabbis who invoked human dignity had very down-to-earth examples in mind.

Thus, Rabba asks Rabbi Hisda whether it is permissible on the Sabbath to carry stones to the outhouse to wipe yourself. Rabbi Hisda replies: "Human dignity is very important ... and it supersedes a negative injunction of the Torah" (BT, *Shabbat* 81a–b). Two points about this example bear close consideration. First, Rabbi Hisda uses the Hebrew equivalent of "human dignity," *kvod ha-briot* (lit., "the dignity of created things"), for something that is quite humble and has to do with relatively petty embarrassment. This supports the claim I am making, which is that, within the Jewish tradition, respecting human dignity has as a central meaning not humiliating people. Nonhumiliation may not exhaust the concept of human dignity, but it strikes me as the paradigm of what respecting human dignity means. At worst, nonhumiliation will be a useful naturalized stand-in for the more grandiose but vaguer concept of "respecting human dignity."

Second, the principle at work in Rabbi Hisda's response is tremendously significant: he says that human dignity is so important that it can override

[14] *Ibid.*, §§ 7–14, pp. 136–9.
[15] Avishai Margalit, *The Decent Society* (Naomi Goldblum, Trans.) (Cambridge, MA: Harvard University Press, 1996), p. 1.

the law. Subsequent interpretation of Rabbi Hisda's dictum limits this principle to rabbinic law, not Torah law – but even that limitation is controversial, because the rabbis also identify some Torah laws that can be overridden in the name of human dignity. So the principle that human dignity can override the law actually turns out to be a very strong one.[16] In contemporary America, where lawyers in the Bush administration claimed the right of the president to override any statute in the lawbook, including the prohibition on torture, it is a remarkable and refreshing counterweight to discover in the Talmud a different kind of legal override – an override in the defense of human dignity rather than in attacks on it.

One important question about nonhumiliation is whether the wrong in humiliating others is purely subjective and psychological. What if the victims do not recognize that they are being humiliated? What if they belong to a culture in which a practice that *we* would find humiliating *they* regard as perfectly normal and natural? Is the notion of humiliation subjective and victim-relative, or objective and universal? If it is subjective, then people who have been beaten down so long that they no longer feel humiliated by it are not really humiliated, and their human dignity has not really been injured.

The subjectivity of humiliation poses a very hard and very deep-cutting challenge to the project of connecting human dignity with universal human rights. This is not the place for a full discussion, but I shall say a few more words about the issue. My own strong intuition is that humiliation is not merely subjective. Let me show why through a thought experiment.

A student drinks too much at a party and passes out. Some malicious wiseacres proceed to undress her and exhibit her naked body to everyone at the party – friends, acquaintances, dormmates, and strangers. Then they put her clothes back on, and when she wakes up and sobers up, nobody tells her what happened. In my view, the most natural and correct thing to say is that she has been humiliated – even if she never finds out and never has any subjective experience of humiliation. In much the same way, I believe that cultural practices of human subordination may be objectively humiliating, even though participants in the practice are so used to it that it does not cause them psychological pain.[17]

---

[16] In this discussion of R. Hisda's response to Rabba, I am drawing on Rabbi Melissa Weintraub, "*Kvod Ha'Briot*: Human Dignity in Jewish Sources, Human Degradation in American Military Custody," T'Ruah: The Rabbinic Call for Human Rights (formerly Rabbis for Human Rights – North America) (2005) (www.truah.org/images/stories/pdf_torture_resources/Human_Dignity_Weintraub_0.pdf).

[17] My view here accords with that of Jon Elster, in the title essay of *Sour Grapes: Studies in the Subversion of Rationality* (Cambridge University Press, 1985). There, Elster defines the notion of "adaptive preference formation," a term that refers to unconscious modification of one's own preferences to accommodate low expectations of what kind of treatment one can realistically hope for.

And this nonpsychological notion of humiliation is the rabbis' view as well. In the same *sugya* that declares that using an insulting nickname for someone in public is the moral equivalent of murder, the rabbis add: "Even when he is accustomed to the nickname" and therefore experiences no (subjective) humiliation (BT, *Bava Metzia*, 58b).

Torture and humiliation in the "war on terrorism"

So far, I have argued for four main propositions: first, that human dignity is a property of human relationships, not a metaphysical fact about human nature; second, that the paradigm case of violating human dignity consists in humiliating someone; third, that humiliation is not, or not only, a matter of subjective psychological pain for the victim; and fourth, that all these ideas make up a central strand of Jewish ethics, at least as I interpret the texts I have discussed.

At this point, I shall turn away from abstract questions about human rights and human dignity and towards my principal practical topic: US practices of torture and cruel, inhuman, and degrading treatment in the war on terrorism.

I begin with some legal background. US law on these issues derives from two major multilateral treaties to which we are party. The first is the Convention Against Torture (CAT), which currently has 155 parties. The second is the Geneva Conventions governing the treatment of wartime captives. All the world's 192 states belong to the Geneva Conventions.

CAT offers a legal definition of torture, which I will simplify slightly: it is the intentional infliction of severe mental or physical pain or suffering.[18] The convention requires states to make official torture a crime, which the United States has done. It also requires states to undertake to prevent cruel, inhuman, or degrading treatment that falls short of torture (which lawyers abbreviate as "CIDT"), although it does not require them to criminalize CIDT. In 2005, the US Congress implemented this clause of the treaty, over strenuous Bush administration objections, and banned CIDT, without criminalizing it.

The Geneva Conventions contain an article, so-called Common Article 3, which applies to al Qaeda detainees and contains similar prohibitions. Article 3 bans torture and cruelty, and it also bans "outrages against personal dignity," including humiliating or degrading treatment. Both treaties therefore distinguish torture from lesser forms of cruelty, which include humiliation and degradation, and both forbid both torture and outrages against personal dignity.

---

[18] The CAT limits its definition to torture carried out by government officials or under color of governmental authority, and also to torture undertaken for certain specific purposes, such as interrogation, punishment, intimidation, or discrimination. For purposes of this discussion, I set these limitations to one side.

It is no secret that US lawyers worked tirelessly for more than five years to loophole their way around these prohibitions so that the CIA can do bad things to terrorist suspects. Several of the "torture memos" became public in 2004, but others were hidden until the Obama administration released them in April 2009. These additional memos provide a detailed description of the CIA's "enhanced interrogation techniques" (EITs) – a bit of doublespeak for torture and humiliation. Through prodigious legal sophistry, Justice Department lawyers concluded that none of the techniques amount to torture, either singly or taken in combination, and – furthermore – that none amount to cruel, inhuman, or degrading treatment.[19]

These conclusions are staggering, given the nature of the techniques. The best known is waterboarding: partially drowning the victim by pouring water over a cloth covering his face, interrupting the process before he dies. Waterboarding, however, is not the only technique described in the torture memos. In addition, the CIA used – and the Justice Department approved – techniques that are obviously humiliating and degrading. Detainees were stripped naked. They were fed for weeks on nothing but liquid dietary supplements. They were hosed down with cold water, grabbed and slapped in the face, and slammed into walls. They were deprived of sleep for up to a week by being shackled upright, in diapers, with manacles around their legs and manacles from their wrists to the ceiling.[20] The bureaucratic prose of the torture memo deserves full quotation:

> The primary method of sleep deprivation involves the use of shackling to keep the detainee awake. In this method, the detainee is standing and is handcuffed, and the handcuffs are attached by a length of chain to the ceiling. The detainee's hands are shackled in front of his body... The detainee's feet are shackled to a bolt in the floor... All of the detainee's weight is borne by his legs and feet during standing sleep deprivation. You have informed us that the detainee is not allowed to hang from or support

[19] These memos are collected in David Cole, *The Torture Memos: Rationalizing the Unthinkable* (New York Review of Books, 2009). Chapters 5 and 8 of this book analyze the sophistry of the memos in some detail. Shortly before the memos were released, the journalist Mark Danner obtained and published the International Committee of the Red Cross's confidential report to the US government about CIA torture, based on interviews with Guantánamo detainees who had not yet had any opportunity to coordinate their stories. International Committee of the Red Cross (ICRC) Report on the Treatment of Fourteen "High Value Detainees" in CIA Custody, February 2007 (www.nybooks.com/icrc-report. pdf). The ICRC report indicates that in execution the CIA's procedures went beyond the techniques described in the memos – for example, they involved slamming detainees into real walls rather than the flexible false walls described in the memos.

[20] Even in the ancient world, sleep deprivation was understood to be a horrible torture. Cicero (*De Officiis* III.xxvii.100) characterizes the execution of Regulus by the Carthaginians through "enforced wakefulness" (*vigilando*) as "exquisite torture" (*exquisita supplicia*).

his body weight with the shackles. . . If the detainee is clothed, he wears an adult diaper under his pants. Detainees subject to sleep deprivation who are also subject to nudity as a separate interrogation technique will at times be nude and wearing a diaper. . . You have informed us that to date no detainee has experienced any skin problems resulting from use of diapers. The maximum allowable duration for sleep deprivation authorized by the CIA is 180 hours, after which the detainee must be permitted to sleep for at least eight hours. You have informed us that to date, more than a dozen detainees have been subjected to sleep deprivation of more than 48 hours, and three detainees have been subjected to sleep deprivation of more than 96 hours; the longest period of time for which any detainee has been deprived of sleep by the CIA is 180 hours.[21]

The torture memos make a point of insisting that during the sleep deprivation the victims were under observation 24 hours a day, supposedly as a safety measure to ensure that their diapers never overflowed and their suffering never crossed the talismanic legal threshold to "severe" (in which case it might count as torture, and the agents who performed it as serious felons). Perhaps this really was the reason; but it cannot escape our notice that being looked at round the clock in this degrading condition only adds to the humiliation.

Next consider the famous Abu Ghraib photographs, readily available on the internet. They show terrified, naked detainees warding off attack dogs with their hands; shackled to the furniture in painful stress positions with women's underpants over their faces; led around on dog leashes; and standing naked in front of a leering female soldier. I trust that nobody will deny the obvious – that the evil depicted in these photographs is the humiliation and degradation of these detainees, the all-out assault on their human dignity.

The US government insists that these abuses were completely unauthorized. The specific instances on the Abu Ghraib night shift may well have been. But according to the Schmidt Report, the Army's official report on abuses at Guantánamo, every one of the four techniques I have just mentioned was authorized at least once at Guantánamo, in the interrogation of "Detainee 063" – a man named Mohammed Al Qahtani.[22] In the case of threatening him with military working dogs, the report tells us that the technique was

---

[21] Memorandum for John A. Rizzo, Senior Deputy General Counsel, CIA, from Steven G. Bradbury, Re: Application of 18 U.S.C. §§ 2340–2340A to Certain Techniques That May Be Used in the Interrogation of a High Value al Qaeda Detainee, May 10, 2005, in Cole, *Torture Memos*, pp. 165–8.

[22] See the Schmidt report [Army Regulation 15–6: Final Report. Investigation into FBI Allegations of Detainee Abuse at Guantánamo Bay, Cuba Detention Facility] (www.defenselink.mil/news/Jul2005/d20050714report.pdf); the interrogation of Qahtani is discussed on pp. 13–21. For a detailed discussion of this interrogation, see Philippe Sands, *The Torture Team: Rumsfeld's Memo and the Betrayal of American Values* (New York: Palgrave, 2008).

authorized by "SECDEF" himself – Secretary of Defense Donald Rumsfeld.[23] Significantly, the Abu Ghraib abuses occurred soon after the Guantánamo commandant was sent to Iraq in order to "Gitmoize" Abu Ghraib. These were not frat boy pranks – they were policies approved at the highest levels of government. Indeed, the Senate Intelligence Committee reports that the CIA's techniques were discussed and approved at "Principals' Meetings" attended by "the Vice President, the National Security Adviser, the Attorney General, the Acting Assistant Attorney General for the Office of Legal Counsel, a Deputy Assistant Attorney General, the Counsel to the President, and the Legal Adviser to the National Security Council."[24]

The four Guantánamo techniques I have mentioned are by no means the only humiliations in the Abu Ghraib photos. The more lurid photos depict naked men piled in pyramids, or smeared from head to toe in feces, or forced to urinate in each other's mouths. None of these tactics were approved by the US government, but it should come as no surprise that once you have begun to dehumanize and degrade people in your control the very idea of limits quickly disappears.

Furthermore, the four techniques were not the only humiliations visited on Al Qahtani. Schmidt also reports that interrogators taunted him that he was homosexual, and that other detainees knew it; they forced him to dance with a male interrogator; they told him that his mother and sister were whores; a female interrogator straddled him and whispered to him about the deaths of fellow Al Qaeda members. Female soldiers took off their battle-dress tops and ran their hands through other detainees' hair, whispering that resistance is futile. According to Schmidt, all these techniques were authorized.[25]

The torture lawyers devoted their energies to showing that although the CIA's techniques may have been deeply unpleasant, they were not "torture," and therefore not crimes. But, as I argued in Chapter 5, there is something deeply wrong, not to mention perverse, about the entire enterprise of trying to draw fine lines between torture and lesser abuses. An essential continuity exists between them, because all have the degradation of their victim as their core. The truth embodied in the CAT and the Geneva Conventions is that torture and humiliation without torture belong together as forms of abuse; the falsehood comes when we imagine that there is a sharp distinction between them just because they are banned by different clauses of the treaties. Indeed,

---

[23] Schmidt report, p. 14.

[24] OLC Opinions on the CIA Detention and Interrogation Program, Submitted by Senator John D. Rockefeller IV for Classification Review, released Apr. 22, 2009 (http://intelligence.senate.gov/pdfs/olcopinion.pdf), p. 7; Jan Crawford Greenburg, Howard L. Rosenberg, and Ariane De Vogue, "Sources: Top Bush Advisors Approved "Enhanced Interrogation," *ABC News*, Apr. 9, 2008 (http://abcnews.go.com/TheLaw/LawPolitics/story?id=4583256&page=1). I should make it clear that the CIA techniques are not the same as the Guantánamo techniques.

[25] Schmidt report, pp. 8, 16, 19.

a recent medical study found absolutely no difference between the traumatic psychological aftereffects of physical torture and humiliation.[26]

The connection between torture and humiliation

Why did US interrogators use humiliation tactics like these? Several reports indicate that they were briefed with a book by the anthropologist Raphael Patai called *The Arab Mind*, which devotes a chapter to the theme that Arab men are sexually modest and particularly sensitive to sexual humiliation.[27] And Schmidt informs us that these were "Ego Down" and "Futility" tactics – the Army's names for tactics designed to break the detainees by making them feel worthless and filling them with despair. It is hard to come up with a better description of assaulting human dignity. But in physical torture too a central defining feature of torture is the victim's humiliation.

Let me begin with what may seem like a peculiar question: what, specifically, characterizes the evil of torture?

As we saw in Chapters 4 and 5, the answer is not simply the fact of severe pain or suffering, although they are obviously evils – and, as I argued in Chapter 5, they are the most fundamental of the evils (the "first among equals" of the evils) coiled up in the torturer's use of pain and suffering to communicate dominance and absolute mastery. The reason that severe pain or suffering is not the specific evil of torture lies in the fact that we are sapient beings. The meaning of pain and suffering, their communicative content – and therefore the nature of the pain as experienced by a being that is sapient as well as sentient – depends on the context in which we experience them. I cited as a contrast to torture the severe pain of natural childbirth, which countless women have chosen even when anesthesia is available. The connection of birth pangs to a joyful or even ecstatic event changes the sensations' character without diminishing their painfulness.

In the case of torture, the connection is with "breaking" the victim. Fear is perhaps the most important evil-intensifier connected with the pain of torture. The torture victim never knows whether his torturer will do even worse things, regardless of any legal restrictions; the uncertainty is perpetual.

And terror itself is closely connected with humiliation, especially when someone else sets about terrifying us. Terror makes us whimper and beg; it makes us lose control of our bowels and bladder. The Abu Ghraib dog-handlers had contests to see who could make a detainee foul himself first.[28]

---

[26] Metin Baçoglu *et al.*, "Torture vs. Other Cruel, Inhuman, and Degrading Treatment: Is the Distinction Real or Apparent?", *Archives of General Psychiatry*, 64 (2007), 277–85.

[27] Jane Mayer, *The Dark Side: The Inside Story of How the War on Terror Turned into a War on American Ideals* (New York: Doubleday, 2008), p. 168.

[28] See footnote 22 in Chapter 3.

The strategic use of terror is one way that torture and humiliation are tightly bound together. But that is not all.

The experience of acute pain is itself degrading because it collapses our world and reduces us to mere prisoners of our bodies (a phenomenon I discussed in Chapter 3). Pain forcibly severs our focus on anything outside of us; it shrinks our horizon to our own body. The world of intense pain is a world in which we are incredibly diminished (and, as the next chapter will show, this is no less true of mental pain).[29] This is degrading in itself, but when it happens in front of spectators, the experience is doubly shameful and humiliating. I vividly recall a visit to some old friends when my back went out. The pain was bad enough that for a few minutes I could not move; but at the same time I felt perfectly, miserably ashamed to be seen in this ridiculous helpless state by my friends and family. It did not even matter that they were sympathetic; obviously, however, it would be infinitely worse if the spectator is an enemy who inflicts the suffering and laughs at you.

Perhaps most significantly, the relation between the torturer and the victim is one of absolute domination and absolute subordination. Recall Jean Améry's observation quoted above in Chapter 4: the torturer "has control of the other's scream of pain and death; he is master over flesh and spirit, life and death."[30] Améry rightly emphasizes the degrading relational character of torture, in addition to the pain and the fear. Torture leaves the victim in a state of abject humiliation. The victim counts as nothing, the torturer as everything. Nothing could be worse, from the standpoint of Jewish ethics, on the interpretation offered here. The denial of human dignity is close to total.

Fraudulent necessity

I now come to an unpleasant fact. Many people approve of torture. A 2009 Pew poll showed that about half of surveyed Americans believe that torture against "suspected terrorists" can often or sometimes be justified, and the number is up since a similar poll in 2005.[31] Not even terrorists – merely *suspected* terrorists.

Oftentimes, supporters of torture appeal to a kind of military necessity, based on the intuition that if torture is the only way to find out where a ticking bomb is hidden, the need to save innocent lives outweighs the moral prohibition against torture.

---

[29] This is one of the themes of Elaine Scarry's powerful book *The Body in Pain: The Making and Unmaking of the World* (Oxford University Press, 1987).

[30] Jean Améry, "Torture," in Améry, *At the Mind's Limits: Contemplations By a Survivor on Auschwitz and Its Realities* (Sidney Rosenfeld and Stella P. Rosenfeld, Trans.) (Bloomington, IN: Indiana University Press, 1980), p. 35.

[31] Pew Forum on Religion and Public Life, Publications, "The Religious Dimensions of the Torture Debate," Apr. 29, 2009 (http://pewforum.org/docs/?DocID=156). For later polling data, and discussion, see Chapter 10.

I have argued in previous chapters that the ticking-bomb scenario is an intellectual fraud; furthermore, that the US government has never identified a genuine ticking-bomb scenario, even when leaking the details would have been to the immense advantage of the Bush administration. The torture memos released in 2009 assert several times that the CIA reserved its "enhanced" techniques for situations of last resort. In fact, however, the CIA's protocols gave detainees only one chance to "provide information on action-able threats and location information on High-Value Targets at large" before beginning "enhanced" interrogation as early as the first day. The same memo notes that "it is difficult to determine conclusively whether interrogations have provided information critical to interdicting specific imminent attacks."[32]

Yet we swallow the bunkum of ticking bombs. Perhaps we accept the "Mel Brooks fallacy" identified in Chapter 2: we do not mind sacrificing other people's rights for our own security, even small gains in security. Yet another danger in the ticking-bomb conversation is that the real source of our pro-torture intuitions is not intelligence gathering, but rage. Consciously or unconsciously, we approve of the torture of terrorists for punitive reasons, and we deceive ourselves into repackaging rage as rationality. We want to see him beg for mercy; we want to humiliate.

If so, it shows how desperately fragile the ethics of respect for human dignity is. When the enemy, or suspected enemy, is in our hands, it is hard to view him as our likeness. The temptation to degrade him just because he is the enemy seems overwhelming. Yet, resisting the temptation comes close to the core of ethics as I have described it here.

---

[32] Memorandum for John A. Rizzo, Senior Deputy General Counsel, CIA, Re: Application of United States Obligations Under Article 16 of the United Nations Convention Against Torture to Certain Techniques That May Be Used in the Interrogation of High Value al Qaeda Detainees, May 30, 2005, in Cole, *Torture Memos*, pp. 234, 237.

7

Mental torture: a critique of erasures in US law

(with Henry Shue)

Introduction

> As flies to wanton boys, are we to th' gods,
> They kill us for their sport.[1]

John McCain's bones may have been broken, but his spirit never was.[2]

Torture can be psychological as well as physical. Prolonged isolation, sensory deprivation, humiliation and sexual degradation, close confinement in coffin-like boxes, and threats to you or those you love all produce horrific mental suffering. The forms it takes are hardly mysterious, and we can describe them in everyday language as well as psychiatric categories: despair, loneliness, disorientation, terror, depression, confusion, claustrophobia, anxiety, and loss of personality. Mental suffering may take the form of clinically recognized psychiatric conditions like post-traumatic stress disorder (PTSD), but it need not.

Both US and international law recognize that torture can be psychological as well as physical. The UN Convention Against Torture and Other Cruel, Inhuman or Degrading Treatment or Punishment (CAT) defines torture as "severe pain or suffering, whether mental or physical,"[3] and the US torture statute likewise recognizes that "severe physical or mental pain or suffering" intentionally inflicted by government agents constitutes torture, a crime that carries sentences from twenty years to life.[4] The similarity is no coincidence: the statute represents Congress' implementation in 1994 of CAT, as required

The main text of this chapter was first published in 2012 – see Acknowledgments.

[1] William Shakespeare, *King Lear*, Act IV, scene i, lines 38–9, reprinted in William Allan Neilson and Charles Jarvis Hill, Eds., *The Complete Plays and Poems of William Shakespeare* (Boston: Houghton Mifflin, 1942), p. 1166.

[2] Senator Fred Thompson, Speech at the Republican National Convention (Sept. 2, 2008), *New York Times*, Sept. 3, 2008 (www.nytimes.com/2008/09/03/us/politics/03thompson-text.html?fta=y&pagewanted=print).

[3] Convention Against Torture and Other Cruel, Inhuman or Degrading Treatment or Punishment, art. 1, opened for signature Dec. 10, 1984, 1465 U.N.T.S. 85 [hereinafter CAT].

[4] See 18 U.S.C. §§ 2340(1), 2340A(a) (2006).

by Article 4 of the convention. The convention and the US torture statute also specify *mens rea* and circumstance in their definitions of the crime of torture, but the "severe physical or mental pain or suffering" formula is the definitional core of what it is that torturers inflict on their victims.

Unfortunately, the law Congress enacted narrows and distorts the meaning of CAT's core formula in the case of mental torture. It includes a cramped, convoluted, and arbitrary definition of mental pain or suffering, so narrow that few techniques of mental torment qualify as torture under the law. In brief – we will discuss the details later – the torture statute restricts mental torture to just four techniques and labels the victim's experience "severe mental pain or suffering" only if it is a prolonged harm the torturer specifically intends to cause.[5] These restrictions are wrongheaded because they have nothing to do with the basic definition of torture as severe pain or suffering. They also make it nearly impossible to prosecute psychological torture, including the most egregious techniques used in the CIA's now-shuttered secret prisons and in Guantánamo.

By itself, the definitional confusion might signify nothing more than a peculiarity in the US criminal statutes against torture. Congress may have tailored its definition around the need to specify elements easily proven in a court of law. However, the confusion runs broader than the criminal law. The legal definition derives from an "understanding" of mental pain and suffering that the US Senate attached to CAT at its ratification – an "understanding" that we shall argue *misunderstands* mental torture and reneges on the US obligation under CAT to criminalize "all acts of torture."[6] Our main aim in this chapter is to expose the fallacies that make US torture law nearly useless for defining and repressing psychological torture.[7] We identify three basic fallacies: the *materialist bias*, that somehow the psychological is less real than the physical and should be viewed with suspicion; the *substitution trick*, according to which mental pain and suffering get defined through their causes and aftermath and not the experience itself; and the *forensic fallacy*, which confuses the due process requirement of narrowness and precision in criminal statutes with defining features of the crime's gravamen itself.

None of these are innocent fallacies. A careful examination of the legislative record reveals no attempt to defend the definition of mental torture on its merits or even to explain its distinctive features. Instead, as we show, one finds repeated concerns that unless the definition of mental torture is written narrowly, US law-enforcement officials might face accusations of torture. In other words, the definition of mental torture was narrowed for reasons of liability screening, not reasons of definitional accuracy.

---

[5] *Ibid.*, §§ 2340(1)-(2).

[6] CAT, note 3 above, art. 4(1) ("Each State Party shall ensure that all acts of torture are offences under its criminal law.").

[7] We use "psychological torture" and "mental torture" interchangeably in this chapter.

During the administration of President George W. Bush, officials approved harsh interrogation tactics after their lawyers assured them that the tactics did not meet the legal definition of the crime of torture. By now it is well understood that government lawyers used questionable interpretive methods to reach their conclusion that stress positions, wall slamming, dousing with cold water, and waterboarding are not severe enough to constitute physical torture. The Justice Department itself has officially condemned these interpretations as "bad judgment," after initially finding them grounds for recommending professional discipline.[8] Regrettably, the law defining mental pain and suffering is itself so flawed that the torture lawyers had little need for frivolous interpretations to absolve interrogators inflicting systematic humiliation, prolonged isolation, threats to "disappear" a detainee, sleep deprivation, and other techniques of psychological torture. The law's definition of mental torture is so narrow that the lawyers had to add only the slightest dash of interpretive exaggeration to reach their conclusions.

Thus, the problem cannot be dismissed as mischief by a handful of lawyers in a single US administration. It runs far deeper than that. The effort to minimize mental torture has continued for twenty years since the time of President Reagan's submission of CAT for Senate ratification in 1988, and its actual ratification six years later in the first Clinton administration.[9] Congress implemented CAT through the Torture Act of 1994 and additionally prohibited torture through the War Crimes Act of 1996, both signed into law by President Bill Clinton.[10] Both statutes incorporated the same flawed definition of mental torture and the same fallacies. The Military Commissions Act (MCA) of 2006 perpetuated the misunderstandings and even piled on additional confusion in its definitions, and the MCA of 2009 left

---

[8] For detailed analysis of the memos, see Chapters 3, 5, and 8 of this book. Focusing on one of the torture memos, the Office of Professional Responsibility (OPR) – the US Department of Justice's internal ethics watchdog – demonstrated in detail how the government lawyers distorted the law. See Office of Professional Responsibility, Investigation into the Office of Legal Counsel's Memoranda Concerning Issues Relating to the Central Intelligence Agency's Use of "Enhanced Interrogation Techniques" on Suspected Terrorists (2009), pp. 159–259. Not everyone agrees that the distortions were unethical: a senior Justice Department official, David Margolis, reviewed the OPR reports critically and downgraded the finding that the government lawyers had committed professional misconduct to a finding of "poor judgment." Memorandum from David Margolis, Associate Deputy Attorney General, US Department of Justice, for the Attorney General, pp. 67–9 (Jan. 5, 2010) (http://judiciary.house.gov/hearings/pdf/DAGMargolisMemo100105.pdf). One of us has rebutted Margolis' analysis: David Luban, "David Margolis Is Wrong," Slate (Feb. 22, 2010, 11:49 a.m.) (www.slate.com/articles/news_and_politics/jurisprudence/2010/02/david_margolis_is_wrong.html).

[9] See Alfred W. McCoy, A Question of Torture: CIA Interrogation, from the Cold War to the War on Terror (New York: Henry Holt, 2006), pp. 100–2.

[10] See 18 U.S.C. §§ 2340–2340A; § 2441.

those misunderstandings intact.[11] Narrowly defining mental torture has been
the consistent US strategy through five presidencies, including the ten years
of two Democratic presidents, Bill Clinton and Barack Obama. As we noted
above, the record reveals a persistent anxiety among US officials that
law-enforcement abuses, punishment practices, and – since 9/11 – interrogation methods might be labeled as torture. Even though the Torture Act is
explicitly limited to conduct that takes place outside the United States, the
drafters seem to have feared the public relations consequences of a legal
standard under which the United States might come to be seen as a nation
that practices torture.

We begin by discussing right and wrong ways to think about mental
pain and suffering and how the law should treat them. Next, we briefly
catalog examples and types of recent US mental torture (Part I). We then
sketch the features of the US legal treatment of torture during the last
quarter of a century and identify the fallacies that underlie it (Parts II–IV).
We finally indicate what is distinctively objectionable about the kind of
mental torture that US laws obscure from view (Part V). This, we argue, is
the special evil of breaking the resistance of a prisoner by breaking
his mind.[12]

---

[11] *Ibid.*, § 2441(d)(2)(E) (defining "serious mental pain or suffering," a lesser category
than "severe mental pain or suffering"); National Defense Authorization Act for Fiscal
Year 2010, Pub. L. No. 111-84, tit. XVIII, 123 Stat. 2190, 2574–614 (2009) (codified as
amended at 10 U.S.C. §§ 948a–950w); Military Commissions Act of 2006, Pub. L. No.
109-366, § 6(b), 120 Stat. 2600, 2633–5 (codified as amended at 18 U.S.C. § 2441).

[12] The mercilessness for which we will, in the end, condemn psychological torture is
suggested in Henry Shue, "Torture," *Philosophy and Public Affairs*, 7 (1978), 124–43.
Most subsequent philosophical discussions of torture, which were relatively rare until the
last few years but have now, depressingly, expanded to a large library, focus on ticking-
bomb scenarios for torture without much attention to the nature of the torture itself or to
which of its features provide the grounds for its wrongfulness. An important article on
such scenarios is Vittorio Bufacchi and Jean Maria Arrigo, "Torture, Terrorism and the
State: A Refutation of the Ticking-Bomb Argument," *Journal of Applied Philosophy*,
23 (2006), 355–73. See also Association for the Prevention of Torture, "Defusing the
Ticking Bomb Scenario: Why We Must Say No to Torture, Always" (2007), p. 11 (www.
apt.ch/content/files_res/tickingbombscenario.pdf) (challenging the underlying assumptions of the ticking-bomb exception and arguing that any "exception to the prohibition of
torture must be categorically rejected"). For recent book-length studies, see Fritz Allhoff,
Terrorism, Ticking Time-Bombs, and Torture: A Philosophical Analysis (University of
Chicago Press, 2012); Bob Brecher, *Torture and the Ticking Bomb* (Oxford: Blackwell,
2007); and Yuval Ginbar, *Why Not Torture Terrorists? Moral, Practical, and Legal Aspects
of the "Ticking Bomb" Justification for Torture* (Oxford University Press, 2008). Both of us
have argued against the distortions that the "ticking-bomb scenario" introduces into
discussions of torture: see Chapters 3 and 4 of this book and Henry Shue, "Torture in
Dreamland," *Case Western Reserve Journal of International Law*, 37 (2006), 231–9.
Notable exceptions to the general tendency to neglect to probe the nature of the torture
itself have been discussed in John T. Parry, *Understanding Torture: Law, Violence, and*

I   Mental pain and suffering

Leaving to one side the elements of *mens rea* and circumstance in CAT's definition of torture, we observe that the drafters constructed it around two pairs of distinctions: pain and suffering, mental and physical. The definition is neither novel nor eccentric: it appears to be modeled on the *Oxford English Dictionary* (1971) definition of "torture" as "severe or excruciating pain or suffering (of body or mind)."[13] A third distinction is implicit in the structure and text of the treaty: pain or suffering that takes the form of torture must be criminalized under Article 4, and cruel, inhuman, or degrading treatment other than torture, which under Article 16 need not be criminalized, must be prevented. We set this third distinction aside and offer a few observations about the first two.

The most obvious point is that "severe pain or suffering" refers to what the torture victim experiences. It does not refer to the technique that caused the experience or to its lingering aftereffects. The pain or suffering, according to the law, may be mental or physical, and the conceptual question is how to distinguish these.

In both the CAT and the US statutes, the phrase is "pain *or* suffering," not "pain *and* suffering." Either pain or suffering can count as torture. This turned out to be an important point in the Bush administration's torture memos, two of which interpreted "pain or suffering" as a unitary concept and, therefore, concluded that if a technique such as waterboarding does not produce physical pain, it does not produce physical suffering either.[14] But of course, forms of

Political Identity (Ann Arbor, MI: University of Michigan Press, 2010); David Sussman, "'Torture Lite': A Response," *Ethics and International Affairs*, 23 (2009), 63–7; David Sussman, "What's Wrong with Torture?", *Philosophy and Public Affairs*, 33 (2005), 1–33; Jessica Wolfendale, "The Myth of 'Torture Lite,'" *Ethics and International Affairs*, 23 (2009), 47–61. See also Chapter 5 of this book. A major historical survey of the varieties of torture is Darius Rejali, *Torture and Democracy* (Princeton University Press, 2007). Other extensive, recent philosophical discussions include Charles Fried and Gregory Fried, *Because It Is Wrong: Torture, Privacy and Presidential Power in the Age of Terror* (New York: Norton, 2010); Richard Matthews, *The Absolute Violation: Why Torture Must Be Prohibited* (Montreal: McGill-Queen's University Press, 2008); Jessica Wolfendale, *Torture and the Military Profession* (Basingstoke: Palgrave Macmillan, 2007). Useful accounts of current interrogation practices include Matthew Alexander with John R. Bruning, *How to Break a Terrorist: The U.S. Interrogators Who Used Brains, Not Brutality, to Take Down the Deadliest Man in Iraq* (New York: Simon & Schuster, 2008); Chris Mackey and Greg Miller, *The Interrogators: Inside the Secret War Against Al Qaeda* (2004); Mark Danner, "US Torture: Voices from the Black Sites," *New York Review of Books* (Apr. 9, 2009) (www.nybooks.com/articles/archives/2009/apr/09/us-torture-voices-from-the-black-sites/) (leaking and analyzing confidential ICRC report on high-value detainees). We are not aware of a conceptual analysis of US legal definitions of torture.

[13] *The Compact Edition of the Oxford English Dictionary* (Oxford University Press, 1971), vol. II, p. 3357.

[14] See Memorandum from Jay S. Bybee, Assistant Attorney General, Office of Legal Counsel, for Alberto R. Gonzales, Counsel to the President (Aug. 1, 2002), in David

158 THE EVILS OF TORTURE

physical suffering exist that are not pain: freezing cold, unbearable heat, itching, nausea, paralysis, aching all over, inability to breathe – all are suffering; none are pain. Inability to breathe gets to the heart of waterboarding, which is controlled suffocation. After the Justice Department withdrew the Bybee–Yoo memoranda, Acting Assistant Attorney General Daniel Levin wrote a substitute memo that conceded "that under some circumstances 'severe physical suffering' may constitute torture even if it does not involve 'severe physical pain.'"[15]

Even though physical pain and suffering are distinguishable, it is less clear that mental pain is different from mental suffering. The US statutory definition of severe mental pain or suffering treats them together, and although we reject that definition in most respects, we have no strong linguistic or moral intuitions that mental pain and mental suffering represent categorically different phenomena. Perhaps a terrible memory that suddenly comes back to the surface with agonizing force would better be described as "mental pain" than "mental suffering"; the phrase "painful memories" belongs to ordinary English with no corresponding phrase for the word "suffering." But we do not perceive a sharp, stable distinction between mental pain and mental suffering, and our discussion will not assume a distinction between the two.

What then is "mental pain or suffering"? How does it differ from physical pain or suffering? Before addressing these questions, we want to ward off several tempting errors and red herrings.

First, we think it is a mistake to get too theoretical or too deep in differentiating the mental from the physical. You do not need a solution to the mind–body problem to draw the CAT's distinction between mental and physical suffering, and it may be that a philosophically adequate solution to the mind–body problem would actually muddy the waters. It might, for example, discredit the CAT's legal distinction by showing that it presupposes an untenable "ghost-in-the-machine" picture of mind's relation to body.[16] Or it might show that deep down it is all ghost or all machine, so that the legal distinction falsifies reality.

Even careful writers are vulnerable to theoretical overclaiming that, in our view, is unnecessary and potentially confusing. Thus, one writer whose article

Cole, Ed., *The Torture Memos: Rationalizing the Unthinkable* (New York Review of Books, 2009), pp. 41, 47, n.3 [hereinafter Bybee–Yoo torture memo]; Memorandum from Jay S. Bybee, Assistant Attorney General, Office of Legal Counsel, for John Rizzo, Acting General Counsel, Central Intelligence Agency (Aug. 1, 2002), in Cole, *Torture Memos*, pp. 106, 118 [hereinafter Bybee–Yoo techniques memo].

[15] Memorandum from Daniel Levin, Acting Assistant Attorney General, Office of Legal Counsel, for James B. Comey, Deputy Attorney General, US Department of Justice (Dec. 30, 2004), in Cole, *Torture Memos*, pp. 128, 141 [hereinafter Levin memo].

[16] The phrase originates in Gilbert Ryle's classic of philosophical behaviorism, Gilbert Ryle, *The Concept of Mind* (London: Hutchinson, 1949), pp. 15–16.

is in other respects a source of insight calls the distinction between physical and psychological torment "untenable" because "all pain is at root psychological – an affliction of feeling whose defining characteristic is that it hurts."[17] He voices this argument to criticize the US disparagement of mental pain and suffering, but although we agree with the conclusion, the argument bites off more theory than it needs to or should.

After all, one could, with equal justification, say that all pain is at root physical because it involves neuron and brain activity – and other writers make precisely that argument.[18] But we doubt that asking what pain is "at root" will shed light on the law, which operates in the theoretical shallows, using ordinary language categories (what theorists call folk psychology). In ordinary language, a searing pain in the shoulder is physical, not mental, and it is not "at root" psychological. Or rather, calling it psychological refers in ordinary speech to etiology, not ontology. It means that the shoulder pain is caused by emotional or mental disturbance, rather than, say, by a bone chip pressing against a nerve. Pain can be psychosomatic without being any the less physical: it is still a sore shoulder, not an achy, breaky heart. Psychosomatic physical pain is obviously *not* what the CAT means by "severe mental pain or suffering."

In our ordinary-language view, mental pain and suffering simply means the kind of pain or suffering we describe by psychological terms like *anxiety, terror, humiliation, despondency, brokenheartedness, grief*, and so on. (We wish we had a handy categorical way of describing these, but we do not). What makes them mental is that the terms name emotional states; what makes them pain and suffering is that they feel bad, and what makes them severe is how bad they feel. There may be vagueness here, but there is no mystery.

Physical pain and suffering have their own vocabularies. With physical pain we talk about bodily regions: it hurts here, not there; it moves around;

[17] Jamie Mayerfeld, "Playing by Our Own Rules: How U.S. Marginalization of International Human Rights Law Led to Torture," *Harvard Human Rights Journal*, 20 (2007), pp. 89–140.
[18] "Thus, to think that psychological torture is *not* an assault on the body is a conceptual error from the outset... [W]hat all torture has in common, regardless of physical or mental appearances, is its assault on the brain... Extreme fear and despair ... are emotional states that are anchored in brain states." Uwe Jacobs, "Documenting the Neurobiology of Psychological Torture: Conceptual and Neuropsychological Observations," in Almerindo E. Ojeda, Ed., *The Trauma of Psychological Torture* (Westport, CT: Praeger, 2008), pp. 163–72, at pp. 164–5. "Torture is speciously categorized as physical ... or as psychological. This is a distinction without a difference. Coercion of any type ... can and often does impact on brain, spinal cord, and organ integrity and therefore has medical consequences." Rona M. Fields, "The Neurobiological Consequences of Psychological Torture," in Ojeda, *Trauma of Psychological Torture*, pp. 139–62, at p. 139.

it's in my shoulder, but I can't pinpoint exactly where. We also talk about physical pain's character – sharp, dull, burning, stabbing, mild, or unbearable. Physical suffering other than pain gets described by terms like *stifling hot, freezing cold, itching,* or *nauseous.* Approaching the CAT's mental–physical distinction through the ordinary language we use to describe pain and suffering avoids the need for theory-laden descriptions that require some account of the mind–body relationship.

Second, we acknowledge that mental pain and suffering can cause physical effects and, vice versa, that physical pain and suffering can cause mental effects – including mental pain and suffering. Loneliness, as induced for example by solitary confinement, floods the body with stress hormones, raises blood pressure, accelerates aging, damages cognition, and weakens the immune system.[19] Thus, the mental torture of prolonged isolation or long-term solitary confinement need not cause purely mental damage. Conversely, physical pain and suffering can cause depression, PTSD, despair, fear, feelings of loneliness and isolation, and inability to concentrate. That makes physical torture a sometime source of mental torture as well.

In our view, though, both these observations are completely consistent with folk psychology's distinction between mental and physical suffering. That *A* causes *B*, or even that *A* invariably causes *B*, does not imply that *A* and *B* are indistinguishable. Of course, if *A* and *B* always co-occur, we may decide to regard them as simply two aspects or pieces of a single thing – call it *C*. We *may* so decide – but intellectual rigor does not compel us to do so, and even if we do switch from "*A–B*" talk to "*C*" talk for scientific purposes, nothing prevents us from retaining the distinction between *A* and *B* for whatever purposes it remains useful. That is how we should think of the distinction between mental and physical torture – a useful one for the pre-theoretical purposes of CAT and for moral discussions of torture, regardless of whether medical investigation eventually proves that the two forms of suffering are, in fact, always yoked together.

Third, some forms of suffering may be both physical and psychological or have aspects of both. Waterboarding, which combines suffocation with panic, is an example. Bombarding prisoners with earsplitting, culturally repugnant rock music for hours on end is another. Forcing prisoners to piss and shit on themselves is a third; the suffering of lying in your own excrement is physical as well as mental. And prolonged sleep deprivation is a fourth:

[19] See John T. Cacioppo and William Patrick, *Loneliness: Human Nature and the Need for Social Connection* (New York: Norton, 2008), pp. 92–109; see also Fields, "Neurobiological Consequences of Psychological Torture" (arguing that feelings of fear and powerlessness can have medical consequences); Stuart Grassian, "Neuropsychiatric Effects of Solitary Confinement," in Ojeda, *The Trauma of Psychological Torture,* pp. 113–26 (discussing the psychological effects of solitary confinement through the story of Jose Padilla).

your body hurts and feels hypersensitive, *and* your mind functions abnormally as your emotions run riot, and your will may collapse. All these techniques have been used by US interrogators, and sleep deprivation was a favorite technique – Guantánamo inmate Mohammed al-Qahtani was kept awake 20 hours a day for 48 days out of 54. The torture memos approved sleep deprivation of up to 180 hours – seven-and-a-half consecutive days and nights – noting that

> to date, more than a dozen detainees have been subjected to sleep depri-
> vation of more than 48 hours, and three detainees have been subjected to
> sleep deprivation of more than 96 hours; the longest period of time for
> which any detainee has been deprived of sleep by the CIA is 180 hours.[20]

Detainees were kept awake naked, diapered, and hanging in chains or, alterna-tively, shackled to a stool "too small to permit the subject to balance himself sufficiently to be able to go to sleep."[21] They were kept under nonstop observa-tion, which the torture memos regarded as a salutary precaution guaranteeing that the suffering would be stopped before it crossed the line into torture,[22] but which common sense would count as an additional humiliation – and, thus, a further candidate for mental torture rather than a precaution against it.

Despite uncertainties in all these examples about whether to label the suffering mental, physical, or both, the distinction between mental and physical suffering remains intact. Borderline cases between concepts do not invalidate the concepts.

Our basic point in this section is simple: folk psychology and ordinary speech recognize psychological states that count as severe pain or suffering for the obvious reason that they feel so bad. We have a rich vocabulary for them: words like *grief, loneliness, heartbreak, terror,* and *despair* only begin to scratch a surface that poets and songwriters explore in its depths. What makes these states count as pain or suffering is the way they feel – their phenomenology. It is not their

[20] Memorandum from Steven G. Bradbury, Principal Deputy Assistant Attorney General, Office of Legal Counsel, for John A. Rizzo, Senior Deputy General Counsel, Central Intelligence Agency (May 10, 2005), reprinted in Cole, *Torture Memos*, pp. 167–8 [hereinafter Bradbury memo]. On the sleep deprivation of al-Qahtani, see US Army Regulation 15–6: Final Report: Investigation into FBI Allegations of Detainee Abuse at Guantánamo Bay, Cuba Detention Facility (2005), pp. 17–18 [hereinafter Schmidt report] (www.defense.gov/news/jul2005/d20050714report.pdf). Even in the ancient world, sleep deprivation was understood to be torture. Cicero (44 BC) characterizes the execution of Regulus by the Carthaginians through "enforced wakefulness" (*vigilando*) as "exquisite torture" (*exquisita supplicia*). Marcus Tullius Cicero, *De Officiis* (T. E. Page and W. H. D. Rouse, Eds., Walter Miller, Trans.) (London: William Heinemann, 1913), pp. 376–8. The Supreme Court described sleep deprivation as torture in *Ashcraft* v. *Tennessee*, 322 U.S. 143, 150 n.6 (1944); the court likened Ashcraft's 36-hour-long interrogation to "the inquisition of the Middle Ages," p. 152, n.8 (quoting *Enoch* v. *Commonwealth*, 126 S.E. 222, 225 (Va. 1925)).

[21] Bradbury memo, note 20 above, p. 166.   [22] *Ibid.*, p. 168.

causes and not their effects that make them pain or suffering. At bottom, our conceptual critique of US law is that its drafters mistakenly defined "severe mental pain or suffering" through a small set of causes and effects, leaving nothing but a blank where the experience itself belongs, and our moral critique is that substituting these causes and effects lets torturers off the hook.

Of course, knowing causes or effects can be important evidence of the type and severity of mental pain or suffering. Consider the horrible example of a man or woman who watches a beloved child die in an accident that the parent's carelessness caused. No sane person can doubt that the parent's mental pain and suffering is as terrible as pain and suffering can be. Without knowing the cause, outsiders might not appreciate the depth of the suffering or understand its character – that it is composed of grief, guilt, self-hatred, and despair. Importantly, you do not need to experience it yourself to know these things. In fact, a poet might use the example figuratively to describe suffering caused by something entirely different. That possibility might tempt us to confuse the cause with the suffering because, here, to name the cause is to describe the suffering. But let us be clear: the mental pain and suffering is the waves of anguish rolling over the parent, not the cause of the anguish. Similar confusions exist in describing physical pain: the word *burning* can be used either to describe a sensation or to name its cause, and, of course, a burning sensation need not be caused by actual burning. Similarly, when we turn from causes to effects, the flashbacks, nightmares, and cognitive deficits experienced by torture survivors with PTSD provide evidence that their pain and suffering must have been severe when they were being tortured, and, of course, these symptoms are themselves forms of mental pain or suffering. However, the PTSD symptoms are not themselves the mental suffering experienced during the trauma.

II   Mental torture in practice: a brief catalog

Before proceeding to our discussion of the law, it will help to put on the table the forms that mental torture actually takes. The legal standard of infliction of severe mental pain or suffering provides the general rubric, but what, in historical experience, have been the methods of mental torture? In particular, what has been the US experience? In the brief part that follows, we focus on mental torture as used in the US conflict with Al Qaeda, not because it is the only, or worst, national practice of mental torture in the world, but because it has been the most prominent topic of public debate in recent years – and, of course, because our topic is US law.

The story of America's involvement with mental torture has been told before, and we will not retell it in detail here.[23] In brief, the CIA and military

[23] Readers may consult McCoy's history of the CIA's involvement, *A Question of Torture*; Darius Rejali's large-scale study, *Torture and Democracy*; and Jane Mayer, *The Dark Side:*

authorities began research into mental torture in the 1950s to understand the baffling phenomenon of patently false confessions that communist regimes were able to elicit from their victims, including Soviet political prisoners and, during the Korean War, captured US service members. How did they do it? How do you "brainwash" someone? The only way to study the KGB techniques was to replicate them, and a surprising amount of research by eminent civilian psychologists was funded by the government for just these purposes. The CIA discovered that seemingly minor manipulations of a prisoner's environment – disruptions of space and time by capriciously varied schedules and environment, isolation, sensory and sleep deprivation, irregular sleep, and extremes of hot and cold – could cause major degradations of the victim's personality. Piling them one on top of the other is even more devastating. Much of this lore was compiled in manuals that later became public, such as the CIA's "Kubark" manual.[24]

The major practical payoff of the experiments (occasionally conducted on unwilling subjects) was the creation of training methods for special forces in how to resist mental torture. In the SERE training – SERE stands for *Survival, Evasion, Resistance, Escape* – R, for "resistance," means precisely training in how to resist a captor's efforts to break you down.[25]

In the wake of 9/11, a pair of psychologists, private consultants to the US government, persuaded officials that the most effective way to interrogate detainees would be through techniques used in SERE training.[26] In other words, SERE was reverse engineered so that protocols designed to teach SEALs how to resist torture were mined for the techniques that the SEALs were being trained to resist. Behavioral science consultation teams, or "biscuits" (BSCTs), were attached to interrogation teams in Guantánamo and elsewhere.[27]

The Inside Story of How the War on Terror Turned into a War on American Ideals (New York: Doubleday, 2008). The brief account that follows comes largely from these sources.

[24] See McCoy, *A Question of Torture*, pp. 22–3, 28–49, 50–3.

[25] See, e.g., U.S. Army, "Soldier Life: Special Forces Training" (www.goarmy.com/soldier-life/being-a-soldier/ongoing-training/specialized-schools/special-forces-training.html). On the development of SERE, see M. Gregg Bloche, *The Hippocratic Myth: Why Doctors Are Under Pressure to Ration Care, Practice Politics, and Compromise Their Promise to Heal* (Basingstoke: Palgrave Macmillan, 2011), pp. 129–32.

[26] The adventures of James Mitchell and Bruce Jessen were first exposed by two major works of investigative journalism. See Katherine Eban, "Rorschach and Awe," *Vanity Fair* (July 17, 2007) (www.vanityfair.com/politics/features/2007/07/torture200707); Jane Mayer, "The Experiment," *New Yorker* (July 11, 2005) (www.newyorker.com/archive/2005/07/11/050711fa_fact4?currentPage=all). For additional discussion based on new interviews with some of the principals, see Bloche, *Hippocratic Myth*, pp. 132–57.

[27] For a detailed description and timeline of these events, see Senate Committee on Armed Services, 110th Congress, Inquiry into the Treatment of Detainees in U.S. Custody (*Committee Print*, 2008). One of the authors (Luban) interviewed an interrogator who had worked in Iraq and asked him about the role of the BSCTs. The interrogator responded that they played a minor role, but that a BSCT had instructed him in how

One result was the repertoire of techniques detailed in the torture memos, used on high-value detainees in the CIA's secret prisons. The Bybee–Yoo techniques memo details ten techniques,[28] and the Bradbury memo expands the list to thirteen, used in combination.[29] Some of these are physical (the belly slap, the facial slap, wall slamming, dousing with cold water, waterboarding), although the goal of piling physical insults atop each other is psychological suffering. Others are purely psychological: enforced nudity, sleep deprivation, and close confinement in small spaces. Consider this passage from the Bybee–Yoo techniques memo:

> You would like to place Zubaydah in a cramped confinement box with an insect. You have informed us that he appears to have a fear of insects. In particular, you would like to tell Zubaydah that you intend to place a stinging insect into the box with him. You would, however, place a harmless insect in the box.[30]

The insect technique is an attempt to exploit a phobia, and, unlike cramped confinement sans insect, it was never employed. Obviously, cramped confinement is itself psychological, although in his careful effort to evade the charge of mental torture, the CIA counsel John Rizzo "informed [Bybee and Yoo] that [the] purpose in using these boxes is not to interfere with [the subject's] senses or his personality, but to cause him physical discomfort."[31] The answer is incredible. Even though confinement in a fixed position will eventually become uncomfortable physically, the claustrophobia and sensory deprivation are the predominant effects. Evidently, all three lawyers were nervous about mental torture. Perhaps they remembered that in George Orwell's *Nineteen Eighty-Four* it was the exploitation of Winston Smith's rat phobia, not physical torture, that finally broke his spirit and made him scream, "Do it to Julia [his lover]."[32]

At Guantánamo, interrogators subjected detainees to a "frequent-flyer" sleep-interruption program in which "[d]etainees were moved dozens of times in just days and sometimes more than a hundred times over a two-week period."[33] The interrogation of Mohammed al-Qahtani included not only the intensive sleep deprivation described earlier, but also a barrage of sexual and other humiliations described in the Schmidt report:

to induce Stockholm syndrome in a detainee. He said it is easy to do but remarked that he personally felt it was immoral and that it reminded him of Arthur Koestler's novel *Darkness at Noon* and Fyodor Dostoevsky's "The Grand Inquisitor."

[28] Bybee–Yoo techniques memo, note 14 above, p. 107.

[29] Bradbury memo, note 20 above, pp. 159–71.

[30] Bybee–Yoo techniques memo, note 14 above, pp. 109.   [31] *Ibid.*, p. 121.

[32] See George Orwell, *Nineteen Eighty-Four* (London: Alfred A. Knopf, 1992), pp. 296–300, 311 (first published in 1949).

[33] Josh White, "Tactic Used After It Was Banned: Detainees at Guantanamo Were Moved Often, Documents Say," *Washington Post* (Aug. 8, 2008) (www.washingtonpost.com/wp-dyn/content/article/2008/08/07/AR2008080703004_pf.html).

Finding # 16b: On 06 Dec 02, the subject of the first Special Interrogation Plan was forced to wear a woman's bra and had a thong placed on his head during the course of the interrogation.

Finding # 16c: On 17 Dec 02, the subject of the first Special Interrogation Plan was told that his mother and sister were whores.

Finding # 16d: On 17 Dec 02, the subject of the first Special Interrogation Plan was told that he was a homosexual, had homosexual tendencies, and that other detainees had found out about these tendencies.

Finding # 16e: On 20 Dec 02, an interrogator tied a leash to the subject of the first Special Interrogation Plan's chains, led him around the room, and forced him to perform a series of dog tricks.

Finding # 16f: On 20 Dec 02, an interrogator forced the subject of the first Special Interrogation Plan to dance with a male interrogator.

. . .

Finding # 16h: On one occasion in Dec 02, the subject of the first Special Interrogation Plan was forced to stand naked for five minutes with females present. This incident occurred during the course of a strip search.[34]

Al-Qahtani was also threatened with a military working dog.[35] Four of these techniques – threatening with a dog, placing women's underwear over the head, forcing nudity in the presence of female soldiers, and leading the victim around on a leash – eventually migrated to Abu Ghraib, where they appeared in iconic and devastating photographs.[36] Eventually, Susan Crawford, the convening authority (that is, the head) of the Military Commissions, refused to prosecute al-Qahtani because "his treatment met the legal definition of torture. And that's why I did not refer the case."[37] This statement was the first, and to our knowledge only, occasion on which a Bush administration official publicly used the word *torture* to describe the treatment of a detainee.

Prolonged isolation is one of the worst techniques; apparently companionship is a basic human need and complete solitude one of the most painful human experiences.[38] According to the US government, isolation became a

---

[34] Schmidt report, note 20 above, p. 19. Schmidt concluded that taken together with 20-hour-a-day interrogations, these techniques were "degrading and abusive," although "this treatment did not rise to the level of prohibited inhumane treatment," p. 20.

[35] *Ibid.*, p. 14.

[36] See Abu Ghraib Prison Photos, *Antiwar.Com* (Feb. 16, 2006) (http://antiwar.com/news/?articleid=2444).

[37] Bob Woodward, "Detainee Tortured, Says U.S. Official: Trial Overseer Cites 'Abusive' Methods Against 9/11 Suspect," *Washington Post* (Jan. 14, 2009) (www.washingtonpost.com/wp-dyn/content/article/2009/01/13/AR2009011303372_pf.html) (quoting Susan J. Crawford).

[38] See Atul Gawande, "Hellhole," *New Yorker* (Mar. 30, 2009) (www.newyorker.com/reporting/2009/03/30/090330fa_fact_gawande) (discussing long-term solitary confinement); see sources cited in note 19 above.

centrally important technique used against the "dirty bomb" conspirator Jose Padilla.[39] Padilla was held in isolation from June 2002 until March 2004, when (with Padilla's Supreme Court case looming) authorities finally permitted a visit from his attorney.[40]

It would be tedious to continue the catalog of techniques. Whether you agree that these techniques are severe enough to qualify as torture, our point in describing them is to make it clear that the United States is no stranger to the deliberate infliction of mental suffering.

We will follow a characterization by Almerindo E. Ojeda, who, reviewing evidence from several countries, finds thirteen forms that mental torture has characteristically taken:

A1. *Isolation*: solitary confinement (no human contact whatsoever) or semi-solitary confinement (contact only with interrogators, guards, and other personnel ancillary to the detention).

A2. *Psychological Debilitation*: the effect of deprivation of food, water, clothes, or sleep, the disruption of sleep cycles, prolonged standing, crouching, or kneeling, forced physical exertion, exposure to temperatures leading to stifling or hypothermia.

A3. *Spatial Disorientation*: confinement in small places; small, darkened or otherwise nonfunctional windows.

A4. *Temporal Disorientation*: denial of natural light; nighttime recreation time; erratic scheduling of meals, showers, or otherwise regular activities.

A5. *Sensory Disorientation*: use of *magic rooms*, i.e., holding facilities or interrogation chambers that induce misperceptions of sensory failure, narcosis, or hypnosis.

A6. *Sensory Deprivation*: use of hooding, blindfolding, opaque goggles, darkness, soundproofing/canceling headsets, nasal masks (possibly deodorized), gloves, arm covers, sensory deprivation tanks or vaults.

A7. *Sensory Assault (Overstimulation)*: use of bright or stroboscopic lights; loud noise (or music); shouting or using public address equipment at close range.

A8. *Induced Desperation*: arbitrary arrest; indefinite detention; random punishment or reward; forced feeding; implanting sense of guilt, abandonment, or "learned helplessness."

A9. *Threats*: to self or to others; threats of death, physical torture, or rendition; mock executions; forced witnessing of torture (visually or aurally).

---

[39] The so-called Jacoby declaration was introduced as evidence to oppose granting Padilla access to counsel. See Declaration of Vice Admiral Lowell E. Jacoby (US Navy), Director of the Defense Intelligence Agency, at 5, Padilla ex rel. *Newman* v. *Bush*, 233 F. Supp. 2d 564 (S.D.N.Y. 2002) (No. 02-Civ-445) (www.docstoc.com/docs/110166680/Declaration-of-Vice-Admiral-Lowell-E-Jacoby-_USN_-Director-of-the) (describing need to maintain relationship of "dependency and trust" between Padilla and interrogators).

[40] See Grassian, "Neuropsychiatric Effects of Solitary Confinement."

A10. *Feral Treatment*: berating victim to the subhuman level of wild animals; forced nakedness; denial of personal hygiene; overcrowding; forced interaction with pests; contact with blood or excreta; bestiality; incest.

A11. *Sexual Humiliation*: forcing the victim to witness or carry out masturbation, copulation, or other forms of sexual behavior.

A12. *Desecration*: forcing victims to witness or engage in the violation of religious practices (irreverence, blasphemy, profanity, defilement, sacrilege, incest, Satanism).

A13. *Pharmacological Manipulation*: nontherapeutic use of drugs or placebos.[41]

Ojeda's catalog may not be exhaustive because human beings have never lacked inventiveness in devising new forms of cruelty. But, it gives some sense of what we are talking about.

III   Obscuring mental pain and suffering

The Senate reservations, understandings, and declarations

The CAT was adopted internationally in 1984, ten years before US ratification. It did not take long before US officials became nervous about the CAT's definition of torture. In 1988, the Reagan administration submitted the CAT for ratification.[42] The report submitted to the Senate Foreign Relations Committee expresses concern that someone might apply the CAT's definition to US law-enforcement practices and particularly to "'police brutality,' [which] while deplorable, does not amount to 'torture.'"[43] This political worry led to several proposed understandings: first, that CAT's exemption of pain and suffering "inherent in or incidental to lawful sanctions"[44] applies to law enforcement as well as punishment and, second, that "in order to constitute torture, an act must be a deliberate and calculated act of an extremely cruel and inhuman nature, specifically intended to inflict excruciating and agonizing physical or mental pain or suffering."[45]

The Foreign Relations Committee rejected the proposed understandings because they "created the impression that the United States was not serious in its commitment to end torture worldwide." The committee singled out the understanding that pain and suffering must be excruciating and agonizing for

---

[41] Almerindo E. Ojeda, "What Is Psychological Torture?", in Ojeda, *The Trauma of Psychological Torture*, pp. 1–23, at pp. 2–3.

[42] Message from the President of the United States Transmitting the Convention Against Torture and Other Cruel, Inhuman or Degrading Treatment or Punishment, S. Treaty Doc. No. 100-20, pp. 3–5 (1988) [hereinafter S. Treaty Doc. No. 100-20].

[43] *Ibid.*, pp. 3–4.   [44] CAT, note 3 above.

[45] S. Treaty Doc. No. 100-20, note 42 above, pp. 4–5. The "understandings" were part of a package of reservations, understandings, and declarations (RUDs).

168 THE EVILS OF TORTURE

"setting too high a threshold of pain for an act to constitute torture."[46] In response, the George H. W. Bush administration deleted the Reagan understanding of physical pain or suffering and proposed a substitute understanding of mental pain or suffering – the very standard that we criticize here.[47] As adopted when the Senate ratified the treaty in 1994, it reads:

II. The Senate's advice and consent is subject to the following understandings, which shall apply to the obligations of the United States under this Convention:

(1)(a) That with reference to Article 1, the United States understands that, in order to constitute torture, an act must be specifically intended to inflict severe physical or mental pain or suffering and that mental pain or suffering refers to prolonged mental harm caused by or resulting from: (1) the intentional infliction or threatened infliction of severe physical pain or suffering; (2) the administration or application, or threatened administration or application, of mind altering substances or other procedures calculated to disrupt profoundly the senses or the personality; (3) the threat of imminent death; or (4) the threat that another person will imminently be subject to death, severe physical pain or suffering, or the administratio [sic] or application of mind altering substances or other procedures calculated to disrupt profoundly the senses or personality.[48]

In brief, the US understandings restrict mental pain and suffering to the prolonged harm caused by physical torture, threats of death or physical torture, mind-altering drugs or their equivalent, and threats to another of death, physical torture, or mind alteration.

Under international law, states can issue any treaty understandings they wish, provided that they are not incompatible with the object and purpose of the treaty.[49] Whether a partial, narrowing construction of the prohibition on

[46] Senate Committee on Foreign Relations, Convention Against Torture and Other Cruel, Inhuman or Degrading Treatment or Punishment, S. Exec. Rep. No. 101-30, at 4, 9 (1990).
[47] Ibid. The other understanding, that "lawful sanctions" includes law enforcement as well as punishment, was retained, although modified "to make it clear that to be 'lawful,' sanctions must also meet the standards of international law."
[48] 136th Congress Rec. S17491-01 (daily edn. Oct. 27, 1990).
[49] See Vienna Convention on the Law of Treaties art. 19(c), opened for signature May 23, 1969, 1155 U.N.T.S. 331 [hereinafter VCLT] (limiting permissible reservations to those not "incompatible with the object and purpose of the treaty"). Although the United States describes its definition of "severe mental pain or suffering" as an understanding, not a reservation, it falls under the convention's definition of a reservation – "a unilateral statement, however phrased or named, made by a State, when signing, ratifying, accepting, approving or acceding to a treaty, whereby it purports to exclude or to modify the legal effect of certain provisions of the treaty in their application to that State," art. 2 (1)(d). This definition and the following paragraph correct the interpretation and analysis offered in Henry Shue, "Target-Selection Norms, Torture Norms, and Growing US Permissiveness," in Hew Strachan and Sibylle Scheipers, Eds., The Changing Character of War (Oxford University Press, 2011), pp. 464–83, at pp. 475–6.

mental torture is compatible with the CAT's object and purpose is a debatable question – a partial prohibition on mental torture is better than nothing, even if it leaves a loophole for tortures that it is the CAT's object and purpose to prohibit. Regardless of how one answers that question, however, such understandings have no effect on the content of international treaty law like the CAT.[50] In 1996, the Netherlands entered an objection to the US understandings: "The Government of the Kingdom of the Netherlands considers the following understandings to have no impact on the obligations of the United States of America under the Convention: II. 1 a[.] This understanding appears to restrict the scope of the definition of torture under article 1 of the Convention."[51] The next day, Sweden lodged a similar objection and cautioned "that the understandings expressed by the United States of America do not relieve the United States of America as a party to the Convention from the responsibility to fulfil the obligations undertaken therein."[52]

As we have seen, the Dutch were exactly right that the US understandings were intended "to restrict the scope of the definition of torture" – specifically, as we have seen, to ward off labeling police brutality as torture.[53] The torture statutes incorporate the language of the understandings with only minor changes. The most dramatic US departure from the convention's language is in the definition of mental torture. As Deputy Assistant Attorney General Mark Richard said to the Senate Foreign Relations Committee in 1990, "It is . . . in regard to the area of mental pain that the definition [of torture] poses the greatest problem."[54]

The substitution trick

One device the Senate used to narrow the crime of torture is a specific-intent requirement, which we discuss below. But it uses two additional means directed solely at the definition of mental torture. One incorporates into the

[50] See VCLT, note 49 above, art. 21(2) ("The reservation does not modify the provisions of the treaty for the other parties to the treaty inter se.").

[51] Declarations and Reservations, Office of the United Nations High Commissioner for Human Rights (https://treaties.un.org/Pages/ViewDetails.aspx?mtdsg_no=IV-9& chapter=4&lang=en#EndDec).

[52] Ibid. We are grateful to Guy Goodwin-Gill for pointing out the prompt Dutch and Swedish objections to the US understandings.

[53] The George H. W. Bush administration shared the Reagan administration's worry that CAT might (in the eyes of some states) reach US law-enforcement practices: "The convention does place U.S. law enforcement officials when traveling overseas at risk of arrest and prosecution in foreign jurisdictions or even extradition to a third country for purported violations committed within the United States." Convention Against Torture: Hearing Before the Senate Committee on Foreign Relations, 101st Congress (1990) [hereinafter CAT SFRC hearing] (statement of Mark Richard, Deputy Assistant Attorney General, US Department of Justice), p. 13.

[54] Ibid.

definition an allegedly necessary effect, and the other incorporates a short list of allegedly necessary causes. Without the effect and one of the specified causes, there is no severe mental pain or suffering and, therefore, no torture regardless of how much mental agony the victim actually experienced.

Note first that the Senate understandings *define* mental pain or suffering as "prolonged mental harm." This restrictive, additional requirement is doubly arbitrary. What the CAT prohibits is the infliction of mental torture; it contains absolutely no requirement that this infliction result in harm other than the pain or suffering itself. The US understandings generate a requirement that would mean that the infliction of the severe pain or suffering, when it is psychological, is unobjectionable unless it has some prolonged additional effect. Or rather, it is unobjectionable because – reading the Senate's language carefully and literally – *it is not mental pain or suffering at all.* "What is real about severe mental pain or suffering if it does not cause harm?", the United States seems to be asking. Further, the severe pain or suffering, when it is mental, in order to be objectionable, not only must result in harm but also the harm must be "prolonged." "What is wrong with severe pain or suffering, provided it is mental, if it does not cause harm that is prolonged?" is the full question. As Mark Richard objected to the Foreign Relations Committee about CAT's definition of torture, "mental suffering is often transitory, causing no lasting harm"[55] – as though that means it is not really mental suffering.

Could it be that the prolonged mental harm in this definition refers to the mental pain or suffering during the torture rather than to an aftereffect? The answer is no. The Senate's definition specifies that the only techniques that count as mental torture are physical torture, threats of a few specified kinds, and procedures like the administration of mind-altering drugs. None of these need be prolonged, and, if they are not, prolonged mental harm can refer only to the aftereffects. To be sure, if prolonged drugging or prolonged physical torture generates severe mental suffering while it is going on, that could by itself count as prolonged mental harm under the Senate's definition even if it had no aftereffects, but that appears to be only a secondary meaning of the Senate's definition.

The Office of Legal Counsel interpreted the language to refer solely to aftereffects. The Bybee–Yoo torture memo explains prolonged mental harm this way:

> For example, the mental strain experienced by an individual during a lengthy and intense interrogation—such as one that state or local police might conduct upon a criminal suspect—would not violate Section 2340(2). On the other hand, the development of a mental disorder such as posttraumatic stress disorder, which can last months or even years, or

---

[55] *Ibid.*, p. 17.

even chronic depression, which also can last for a considerable period of time if untreated, might satisfy the prolonged harm requirement.[56]

Thus, the Bybee–Yoo torture memo concluded, "For purely mental pain or suffering to amount to torture under Section 2340, it must result in significant psychological harm of significant duration, e.g., lasting for months or even years."[57] The Levin memo disagreed that the harm must last months or years but continued to deny that the prolonged mental harm "is to be presumed any time one of the predicate acts occurs" and continued to insist that it "must extend for some period of time" to pass the legal threshold.[58]

Evidently, what in plain language would be called mental pain or suffering does not exist unless it actually produces prolonged mental harm as an after-effect, and the aftereffect is the only mental pain or suffering the Senate understandings recognize. The understandings retain words from the CAT while assigning them a completely different reference – namely, what would ordinarily be considered one of the possible effects of pain and suffering. If prolonged harm does not result, the pain or suffering never existed. We will refer to this as the *substitution trick* – the trick of substituting a possible effect for its cause so that the cause itself ceases to constitute torture.[59] The result is the attempted erasure of any infliction of mental pain or suffering that does not leave behind harm – in the case of psychological torture, prolonged harm – in defiance of the CAT's prohibition of inflicting severe mental pain or suffering.

The materialist bias

Notice that the law contains no corresponding requirement for physical pain or suffering – no claim that unless physical torture produces some additional effect like scarring or maiming or, for that matter, prolonged mental harm it is not pain or suffering. Of course, we have learned that US interrogators in Iraq posted a placard in their interrogation chamber reading "NO BLOOD, NO FOUL," but that cynical slogan meant only that torture that leaves no

---

[56] Bybee–Yoo torture memo, note 14 above, p. 49. For a powerful critique of this argument, and the Bybee–Yoo construal of mental torture, see Kate Riggs, Richard Blakeley, and Jasmine Marwaha, "Prolonged Mental Harm: The Torturous Reasoning Behind a New Standard for Psychological Abuse," *Harvard Human Rights Journal*, 20 (2007), 263–92.

[57] Bybee–Yoo torture memo, note 14 above, p. 41.

[58] Levin memo, note 15 above, pp. 145–6. Levin points out that cases under the Torture Victim Protection Act are consistent with this interpretation – some decisions point to persisting symptoms to find mental torture, and one case denies that a single night of death threats inflicted prolonged mental harm (pp. 147–8, citing *Villeda Aldana* v. *Fresh Del Monte Produce, Inc.*, 305 F. Supp. 2d 1285, 1294–95 (S.D. Fla. 2003), affirmed in part, vacated in part, 416 F.3d 1242 (11th Cir. 2005)).

[59] This term was first used in Shue, "Target-Selection Norms." In this chapter, we will subsequently broaden the definition to include the substitution of causes for effects as well as effects for causes.

scars is hard to prove, not that it is not torture.[60] Claiming that it is not torture would be too obviously incredible, given the notoriety of bloodless methods such as water torture and electrical shocks.[61] Somehow, though, requiring an additional, prolonged harm seems less incredible in the case of mental torture, and the question is why. The implication is clear: the entire conception of psychological torture – the infliction of severe mental pain or suffering – must be viewed with suspicion. We will refer to this as the *materialist bias* in the US position: the implication is that even desperate psychological distress is not quite as real as physical pain or suffering.[62] To paraphrase Bertrand Russell's caricature of vulgar materialism, "Never mind, it's all matter." The materialist bias is our hypothesis to explain a number of the oddities in the law, including the specific substitution trick employed here. The generic form of the trick is the replacement of one thing by another; this specific instance is the replacement of the mental by the physical.

We can hear echoes of the materialist bias in the Bush Justice Department's treatment of physical suffering as well: the Bybee–Yoo torture memo denied that it exists separate from physical pain, and, even when the Levin memo restored the category of suffering, it added a requirement that physical suffering be prolonged, which allowed the CIA to claim that waterboarding in short sessions was not torture.[63] That requirement of extended duration has no basis in the torture statute and is, in fact, inconsistent with the torture statute.[64] But apparently the memo's authors thought physical suffering that is

[60] See Eric Schmitt and Carolyn Marshall, "In Secret Unit's 'Black Room,' a Grim Portrait of U.S. Abuse," *New York Times* (Mar. 19, 2006) (www.nytimes.com/2006/03/19/international/middleeast/19abuse.html). Task Force 6-26's "adage" was "if you don't make them bleed, they can't prosecute for it."

[61] See, generally, Rejali, *Torture and Democracy*, pp. 65–401 (providing a comprehensive history of "clean" or "stealth" torture).

[62] Jacobs, "Documenting the Neurobiology of Psychological Torture", pp. 167–8 (pointing out the prevalence of the materialist bias).

[63] See Levin memo, note 15 above, pp. 141–3.

[64] *Ibid.*, p. 147. The memo read a requirement into the statute that physical suffering must be "of some extended duration" to constitute torture. Not only is there no support for this requirement in the statute, but also the structure of the statute rules it out: under ordinary rules of statutory construction, that the statute explicitly builds a duration requirement into the definition of mental torture but not physical torture means that there is no such requirement in the definition of physical torture. See 18 U.S.C. § 2340 (2006); cf. *Chevron U.S.A., Inc.* v. *Echazabal*, 536 U.S. 73, 81 (2002) (explaining the *expressio unius* canon that "an omission bespeaks a negative implication"). This flawed analysis, conjuring a statutory requirement out of thin air, proved convenient and indeed essential for permitting waterboarding. Levin's successor, Steven G. Bradbury, used the Levin memo's duration requirement to exclude waterboarding as a form of torture because waterboarding sessions are short. See Bradbury memo, note 20 above, pp. 193–4. In a remarkable piece of legal detective work, Marty Lederman correctly guessed this deeply hidden connection between Levin's extended-duration requirement and waterboarding, more than two years before the Obama administration released Bradbury's memo. Lederman's

not pain is not real unless it is prolonged and, therefore, treated it on a par with mental pain and suffering. The materialist bias strikes again.

The materialist bias dates back to the Reagan administration's original submission of the CAT to the Senate in 1988:

> Mental pain and suffering is, however, a relatively more subjective phenomenon than physical suffering. Accordingly, in determining when mental pain and suffering is of such severity as to constitute torture, it is important to look to other, more objective criteria such as the degree of cruelty or inhumanity of the conduct causing the pain and suffering.[65]

We want to acknowledge that one clause of the Senate's reservations, understandings, and declarations (RUDs) may, if correctly interpreted, escape distortion by the materialist bias. We saw above that, among the enumerated possible causes of prolonged mental harm, is "the administration or application ... of mind altering substances or other procedures calculated to disrupt profoundly the senses or the personality." This recognition that profound disruption of the senses or the personality is a significant mental harm could be an important tear in the veil obscuring mental phenomena. Everything turns on how broadly "the administration or application ... of ... other procedures calculated to disrupt profoundly the senses or the personality" can reasonably be construed. Although the statute does not explain what "other procedures calculated to disrupt profoundly the senses or the personality" refers to, the category would surely include nonpharmaceutical interventions such as electrical stimulation of the brain, surgical procedures like lobotomies, and prolonged sensory deprivation. These nonpharmaceutical interventions may be all the drafters intended to include. However, if the category were expanded to include all psychological techniques designed to break the victim's personality, it would avoid the materialist bias that corrupts the remainder of the law. How expansively to read this clause is an important question to which we return briefly below.

The four causes

The idea that mental pain and suffering must be defined by the kind of conduct that causes it brings us to the second way US law minimizes the mental pain and suffering that can count as torture. The US understandings of mental pain and suffering limit it to the mental pain and suffering arising from one of four causes and from nothing else.

---

prophetic blog post was the first publication to explain the point of Levin's puzzling rewrite of the statute. See Marty Lederman, "Yes, It's a No-Brainer: Waterboarding *Is* Torture," *Balkinization* (Oct. 28, 2006, 11:07 a.m.) (http://balkin.blogspot.com/2006/10/yes-its-no-brainer-waterboarding-is.html).

[65] S. Treaty Doc. No. 100-20, note 42 above, p. 3.

Why such a short, exclusive list? Why should we suppose that severe mental pain or suffering could be caused in only four ways? The causes in the list quoted above are highly specific: use or threatened use of drugs or other mind-altering procedures, use or threat of physical torture, threats of the imminent death of the victim, and threats that someone other than the victim will imminently suffer death, physical torture, or administration of mind-altering drugs or something similar. The obvious question about these four required causes is why precisely only these? What about a threat of imminent rape? What about being prevented permanently from performing required religious observances – never being allowed to pray properly, for example? What about being required to perform sexual acts considered perverse and disgusting? We see no good reason to think that only the few threats and actions that happen to be listed in the US understandings can cause severe mental pain or suffering. The four causes enumerated in the law arbitrarily narrow what could count as mental pain or suffering and ignore most of the ways that interrogators standardly impose extreme psychological stress, such as prolonged isolation and sleep deprivation. This restriction, too, is a substitution trick.

To see just how arbitrary this list is and what latitude it gives interrogators, consider a threat that an interrogator made to Guantánamo detainee Mohamedou Ould Slahi (or Salahi), both in person and in writing, as described in an official military report: "U.S. authorities in conjunction with authorities from the country of origin of the subject . . . would interrogate the mother of the subject. . . The letter further indicated that if his mother was uncooperative she would be detained and transferred to U.S. custody at GTMO [Guantánamo Bay] for long term detention."[66] Analyzing this threat to the victim's mother, the report explains that it received legal approval:

> As written the letter does contain a threat to detain the subject of the second special interrogation's mother but does not contain any threat on her life or that of her family. . .

> [The Special Team Chief] claims that he cleared the plan with the senior judge advocate. . . Considering the actual content of the letter, it is reasonable to conclude that the JAG [officer of the Judge Advocate General's Corps] advised that the letter was a proper deception and therefore additional approval was not required.[67]

The JAG was simply following the letter of the law, and the investigator concluded that the threat did "not rise to the level of torture as defined under U.S. law."[68]

[66] Schmidt report, note 20 above, p. 24.
[67] Ibid., pp. 25–6. A "JAG" is a US military lawyer, a member of the Judge Advocate General's Corps.
[68] Ibid., p. 26.

The first of the four required causes is especially notable: mental pain or suffering can be caused by "the intentional infliction or threatened infliction of severe physical pain or suffering" – that is, by physical torture or threats of physical torture. This cause seems designed to say that the only mental pain we are prepared to take seriously, apart from two or three special cases like the terror produced by threats of imminent death and the hallucinatory nightmares produced by mind-altering drugs, is mental pain produced by physical pain. Apart from these, only physical pain really counts. "Do you claim to be undergoing mental suffering? Show me the physical pain that produced it." This approach is once again the materialist bias: if nothing is wrong with your body, nothing can be wrong with your spirit.[69]

Consider another threat made to Salahi:

> Interrogator's colleagues are sick of hearing the same lies over and over and are seriously considering washing their hands of him. Once they do so, he will disappear and never be heard from again. Interrogator assured detainee again to use his imagination to think of the worst possible scenario he could end up in. He told Detainee that beatings and physical pain are not the worst thing in the world. After all, after being beaten for a while, humans tend to disconnect the mind from the body and make it through. However, there are worse things than physical pain. Interrogator assured Detainee that, eventually, he will talk, because everyone does. But until then, he will very soon disappear down a very dark hole. His very existence will become erased. His electronic files will be deleted from the computer, his paper files will be packed up and filed away, and his existence will be forgotten by all. No one will know what happened to him and, eventually, no one will care.[70]

This horrifying threat, too, was deemed not to "rise to the level of torture as defined under U.S. law" – probably correctly because of the materialist bias in the law, and because threats of oblivion are not threats of death, torture, or drugging.[71]

Unfortunately, Congress wrote both the same required effect and the same required causes into the torture statute's provision on mental torture, without similarly imposing either a specific effect or a specific cause requirement on

---

[69] For more on this general subject, see Derek S. Jeffreys, *Spirituality and the Ethics of Torture* (New York: Palgrave Macmillan, 2009).

[70] Schmidt report, note 20 above, p. 25.

[71] *Ibid.*, p. 26. Eventually, US District Judge James Robertson (in a classified opinion) ordered Salahi freed because the government lacked evidence to detain him. *Salahi v. Obama*, 710 F. Supp. 2d 1, 15–16 (D.D.C.), vacated, 625 F.3d 745 (D.C. Cir. 2010); see Carol Rosenberg, "Judge Orders Release of Detainee Abused at Guantánamo," *Miami Herald* (Mar. 22, 2010) (www.miamiherald.com/2010/03/22/1551648/judge-orders-detainee-abused-at.html). The US Court of Appeals for the District of Columbia Circuit vacated and remanded the case, and Salahi remains in custody. See *Salahi v. Obama*, 625 F.3d 745, 753 (D.C. Cir. 2010). Oblivion may yet loom.

physical pain or suffering. There is no plainer example of the materialist bias: mental pain and suffering are made much more difficult to demonstrate than physical. One slight difference between the torture statute and the Senate's understandings of the CAT is that, where the latter makes prolonged mental harm resulting from the four enumerated causes the definition of "mental pain or suffering," the statute makes it the definition of "severe mental pain or suffering."[72] Arguably, this is a slight improvement because it might be taken as a gloss on the meaning of "severe" rather than the meaning of "mental pain or suffering," but it still radically redefines "severe mental pain or suffering" to mean one of its possible effects – prolonged mental harm. Consequently, inflicting severe mental pain or suffering itself is not categorically prohibited! All that US law prohibits is prolonged mental harm caused in a few arbitrarily specified ways, not all the infliction of severe mental pain or suffering prohibited by international law. Through the substitution trick, the possible effect, the harm, has replaced the cause, the infliction of the mental pain and suffering.

Second, the torture statute uses the same arbitrary list of four possible causes of severe mental pain or suffering that were presented in the President George H. W. Bush-era ratification understandings accepted by the Clinton administration. Someone who was simply caused severe mental pain or suffering, in the ordinary sense of these words, by any means other than the four listed would not count as having been tortured. This result, we fear, is precisely the point.

As if these contortions were not sufficient, Congress allowed them to infect the US War Crimes Act, which also prohibits torture.[73] The War Crimes Act was enacted in 1996, to (belatedly) implement the Geneva Conventions, just as the torture statute was enacted to implement the CAT. Torture can of course be practiced outside the context of war. Many governments torture their own citizens when there is no war. But torture of adversaries during an armed conflict was recognized as a war crime long before the CAT. The 1949 Geneva Conventions recognize torture during an international armed conflict as a "grave breach" that must be criminalized;[74] they also include an article (known

---

[72] Compare 18 U.S.C. § 2340(2), with 136th Congress Rec. S17491-01 (daily edn. Oct. 27, 1990).

[73] See 18 U.S.C. § 2441(d)(2)(E).

[74] The four Geneva Conventions of August 12, 1949, usually abbreviated as "GCs" and designated by their number, define "grave breaches"; all these definitions include torture as a grave breach. See Geneva Convention for the Amelioration of the Condition of the Wounded and Sick in Armed Forces in the Field, art. 50, Aug. 12, 1949, 75 U.N.T.S. 31 [hereinafter GC I]; Geneva Convention for the Amelioration of the Condition of Wounded, Sick and Shipwrecked Members of Armed Forces at Sea, art. 51, Aug. 12, 1949, 75 U.N.T.S. 85 [hereinafter GC II]; Geneva Convention Relative to the Treatment of Prisoners of War, art. 130, Aug. 12, 1949, 75 U.N.T.S. 135 [hereinafter GC III]; Geneva Convention Relative to the Protection of Civilian Persons in Time of War, art. 147, Aug. 12, 1949, 75 U.N.T.S. 287 [hereinafter GC IV]. The four GCs all require the parties

as common Article 3 because it appears under that number in all four Geneva Conventions) that prohibits torture and outrages to human dignity in non-international armed conflicts as well.[75] In its original version, the US War Crimes Act prohibited all grave breaches and all violations of common Article 3, but, after the Supreme Court's 2006 *Hamdan* v. *Rumsfeld* decision, which declared that common Article 3 applies to the US conflict with Al Qaeda and the Taliban,[76] Congress retroactively weakened the statute to ensure impunity to US interrogators.[77] This weakening was part of the Military Commissions Act (MCA) of 2006, and Congress left the weakening of the War Crimes Act intact in the 2009 MCA.[78]

At first glance, the War Crimes Act seems to have taken a giant step forward compared to the torture statute. As we have explained above, the latter redefines severe mental pain or suffering as one of its possible effects – namely, "prolonged mental harm caused by or resulting from [only the usual four sources]."[79] The War Crimes Act, by contrast, seems to have the distinct merit of returning to the standard practice of keeping cause and effect separate, defining torture as "the act of a person who commits, or conspires or attempts to commit, an act specifically intended to inflict severe physical or mental pain or suffering."[80]

---

to "undertake to enact any legislation necessary to provide effective penal sanctions for persons committing, or ordering to be committed, any of the grave breaches of the present Convention." See GC I, art. 49; GC II, art. 50; GC III, art. 129; GC IV, art. 146. These articles also make grave breaches universal-jurisdiction offenses.

[75] *Ibid.* GC I, art. 3; GC II, art. 3; GC III, art. 3; GC IV, supra note 74, art. 3.

[76] 548 U.S. 557, 631–2 (2006).

[77] "The amendments made by this subsection ... shall take effect as of November 26, 1997," Military Commissions Act of 2006, Pub. L. No. 109-366, § 6(b)(2), 120 Stat. 2600, 2635. In other words, Congress decriminalized certain common Article 3 violations committed by US personnel retroactively to the putative beginning of the "war on terrorism." To further ensure impunity for US torturers, Congress stripped jurisdiction from the federal courts over action against "the United States or its agents relating to any aspect of the detention, transfer, treatment, trial, or conditions of confinement of an alien who is or was detained by the United States and has been determined by the United States to have been properly detained as an enemy combatant or is awaiting such determination." 28 U.S.C. § 2241(e)(2) (2006). A year earlier, in the Detainee Treatment Act of 2005, Congress enacted an impunity provision entitled "Protection of United States Government personnel engaged in authorized interrogations," which specifies that "it shall be a defense that such officer, employee, member of the Armed Forces, or other agent did not know that the practices were unlawful and a person of ordinary sense and understanding would not know the practices were unlawful. Good-faith reliance on advice of counsel should be an important factor, among others, to consider in assessing whether a person of ordinary sense and understanding would have known the practices to be unlawful." 42 U.S.C. § 2000dd-1(a) (2006).

[78] See National Defense Authorization Act for Fiscal Year 2010, Pub. L. No. 111-84, tit. XVIII, 123 Stat. 2190, 2574–2614 (2009) (codified as amended at 10 U.S.C. §§ 948a–950w).

[79] 18 U.S.C. § 2340(2) (2006).   [80] *Ibid.* § 2441(d)(1)(A).

Unfortunately, these appearances are deceiving because the drafters define severe mental pain or suffering by reference to the definition in the torture statute.[81] So the real definition of torture in the War Crimes Act now is an act specifically intended to inflict prolonged mental harm (but only from one of the usual four sources)![82] Once again, the mental pain or suffering itself has completely disappeared, having been redefined as the harm that sometimes results from mental pain or suffering.

As mentioned earlier, the four causes would not be so narrow as they are often assumed to be if the second cause, "the administration or application, or threatened administration or application, of mind altering substances or other procedures calculated to disrupt profoundly the senses or the personality," were interpreted to include all systematic procedures designed to produce profound disruption of the personality. Why should other procedures calculated to disrupt profoundly the senses or the personality not include, for example, the careful contrivance of prolonged isolation and sleep deprivation frequently employed in Guantánamo? Reading the language inclusively would go partway towards redeeming the RUDs and the torture statute, although the statute would still gratuitously require prolonged mental harm as an aftereffect.

In fact, surveyed torture victims rated nonphysical torture (for example, isolation or being pelted with urine or feces) as bad as the worst physical torture they endured, and victims of psychological abuse exhibit similar rates of PTSD and clinical depression.[83] But it is important to understand that

---

[81] *Ibid.*, § 2441(d)(2)(A).

[82] See also Executive Order No. 13,440, 3 C.F.R. 229 (2007) (interpreting the meaning of common Article 3 and its applicability to the CIA). Section 3(b)(i)(A) defines torture by the torture statute while Section 3(b)(i)(B) adds torture as defined in the War Crimes Act; both incorporate the same flawed definition of mental torture. President Bush's executive order did make some progress by classifying "willful and outrageous acts of personal abuse done for the purpose of humiliating or degrading the individual," as well as "acts intended to denigrate the religion, religious practices, or religious objects of the individual," as violations of common Article 3 (§§ 3(b)(i)(E)–(F)). These are forms of psychological torture, and it is noteworthy that the order prohibited them, although it did not call them torture. It is unclear whether the order would find that the sexual humiliations visited on al-Qahtani, such as dressing him in a bra, calling his mother a whore, and stripping him naked in front of women, would be prohibited. The test is whether they are "so serious that any reasonable person, considering the circumstances, would deem the acts to be beyond the bounds of human decency, such as sexual or sexually indecent acts undertaken for the purpose of humiliation, forcing the individual to perform sexual acts or to pose sexually, [or] threatening the individual with sexual mutilation" (§ 3(b)(i)(E)). On his second day in office, President Obama revoked Executive Order 13,440. See Executive Order No. 13,491, 3 C.F.R. 199 (2009).

[83] See Metin Başoğlu, "A Multivariate Contextual Analysis of Torture and Cruel, Inhuman, and Degrading Treatments: Implications for an Evidence-Based Definition of Torture," *American Journal of Orthopsychiatry*, 79 (2009), 135–45, at 141–2; Metin Başoğlu, Maria Livanou, and Cvetana Crnobaric, "Torture vs Other Cruel, Inhuman, and Degrading

neither of these observations cures the fundamental confusion caused by replacing mental suffering with its aftereffects. Moreover, the substitution trick would require prosecutors trying to prove that a victim had experienced severe mental pain or suffering to prove that the victim had suffered prolonged psychological damage caused by the torture. Proving causation is often diffi-cult in injury cases, so the substitution trick creates a needless hurdle to the prosecution and deterrence of torture.[84]

Limiting torture to the handiwork of sadists

The most important device for setting an impossibly high threshold for mental torture is the specific-intent requirement built into both the Senate understandings attached to the CAT and the torture statute. To commit torture, a defendant must specifically intend the act to cause severe pain or suffering. Of course, some intent-based *mens rea* requirement is necessary to rule out cases in which, for example, a heart surgeon performs a bypass operation that foreseeably results in severe pain after the anesthetic wears off.[85] The surgeon has performed an act that that she knows will result in severe pain, but she is obviously not a torturer – she intended the surgery but not the pain. Including the specific-intent requirement guards against mis-labeling cardiac surgery as torture, and the CAT itself includes an intent requirement. That is all to the good.[86]

Treatment: Is the Distinction Real or Apparent?", *Archives of General Psychiatry*, 64 (2007), 277–85, at 283. We do not, however, accept the implication of the former paper that the established international definitions, as distinguished from the arbitrary US definitions, require change. See Başoğlu, "A Multivariate Contextual Analysis," pp. 142–3; see also Ojeda, *The Trauma of Psychological Torture* (presenting analyses of psychological torture in a variety of contexts).

[84] Of course, the statute does not require proof that the victim actually suffered severe pain or suffering, but only that the accused performed actions with the specific intent of causing the severe pain or suffering. See 18 U.S.C. § 2340(1). Practically, however, a mental-torture prosecution where the prosecutor could not argue that the victim had actually experienced severe pain or suffering caused by the torture would be hopeless, and no prosecutor would ever go forward with a case in which the victim would testify that it really was not all that bad. Thus, in the real world, a prosecution for mental torture would have to include evidence that the victim had suffered prolonged mental damage caused by the torture.

[85] We briefly discuss the exact nature of the intent requirement in note 108 below.

[86] In the case of mental pain and suffering, an intent requirement is necessary so that interrogation does not get labeled torture whenever the subject suffers intense pangs of remorse for having ratted out his comrades. After all, any interrogation in which the subject gives up information that he would prefer not to may cause severe mental suffering in the form of feelings of guilt and remorse, not to mention agonies of indecision during the interrogation as he decides whether to give up the information that the interrogator wants from him. That tension, by itself, does not automatically make a successful interrogation mental torture. The difference is that in a legitimate, noncoercive interrogation, the

The trouble arises because Congress coupled the specific-intent requirement with a concept of torture artificially diluted by the materialist bias and narrowed by the substitution trick. An act counts as mental torture only if it is "specifically intended to inflict severe ... mental pain or suffering," where the latter has been defined as "prolonged mental harm" caused by one of the four specified means.[87]

The result defies sense. According to this definition, interrogators engaged in psychological abuse have not committed torture unless they specifically intend to prolong the severe pain or suffering beyond the interrogation. Why would interrogators intend pain or suffering that lingers unless they are sadists? Even the most ruthless "normal" interrogator, deliberately aiming to inflict severe mental suffering on a victim, does so only in order to extract information, not in order to prolong the suffering after the interrogation is over. Through its substitution tricks, Congress has built an absurd requirement into the torture statute, defining torture so narrowly that only the handiwork of sadists could satisfy the definition. Plainly, Congress ought to repeal these flawed and narrow characterizations of psychological torture before many more torturers stride through the gate that the law has flung wide open.

IV   The forensic fallacy

Before accepting this critique, however, we must consider a possible response. Congress was writing a criminal law carrying heavy penalties. Elementary considerations of due process, embodying the principle of legality accepted worldwide (*nulla crimen sine lege*), require precision in drafting criminal statutes to ensure the legislature has defined elements susceptible to proof or disproof in a court of law. That is how the Clinton administration explained its understanding of mental torture in its 1999 report to the UN's Committee Against Torture:

> The intentional infliction of "mental" pain and suffering is appropriately included in the definition of "torture" to reflect the increasing and deplorable use by States of various psychological forms of torture and ill-treatment such as mock executions, sensory deprivations, use of drugs, and confinement to mental hospitals. As all legal systems recognize, however, assessment of mental pain and suffering can be a very subjective undertaking. There was some concern within the U.S. criminal justice community that in this respect the Convention's definition regrettably fell short of the constitutionally required precision for defining criminal

interrogator does not intend to cause the suffering or to use the suffering as an instrument to induce the victim to talk. If the subject of interrogation felt no pangs of remorse about confessing, a decent interrogator would not be disappointed.

[87] 18 U.S.C. §§ 2340(1)-(2).

offenses. To provide the requisite clarity for purposes of domestic law, the United States therefore conditioned its ratification upon [the Senate's understandings quoted above].[88]

This rationale was the same one that Deputy Assistant Attorney General Mark Richard gave to the Senate Foreign Relations Committee hearing on the CAT in 1990:

> The basic problem with the convention, one that permeates largely all of our concerns at the Department of Justice, is its imprecise definition of torture, especially as that term is applied to actions which result solely in mental anguish. This definitional vagueness makes it doubtful that the United States can, consistent with constitutional due process constraints, fulfill its obligation under the convention to adequately engraft the definition of torture into the domestic criminal law of the United States.[89]

He added, "Mental pain is by its nature subjective. Action that causes one person severe mental suffering may seem inconsequential to another person."[90]

Superficially, this argument has some merit. What is to prevent someone from falsely claiming that her mental suffering was severe when it actually was not? It is just her word against the defense about what she experienced. Requiring a showing of prolonged mental harm – for example, a clinical diagnosis of depression or PTSD – provides the kind of independent evidence that a court of law can evaluate. Similarly, limiting the acts constituting mental torture to a small set that everyone can recognize as what the Reagan administration called a "deliberate and calculated act of an extremely cruel and inhuman nature,"[91] diminishes the possibility of wrongful convictions.

But on closer inspection, the argument fails. For one thing, the kinds of evidence that might show severe mental pain or suffering are hardly anomalies in courts of law: they will include, for example, third-party observations of the victim's behavior, evidence by expert psychologists who have observed large numbers of torture victims, and, conceivably, testimony by others who have experienced the same forms of abuse. If witnesses testify credibly that

---

[88] US Department of State, Initial Report of the United States of America to the UN Committee Against Torture pt. II.A (1999) (www.state.gov/www/global/human_rights/torture_articles.html).

[89] CAT SFRC Hearing, note 53 above, p. 12. State Department Legal Adviser Abraham Sofaer offered the same explanation: "If the Convention were simply a political statement, imprecision would cause no difficulties. However, because the Convention is a legal instrument and creates legal obligations, and especially because it requires establishment of criminal penalties under our domestic law, we must pay particular attention to the meaning and interpretation of its provisions, especially concerning the standards by which the Convention will be applied as a matter of U.S. law" (p. 8) (statement of Abraham D. Sofaer, Legal Adviser, US Department of State).

[90] Ibid., p. 17 (statement of Mark Richard, Deputy Assistant Attorney General).

[91] S. Treaty Doc. No. 100-20, note 42 above, pp. 4–5.

they observed a detainee lying on the floor in a pile of his own hair which he had pulled out or publicly "masturbating like a monkey in the zoo" – as agents reported from Guantánamo and a CIA "black site"[92] – that seems like an objective indicator of severe mental suffering, one that should have been apparent to the interrogator at the time and provides evidence of intent. So too when a "detainee threw himself on the floor and started banging his head" because his Guantánamo interrogator rubbed red ink on his shoulder and told him it was her menstrual blood.[93] This evidence seems like objective evidence of a subjective state, fully open to a court to evaluate. As for the victim's own testimony, juries assess witness credibility every day, including disputed testimony that cannot be corroborated by other sources, like a date-rape victim's testimony that she never consented to sex.

Notice that in physical-torture cases, juries would be compelled to make an equally subjective determination about whether physical pain or suffering was severe enough to count as torture. Of course, there might be borderline cases (is a belly slap torture?) but, importantly, there might be clear cases as well. To regard the severity of mental suffering as more subjective than the severity of physical suffering is simply the materialist bias.

So too, jurors apply vague standards, such as the "reasonable person" standard, every day in courts of law. They do it in the obvious way: they put themselves in the shoes of a reasonable person and ask themselves what they would do if they were in the situation. This kind of exercise in imaginative identification with another person is the everyday work of jurors and judges. Evaluating the severity of suffering is no different. Would jurors think that partial drowning is severe suffering? Would they think so after hearing testimony from a dozen former Navy SEALs who were waterboarded in survival training and who say, "Yes, it was torture" (or, "No, it wasn't all that bad")? This decision is not much different, and not notably less subjective, than whether weeks of sexual humiliations or solitary confinement cause severe mental suffering.

In any case, the worry about subjectivity and false accusations does not explain why the prohibited forms of mental torture are just the four listed in the statute or why "prolonged mental harm," which the law requires fact-finders to evaluate, is any less subjective a category than severe mental pain or suffering. The legal solution simply does not match the problem it purports to solve, and the argument does not show that the problem is a real one.

Finally, both the problem and the solution seem tailored for a specific political purpose: screening the United States from the political embarrassment of having official practices labeled "torture." The legal adviser Sofaer explained to the Senate that one concern about the CAT was the possibility of

[92] See Mayer, "The Experiment," note 26 above, p. 175 (quoting a former CIA officer).
[93] Schmidt report, note 20 above, p. 8.

accusations against US law-enforcement personnel: "We believe that such complaints are likely to be frivolous, and aimed at embarrassing the United States rather than at rectifying the form of injustice with which the Convention was intended to deal."[94] This worry, however, is a public-relations concern, not a due-process concern.

Earlier, we saw that the Reagan administration had raised worries about excessive subjectivity in the concept of mental torture because of potential accusations of torture in cases of police brutality. By the time of the Clinton administration, these concerns had spread from police to prisons because of the European Court of Human Rights' decision in the 1989 *Soering* v. *United Kingdom* case, which declared that confinement in a US death row violates the European Convention on Human Rights' prohibition of torture and inhuman or degrading treatment.[95] The opinion generated consternation and outrage in the US government[96] because it treated a psychological experience – the "death-row phenomenon" – as inhuman treatment bordering on torture.[97] *Soering* played a role as the State Department shepherded the CAT through the Senate.[98] Of course, the CAT does not apply only to US officials; indeed, because the statute is limited to torture committed outside US territory, it will apply pre-eminently to torture committed by others.[99] So far, the only

---

[94] CAT SFRC Hearing, note 53 above, p. 9 (statement of Abraham D. Sofaer, Legal Adviser, US Department of State).

[95] *Soering* v. *United Kingdom*, 11 Eur. Ct. H.R. 439, 478 (1989). In *Soering*, the European Court prohibited the extradition of a German teenager to face capital charges in Virginia – he and his girlfriend were charged with murdering her parents – because of the "death-row phenomenon" of psychological suffering as the inmate awaits execution (pp. 459–61). The court found it to violate Article 3 of the European Convention on Human Rights, the prohibition on torture and inhuman or degrading treatment (p. 478). (For legal reasons, the European Court could not find that the death penalty itself violates the European Convention on Human Rights.)

[96] See, e.g., CAT SFRC Hearing, note 53 above, p. 39 (testimony of Abraham D. Sofaer, Legal Adviser, US Department of State) (responding to a question from Senator Frank Murkowski that "the decision in the Soering case . . . is just unreasonable, we believe, and we do not adhere to it, and we will never adhere to it").

[97] See *Soering* v. *United Kingdom*, 11 Eur. Ct. H.R. at 478.

[98] So we were told by David P. Stewart, who, as an attorney adviser in the State Department's Legal Adviser's Office, was charged with shepherding the CAT through the Senate. According to Abraham D. Sofaer, the State Department's Legal Adviser in the George H. W. Bush administration, the US RUDs concerning cruel, inhuman, or degrading treatment were inserted in response to *Soering*. CAT SFRC Hearing, note 53 above, p. 11 (statement of Abraham D. Sofaer, Legal Adviser, US Department of State).

[99] See 18 U.S.C. § 2340A(a) (2006). This provision makes clear that the crime of torture being created under US law applies only to acts "outside the United States." The rationale for this restriction is supposed to be that torture committed inside the United States has already been criminalized by various other laws, even if not under the name of torture. This rationale assumes that these various US laws embody an understanding of torture that is the same as, or superior to, the understanding in the international documents, an

prosecution under the torture statute is that of "Chuckie" Taylor, the son of former Liberian president Charles Taylor.[100] But this fact itself highlights how political the focus on US public-relations issues is – far removed from a good-faith, dispassionate concern about due process for defendants.

But suppose we agree that Congress might justifiably tighten up the CAT's definitions for due-process reasons. *That would have nothing to do with the correct definition of mental pain or suffering.* Thinking otherwise is what we call the *forensic fallacy* – confusing the due-process requirement of narrowness and precision in criminal statutes with defining features of torture.

The result of the forensic fallacy is that concepts of right and wrong are weakened. Then, there is a baleful feedback effect: the criminal law definition, cramped and narrowed, now becomes the "legal definition" more generally, and then the policy definition. In 2006, President George W. Bush stated, "I want to be absolutely clear with our people, and the world: The United States does not torture. It's against our laws, and it's against our values. I have not authorized it – and I will not authorize it."[101] The president was echoing a similar statement he made soon after Abu Ghraib: "America stands against and will not tolerate torture... Torture is wrong no matter where it occurs, and the United States will continue to lead the fight to eliminate it every-where."[102] And yet, President Bush fully acknowledges that he authorized the CIA's techniques and would do it again.[103] Apparently, "the United States does not torture" means that the United States does not do anything that the torture statute (as interpreted by administration lawyers) criminalizes. Ironically, criminalizing mental torture – which the CAT requires and which seems like the obvious, civilized thing the law should do – leads us to misunderstand what torture is. This misunderstanding, in turn, feeds back to affect the law. When the Office of Legal Counsel withdrew the Bybee–Yoo torture memo, the Levin memo that replaced it conspicuously declined to address two of its most radical conclusions: that the president's commander-in-chief authority allows him to override criminal statutes and that the self-defense and necessity defenses are available to accused torturers. Rather than replacing the Bybee–Yoo arguments with a better analysis, Levin ducked the issues because "consideration [of these issues] would be inconsistent with

---

assumption that we find highly dubious. The torture statute applies whenever "(1) the alleged offender is a national of the United States; or (2) the alleged offender is present in the United States, irrespective of the nationality of the victim or alleged offender."

[100] See *United States* v. *Belfast*, 611 F.3d 783, 803–13 (11th Cir. 2010) (upholding the conviction under the torture statute of Roy Belfast, also known as Chuckie Taylor).

[101] President George W. Bush, Address from the East Room: President Discusses Creation of Military Commissions to Try Suspected Terrorists (Sept. 6, 2006) (georgewbush-whitehouse.archives.gov/news/releases/2006/09/20060906-3.html).

[102] Statement on United Nations International Day in Support of Victims of Torture, *Weekly Compilation of Presidential Documents*, 40 (June 26, 2004), 1167–8.

[103] George W. Bush, *Decision Points* (London: Virgin Books, 2011), p. 171.

the President's unequivocal directive that United States personnel not engage in torture."[104] And yet, as he wrote these words, Levin was perfectly aware of the mental and physical tortures that the Bybee–Yoo techniques memo had approved, and his memo also approves them.[105] The forensic fallacy corrupts the extralegal concept of torture and that leads to corruption of the law itself.

Another example of the forensic fallacy appears in removal cases in which people facing deportation petition for relief under the CAT because they will be subjected to severe pain or suffering in the brutal prisons of their country of origin.[106] Courts denying relief to Haitians have focused on the specific-intent requirement in the torture statute and concluded that even if "severe pain was the 'only plausible consequence' of a petitioner's imprisonment in a Haitian prison" this pain would not constitute torture because the petitioner cannot show that officials specifically intend to inflict severe pain or suffering on him; thus, the petitioner gets no CAT protection.[107] But the specific-intent requirement was inserted in US law for due-process reasons, and to regard a protection in criminal prosecution as a defining feature of torture in the question of removal is the forensic fallacy – doubly so, because the US specific-intent requirement is significantly narrower than the *mens rea* element in Article 1 of the CAT.[108]

---

[104] Levin memo, note 15 above, p. 130.   [105] *Ibid.*, p. 130, n.8.

[106] Article 3 of the CAT (note 3 above) prohibits states from returning someone to a state where "there are substantial grounds for believing that he would be in danger of being subjected to torture." Congress implemented Article 3 in the Foreign Affairs Reform and Restructuring Act of 1998. See Pub. L. No. 105-277, div. G, tit. XXII, § 2242, 112 Stat. 2681, 2681–761, 2681–822–23 (codified as a note to 8 U.S.C. § 1231 (2006)).

[107] *Pierre* v. *Attorney General*, 528 F.3d 180, 184, 190–1 (3d Cir. 2008) (en banc) (quoting *Lavira* v. *Attorney General*, 478 F.3d 158, 170 (3d Cir. 2007)); see also *Auguste* v. *Ridge*, 395 F.3d 123, 142–3 (3d Cir. 2005) (holding that the shared consensus of the president and the Senate that the CAT's definition of torture included a specific-intent requirement governed the domestic implementation of the treaty); *J-E-*, 23 I. and N. Dec. 291 (2002) (relying on the Senate's ratification resolution in inferring a specific-intent requirement in the definition of torture).

[108] Article 1 of the CAT uses "intentionally" where 18 U.S.C. § 2340 uses "specifically intended." Compare 18 U.S.C. § 2340(1) (2006), with the CAT, note 3 above. "Intentionally" does not have the same meaning in all legal systems; as State Department Legal Adviser Abraham Sofaer notes, "The Convention was negotiated on a multilateral basis ... and differing points of view and differing legal systems are necessarily reflected in the final text." CAT SFRC Hearing, note 53 above, p. 8 (statement of Abraham D. Sofaer, Legal Adviser, US Department of State). In the German legal system, "intention" (*Vorsatz*) is a significantly broader concept than specific intent or even intention as defined in the Model Penal Code. *Vorsatz* includes not only US-style intention (*dolus directus*, in German terminology) and specific intent (*dolus specialis*) but also *dolus eventualis*, the nearest German equivalent to "recklessness." Greg Taylor, "Concepts of Intention in German Criminal Law," *Oxford Journal of Legal Studies*, 24 (2004), 99–127, at 106. *Dolus eventualis* means acting in awareness of an unjustifiable risk and being reconciled to that risk (pp. 101–6). Arguably, under this broader concept of intention,

V   Grasping why inflicting mental pain and suffering ought to be illegal

We are so far only assuming, of course, the reasonableness of the international consensus that psychological torture is to be absolutely prohibited just as physical torture is. But is psychological torture really that bad? We need first to remember one of the respects in which all torture, physical and psychological, is especially awful. It is common for people to say that, of course, being killed is far worse than being tortured. Being killed must be terrible – we hope never to be killed. But torture has its own special terrors. People also often say that what they fear is not so much death but dying. It is one thing to have gone; it is another to continue to survive but in despair and with no grounds for hope. One of the special terrors of torture is that, like dying, as distinguished from death, being tortured is a continuing process, not a single event or a final state. It is a process filled with dread, despair, hopelessness, and the awful awareness that one has absolutely no control over one's own condition. One can try to end the torture by trying to cooperate, but the torturer may well not be convinced and may well not admit it even if he is. Like the flies to the wanton boys, and like us to the gods, in the words of Shakespeare's blinded Gloucester quoted at the beginning of this chapter, the victim is the torturer's plaything. The vulnerability is absolute, and the mental suffering accompanying that awareness is awful.

One is, of course, rarely in full control of one's fate – the panic at the recent world financial crisis in part reflected many people's frightening sense of having lost any firm grip on how their lives would go in the future. But the fear of a depleted pension is nothing to the fear that one's own self will be undermined so that one will not retain even the underlying psychological integrity necessary for having desires and beliefs that are one's own, much less the psychological capacity (the agency) to act effectively on them. The fear is that one will be returned to the infantile state of being an uncoordinated bundle of desires and dreads with no integral self to organize them.

Think of a practice other than torture that is utterly wrong and ought universally to be prohibited – say, slavery. The slave is at the mercy of her owner. She works when and where he says. She gives him sexual pleasure when and

the brutal conditions in Haitian prisons may well count as torture under the CAT. German jurisprudence is widely influential in Europe and Latin America, and the International Criminal Court (ICC) has interpreted "intention" in the German meaning to include *dolus eventualis*. *Prosecutor* v. *Lubanga*, Case No. ICC-01/04-01/06, Decision on the Confirmation of Charges, P 352 (Jan. 29, 2007) (www.icc-cpi.int/iccdocs/doc/doc266175.pdf). (However, subsequent to the original publication of this chapter, another chamber of the ICC reversed this finding and excluded *dolus eventualis* from intention. *Prosecutor* v. *Bemba*, Case No. ICC-01/05-01/08-424, Decision Confirming Charges Pursuant to Article 61(7)(a) and (b) of the Rome Statute on the Charges of the Prosecutor Against Jean-Pierre Bemba Gombo, Pre-Trial Chamber II (June 15, 2009, § 360).)

where he says. In an obvious sense, slaves have their wills controlled by their masters; they are subject to the lash, to punitive mutilation, to other tortures designed to deter rebelliousness, and to the market in persons.[109] But even defenders of slavery condemned unlimited cruelty to slaves.[110] Living in fear of being whipped or sold away from their family and loved ones, slaves learn to give up much hope of fulfilling their dreams and goals. But their personality structures remain intact so that they are capable of having dreams of manumission and goals that are meaningfully their own, even if they are virtually certain that they will never actualize them.[111]

Psychological torture, in contrast, undermines the structure of the personality – it literally breaks apart the self, unhinging its parts from each other.[112] The victim is reduced to a quivering bundle of fears, driven to try to please – that is, to try to fulfill the wishes of others – with few wishes of her own, except release from the awful psychological stresses that are being systematically and relentlessly imposed by all-powerful others. This stress goes far beyond what slavery involved and gives new meaning to being at the mercy of someone else.

This complete breaking of the spirit is the goal of psychological torture and the distinctive methods of torture now widely practiced: the breaking of "resistance" – that is, the self – and rapid "regression" to a childlike state of pure desire to please those who completely control one's fate – one's torturers.[113] Is this worse than death? It hardly matters because it is too terrible to be permitted, much less to have been adopted as state policy and protected by legal fallacies as it now has been in the United States.

Consider just a few concrete examples of what following the basic CIA paradigm means.[114] A memo from a shocked FBI agent at Guantánamo to the Office of General Counsel of the FBI in August 2004 said the following:

[109] See Ira Berlin, *Many Thousands Gone: The First Two Centuries of Slavery in North America* (Cambridge, MA: Harvard University Press, 1998), pp. 115–16.

[110] See, generally, Moses I. Finley, *Ancient Slavery and Modern Ideology* (Brent D. Shaw, Ed.) (Princeton, NJ: Markus Wiener, 1998), pp. 189–90 (noting humanitarian rhetoric in ancient writers, although criticizing it for reinforcing the institution of slavery rather than weakening it); Mark V. Tushnet, *The American Law of Slavery 1810–1860: Considerations of Humanity and Interest* (Princeton University Press, 1981) (arguing that "Southern slave law as a whole can be viewed as reproducing this interplay between humanity and interest" (pp. 5–6), and analyzing examples of a limited humanitarianism in Southern beliefs about the treatment of slaves).

[111] Many slave songs express both the dreams and the painful awareness that they almost certainly never will be. An example is "No More Auction Block for Me" – for lyrics, see Berlin, *Many Thousands Gone*, p. xii. On the prospect of manumission and the "ambiguity" it created in ancient slavery, see Finley, *Ancient Slavery and Modern Ideology*, pp. 164–6. Finley, it should be noted, completely rejects the notion that the practice of slavery was in any sense "humanitarian."

[112] See McCoy, *A Question of Torture*, pp. 50–3.   [113] *Ibid.*, ch. 2.

[114] We are not suggesting that the psychological torture illustrated below was carried out by CIA agents. Rather it was carried out by people who had become convinced that the CIA

As requested, here is a brief summary of what I observed at GTMO[.]

On a couple of occassions [sic], I entered interview rooms to find a detainee chained hand and foot in a fetal position to the floor, with no chair, food, or water[.] Most times they had urinated or defacated [sic] on themselves, and had been left there for 18[–]24 hours or more[.] On one occassion [sic], the air conditioning had been turned down so far and the temperature was so cold in the room, that the barefooted detainee was shaking with cold[.] When I asked the MP's [military police] what was going on, I was told that interrogators from the day prior had ordered this treatment, and the detainee was not to be moved[.] On another occassion [sic], the A/C had been turned off, making the temperature in the unventilated room probably well over 100 degrees[.] The detainee was almost unconcious [sic] on the floor, with a pile of hair next to him[.] He had apparently been literally pulling his own hair out throughout the night[.] On another occassion [sic], not only was the temperature unbearably hot, but extremely loud rap music was being played in the room, and had been since the day before, with the detainee chained hand and foot in the fetal position on the tile floor[.][115]

This FBI agent is describing techniques, such as chaining on the floor in a fetal position and being allowed to lie in one's own excrement, designed to reduce victims to an infantile state. The victim who was pulling out his own hair during the night seems to have been reduced to some such subadult state.

Alfred McCoy reports the following about the interrogation at Guantánamo of "Detainee 063" (Mohammed al-Qahtani): "Playing upon Arab attitudes towards dogs, the Guantánamo guards, in their [interrogation log] entry for December 20, 2002, wrote: 'Began teaching the detainee lessons such as stay, come, and bark to elevate his social status up to that of a dog. Detainee became very agitated.'"[116] This activity was at 11:15 a.m. At 10:00 p.m. the same day, he was forced to stand naked in front of female interrogators on the pretext that he needed to be strip-searched:

paradigm is modern, scientific, and superior. How this model came to be adopted in recent years, even by some people in the US military, which has a strong tradition of opposition to torture in general and psychological torture in particular, is a tangled story that cannot be repeated here. McCoy, *A Question of Torture* goes most thoroughly into the techniques themselves and the famous psychologist Donald O. Hebb's theory of regression to an infantile state, on which they rest. But see Mayer, "The Experiment," note 26 above; Philippe Sands, *Torture Team: Rumsfeld's Memo and the Betrayal of American Values* (New York: Palgrave Macmillan, 2008); Ojeda, *The Trauma of Psychological Torture*.

[115] Email from [redacted name] to Valerie E. Caproni, General Counsel, Federal Bureau of Investigation (www.aclu.org/sites/default/files/torturefoia/released/FBI.121504.5053. pdf). Large numbers of similar memos are available in Jameel Jaffer and Amrit Singh, *Administration of Torture: A Documentary Record from Washington to Abu Ghraib and Beyond* (New York: Columbia University Press, 2007).

[116] McCoy, *A Question of Torture*, pp. 127–8. For an official account of the interrogation tactics used on this prisoner, see Schmidt report, note 20 above, pp. 13–21.

> The detainee was strip-searched. Initially he was attempting to resist the guards. After approximately five minutes of nudity the detainee ceased to resist... He stated that he did not like the females viewing his naked body while being searched and if felt [sic] that he could have done something about it then he would have.[117]

Philippe Sands summarizes in chilling detail the treatment of Detainee 063 over fifty-one days of intense interrogation, which included being forced to view "girly" magazines that he found offensive, forced to stand and face the American flag while the national anthem was played, and denied permission to pray.[118] On January 11, 2003, the fiftieth straight day of interrogation, usually for twenty hours per day, the interrogation log says:

> Source received haircut. Detainee did not resist until the beard was cut. Detainee stated he would talk about anything if his beard was left alone. Interrogator asked detainee if he would be honest about himself. Detainee replied 'if God wills.' Beard was shaven. A little water was poured over the detainee's head to reinforce control and wash the hair off. Interrogator continued the futility approach. The detainee began to cry when talking.[119]

All this relentless sexual and religious humiliation was designed to demonstrate to the victim his utter powerlessness – futility – and undermine his sense of self, his sense of being an autonomous agent who could have and act on his own beliefs, such as covering himself in the presence of women and praying when he believed he should. It is completely incredible, we think, that reducing a person to such a state of powerlessness and inflicting on him the painful awareness that he has beyond all doubt been brought so low – he cannot even keep his clothes on when he believes it is shameful to have them off – does not count as torture unless, in addition to suffering the state itself, the person also suffers some other prolonged harm (and indeed suffers it because the prolonged harm was specifically intended to be the result of the destruction of agency).

As a result of his torture, which included strong elements of psychological torture in one of the CIA's black sites, Abu Zubayda, the purported Al Qaeda logistics chief (whose real name is Zayn al-Abidin Muhammed Hussein), had evidently been caused to regress, at least temporarily, to a juvenile state:

> As one former CIA officer put it, and another confirmed, "He spent all of his time masturbating like a monkey in the zoo. He went at it so much, at some point I heard he injured himself. They had to intervene. He didn't care that they were watching him. I guess he was bored, and mad."

> Another source said, "He masturbated constantly. A couple of guards were worried about it... This was closed circuit. He complained to the

---

[117] Sands, *Torture Team*, p. 106 (omissions in original).   [118] *Ibid.*, pp. 10–12.
[119] *Ibid.*, p. 154.

interrogator that he would never have the chance to feel a woman's touch
again, and lament that he would never have children."[120]

This is a man who has been driven into despair – broken, left with no shame
and only a pitiful desire repeatedly to perform one of the few pieces of effective
behavior still allowed to him.

Part of the special wrongfulness of torture lies, then, in the limitlessness of
the extent to which the victim is at the mercy of the torturer, who never relents
until he himself, for his own reasons, chooses to end the terror that this torture
implants in the victim. The victim can attempt to end the torture by trying to
give the torturer what the victim thinks the torturer wants, but the torturer
decides entirely for himself what he wants at any given time, and whether he
believes he has it all. The victim may well guess wrong about what the torturer
wants, and often the victim does not have what the torturer wants in any case,
especially, of course, if the victim is not who the torturer thinks he is or has not
done what the torturer suspects he has done. All power remains with the
torturer, who may move the goal posts as often and as far as he wishes. The
victim is utterly at his mercy. Unlike even war, torture has no natural end. It
ends when the torturer chooses to end it. The tyranny of torture is absolutely
arbitrary in degree and duration. And if it has the power of the state behind it,
the vulnerability of the victim is absolute as well. The victim's agency, his
effective self, is at least for some time eliminated. The awareness of being a
broken person is an extreme form of mental suffering – profound regret at
what has been lost and deep despair about what may next come.

We may appear now to be launching our own attempt to perform a
substitution trick.[121] Above, we criticized the statutes for substituting "prolonged mental harm" for "mental pain or suffering." Now we are noting that
severe mental pain or suffering can lead to unhinging the self – profoundly
undermining the personality structure. Are we trying to suggest that severe
mental pain or suffering is just an undermining of the personality structure,
which would imply that apparently severe mental pain or suffering that did
not succeed in unhinging the self of the victim would not count as severe
mental pain or suffering? Not at all – severe mental pain or suffering remains
severe mental pain and suffering; it is an awful experience undergone, not the
likely damaging results of undergoing it. Not all severe mental pain or
suffering leaves its victim psychologically broken. Mental torture, like physical
torture, sometimes fails. The point is that breaking resistance by producing
psychological regression is the contemporary rationale for mental torture and
specifies the goal pursued. Mental torture that fails to attain its goal is still
mental torture, and, presumably, no one would suggest that torture should be
punished only if it succeeds (nor does the statute require it). We are, in effect,

---

[120] Mayer, "The Experiment," note 26 above, p. 175.
[121] We are grateful to Stephen Nathanson for noting this possible misunderstanding.

attempting to overcome any remaining materialist bias by explaining another respect in which mental torture is extremely objectionable. Neither the means nor the end is "subjective" in any respect that makes either in the least unreal. The collapse of a personality may be in a literal sense subjective, but it is utterly real. Allowing the state to use severe mental pain or suffering is allowing it to employ an inherently awful tool – the experience of severe mental pain or suffering – that is capable sometimes of attaining an awful goal – destroying the psychological identity of its target. This technique is objectionable even when it fails and all the more so when it succeeds. And there are other reasons why mental torture must be controlled.

The infliction of physical pain was the old-fashioned and crude means of bringing merciless pressure to bear, but up-to-date and sophisticated means of pressure can involve relatively little physical pain and instead use overpowering psychological stress. Distinctively, contemporary torture aims to break the person without breaking his bones.[122] One advantage of psychological torture, then, is that it protects the torturers against being brought to justice by minimizing physical evidence.

The disadvantage is that, if anything, psychological torture may be even less reliable as a method of gaining accurate information than physical torture. Consider an instructive example involving sleep deprivation:

> A Prince George's County[, Maryland,] jury awarded $6.38 million Thursday to a man who falsely confessed to killing his wife following 38 hours of interrogation by the Prince George's County police, according to the man's attorneys.
>
> Keith Longtin spent more than eight months in jail after he told police he killed his wife, Donna Zinetti, in 1999 following a marathon interrogation in which he wasn't allowed to sleep. DNA evidence later exonerated Longtin and led to the arrest and conviction of a Washington, D.C., man.
>
> Longtin's case was one of several in which the Prince George's police obtained false confessions through extensive interrogations.[123]

Here we have a nice experiment on reliability: a man, facing life in prison or the death penalty if convicted, who nevertheless falsely confesses to raping his own wife in the woods and slashing her face and throat thirteen times.[124] Longtin had nothing to gain and everything to lose by the confession – his

---

[122] The old and the new, the physical and the psychological, are, of course, often combined in fact, although the physical is still usually kept "clean" – that is, leaving no permanent scars or marks. Water torture – recently given the cute new name *waterboarding* – combines psychological terror and physical pain but leaves no marks. Psychological torture tends to be clean – enhancing its deniability – but not all clean torture is psychological. We are grateful to Jeremy Waldron for discussion of this point.

[123] "$6 Million Awarded in False Confession Lawsuit," MSNBC.Com (Aug. 31, 2006, 9:35:50 p.m.) (www.msnbc.msn.com/id/14609924/).

[124] *Ibid.*

liberty or life, his reputation, and the respect and affection of anyone who knew him – but even with all those incentives lined up against a false confession, sleep deprivation broke him down.

Once the victim's spirit is broken, he becomes desperate to please the torturer and to give him whatever the victim believes he wants. That might be accurate information, but it might be nothing more than a desperate guess about what will satisfy the interrogator. The unreliability of the results of psychological torture is a predictable result of the fact that CIA "experts" copied their supposedly innovative methods of psychological torture from techniques developed by communist regimes to induce false confessions.[125] The illogic of the assumption that a method that will cause false confessions will somehow yield accurate and timely information useful in preventing terrorist attacks is stunning.[126]

So something else wrong with psychological torture is that it could only conceivably be justified if it reliably produced useful results, but it is not generally reliable for reasons that are perfectly obvious: the victim's motivation is to please, not to provide accurate information. US Army manuals have for years pointed out the unreliability of all torture.[127] The fact that the spirit of

[125] See Scott Shane and Mark Mazzetti, "In Adopting Harsh Tactics, No Look at Past Use," *New York Times*, Apr. 22, 2009 (www.nytimes.com/2009/04/22/us/politics/22detain. html?pagewanted=all) (noting Bush administration's unawareness that methods were partly copied from those used against American POWs in the Korean War to wring false confessions).

[126] The psychologist who devised the "enhanced" interrogation program believed in a learned-helplessness model, according to which, once an interrogation victim has been broken and reduced to helpless despair, the interrogator can use small rewards and punishments to shape the victim's responses. The same psychologist acknowledged that the CIA never tested the reliability of the model – ironically, because of concerns that scientific testing would be unethical. Bloche, *The Hippocratic Myth*, p. 133; M. Gregg Bloche, editorial, "Torture-Lite: It's Wrong, and It Might Work," *Washington Post* (May 27, 2011) (www.washingtonpost.com/opinions/torture-lite-its-wrong-and-it-might-work/2011/05/19/AGWIVzCH_story.html). The model acknowledges that learned helplessness cannot be counted on to provide reliable information in a short amount of time. See Bloche, "Torture-Lite." Following up false leads can divert the energies of large numbers of personnel and, in that way, can actually damage national security. Ron Suskind reports that precisely this diversion happened during the interrogation of Abu Zubaydah. Ron Suskind, *The One Percent Doctrine: Deep Inside America's Pursuit of Its Enemies Since 9/11* (New York: Simon & Schuster, 2006), pp. 115–16. (reporting that "thousands of uniformed men and women raced in a panic to each … target" that Zubaydah told his interrogators about).

[127] See, e.g., Headquarters, Department of the Army, Field Manual 34–52: Intelligence Interrogation 1–8 (1992) (www.fas.org/irp/doddir/army/fm34-52.pdf). This version of the field manual was superseded by another version in 2006. See Headquarters, Department of the Army, Field Manual 2–22.3: Human Intelligence Collector Operations (2006) (www.cfr.org/intelligence/human-intelligence-collector-operations-us-army-field-manual-intelligence-interrogations/p11394).

the victim of psychological torture has been broken explains why he will say or do utterly anything that he guesses will please the torturer.

But the predictable unreliability of psychological torture – its failure in many cases to produce valuable information – is not the main reason for its distinctive wrongfulness. The main reason is its mercilessness – the limitlessness of the invasion of one person by others. Psychological torture is not finished until a person is broken. Its practitioners constantly talk about "overcoming resistance" and producing "rapid regression." "Overcoming resistance" means destroying the integrity of the self, eliminating the agency that is presupposed by autonomy or freedom of the will. Psychological torture literally destroys the self without destroying – and, sometimes, without even seriously injuring – the physical body. The victim need not suffer any bruises or lacerations and need not lose any fingernails or sexual organs – he simply loses his self, which is "broken" so that "resistance" can be overcome.

Psychological torture employed by the state is government occupation of the human soul.[128] It is the ultimate assertion of arbitrary state power– a kind of power that kings in the Dark Ages could only fantasize about. Interrogators in the twenty-first century are living out the wildest fantasies of medieval kings. Those whose quivering souls have been occupied by government agents may wish that their bodies had been put on the rack instead. We have laws restraining the behavior of governments that have occupied the land of others, but nothing would restrain those who have seized control of others' souls if we were to ignore psychological torture except when it both is specifically intended to cause, and does in fact cause, prolonged additional harm, as current US law requires.

Morality is about limits – he who will stop at nothing has no morality. A moral limit on government is the prohibition on brutality even during the exercise of coercion. Law, as noted by Jeremy Waldron, is about the exercise of power without brutality:

> The prohibition on torture is expressive of an important underlying policy of the law, which we might try to capture in the following way: Law is not brutal in its operation. Law is not savage. Law does not rule through abject fear and terror, or by breaking the will of those whom it confronts. If law is forceful or coercive, it gets its way by nonbrutal methods which respect rather than mutilate the dignity and agency of those who are its subjects... [People] will not be herded like cattle or broken like horses; they will not be beaten like dumb animals or treated as bodies to be manipulated. Instead, there will be an enduring connection between the spirit of law and respect for human dignity – respect

---

[128] "Such government occupation of the self is at odds with constitutional mandate." Seth F. Kreimer, "Too Close to the Rack and the Screw: Constitutional Constraints on Torture in the War on Terror," *University of Pennsylvania Journal of Constitutional Law*, 6 (2003), 278–325, at 299.

for human dignity even in extremis, where law is at its most forceful and its subjects at their most vulnerable.[129]

The state sometimes coerces people. This realization, after all, is part of the point: if we did not sometimes need an institution with the authority to coerce, we would not need any institution recognizable as a state. Brutal physical beatings can be awful, but the ultimate brutality is an assault on the integrity of the self – the elimination of the complex person that someone has, over the course of his life, become, and its replacement with the simple child he once was. But US law does nothing to protect us from the mental pain and suffering that is the kind of torture that slick, modern torturers are most likely to use against us when the state wants to control us inside as well as out.

[129] Jeremy Waldron, "Torture and Positive Law: Jurisprudence for the White House," *Columbia Law Review*, 105 (2005), 1681–1750, at 1726–7.

IV

Complicity in torture

8

The torture lawyers of Washington

Preface

I wrote this chapter for my book *Legal Ethics and Human Dignity*, a book about the ethics of the legal profession. It provided an extended case study of one of the main themes of that book, the central role that lawyers providing legal advice to clients play in maintaining the rule of law – or, in this case, subverting the rule of law. The chapter had a second purpose as well, pulling together in a single place a substantive history and critique of all the main torture memos available at the time. Its critique of the Bybee and Levin memos overlaps with, but also extends, the arguments detailed in Chapter 3 of this volume, which I also presented in longer form in Karen J. Greenberg's *The Torture Debate in America*.[1]

At the time I wrote this chapter, however, not all the torture memos were known. The Bybee memo referred to another secret memo applying its arguments to specific CIA interrogation techniques, which was not made public. In addition, though, the Office of Legal Counsel's head Steven G. Bradbury wrote three more torture memos in 2005, and these were unknown when I wrote this chapter. One of these memos revisited the secret Bybee–Yoo "techniques" memo, and once again declared that none of the CIA's "enhanced" interrogation techniques amount to torture. The second found that the same would be true even if the techniques were used in combination. And the third found that the techniques, singly or in combination, would not constitute cruel, inhuman, or degrading treatment other than torture.[2] These three memoranda – revoked by the Obama administration and then released to the public in 2009 – reach conclusions just as radical as the Bybee–Yoo memoranda, but drew far less criticism. In part that is because the Bradbury memoranda did not include discussions of the commander-in-chief power or of criminal defenses, which

---

The main text of this chapter was first published in 2007, and the appendix in 2009 – see Acknowledgments.

[1] See David Luban, "Liberalism, Torture, and the Ticking Bomb," in Karen J. Greenberg, Ed., *The Torture Debate in America* (Cambridge University Press, 2006), pp. 55–83, an expansion of Chapter 3.

[2] I have criticized this latter argument in Chapter 5 of this book.

were among the most inflammatory portions of the Bybee–Yoo memoranda. But also, the Bradbury memoranda were less obviously tendentious in their handling of legal materials.[3]

One major update to the present chapter would therefore be a discussion of the Bradbury memos.[4] After they were released in 2009, I was asked to testify to the US Senate Judiciary Committee, and I included a critique of the Bradbury memos in my testimony. Because it has not been published (except in the Congressional Record), I am including that testimony as an appendix to the present chapter; the testimony also recapitulates in summary form my arguments about the Bybee memo and, more generally, about the ethical responsibilities of lawyers in the advisory role.

With the release of the Bradbury memos, we also learned the details of the CIA's techniques. The present chapter relied on a news report about the techniques that listed only six of them; the Yoo "techniques" memo discusses ten such techniques, and Bradbury's memos discuss thirteen.

One other update. The present chapter criticizes an interpretation of the Bush administration's analysis of the law against cruel, inhuman, and degrading treatment short of torture. When I wrote the chapter, the only source discussing the administration's legal theory was a letter to the US Senate. As this chapter reports, the Senate closed the loopholes on which the theory relied. The Bradbury memorandum therefore needed to find a different theory to reach its conclusion that the CIA's techniques are not cruel, inhuman, or degrading. This is the theory that I criticize in Chapter 5, according to which having a valid national security justification for the interrogations means that they do not "shock the conscience," and therefore do not meet the legal test for cruelty.

THE TORTURE LAWYERS OF WASHINGTON

Revelations of torture and sexual humiliation at Abu Ghraib erupted into the news media at the end of April in 2004, when the reporter Seymour Hersh exposed the scandal in *The New Yorker* magazine and CBS News broadcast the notorious photographs. Five weeks later, with the scandal still at the center of media attention, the *Wall Street Journal* and the *Washington Post* broke the story of the Bybee memo – the secret "torture memo," written by elite lawyers in the US Department of Justice's Office of Legal Counsel (OLC), which

---

[3] They still made major mistakes, including the omission of a leading federal case that described an interrogation technique identical to waterboarding as "torture." See the appendix to this chapter.

[4] The only published analyses of the Bradbury memos are David Cole's preface to Cole, *The Torture Memos: Rationalizing the Unthinkable* (New York Review of Books, 2009) and Cole's article, "The Sacrificial Yoo: Accounting for Torture in the OPR Report," *Journal of National Security Law and Policy*, 4 (2010), 455–64.

legitimized all but the most extreme techniques of torture, planned possible criminal defenses to charges of torture, and argued that if the president orders torture it would be unconstitutional to enforce criminal prohibitions against the agents who carry out his commands. (The memo, written to then White House counsel Alberto Gonzales, went out over the signature of OLC head Jay S. Bybee, but apparently much of it was drafted by John Yoo, a law professor working in the OLC at the time. Before the Abu Ghraib revelations, Bybee left OLC to become a federal judge, and Yoo returned to the academy.)

Soon after, more documents about the treatment of war on terrorism detainees were released or leaked – a stunning and suffocating cascade of paper that has not stopped, even after two years. When Cambridge University Press published *The Torture Papers* a scant six months after the exposure of the Bybee memo, it included over 1,000 pages of documents.[5] Even so, *The Torture Papers* was already out of date when it was published. For that matter, so was a follow-up volume published a year later.[6] No doubt a third volume, collected now (November 2006), would also be outdated by the time it was distributed. The reason is simple: the lawyers continue to lawyer away.

In *Legal Ethics and Human Dignity*, I offered an argument about the jurisprudential and ethical importance of lawyers giving candid, independent advice about the law. This chapter will provide a case study of moral failure. The chapter will help us address questions such as: (1) What does candid, independent advice entail? (2) Given a contentious legal issue, how much leeway does the candid adviser have to slant the law in the client's direction? (3) What is the difference between illicitly slanted advice and advice that is merely wrong?

But in setting out these questions, I do not mean to gloss over the most basic reason for writing about the torture lawyers in a book about legal ethics and human dignity. Torture is among the most fundamental affronts to human dignity, and hardly anything lawyers might do assaults human dignity more drastically than providing legal cover for torture and degradation. We would have to go back to the darkest days of World War II, when Hitler's lawyers laid the legal groundwork for the murder of Soviet POWs and the forced disappearance of political suspects, to find a comparably heartless use of legal

---

[5] Karen J. Greenberg and Joshua L. Dratel, Eds., *The Torture Papers: The Road to Abu Ghraib* (Cambridge University Press, 2005).

[6] Greenberg, *The Torture Debate in America*. The second volume contains eight additional memoranda, but does not include such crucial documents as the Schmidt report on interrogation techniques used in Guantánamo, US Attorney General Alberto Gonzales' written responses to US senators at his confirmation hearings about the legality of cruel, inhuman, or degrading treatment that falls short of torture, official correspondence surrounding these and other issues, or the responses offered by the US government to the UN's Committee Against Torture in May 2006. Nor does it contain major US legislation enacted while the book was in press, such as the Detainee Treatment Act of 2005 and the Military Commissions Act of 2006.

technicalities (and, as Scott Horton has demonstrated, the legal arguments turn out to be uncomfortably similar to those used by Bush administration lawyers[7]). The most basic question, then, is whether the torture lawyers were simply doing what lawyers are supposed to do. If so, then so much for the idea that the lawyer's role has any inherent connection with human dignity.

If the law clearly and explicitly permitted or required torture, legal advisers would face a terrible crisis of conscience, forced to choose between resigning, lying to their client about the law, or candidly counseling that the law permits torture. But that was not the torture lawyers' dilemma. Faced with unequivocal legal prohibitions on torture, they had to loophole shamelessly to evade the prohibitions, and they evaded the prohibitions because that was the advice their clients wanted to receive. With only a few exceptions, the torture memos were disingenuous as legal analysis, and in places they were absurd. The fact that their authors include some of the finest intellects in the legal profession makes it worse, because their legal talent rules out any whiff of the "empty head, pure heart" defense. Possibly they believed that, confronted by terrorists, morality actually required them to evade the prohibitions on torture, a position frankly defended by some commentators.[8]

But the torture lawyers never admitted anything of the sort. Professor Yoo, for example, continues to maintain the pretense of lawyering as usual, and flatly denies that he was offering morally motivated advice.[9] The issue, then, is

[7] Scott Horton, "Through a Mirror, Darkly: Applying the Geneva Conventions to 'A New Kind of Warfare,'" in Greenberg, *The Torture Debate*, pp. 136–50.

[8] See, e.g., Charles Krauthammer, "It's Time to Be Honest About Doing Terrible Things," *Weekly Standard*, Dec. 5, 2005; David Gelernter, "When Torture Is the Only Option," *Los Angeles Times*, Nov. 11, 2005; Jean Bethke Elshtain, "Reflections on the Problem of 'Dirty Hands,'" in Sanford Levinson, Ed., *Torture: A Collection* (Oxford University Press, 2004), pp. 77–92, at pp. 87–8. In Elshtain's words, "Far greater moral guilt falls on a person in authority who permits the deaths of hundreds of innocents rather than choosing to 'torture' one guilty or complicit person... To condemn outright ... coercive interrogation, is to lapse into a legalistic version of pietistic rigorism in which one's own moral purity is ranked above other goods. This is also a form of moral laziness."

[9] In an interview, Professor Yoo said: "At the Justice Department, I think it's very important not to put in an opinion interpreting a law on what you think the right thing to do is, because I think you don't want to bias the legal advice with these other considerations. Otherwise, I think people will question the validity of the legal advice. They'll say, 'Well, the reason they reached that result is that they had certain moral views or certain policy goals they wanted to achieve.' And actually I think at the Justice Department and this office, there's a long tradition of keeping the law and policy separate. The department is there to interpret the law so that people who make policy know the rules of the game, but you're not telling them what plays to call, essentially... I don't feel like lawyers are put on the job to provide moral answers to people when they have to choose what policies to pursue." *Frontline Interview with John Yoo* (Oct. 18, 2005) (www.pbs.org/wgbh/pages/frontline/torture/interviews/yoo.html). "'The worst thing you could do, now that people are critical of your views, is to run and hide. I agree with the work I did. I have an obligation to explain it,' Yoo said from his Berkeley office. 'I'm one of the few people who

not whether lawyers may deceive their clients about the law in order to manipulate the clients into doing the right thing by the lawyer's lights. Although that is an interesting and important question, the torture memoranda raise a different one: whether lawyers may spin their legal advice because they know spun advice is what their clients want.[10]

To grasp just how spun the advice was, it will be necessary to dwell on legal details to a greater extent than in other chapters in this book, even though the technicalities are of no lasting interest. The devil lies in the details, and without the details we cannot study the devil. Only the details permit us to discuss the difference between a memo that "gets the law wrong," but argues within acceptable legal parameters, and one that cannot be understood as anything more than providing political cover for a client's position. And that is the most fundamental distinction this chapter considers.

The background

To understand the work of the torture lawyers, it is crucial to understand two pieces of legal background: the worldwide criminalization of torture, and the overall movement of legal thought by the United States government in the wake of September 11, 2001.

Governments have tortured people, often with unimaginable cruelty, for as long as history has been recorded. By comparison with the millennia-long "festival of cruelty" (Nietzsche), efforts to ban torture are of recent vintage. The eighteenth-century penologist Beccaria (widely read and admired by Americans in the eighteenth century) was among the first to denounce torture, both as a form of punishment and as a method for extracting confessions; and European states legally abolished torture in the nineteenth century.[11] Legal

---

is willing to defend decisions I made in government.'" Peter Slevin, "Scholar Stands by Earlier Writings Sanctioning Torture, Eavesdropping," *Washington Post*, Dec. 26, 2005, p. A3. Discussing the torture memo, Yoo added, "The lawyer's job is to say, 'This is what the law says, and this is what you can't do.'" In other words, it is lawyering as usual, not unusual lawyering for moral purposes. (Oddly enough, however, when the US Supreme Court rejected Yoo's argument that the Geneva Conventions do not protect Al Qaeda captives, Professor Yoo complained that "What the court is doing is attempting to suppress creative thinking." Adam Liptak, "The Court Enters the War, Loudly," *New York Times*, July 2, 2006, section 4, p. 1. Obviously, to call arguments "creative thinking" implies legal novelty, the antithesis of the straightforward "this is what the law says" that Yoo had previously used to describe his work.)

[10] This chapter therefore overlaps with another essay I wrote on torture and the torture lawyers: David Luban, "Liberalism, Torture, and the Ticking Bomb," *Virginia Law Review*, 91 (2005), 1425–61 (reprinted as Chapter 3 above). In a few parts of this chapter, I draw on the earlier paper.

[11] See the opening chapters of Michel Foucault, *Discipline and Punish: The Birth of the Prison* (Alan Sheridan, Trans.) (New York: Vintage Books, 1977).

abolition did not necessarily mean real abolition: Germany practiced torture throughout the Third Reich, France tortured terrorists and revolutionaries in Algeria during the 1950s and 1960s, and the UK engaged in "cruel and degrading" treatment of IRA suspects until the European Court of Human Rights ordered it to stop in 1977. The phenomenon is worldwide: states abolish and criminalize torture, but scores of states, including democracies, engage in it anyway. Nevertheless, the legal abolition of torture marked a crucial step towards whatever practical abolition has followed; and it drove underground whatever torture persists in a great many states.

The post-World War II human-rights revolution contributed to the legal abolition of torture. The Nuremberg trials declared torture inflicted in attacks on civilian populations to be a crime against humanity, and the 1949 Geneva Conventions not only banned the torture of captives in international armed conflicts, but they also declared torture to be a "grave breach" of the conventions, which parties are required to criminalize. Alongside Geneva's anti-torture rules for international armed conflicts, Article 3 of Geneva (called "common Article 3" because it appears in all four Geneva Conventions) prohibits mistreating captives in armed conflicts "not of an international character" – paradigmatically, civil wars, which throughout history have provoked savage repressions.[12] Common Article 3 is particularly remarkable because prohibitions on what sovereign states can do within their own territory in times of crisis are few and far between. And US law classifies the torture and cruel treatment forbidden by common Article 3, along with grave breaches of Geneva, as war crimes carrying a potential death sentence.[13]

---

[12] The Nuremberg Charter did not in those terms declare torture a crime against humanity; but torture fell under the rubric of "inhumane acts" in the list of crimes against humanity found in Article 6(c); furthermore, Allied Control Council Law No. 10, the occupying powers' domestic law version of the Nuremberg Charter used in other postwar trials, did name torture (along with rape and imprisonment) as a crime against humanity. The Third and Fourth Geneva Conventions include "torture or inhuman treatment" among the "grave breaches" that must be criminalized: see Geneva Convention III (on the rights of POWs), articles 129–30, and Geneva Convention IV (on the rights of civilians), articles 146–7. Article 3, common to all four Geneva Conventions, prohibits "mutilation, cruel treatment and torture" as well as "outrages upon personal dignity, in particular humiliating and degrading treatment."

[13] 18 U.S.C. § 2441. Until the Military Commissions Act (MCA) of 2006, this section declared all violations of common Article 3 to be war crimes. The MCA decriminalized humiliating and degrading treatment, along with the practice of subjecting detainees to sentences and punishments resulting from unfair trials – both common Article 3 violations, but now no longer federal war crimes. Indeed, the MCA retroactively decriminalizes these violations back to 1997. The reason for decriminalizing these two Article 3 violations is, unfortunately, rather obvious. The MCA establishes military commissions to try detainees, and apparently its drafters wanted to insulate those who establish and serve on the commissions from potential criminal liability if a federal court ever finds the commissions unfair. (Decriminalizing the subjection of detainees to unfair trials is a

In addition, the United States, together with almost 150 other states, has ratified the International Covenant on Civil and Political Rights, which flatly prohibits torture and inhumane treatment.[14]

The most decisive step in the legal prohibition of torture took place in 1987, when the international Convention Against Torture (CAT) entered into force. Today, 155 states have joined the CAT, and another 81 have signed. Several features of the CAT turn out to be particularly important for understanding the work of the torture lawyers. First, the CAT provides a legal definition of official torture as the intentional infliction of severe physical or mental pain or suffering on someone, under official auspices or instigation (Article 1). This was the definition that the Bybee memo had to loophole its way around. CAT requires its parties to take effective steps to prevent torture on territories within their jurisdiction (Article 2(1)), and forbids them from extraditing, expelling, or returning people to countries where they are likely to face torture (Article 3). Parties must criminalize torture (Article 4), create jurisdiction to try foreign torturers in their custody (Article 5), and create the means for torture victims to obtain compensation (Article 14). A party must also "undertake to prevent in any territory under its jurisdiction other acts of cruel, inhuman or degrading treatment or punishment which do not amount to torture" (Article 16) – a requirement that the torture lawyers loopholed with tenacious ingenuity.

Strikingly, the CAT holds that "no exceptional circumstances whatsoever, whether a state of war or a threat of war, internal political instability or any other public emergency, may be invoked as a justification of torture" (Article2(2)).

---

noteworthy step, because the United States convicted and punished Japanese officers after World War II for illegitimately stripping downed US airmen of Geneva Convention status, trying them unfairly, and executing them. See *Trial of Lieutenant-General Shigeru Sawada and Three Others, United States Military Commission, Shanghai* (1946), in United Nations War Crimes Commission, *Law Reports of Trials of War Criminals*, 5 (1948), p. 1.) And, as we shall see below, US interrogators employed humiliation tactics in interrogating Guantánamo detainees. After the US Supreme Court found that common Article 3 applies to detainees in the war on terrorism, the awkward result was that, without retroactive decriminalization, all those who engaged in humiliation tactics, together with officials who authorized the use of such tactics, were federal war criminals.

[14] "No one shall be subjected to torture or to cruel, inhuman or degrading treatment or punishment." ICCPR, G.A. res. 2200A (XXI), 21 U.N. GAOR Supp. (No. 16) at 52, U.N. Doc. A/ 6316 (1966), 999 U.N.T.S. 171, *entered into force* Mar. 23, 1976, Article 7. The United States, however, does not believe that the ICCPR applies outside US jurisdiction, or during armed conflicts. For a careful argument defending this point of view, see Michael J. Dennis, "Application of Human Rights Treaties Extraterritorially During Times of Armed Conflict and Military Occupation," *American Journal of International Law*, 99(1) (2005), 119–41. For the alternative point of view, see United Nations Human Rights Committee, General Comment No. 31 on Article 2 of the Covenant: The Nature of the General Legal Obligation Imposed on States Parties to the Covenant: 21 Apr. 2004, CCPR/C/74/CRP.4/Rev.6. (General Comments).

What makes this article striking, of course, is its rejection of the most common excuse states offer when they torture: dire emergency. Article 2(2) commits the parties to the CAT to the understanding that the prohibition on torture is not merely a fair-weather prohibition. It holds in times of storm and stress, and by ratifying the convention, states agree to forgo torture even in "new paradigm" wars.[15] With the worldwide adoption of the CAT, torture became an international crime.

The United States signed the CAT in 1988, and the Senate ratified it in 1994. However, the Senate attached declarations and reservations to the CAT, including a declaration that none of its substantive articles is self-executing. That means the articles do not take effect within the United States until Congress implements them with appropriate legislation. Congress did implement several of the articles. Most significantly, it passed a pair of criminal statutes, defining torture along the lines laid down by the CAT and making torture outside the United States a serious federal felony.[16]

What about torture within the United States? Long before the CAT, US domestic law outlawed torture, although not by name. The US Constitution forbids cruel and unusual punishment, and the Supreme Court held that official conduct that "shocks the conscience" violates the constitutional guarantee of due process of law.[17] Ordinary criminal prohibitions on assault and mayhem straightforwardly prohibit torture, and US military law contains parallel prohibitions. When foreign victims sued their home-state torturers in US courts, the courts found no difficulty in denouncing "the dastardly and totally inhuman act of torture."[18] If police investigators sometimes continue to give suspects the third degree in the backrooms of station houses, no one prior to the torture memos doubted that this broke the law; the torture in 1997 of Abner Louima by New York City police officers led to a 30-year sentence for the ringleader. If US agents abroad engaged in torture, nobody admitted it; and when federal agents allegedly tortured a criminal suspect

---

[15] Stunningly, however, in May 2006 the US State Department's legal adviser informed the UN Committee Against Torture that the United States has never understood the CAT to apply during armed conflicts. Opening Remarks by John B. Bellinger III, Legal Adviser, US Department of State, Geneva, May 5, 2006 (www.state.gov/j/drl/rls/68557.htm). He based this view on statements made by US representatives at the negotiations that created the CAT. The United States was apparently worried that the CAT would displace international humanitarian law, including the Geneva Conventions. However, the Senate did not include this limitation among the reservations, declarations, and understandings it attached to CAT at ratification, so these isolated statements from the legislative history have no legal significance. This is particularly important given that US law currently maintains that international humanitarian law does not apply to the war on terrorism, and so there is nothing for the CAT to displace. [2014 update: In 2013, the United States reversed this position. Periodic Report of the United States of America to the UN Committee Against Torture (Third, Fourth, and Fifth Reports) (Aug. 12, 2013), § 14.]

[16] 18 U.S.C. §§ 2340–2340A.   [17] Rochin v. California, 345 U.S. 165, 172 (1952).

[18] Filartiga v. Pena-Irala, 630 F.2d 876, 883 (2d Cir. 1980).

while bringing him to the United States, the court held that he could not be tried if the allegations were true – a rare exception to the long-standing rule of the US courts that people brought for trial illegally can still stand trial.[19]

This is not to say that, when it comes to torture, the United States was squeaky clean. In 1996, the Pentagon admitted that the School of the Americas, in Fort Benning, Georgia – a US-run training school for Latin American military forces – had for years used instructional manuals that advocated torture; and there have been many allegations over the years of US "black ops" involving torture.[20] Nevertheless, until the torture lawyers began making the legal world safe for brutal interrogations, the United States was one of the leading campaigners in the worldwide effort to place torture beyond the pale of permissibility. Afterward, although the US government insists it has not backed down an iota in rejecting torture, the protestations ring hollow, and everyone understands that US officials can proclaim them only because the torture lawyers have twisted words like "torture," "cruel, inhuman, and degrading," and "humane" until they no longer mean what they say.[21]

The result

In the war on terrorism, CIA techniques for interrogating high-value captives reportedly include waterboarding, a centuries-old torture technique of near-drowning. Tactics also include "long time standing" ("Prisoners are forced to stand, handcuffed and with their feet shackled to an eye bolt in the floor for more than 40 hours"), and "the cold cell" ("The prisoner is left to stand naked in a cell kept near 50 degrees. Throughout the time in the cell the prisoner is

---

[19] *U.S. v. Toscanino*, 500 F.2d 267 (2d Cir. 1974).

[20] See, e.g., Dana Priest, "US Instructed Latins on Executions, Torture," *Washington Post*, Sept. 21, 1996; Alfred W. McCoy, *A Question of Torture: CIA Interrogation, from the Cold War to the War on Terror* (New York: Henry Holt, 2006); Jennifer Harbury, *Truth, Torture, and the American Way: The History and Consequences of US Involvement in Torture* (Boston, MA: Beacon Press, 2005).

[21] I discuss some of these redefinitions in David Luban, "Torture, American-Style," *Washington Post*, Nov. 27, 2005, p. B1. At his confirmation hearing, Attorney General Gonzales redefined "cruel, inhuman, and degrading" treatment so that conduct outside US borders does not count. He also defined "humane" treatment as involving nothing more than providing detainees with food, clothing, shelter, and medical care; consistent with this view, the Army's Schmidt report concluded that intensive sleep deprivation, blasting detainees with ear-splitting rock music, threatening them with dogs, and humiliating them sexually "did not rise to the level of being inhumane treatment." *Army Regulation 15–6 Final Report: Investigation of FBI Allegations of Detainee Abuse at Guantanamo Bay, Cuba Detention Facility* [hereafter Schmidt report], p. 1 (www.defense.gov/news/jul2005/ d20050714report.pdf). Legal obligations were defined so narrowly that US officials could truthfully say that the United States complies with its legal obligations, simply because it hardly has any to comply with.

doused with cold water.")[22] All these techniques surely induce the "severe suffering" that the law defines as torture. Consider "long time standing." In 1956, the CIA commissioned two Cornell Medical Center researchers to study Soviet interrogation techniques. They concluded: "The KGB simply made victims stand for eighteen to twenty-four hours – producing 'excruciating pain' as ankles double in size, skin becomes 'tense and intensely painful,' blisters erupt oozing 'watery serum,' heart rates soar, kidneys shut down, and delusions deepen."[23]

More important, perhaps, than authorizations of specific tactics are open-ended, tough-sounding directives that incite abuse without explicitly approving it, such as a 2003 e-mail from headquarters to interrogators in Iraq: "The gloves are coming off, gentlemen, regarding these detainees. Col. Boltz has made it clear we want these individuals broken."[24] In response, a military interrogator named Lewis Welshofer accidentally smothered an uncooperative Iraqi general to death in a sleeping bag – a technique that he claimed his commanding officer approved. Welshofer was convicted of negligent homicide, for which he received a slap on the wrist: a written reprimand, 2 months' restriction to base, and forfeiture of $6,000 in pay. The commanding officer who approved the sleeping-bag interrogation suffered no adverse consequences.[25] Similarly, Manadel Jamadi, a suspected bomb-maker, whose

[22] Brian Ross and Richard Esposito, "CIA's Harsh Interrogation Techniques Described," *ABC News*, Nov. 18, 2005 (http://abcnews.go.com/Blotter/Investigation/story? id=1322866). At least one Afghani captive reportedly died of hypothermia in a CIA-run detention facility after being soaked with water and shackled to a wall overnight. Bob Drogin, "Abuse Brings Deaths of Captives into Focus," *Los Angeles Times*, May 16, 2004. The US government has never officially acknowledged which techniques it uses. However, in a September 2006 speech, President Bush for the first time admitted that the CIA held high-value detainees in secret sites, and interrogated them by "an alternative set of procedures," which he described as "tough . . . and safe . . . and lawful . . . and necessary." Office of the Press Secretary, The White House, "President Discusses Creation of Military Commissions to Try Suspected Terrorists," Sept. 6, 2006 (http://georgewbush-whitehouse. archives.gov/news/releases/2006/09/20060906-3.html). Subsequently, the government argued that revelation of the techniques could cause "exceptionally grave damage" to national security – so much so, that detainees should not be permitted to tell their own civilian lawyers what was done to them. Declaration of Marilyn A. Dorn, Information Review Officer, CIA, in *Majid Khan* v. *George W. Bush*, US District Court, District of Columbia, Civil Action 06-CV-1690, Oct. 26, 2006 (http://balkin.blogspot.com/khan. dorn.aff.pdf); Respondents' Memorandum in Opposition to Petitioner's Motion for Emergency Access to Counsel and Entry of Amended, Protective Order, in *Khan* v. *Bush* (http:// balkin.blogspot.com/khan.doj.brief.pdf).

[23] Quoted in Alfred W. McCoy, "Cruel Science: CIA Torture and US Foreign Policy," *New England Journal of Public Policy*, 19 (2005), 209–62, at 219.

[24] CBS News, "Death of a General," Apr. 9, 2006 (www.cbsnews.com/stories/2006/04/06/ 60minutes/main1476781_page2.shtml).

[25] *Ibid.* See also David R. Irvine, "The Demise of Military Accountability," *Salt Lake Tribune*, Jan. 29, 2006.

ice-packed body was photographed at Abu Ghraib next to a grinning soldier, was seized and roughed up by Navy SEALS in Iraq, and then turned over to the CIA for questioning. At some point, either the SEALS or the CIA interrogator broke Jamadi's ribs; then he was hooded and hung by his wrists twisted behind his back until he died. The CIA operative has still not been charged two years after Jamadi's death. And the SEAL leader was acquitted, exulting afterward that "what makes this country great is that there is a system in place and it works."[26] It worked as well in another notorious case of prisoner abuse, when two young Afghanis

> were found dead within days of each other, hanging by their shackled wrists in isolation cells at the [US military] prison in Bagram, north of Kabul. An Army investigation showed they were treated harshly by interrogators, deprived of sleep for days, and struck so often in the legs by guards that a coroner compared the injuries to being run over by a bus.[27]

The investigation stalled because "officers and soldiers at Bagram differed over what specific guidelines, if any, applied," an ambiguity that "confounded the Army's criminal investigation for months and ... gave the accused soldiers a defense."[28]

In addition to harsh interrogations by its own personnel, the United States has engaged in "extraordinary renditions," where detainees are sent to other countries for interrogation by local authorities of sinister reputation. The practice, nicknamed "outsourcing torture," has existed since the Clinton administration, but accelerated dramatically in the war on terrorism.[29] Several detainees, seized by mistake, rendered, and later released, describe torture

[26] Jane Mayer, "A Deadly Interrogation," New Yorker, Nov. 14, 2005; John McChesney, "The Death of an Iraqi Prisoner," National Public Radio, All Things Considered, Oct. 27, 2005 (www.npr.org/templates/story/story.php?storyId=4977986); Seth Hettena, "SEAL Acquitted in Iraqi's Beating," Boston Globe, May 28, 2005 (www.boston.com/news/nation/articles/2005/05/28/seal_acquitted_in_iraqis_beating/).

[27] Tim Golden, "Years After 2 Afghans Died, Abuse Case Falters," New York Times, Feb. 13, 2006.

[28] Ibid., p. A11.

[29] Jane Mayer, "Outsourcing Torture," New Yorker, Feb. 5, 2004. See also an interview with Michael Scheuer, an ex-CIA officer who helped develop the program: Thomas Kleine-Brockhoff, "Die CIA hat das Recht, jedes Gesetz zu brechen," Die Zeit (Hamburg), Dec. 28, 2005 (www.zeit.de/2006/01/M__Scheuer). An English translation is available (http://sternfels.blogspot.com/2006/01/translation-of-michael-scheuer.html). An investigation has revealed, perhaps unsurprisingly, that several European countries whose governments expressed shock at revelations that their bases and airports formed part of the secret CIA rendition network actually were colluding with the United States. Council of Europe Parliamentary Assembly, Committee on Legal Affairs and Human Rights, Alleged Secret Detentions and Unlawful Inter-State Transfers Involving Council of Europe Member States, Draft report by Dick Marty, June 7, 2006 (http://assembly.coe.int/committeedocs/2006/20060606_ejdoc162006partii-final.pdf).

inflicted on them.[30] In May 2006, the State Department's legal adviser made explicit what observers had long surmised: that US lawyers believe the torture convention's ban on returning people to states where they face torture does not cover cases where the person is rendered from a country other than the United States.[31]

Thus, "We don't torture" comes with an asterisked proviso: "It depends who you mean by 'we,' and it depends what you mean by 'torture.'" Likewise, "The United States obeys its legal obligations" comes with the unspoken qualification "which is easy because we hardly have any." The provisos are the torture lawyers' handiwork. They allow politicians to profess great respect for law and human rights, while operating without the fetters that their noble words suggest.

How did we get here?

The post-9/11 legal response

The torture lawyers went into overdrive in the wake of the 9/11 attacks, producing a flood of documents in a remarkably short time. As an article in the *New York Times* explains,

> The administration's legal approach to terrorism began to emerge in the first turbulent days after Sept. 11, as the officials in charge of key agencies exhorted their aides to confront Al Qaeda's threat with bold imagination.
>
> "Legally, the watchword became 'forward-leaning,'" said a former associate White House counsel, Bradford Berenson, "by which everybody meant: 'We want to be aggressive. We want to take risks.'"

[30] The best known is Maher Arar. See Mayer, "Outsourcing Torture"; Katherine R. Hawkins, "The Promises of Torturers: Diplomatic Assurances and the Legality of 'Rendition,'" *Georgetown Immigration Law Journal*, 20 (2006), 213–68. Another was Khaled El-Masri, a German cab driver seized while on holiday in Macedonia, turned over to US agents, and held for months in Afghanistan. See "Extraordinary Rendition," *Harper's Magazine*, Feb. 2006, pp. 21–4 (excerpting El-Masri's statement). His was a case of mistaken identity, which created a sensation in Germany after he was released. US courts refused to hear lawsuits filed by Arar and El-Masri, on the astonishing basis that revealing "state secrets" about gross government misconduct could embarrass the United States and therefore be bad for national security. *Arar* v. *Ashcroft*, 414 F.Supp.2d 250, 281–3 (E.D.N.Y. 2006); *El-Masri* v. *Tenet*, E.D. Va., Case 1:05cv1417 (memorandum opinion of Ellis, J., May 12, 2006). Another rendition victim, Laid Saidi, claims that his US captors transported him to Afghanistan, hung him by his wrists for five days, and released him only after sixteen months, Craig S. Smith and Souad Mekhennet, "Algerian Tells of Dark Odyssey in US Hands," *New York Times*, July 7, 2006 (www.nytimes.com/2006/07/07/world/africa/07algeria.html?pagewanted=all&_r=0).

[31] List of Issues to Be Considered During the Examination of the Second Periodic Report of the United States of America: Response of the United States of America, pp. 32–7 (2006) (www2.ohchr.org/english/bodies/cat/docs/AdvanceVersions/listUSA36_En.pdf).

The challenge resounded among young lawyers who were settling into important posts at the White House, the Justice Department and other agencies.[32]

As an example of "forward-leaning" legal strategy, the article cites an OLC memorandum by John Yoo on how to overcome constitutional objections to the use of military force against terrorists within the United States – for example, "to raid or attack dwellings where terrorists were thought to be, despite risks that third parties could be killed or injured by exchanges of fire."[33] Yoo wrote the memo just ten days after 9/11. The article explains that "lawyers in the administration took the same 'forward-leaning' approach to making plans for the terrorists they thought would be captured."[34]

Related to the "forward-leaning" strategy is what Ron Suskind refers to as "the Cheney doctrine" or "the one percent doctrine," allegedly formulated by the US vice president in November 2001. In Suskind's words, "If there was even a one percent chance of terrorists getting a weapon of mass destruction ... the United States must now act as if it were a certainty."[35] "It's not about our analysis, or finding a preponderance of evidence," Suskind quotes Cheney as saying. "It's about our response."[36] Suskind asserts that the Cheney doctrine formed the guiding principle in the war on terrorism. It carries far-reaching implications for the interrogation of captives: if even a minute chance of catastrophe must be treated as a certainty, every interrogation becomes a ticking time-bomb case – and ticking time-bomb cases are the one situation where many people who otherwise balk at torture reluctantly accept that breaking the taboo is morally justified.

The most crucial portions of the "forward-leaning" strategy – which included not only interrogation issues but military tribunals and the applicability of the Geneva Conventions as well – were formulated in near-total secrecy by a small group of like-minded administration lawyers, intentionally excluding anticipated dissenters in the State Department and the JAG Corps.[37] Indeed, when the chief JAG officers of the four military services learned of the Bybee memo months after the fact, they responded with forceful criticism and barbed reminders that "OLC does not represent the services; thus, understandably, concern for service members is not reflected in

---

[32] Tim Golden, "After Terror, a Secret Rewriting of Military Law," *New York Times*, Oct. 24, 2004, p. A12. The lawyers were political conservatives, mostly veterans of the Federalist Society and clerkships with Justices Scalia and Thomas, and Judge Laurence Silberman. Some sources for the article stated that their "strategy was also shaped by longstanding political agendas that had relatively little to do with fighting terrorism," such as strengthening executive power and halting US submission to international law.

[33] *Ibid.* This memo was released (and revoked) by the Obama administration.   [34] *Ibid.*

[35] Ron Suskind, *The One Percent Doctrine: Deep Inside America's Pursuit of Its Enemies Since 9/11* (New York: Simon & Schuster, 2006), p. 62.

[36] *Ibid.*   [37] Golden, "After Terror," pp. 12–13.

their opinion."[38] The chief Air Force JAG reminded the Secretary of the Air Force that "the use of the more extreme interrogation techniques simply is not how the US armed forces have operated in recent history. We have taken the legal and moral 'high road' in the conduct of our military operations regardless of how others may operate."[39] (This, by the way, is exactly the kind of moral reminder that a good lawyer ought to give clients.) Nevertheless, where in past administrations OLC weighed in only after relevant federal agencies had addressed legal questions, now the OLC "frequently had a first and final say."[40] The Bush administration took pains to bypass legal advice it did not want to hear, and Vice President Dick Cheney's lead counsel, David Addington, was particularly suspicious that JAGs are too independent.[41] In 2006 it emerged that Defense Secretary Donald Rumsfeld had quietly signed off on a torture-permissive working-group report without ever notifying officials who objected to it (and who were in the working group), including Navy general counsel Alberto Mora. Mora had argued for months against cruel or degrading interrogation techniques. He thought he had won his argument when Defense Department general counsel William Haynes wrote to a US senator that the military would not use abusive tactics. But Haynes, who had previously approved intimidation with dogs, forced nudity, and sleep deprivation, outmaneuvered Mora.[42] In the words of the reporter Jane Mayer, "Legal critics within the administration had been allowed to think that they were engaged in a meaningful process; but their deliberations appeared to have been largely an academic exercise, or, worse, a charade."[43] Nor did Abu Ghraib change the Bush administration's desire to keep politically independent JAG officers out of the advisory loop. In response to Abu Ghraib, the US Congress enacted legislation that prohibited Defense Department officials

[38] Memorandum from Brigadier General Kevin M. Sankuhler (USMC) for the General Counsel of the Air Force, Feb. 27, 2003, reprinted in Greenberg, *The Torture Debate*, p. 383.

[39] Memorandum from Major General Jack L. Rives for the Secretary of the Air Force, Feb. 5, 2003, reprinted in Greenberg, *The Torture Debate*, p. 378.

[40] Golden, "After Terror," p. 13.

[41] Chitra Ragavan, "Cheney's Guy," *US News and World Report*, May 29, 2006 (http://chitraragavan.com/usnews/29addington.pdf). According to Ragavan, Addington has been the most powerful and influential of the torture lawyers, a view confirmed by many sources in Jane Mayer's detailed article on Addington: Jane Mayer, "The Hidden Power," *New Yorker*, July 6, 2006 (www.newyorker.com/archive/2006/07/03/060703fa_fact1?currentPage=all).

[42] Mora's battle is described in Jane Mayer, "Annals of the Pentagon: The Memo," *New Yorker*, Feb. 27, 2006 (www.newyorker.com/fact/content/articles/060227fa_fact). Haynes' approval is in Greenberg and Dratel, *Torture Papers*, p. 237; the list of techniques he recommended is on pp. 227–8.

[43] Mayer, "Annals of the Pentagon." The working group report is in Greenberg and Dratel, *Torture Papers*, pp. 241–359.

from interfering with JAG officers offering independent legal advice.[44] But although President Bush signed the legislation, his signing statement implied that the executive branch would not abide by these prohibitions.[45]

The post-9/11 OLC used the catastrophe to advance an extraordinarily militant version of executive supremacy – an agenda that, even before 9/11, had preoccupied Yoo, Cheney, and Addington.[46] Just two weeks after 9/11, a Yoo memorandum concluded "that the President has the plenary constitutional power to take such military actions as he deems necessary and appropriate to respond to the terrorist attacks upon the United States on September 11, 2001." No statute, he added, "can place any limits on the President's determinations as to any terrorist threat, the amount of military force to be used in response, or the method, timing, and nature of the response. These decisions, under our Constitution, are for the President alone to make."[47] This bold assertion prefigures the Bybee memo, because it clearly implies that the decision whether to torture would be "for the President alone to make." The conclusion reappeared in one of the Bybee memo's most controversial sections, which argued that the criminal laws against torture could not be enforced against interrogators authorized by the president.[48]

One of the first steps the administration took was to strip Geneva Convention protections from Al Qaeda and Taliban captives (a position eventually rejected by the Supreme Court in June 2006, when the court held that common Article 3 of Geneva applies in the war on terrorism and therefore protects even Al Qaeda captives).[49] In January 2002, the OLC concluded that the president has unilateral authority to suspend the Geneva Conventions, and that customary international law (which incorporates Geneva protections) has no purchase on US domestic law – a deeply controversial position favored by some conservative academics but never accepted by mainstream

---

[44] 10 U.S.C. §§ 3037, 5046, 5148, and 8037.

[45] Statement on signing the Ronald W. Reagan National Defense Authorization Act for Fiscal Year 2005, Oct. 28, 2004 (www.highbeam.com/library/docfree.asp?DOCID=1G1: 125646055&ctrlInfo=Round19%3AMode19b%3ADocG%3AResult&ao=). On Bush's use of signing statements, see Charlie Savage, "Bush Challenges Hundreds of Laws," *Boston Globe*, Apr. 30, 2006 (www.boston.com/news/nation/washington/articles/2006/04/30/bush_challenges_hundreds_of_laws/).

[46] In an article about Addington, Chitra Ragavan writes, "The 9/11 attacks became the crucible for the administration's commitment to restoring presidential power and prerogative." Ragavan, "Cheney's Guy." Mayer likewise emphasizes that Addington and his boss Dick Cheney both believe that the presidency had been wrongly weakened from the Nixon administration on. Mayer, "The Hidden Power."

[47] Memorandum from John C. Yoo to Timothy Flanigan, Deputy Counsel to the President, Sept. 25, 2001, reprinted in Greenberg and Dratel, *Torture Papers*, p. 24.

[48] Memorandum from Jay S. Bybee to Alberto R. Gonzales, Aug. 1, 2002 [henceforth: Bybee memo], reprinted in Greenberg and Dratel, *Torture Papers*, p. 204.

[49] *Hamdan v. Rumsfeld*, 548 U.S. 557, 630–31 (2006).

lawyers or the Supreme Court.[50] In any event, two memos argued that the Geneva Conventions do not apply to Al Qaeda or the Taliban, because Al Qaeda is not a state and the Taliban are unlawful combatants. The president quickly adopted this position.[51] However, the president added, because "our Nation has been and will continue to be a strong supporter of Geneva and its principles ... the United States Armed Forces shall continue to treat detainees humanely and, to the extent appropriate and consistent with military necessity, in a manner consistent with the principles of Geneva."[52] Critics quickly noticed that this order applies only to the armed forces, not the CIA, and that the phrase "consistent with military necessity" creates a loophole for harsh interrogation. The carefully crafted phrasing, which makes the document superficially appear more protective of detainees than it actually is, was more handiwork of the White House torture lawyers. A few months later, Attorney General Gonzales qualified the protection even more dramatically when he stated that "humane" treatment of detainees need consist of nothing more than providing them with food, clothing, shelter, and medical care.[53]

Stripping away Geneva protections from the detainees was crucial to all the further work of the torture lawyers. It was essential that as few detainees as possible be classified as POWs under the Third Geneva Convention, because POW status protects them not only from torture but also from all forms of coercive questioning. Indeed, Article 17 provides that "prisoners of war who refuse to answer may not be threatened, insulted, or exposed to unpleasant or disadvantageous treatment of any kind." Stripping away common Article 3 protections against torture and humiliation was equally essential if harsh interrogators were to avoid war crimes charges: as we have seen, violations of common Article 3, like grave breaches of the Geneva Conventions, were war crimes under federal law. Bybee and Yoo argued that because the global war on terrorism (the "GWOT") is international, common Article 3 does not apply, because Article 3 is limited to armed conflicts "not of an international character."[54] (This is the interpretation the Supreme Court eventually rejected in June 2006.) These early opinions set the stage for the torture memos that followed.

---

[50] Memorandum from Bybee to Gonzales, Jan. 22, 2002, reprinted in Greenberg and Dratel, *Torture Papers*, pp. 91, 93, 112–13.

[51] *Ibid.*, p. 136; Memorandum from President Bush to the Vice President and other officials, Feb. 7, 2002, in Greenberg and Dratel, *Torture Papers*, pp. 134–5.

[52] *Ibid.*, p. 135.

[53] "The President said – for example on March 31, 2003 – that he expects detainees to be treated humanely. As you know, the term 'humanely' has no precise legal definition. As a policy matter, I would define humane treatment as a basic level of decent treatment that includes such things as food, shelter, clothing, and medical care." Written response of Alberto R. Gonzales to questions posed by Senator Edward M. Kennedy, question #15, Jan. 2005.

[54] Memorandum from Jay S. Bybee to Alberto Gonzales and William Haynes II, Jan. 22, 2002, in Greenberg and Dratel, *Torture Papers*, pp. 85–9.

The Bybee torture memo

Unquestionably, the Bybee memo is the most notorious of the memos and advisory opinions dealing with abuse of detainees. According to John Yoo, the memo was written because the CIA wanted guidance on how far it could go interrogating high-value Al Qaeda detainees; the United States had already captured Abu Zubaydah, believed by some to be a top Al Qaeda leader.[55] Apparently, the CIA wanted to go quite far. Abu Zubaydah's captors reportedly withheld pain medication from him – he was wounded when he was captured – and the CIA wanted to know whether it would be illegal to waterboard him.[56] Evidently, eager as CIA interrogators might have been to take the gloves off, they were unwilling to do so without a legal opinion to back them up. The OLC did not disappoint. But it would be a mistake to suppose that the OLC was acting on its own: lawyers and other officials in the White House, the vice president's office, and the National Security Council also vetted the torture memo.[57]

The Bybee memo provided maximum reassurance of impunity to nervous interrogators. It concluded that inflicting physical pain does not count as torture until the pain reaches the level associated with organ failure or death; that inflicting mental pain is lawful unless the interrogator specifically intends it to last months or years beyond the interrogation; that utilizing techniques known to be painful is not torture unless the interrogator specifically intends the pain to be equivalent to the pain accompanying organ failure or death; that enforcing criminal laws against presidentially authorized torturers would be unconstitutional; that self-defense includes torturing helpless detainees in the name of national defense; and that torture in the name of national security may be legally justifiable as the lesser evil, through the doctrine of necessity.

[55] Yoo interview on *Frontline*, note 9 above.

[56] Don Van Natta *et al.*, "Questioning Terror Suspects in a Dark and Surreal World," *New York Times*, Mar. 9, 2003, p. A1; Douglas Jehl and David Johnston, "White House Fought New Curbs on Interrogations, Officials Say," *New York Times*, Jan. 13, 2005, pp. A1, A16. Suskind reports that Zubaydah received first-rate medical care, but quotes a CIA official who said, "He received the finest medical attention on the planet. We got him in very good health, so we could start to torture him." Suskind, *One Percent Doctrine*, p. 100. Suskind also describes "[CIA Director George] Tenet's months of pressure on his legal team" to permit harsh interrogation, pp. 100–1. See also Dana Priest, "Covert CIA Program Withstands New Furor," *Washington Post*, Dec. 30, 2005, p. A1 (describing aggressive positions taken by CIA lawyers). The Zubaydah interrogation, however, proved disappointing: Zubaydah proved not to be a big fish – an FBI specialist on Al Qaeda described him as a meet-and-greet guy, "Joe Louis in the lobby of Caesar's Palace, shaking hands." Suskind, *One Percent Doctrine*, p. 100. Furthermore, he was insane (pp. 95–6, 100). Eventually, he revealed the name of dirty-bomb suspect Jose Padilla – but only after harsh interrogation had stopped and interrogators switched to a different tactic, arguing religion with Zubaydah (pp. 116–17). Suskind's account contradicts President Bush's assertion that "alternative interrogation procedures" were "necessary" to break Zubaydah. Bush speech, note 22 above. See also p. 92 above.

[57] Dana Priest, "CIA Puts Harsh Tactics on Hold," *Washington Post*, June 27, 2004, p. A1.

These conclusions range from the doubtful to the loony. Some can be supported by conventional, if debatable, legal arguments. These include the analysis of mental torture, which has some support in the language of the statute, and the discussion of specific intent, where the OLC seizes on one of two standard readings of the doctrine but, quoting authorities quite selectively, ignores the other.

Others, however, have the mad logic of the Queen of Hearts' arguments with Alice. The analysis of self-defense, for example, inverts a doctrine permitting last-resort defensive violence against assailants into a rationale for waterboarding bound and helpless prisoners. The OLC cites no conventional legal authority for this inversion, for the simple reason that there is none. Although the OLC claimed to base its analysis on the teachings of "leading scholarly commentators" (again: "some commentators"), in fact there is only one such commentator, and OLC flatly misrepresents what he says.[58] Although Professors Eric Posner and Adrian Vermeule quickly published a *Wall Street Journal* editorial describing the memo's arguments as "standard lawyerly fare, routine stuff,"[59] theirs was a distinctly minority view that seemed plainly to be an exercise in political damage control.[60]

---

[58] The commentator is Michael S. Moore, "Torture and the Balance of Evils," *Israel Law Review*, 23 (1989), 280–344, at 323. Here is what the OLC says: "Leading scholarly commentators believe that interrogation of such individuals using methods that might violate [the anti-torture statute] would be justified under the doctrine of self-defense." Greenberg and Dratel, *Torture Papers*, p. 211, citing Moore. And here is what Moore actually says on the page the OLC cites: "*The literal law of self-defense is not available to justify their torture*. But the principle uncovered as the moral basis of the defense may be applicable" (emphasis added). The OLC states that "the doctrine of self-defense" would justify torture, where Moore says, quite literally, the opposite. Note also the difference between the OLC's assertive "would be justified" and Moore's cautious "may be applicable."

[59] Eric Posner and Adrian Vermeule, "A 'Torture Memo' and Its Tortuous Critics," *Wall Street Journal*, July 6, 2004.

[60] The Bybee memo provoked a flurry of commentary, almost entirely negative. Along with my own paper "Liberalism, Torture, and the Ticking Bomb," Chapter 3 above, see, e.g., Julie Angell, "Ethics, Torture, and Marginal Memoranda at the DOJ Office of Legal Counsel," *Georgetown Journal of Legal Ethics*, 18 (2005), 557–70; Richard B. Bilder and Detlev A. Vagts, "Speaking Law to Power: Lawyers and Torture," *American Journal of International Law*, 98 (2004), 689–95; Kathleen Clark, "Ethical Issues Raised by the OLC Torture Memorandum," *Journal of National Security Law and Policy*, 1 (2005), 455ff.; Kathleen Clark and Julie Mertus, "Torturing the Law: The Justice Department's Legal Contortions on Interrogation," *Washington Post*, June 20, 2004, p. B3; Christopher Kutz, "The Lawyers Know Sin: Complicity in Torture," in Greenberg, *The Torture Debate*, pp. 241–7; Jesselyn Radack, "Tortured Legal Ethics: The Role of the Government Advisor in the War on Terrorism," *University of Colorado Law Review*, 77 (2006), 1ff.; Michael D. Ramsey, "Torturing Executive Power," *Georgetown Law Journal*, 93 (2005), 1213ff.; Robert K. Vischer, "Legal Advice as Moral Perspective," *Georgetown Journal of Legal Ethics*, 19 (2006), 225ff.; Jeremy Waldron, "Torture and the Common Law: Jurisprudence for the White House," *Columbia Law Review*, 105 (2005), 1681–1750; Ruth Wedgwood

THE TORTURE LAWYERS OF WASHINGTON

By ordinary lawyerly standards, the Bybee memo was, in Peter Brooks' words, "textual interpretation run amok – less 'lawyering as usual' than the work of some bizarre literary deconstructionist."[61] Even the OLC – after Jack Goldsmith (a sometimes coauthor of Professor Posner) took over from Jay Bybee – did not regard the Bybee memo as standard lawyerly fare. In an unusual move, it publicly repudiated the memo a few months after it was leaked.

This is not the place to offer a detailed analysis of the Bybee memo (which I have done elsewhere).[62] To illustrate its eccentricity, I will pick just two examples: the organ-failure definition of "severe pain," and one curious portion of its discussion of the necessity defense.

The amazing fact about the organ-failure definition is that Yoo and his coauthors based it on a Medicare statute that has nothing whatsoever to do with torture. The statute defines an emergency medical condition as one in which someone experiences symptoms that "a prudent lay person . . . could reasonably expect" might indicate "serious impairment to bodily functions, or serious dysfunction of any bodily organ or part." The statute specifies that severe pain is one such symptom. In an exquisite exercise of legal formalism run amok, the memo infers that pain is severe only if it is at the level indicating an emergency medical condition. The authors solemnly cite a Supreme Court decision to show that Congress' use of a phrase in one statute should be used to interpret its meaning in another. Months later, when the OLC withdrew the Bybee memo and substituted the Levin memo, the substitute memo rejected this argument and pointed out the obvious: that the Medicare statute was a definition of an emergency medical condition, not of severe pain, and the difference in context precludes treating it as an implicit definition of severe pain.[63] The organ-failure definition, perhaps more than any other portion of the Bybee memo, involved lawyering that cannot be taken seriously. It seems obvious that the OLC lawyers simply did an electronic search of the phrase "severe pain" in the United States Code and came up with the healthcare statutes (the only ones other than torture-related statutes in the entire code to employ the phrase). Then they decided to see how clever they could get. The result is a parody of legal analysis.

The discussion of the necessity defense is bizarre for a different reason. Looked at dispassionately, necessity offers the strongest defense of torture on

and R. James Woolsey, "Law and Torture," *Wall Street Journal*, June 28, 2004; W. Bradley Wendell, "Legal Ethics and the Separation of Law and Morals," *Cornell Law Review*, 91 (2005), 67ff.

[61] Peter Brooks, "The Plain Meaning of Torture?", *Slate*, Feb. 9, 2005 (www.slate.com/id/2113314).

[62] I offer a detailed analysis of the memo in "Liberalism, Torture, and the Ticking Bomb," in Greenberg, *The Torture Debate*, pp. 55–68.

[63] Levin memo, in Greenberg, *The Torture Debate*, pp. 367–8, and n.17.

normative grounds. The necessity defense justifies otherwise criminal conduct undertaken to prevent a greater evil, and in extreme cases it is at least thinkable that torture might be the lesser evil.[64]

However, the Bybee memo's authors were not content to argue for the possibility of the necessity defense. They also threw in the argument that even though the necessity defense is available to torturers, it would not necessarily be available in cases of abortion to save a woman's life.[65] At this point, the partisan political nature of the document becomes too obvious to ignore. It is the moment when the clock strikes thirteen. Opposition to abortion was an article of faith in the Ashcroft Justice Department, and apparently the OLC lawyers decided to try for a "two-fer" – not only providing a necessity defense for torture, but throwing in a clever hip-check to forestall any possibility that their handiwork might be commandeered to justify life-saving abortions if a legislature ever voted to outlaw them. Even abortion opponents are likely to balk at the thought that torture might be a lesser evil than abortion to save a mother's life. But this was the conclusion that the OLC aimed to preserve.

---

[64] I should also note, however, that the claim that the necessity defense is available for the crime of torture runs flatly contrary to the official opinion of the US government in its 1999 report to the UN Committee Against Torture, a fact that the Bybee memo chooses not to mention: "US law contains no provision permitting otherwise prohibited acts of torture or other cruel, inhuman or degrading treatment or punishment to be employed on grounds of exigent circumstances (for example, during a 'state of public emergency') or on orders from a superior officer or public authority." US Department of State, *Initial Report of the United States of America to the UN Committee Against Torture* (1999), quoted in John T. Parry, "Escalation and Necessity: Defining Torture at Home and Abroad," in Levinson, *Torture: A Collection*, pp. 145–64, at pp. 150, 162 n.34. The memo also ignores a Supreme Court opinion decided just three months earlier, asserting that it is an "open question" whether the necessity defense is ever available for a federal crime without the statute specifically making it available (and the court's language suggests that the answer might turn out to be no). *United States* v. *Oakland Cannabis Buyers' Coop*, 532 U.S. 483, 490 (2001). I am grateful to Marty Lederman for calling these documents to my attention.

[65] Bybee memo, in Greenberg and Dratel, *Torture Papers*, p. 209. In addition to its blatant political pandering, the argument is also garbled to the point of incoherence. When Congress enacted the US antitorture statutes, it broadened the CAT's definition of torture. Whereas the CAT defines torture as the infliction of severe pain for reasons such as interrogation, intimidation, punishment, or discrimination, the US statute drops these reasons and bans torture regardless of why it is inflicted. Congress decided that all torture is criminal, not just torture for certain reasons. In other words, Congress evidently concluded that nothing can justify torture. The OLC reads the Congressional emendation of the CAT's language in the opposite way, concluding that "Congress has not explicitly made a determination of values *vis-à-vis* torture." This sentence is opaque and clumsy; it is hard to speak clearly when you are fudging. The next sentence is even worse, bordering on gibberish: "In fact, Congress explicitly removed efforts to remove torture from the weighing of values permitted by the necessity defense."

The Levin memo

But Bybee's is not the only torture memo that deserves similar judgments. On the eve of Alberto Gonzales' confirmation hearing as attorney general, the Justice Department abruptly withdrew the Bybee memo and replaced it with another OLC opinion, the Levin memo.[66] The OLC lawyer Daniel Levin vehemently denounced torture, retracted Bybee's specific intent analysis, rejected the "organ-failure" definition of severe pain, and no longer argued that it would be unconstitutional to prosecute presidentially authorized torturers. In all these respects, the Levin memo sounded more moderate than Bybee, and perhaps restored a measure of credibility to the OLC. Furthermore, the Levin memo does not indulge in stretched, bizarre, or sophistical arguments – with one striking exception I shall note shortly.

Read closely, however, the Levin memo makes only minimum cosmetic changes to the bits of the Bybee memo that drew the worst publicity. Levin does not point out the weaknesses in Bybee's criminal-defense arguments; he simply never discusses possible defenses to criminal charges of torture.[67] The memo likewise ducks the presidential-power question rather than changing Bybee's answer. And, although Levin explicitly contradicts Bybee's conclusion that pain must be excruciating to be severe, every one of the memo's illustrations of "severe pain" is, in fact, excruciating: "severe beatings to the genitals, head, and other parts of the body with metal pipes, brass knuckles, batons, a baseball bat, and various other items; removal of teeth with pliers ... cutting off ... fingers, pulling out ... fingernails" and similar atrocities.[68] These barbaric illustrations are the only operational guidance Levin has to offer on how to tell when pain is "severe," and they obviously suggest that milder techniques are not torture. While Levin's legal reasoning marks a return to normalcy, the opinion provides ample cover for interrogators who "merely" waterboard detainees or deprive them of sleep for weeks. Indeed, Levin specifically states that he has "reviewed this Office's prior opinions addressing issues involving treatment of detainees and do[es] not believe that any of their conclusions would be different under the standards set forth in this memorandum."[69] This includes another, still secret, August 2002 OLC opinion on specific interrogation techniques used by the CIA, believed to include waterboarding.[70]

---

[66] It is reproduced in Greenberg, *The Torture Debate*, p. 361.

[67] *Ibid.*, p. 376. He does say that "there is no exception under the statute permitting torture to be used for a 'good reason.'" This might be read to suggest that the defenses of necessity and self-defense are unavailable, but the context suggests otherwise.

[68] *Ibid.*, p. 369.   [69] *Ibid.*, p. 362, n.8.

[70] See Opening Statement of Senator Carl Levin at the Personnel Subcommittee Hearing on Military Commissions, Detainees and Interrogation Procedures, July 14, 2005 (www.levin. senate.gov/newsroom/press/release/?id=df0f205c-2a00-40ff-a8a4-e0a3908e1d08) (referring to a second, still secret, Bybee memo). Bush administration officials also stated that

Indeed, at one point the Levin memo indulges in the kind of frivolous statutory interpretation that was the hallmark of the Bybee memo it replaced – and that is a carefully crafted paragraph that reads a nonexistent word into the torture statute which would render it inapplicable to waterboarding.[71] Recall that the torture statutes define torture to include both severe physical pain and severe physical suffering. Waterboarding, by duplicating the experiences of drowning, would presumably fall under the "suffering" prong of this definition rather than the "pain" prong. And the suffering must indeed be severe: according to CIA sources, Khalid Sheikh Mohammed (KSM), the architect of 9/11, "won the admiration of interrogators when he was able to last between two and two-and-a-half minutes before begging to confess"; CIA agents who underwent waterboarding all broke in less than fifteen seconds.[72]

Enter the Levin memo, which concludes that "to constitute torture, 'severe physical suffering' would have to be a condition of some extended duration or persistence as well as intensity."[73] That would exclude any technique that breaks victims in a matter of seconds or minutes, such as waterboarding. But in fact, the torture statute contains no mention whatever of "extended duration or persistence." This is especially striking because the statute does state that *mental* pain and suffering must be "prolonged" to count as torture – but it never says that physical pain or suffering must be prolonged. The authors of the Levin memo simply made up the duration requirement out of whole cloth.

The Beaver memo

Next consider the memorandum written for the Defense Department by Lieutenant Colonel Diane Beaver (a JAG legal adviser at Guantánamo), on the legality of specific interrogation techniques. Like the Bybee memo, Beaver's was written to respond to a specific request by interrogators who were having a

Michael Chertoff, then head of the Justice Department's Criminal Division, consulted on the second Bybee memo, which permitted waterboarding. David Johnston, Neil Lewis, and Douglas Jehl, "Security Nominee Gave Advice to the C.I.A. on Torture Laws," *New York Times*, Jan. 29, 2005 (www.nytimes.com/2005/01/29/politics/29home.html?page-wan-ted=1&ei=5090&en=8b261a9df1338e4a&ex=1264741200&partner=rssuserland).

[71] I am grateful to Marty Lederman for pointing out the connection between this portion of the Levin memo and waterboarding. See Lederman, "Yes, It's a No-Brainer: Waterboarding Is Torture," *Balkinization*, Oct. 28, 2006 (http://balkin.blogspot.com/2006/10/yes-its-no-brainer-waterboarding-is.html).

[72] Brian Ross and Richard Esposito, "CIA's Harsh Interrogation Techniques Described," *ABC News*, Nov. 18, 2005 (http://abcnews.go.com/WNT/Investigation/story?id=1322866&page=1). On the treatment of KSM, see James Risen, *State of War: The Secret History of the CIA and the Bush Administration* (New York: Simon & Schuster, 2006), pp. 32–3. Risen asserts that CIA agents inflicted hundreds of abuses each week on KSM, and quotes one source who said that it was the accumulation of so many abuses that made the interrogation program torture.

[73] Greenberg, *The Torture Debate*, p. 371.

hard time "breaking" a high-value Al Qaeda detainee; it was then forwarded to the Pentagon. In this case, the detainee was Mohammed Al-Qahtani (or Kahtani), one of the "twentieth hijackers" who tried but failed to participate in 9/11. Qahtani was detained at Guantánamo, and in 2002 a series of requests went from Guantánamo to Washington for approval of harsh interrogation techniques.[74] Eventually, Qahtani was subjected to a wide variety of sexual humiliations, intensive sleep deprivation (20-hour-a-day interrogations for 48 out of 54 days, interrupted only when Qahtani's pulse-rate plummeted), and months of isolation. He was shot up with three-and-a-half bags of intravenous fluid and forced to urinate on himself; leashed and made to do dog tricks; threatened with working dogs (a technique specifically approved by Defense Secretary Donald Rumsfeld, who closely followed the interrogation of Qahtani[75]); straddled by a female interrogator who taunted him about the deaths of other Al Qaeda members; made to wear a thong on his head and a bra; stripped naked in front of women; and bombarded with ear-splitting "futility music" (the Army's term) by Metallica and Britney Spears.[76] A subsequent US Army report concluded that none of these techniques are "inhumane."[77] (Nor is "futility music" the most bizarre Guantánamo tactic: FBI agents have reported seeing interrogators force detainees to watch homosexual porn movies.[78])

Some of these techniques, including the dog threats, leading detainees around on a leash, placing women's underwear on detainees' heads, and forced nudity, migrated to Abu Ghraib, where soldiers memorialized them in photos that soon became notorious throughout the world. In General Randall Schmidt's words, "Just for the lack of a camera, it would sure look like Abu Ghraib."[79] Compelling evidence suggests that the migration resulted when the Guantánamo commander, General Geoffrey Miller, was sent to Iraq to

[74] Greenberg and Dratel, *Torture Papers*, pp. 223–8.

[75] Michael Scherer and Mark Benjamin, "What Rumsfeld Knew," *Salon.com*, Apr. 14, 2006 (www.salon.com/news/feature/2006/04/14/rummy/index_np.html). This article is based on an Army inspector-general's report Salon obtained through the Freedom of Information Act.

[76] These techniques (and the Army's judgment that they were approved) are described in the Army's own report, the so-called Schmidt report, note 21 above. Most of this report remains classified, but a 30-page summary has been released and is available online (www.defense.gov/news/jul2005/d20050714report.pdf). See also Adam Zagorin et al., "Inside the Interrogation of Detainee 063" and "Excerpts from an Interrogation Log," both in *Time Magazine*, June 20, 2005. The forced urination is described in the latter articles but not in the Schmidt report.

[77] Schmidt report, note 21 above.

[78] See documents obtained under the Freedom of Information Act by the American Civil Liberties Union (ACLU) (www.aclu.org/human-rights/new-documents-provide-further-evidence-senior-officials-approved-abuse-prisoners-guanta).

[79] Quoted in Scherer and Benjamin, "What Rumsfeld Knew."

"Gitmoize" intelligence operations there (although Miller denies it).[80] If so, the implications are enormous: it would mean that Abu Ghraib does not represent merely the spontaneous crimes of low-level sadists, but rather the unauthorized spillover of techniques deliberately exported from Guantánamo to Iraq as a high-level policy decision.[81] That would imply a direct causal pathway connecting the advice of the torture lawyers to the Abu Ghraib abuses via General Miller. (A former State Department official traces the policy back to Cheney's then general counsel David Addington.[82])

Beaver labeled her memorandum a "legal brief" on counterresistance strategies, and a brief rather than an impartial legal analysis is indeed what she wrote. Beaver rightly observes that interrogations must meet US constitutional standards under the Eighth Amendment. To identify these standards, she analyzes the 1992 Supreme Court decision *Hudson* v. *McMillian*.[83] *Hudson* addressed the question whether mistreatment of prisoners must cause serious injury to violate the constitutional prohibition on cruel and unusual punishment, and its answer was no: even minor injuries can violate the Eighth Amendment if guards inflict them for no good reason. (A good reason would consist of subduing a violent inmate.) Beaver's analysis of the case virtually flips it upside down, and the message she draws from *Hudson* is that mistreatment is unconstitutional only if there is no "good faith legitimate governmental interest" at stake and the interrogator acted "maliciously or sadistically for the very purpose of causing harm."[84] Obviously, any interro-

---

[80] Janice Karpinski, the commander of the military police unit implicated in the Abu Ghraib abuses, claims that General Miller told her his job was to "GTMO-ize" or "Gitmoize" Abu Ghraib; Miller denies he ever used that phrase. Mark Benjamin, "Not So Fast, General," *Salon. com*, Mar. 7, 2006 (www.salon.com/news/feature/2006/03/07/major_general/index_np.html). However, the mandate Miller received from Rumsfeld was to replicate his Gitmo intelligence successes in Iraq. John Barry *et al.*, "The Roots of Torture," *Newsweek*, May 24, 2004; see also Josh White, "Army General Advocated Using Dogs at Abu Ghraib, Officer Testifies," *Washington Post*, July 28, 2005, p. A18 (testimony by top military police operations officer at Abu Ghraib that Miller "was sent over by the secretary of defense to take their interrogation techniques they used at Guantánamo Bay and incorporate them into Iraq"). The Fay–Jones Report on Abu Ghraib likewise concludes that it is possible that interrogation techniques had migrated from Guantánamo to Abu Ghraib. Greenberg and Dratel, *Torture Papers*, p. 1004. And Donald Rumsfeld briefed Miller on the Department of Defense's working group report on interrogation techniques. Mayer, "Annals of Pentagon" (note 42 above). According to one released detainee, inmates received the worst treatment during Miller's command at Guantánamo. Jackie Northam, "Leaving Guantánamo: Enduring a Harsh Stay," National Public Radio, *All Things Considered*, May 22, 2006.

[81] For analysis along these lines, see Mark Danner, *Torture and Truth: America, Abu Ghraib and the War on Terror* (New York Review of Books, 2004).

[82] "Former Powell Aide Links Cheney's Office to Abuse Directives," *International Herald-Tribune*, Nov. 3, 2005.

[83] 503 U.S. 1 (1992).   [84] Greenberg and Dratel, *Torture Papers*, p. 232.

gation technique, no matter how brutal, passes this test if the interrogator's sole purpose is to extract intelligence. Beaver inverted a Supreme Court decision designed to broaden the protections of prisoners and read it to narrow them dramatically.

And indeed, Beaver proceeded to legitimize every proposed technique, including "the use of a wet towel to induce the misperception of suffocation" – a version of waterboarding. Oddly, Beaver adds that "The use of physical contact with the detainee ... will technically constitute an assault," but immediately goes on to "recommend that the proposed methods of interrogation be approved."[85] In other words, her memo on the legality of interrogation techniques concludes by recommending government approval of a felony.

The draft Article 49 opinion

After Jay Bybee's departure, Jack Goldsmith, a distinguished University of Chicago law professor (now a Harvard law professor), took over the leadership of the OLC. Goldsmith took several courageous stands against administration hard-liners, stands for which he reportedly had to withstand the fury of David Addington, Cheney's volcanic general counsel, regarded by many as the hardest of hard-liners.[86] As early as December 2003, before the Abu Ghraib scandal and the leak of the Bybee memo, Goldsmith advised the government not to rely on a March 2003 memo by John Yoo that had directly influenced the Defense Department's working group on interrogation.[87] And it was under Goldsmith's leadership that the OLC repudiated the Bybee memo. Some regard Goldsmith as an unsung hero in the torture debates.

Nevertheless, Goldsmith too drafted a memorandum that exemplifies the kind of loophole legalism I object to in the other memoranda. (Let me emphasize, however, that Goldsmith's draft was never given final approval, and that could indicate that Goldsmith thought better of it.) Written in March 2004, it concerned the question of whether detainees in Iraq could be temporarily sent out of the country for interrogation, despite plain language in Article 49 of the Fourth Geneva Convention stating:

---

[85] *Ibid.*, p. 235.

[86] Daniel Kleidman, Stuart Taylor, Jr., and Evan Thomas, "Palace Revolt," *Newsweek*, Feb. 6, 2006. On David Addington's role, see Ragavan, "Cheney's Guy," and Mayer, "The Hidden Power," both in note 41 above.

[87] In February 2005, the OLC formally retracted this latter Yoo memo (OLC letter from Daniel Levin to William J. Haynes II, Feb. 4, 2005, regarding the Yoo memo of Mar. 14, 2003). The March 14, 2003 Yoo memo and Levin's letter were released by the Obama administration in 2009.

Individual or mass forcible transfers, as well as deportations of protected
persons from occupied territory to the territory of the Occupying Power
or to that of any other country, occupied or not, are prohibited, regardless
of their motive.[88]

Goldsmith divided the memo into two sections, one on whether Article 49
would prevent US authorities from deporting illegal aliens in Iraq "pursuant to
local immigration law," and one on whether removing protected civilians from
Iraq for interrogation violates Article 49.

In answer to the first question, Goldsmith contends that the drafters of
Article 49 could not have meant to ban the removal of illegal aliens under an
occupied state's immigration law. That conclusion sounds uncontroversial.
But we should not forget that during World War II, the removal of illegal
aliens under an occupied state's immigration law included deporting stateless
Jewish refugees from Vichy France to death camps in the East. The Vichy
government and the German occupation authorities made a point of beginning with stateless Jews, in order to fit the deportations under the rubrics of
immigration law.[89] It is a little hard to believe that the drafters of Article
49 were oblivious of the Nazis' studied policy of using immigration law to
facilitate the deportation of Jews to Auschwitz.[90] In this matter, a little

[88] The *Washington Post* reports that Goldsmith had written an opinion five months earlier
concluding that a ghost detainee named Rashul could not be removed from Iraq. By that
time the CIA had already spirited Rashul away to Afghanistan, and after Goldsmith's
opinion they quickly returned him to Iraq. According to an intelligence source, "That
case started the CIA yammering to Justice to get a better memo." Dana Priest, "Memo
Lets CIA Take Detainees Out of Iraq," *Washington Post*, Oct. 24, 2004, pp. A1, A21.
However, Professor Goldsmith has informed me that this account is seriously defective:
there was no previous memo on the topic, and he did not give in to any pressure. (Private
e-mail communications, Aug. 27 and 29, 2006.) The CIA's deputy inspector general "told
others she was offended that the CIA's general counsel had worked to secure a secret
Justice Department opinion in 2004 authorizing the agency's creation of 'ghost detainees' – prisoners removed from Iraq for secret interrogations without notice to the
International Committee of the Red Cross – because the Geneva Conventions prohibit
such practices." R. Jeffrey Smith, "Fired Officer Believed CIA Lied to Congress," *Washington Post*, May 14, 2006. Priest's article states that even though the draft was never
released, the CIA relied on it to remove a dozen Iraqis from the country. However, other
sources assert that the dozen detainees were not Iraqis. Douglas Jehl, "The Conflict in
Iraq: Prisoners; U.S. Action Bars Rights of Some Captured in Iraq," *New York Times*,
Oct. 26, 2004.
[89] This was the accord between Vichy and the Nazis of July 4, 1942, described in Michael R.
Marrus and Robert O. Paxton, *Vichy France and the Jews* (New York: Basic Books, 1981),
p. 249.
[90] Indeed, embedded in a footnote, Goldsmith quotes a Norwegian delegate "regarding the
plight of 'ex-German Jews denationalized by the German Government who found
themselves in territories subsequently occupied by the German Army.'" Greenberg and
Dratel, *Torture Papers*, p. 376, n.11. The trouble is that Goldsmith's sole point in
including this quotation is to buttress his argument that deportation implies

historical sense would perhaps have given some moral clarity to the role of the OLC in approving the removal of "illegal aliens" from Iraq. Goldsmith's argument would have legalized the deportation of Anne Frank.

For that matter, Goldsmith never questions whether forcible removal by US forces of foreign captives taken in Iraq actually *does* accord with Iraqi immigration law. It does not sound terribly likely, unless some conscientious American lawyer hastily rewrote Iraqi immigration law. Without the unarticulated premise that the US interest in Article 49 is nothing more than learning its implications for immigration enforcement, this portion of the memo has no point – unless, perhaps, "enforcement of immigration law" is the legal hook on which rendition of foreign insurgents hangs.

Goldsmith then turns to the question of whether Article 49 forbids sending Iraqi captives outside the country for interrogation, to which his answer is no. First he argues that "transfer" and "deportation" both imply permanent or at least long-term uprooting, not temporary removal for interrogation. To show this, he quotes authorities who indicate that uprooting and resettling people violates Article 49.[91] However, none of his sources suggest that resettlements are the only forcible transfers or deportations that violate Article 49, and so this argument by itself amounts to very little.

To show that Article 49 permits temporary transfers, Goldsmith argues that reading Article 49 to forbid all forcible transfers is inconsistent with Article 24, which says that occupiers must facilitate the reception of youthful war orphans in a neutral state.[92] If Article 24 permits occupiers to evacuate war orphans, he reasons, then Article 49 cannot possibly mean to forbid *all* forcible transfers, such as sending Iraqi nationals to Afghanistan for interrogation.

Unsurprisingly, no commentator before Goldsmith ever noticed an "inconsistency" between the duty to evacuate war orphans and the obligation not to deport or forcibly transfer captives. No one would reasonably describe parents sending their child to safety as a "forcible transfer" or "deportation." Nor, therefore, is it a forcible transfer or deportation when a child is moved out of harm's way by responsible adults acting *in loco parentis*. The authorities acting *in loco parentis*, not the child, are the responsible decision-makers, so long as they are aiming at the child's well-being. Goldsmith's analogy between captives sent to be interrogated and children sent to safety boggles the mind – and that analogy is the sole basis of his argument that if Geneva does not forbid the latter it does not forbid the former. Like the Bybee memo's organ-failure definition of "severe pain," this is legal formalism divorced from sense.

denationalization. He overlooks the more important point: the horrific history of using immigration law as a fig leaf for something far more sinister.

[91] *Ibid.*, p. 376.   [92] *Ibid.*, pp. 376–7.

A second argument dispenses more senseless formalism. Goldsmith turns to two other Geneva articles, one protecting impressed laborers and the other protecting people detained for crimes. Among their protections, both articles prohibit such people from being sent abroad. According to Goldsmith, if Article 49 really meant to forbid any and all temporary removals out of state, these two articles would become redundant, and therefore "meaningless and inoperative."[93]

The short response is: no, they would not. The two articles say, in effect, that Article 49's protection against forcible removal applies even to persons detained for a crime or lawfully impressed into labor. The articles ward off potential misreadings of Article 49 that find implied exceptions to it for impressed laborers or accused criminals. In that way, the two articles strengthen and clarify Article 49 – and, unsurprisingly, that is precisely how the Red Cross's official commentary to the Geneva Conventions explains the relationship among the three articles.[94]

Goldsmith rejects the commentary's explanation because Article 49 must not be read to make the other articles superfluous.[95] Evidently, he believes that the antiredundancy canon articulated in a 1933 US Supreme Court opinion trumps all other rules of treaty interpretation. However, the canons of treaty interpretation explicitly recognized in the international law of treaties empha- size "good faith [interpretation] in accordance with the ordinary meaning to be given to the terms of the treaty in their context and in the light of its object and purpose"[96] – the very form of interpretation so conspicuously absent from Goldsmith's memo. The antiredundancy canon he relies on appears nowhere in the Vienna Convention, not even its article on supplementary means of interpretation.

Finally, Goldsmith observes that a separate clause of Article 49 forbids occupying powers from deporting or transferring its own civilians *into* occupied territory. Presumably (he argues), that prohibition does not prevent the occupier from bringing civilian contractors or NGOs in for the short term. Hence, in this latter clause, the words "transfer" and "deport" do not encompass short-term transfers and deportations. Thus, these words do not

---

[93] *Ibid.*, pp. 378–9. According to Article 51, impressed laborers can be compelled to work "only in the occupied territory where the persons whose services have been requisitioned are," and Article 76 requires that people accused or convicted of offenses can be detained only in the occupied country.

[94] Jean S. Pictet, *Commentary on the Geneva Conventions of 12 August 1949* (Geneva: ICRC, 1958), vol. IV, pp. 279, 298, 363.

[95] He rejects the commentary's construction in Greenberg and Dratel, *Torture Papers*, p. 379, n.13.

[96] Vienna Convention on the Law of Treaties, Articles 31 and 32. Although the United States is not a party to the Vienna Convention, it accepts its sections on treaty interpret- ation as customary international law. Restatement (Third) of the Foreign Relations Law of the United States, § 325.

encompass short-term transfers of persons out of the country either, because "there is a strong presumption that the same words will bear the same meaning throughout the same treaty."[97]

Perhaps so, although the only legal authority Goldsmith cites for this "strong presumption" is a US Supreme Court dictum saying something different.[98] In opinions Goldsmith does not cite, the court recognizes that in the interpretation of federal statutes, the same-words-same-meaning "presumption ... is not rigid and readily yields" to good reasons for distinguishing meanings in different contexts.[99] But even if there were a rigid same-words-same-meaning presumption, it hardly follows that words with the same meaning coincide in every respect. If a building code specifies safety requirements for "the cellar of a house" in one paragraph, obviously in that paragraph the word "house" refers only to houses with cellars. But it would be absurd to suppose that in other clauses of the code, dealing with other issues, the word "house" likewise refers only to houses with cellars. The word's core meaning covers both houses with cellars and houses with none. In precisely the same way, the fact that in one paragraph of the Fourth Geneva Convention the word "transfer" can refer only to long-term transfers implies nothing about its referent in a very different context. The word's core meaning – moving people from one place to another – covers both long-term and short-term transfers. Tellingly, Goldsmith fails to mention the Red Cross Commentary's observation that in the paragraph prohibiting occupiers from transferring or deporting their own civilians into occupied territory "the meaning of the words 'transfer' and 'deport' is rather different from that in which they are used in the other paragraphs of Article 49."[100]

I describe these admittedly arcane details of Goldsmith's memo because I have heard scholars who despise the Bybee memo hold up Goldsmith's as the gold standard of what a pro-administration OLC memo ought to look like. It is no such thing. Like the Bybee memo, it reaches a preordained conclusion by kabbalistic textual manipulations. The basic recipe in both memos is the same: lean heavily on "structural" canons of construction, take unrelated bits

---

[97] Greenberg and Dratel, *Torture Papers*, p. 377.

[98] *Air France* v. *Saks*, 470 U.S. 392, 398 (1985). In the passage Goldsmith cites, the court says that different words in a treaty presumptively refer to different things. That is the logical converse of Goldsmith's principle, and neither implies the other. For good reason, then, Goldsmith cites this case with a "cf." Presumably, if better authority existed, he would have cited it.

[99] *General Dynamics Land Systems* v. *Cline*, 540 U.S. 581, 595–8 (2004). For an even stronger statement to the same effect, see the unanimous opinion in *Robinson* v. *Shell Oil Co.*, 519 U.S. 337, 343–4 (1997).

[100] Pictet, *Commentary on the Geneva Conventions*, vol. IV, p. 283. Pictet is pointing to the difference between transferring people into a country and transferring people out, but that does not matter, because the point is that the meaning of words (especially nontechnical terms like "transfer") can shift from context to context.

of law having to do with very different problems, read them side by side as though a legislator had intended to link them, and spin out "consequences," "interpretations," and "contradictions." Where Bybee and Yoo interpret "severe" in the torture statute by looking at a Medicare statute, Goldsmith combines a treaty clause dealing with forcible transfer and a different clause dealing with war orphans to generate an imaginary contradiction. Neither memo writer asks the most basic interpretive question: *What is the point of this law?* To ask that question would have been fatal, because the object of both documents is to protect individuals in the clutches of their enemies, and here the captors – the OLC's "client" – wanted to unprotect them. Unmooring a law from its point leaves only the formal techniques of textual manipulation to interpret it.

At one point, however, Goldsmith pushes back against detainee abuse. In a final footnote at the end of his draft, Goldsmith warns that some removals of prisoners might indeed violate Article 49 and constitute war crimes.[101] He also includes a reminder that a prisoner transferred out of Iraq for interrogation does not lose "protected person" benefits. These are important warnings, and they buttress reports of Goldsmith's admirably anodyne role in resisting "the program" (as executive branch officials chillingly refer to their detention, interrogation, and rendition policies).

But then why not say specifically that those benefits include those of Article 31: "No physical or moral coercion shall be exercised against protected persons, in particular to obtain information from them or from third parties"? Is it because a memo that explicitly said, "On the contrary, we believe he would ordinarily retain his Article 31 right against any form of coercive interrogation" would defeat the purpose of removing prisoners from Iraq? Why bury his vague warning in a footnote at the end of the memorandum? Why not quote Article 31 *in the text*, and point out that no form of coercive interrogation is permitted under Geneva IV?

It seems to me that the most charitable interpretation is that Goldsmith was working among hard-liners, and could subvert abusive interrogation only in a subtle and inconspicuous way. That may be the best an OLC lawyer could hope for. (Indeed, perhaps the OLC never adopted his draft memo because even subtle and inconspicuous subversion was more than the OLC's clients could stomach.) But a huge potential for self-deception exists in this strategy. To bury a warning risks its dismissal. And to say, in effect, "You can forcibly remove detainees from Iraq for interrogation, but it is up to you to make sure that the interrogation does not include coercion," comes awfully close to Tom Lehrer's Wernher von Braun ("'Once the rockets are up, who cares where they come down? / That's not my department,' says Wernher von Braun").

---

[101] Greenberg and Dratel, *Torture Papers*, pp. 379–80, n.14.

Cruel, inhuman, or degrading treament

Interrogation techniques such as sexual humiliation do not fall under the legal definition of torture, or under most people's informal understanding of what torture is. They do, however, constitute degrading treatment, one of the three subcategories of the "cruel, inhuman or degrading treatment" banned by the CAT. (Jurists abbreviate the treaty phrase "cruel, inhuman or degrading treatment or punishment which does not amount to torture" by the acronym "CIDT.") So do many other forms of "torture lite." Arguably, the legality of CIDT matters more for US interrogation practices than the torture statutes do.

As we have seen, the torture convention obligates parties to "undertake to prevent" CIDT, but it does not require criminalizing CIDT, and the United States has never made CIDT a crime. To be sure, CIDT violates common Article 3 of the Geneva Conventions, and that made it a US war crime. But, in 2006, the US Congress decriminalized humiliating and degrading treatment of detainees.

The requirement to "undertake to prevent" CIDT nevertheless remains an international legal obligation of the United States; and, while the duties it entails are vague, the obligation surely rules out deliberately engaging in CIDT. However, at his confirmation hearing for Attorney General, Alberto Gonzales offered a startling legal theory about why that obligation does not apply. When the US Senate ratified the torture convention, Gonzales explained, it added the reservation that CIDT means the cruel, inhuman, or degrading treatment forbidden by the Constitution's Eighth Amendment ban on cruel and unusual punishments and Fifth Amendment ban on conduct that shocks the conscience. But the Eighth Amendment applies only to punishment, and the Supreme Court has held, in other unrelated contexts, that the Fifth Amendment does not protect aliens outside US territory. Therefore, in Gonzales's words, "the Department of Justice has concluded that ... there is no legal prohibition under the CAT of cruel, inhuman or degrading treatment with respect to aliens overseas." He reiterated the argument in written responses to senatorial questions.[102]

The argument is startling because it seems obvious that the Senate's reservation intended nothing of the sort. Before Gonzales' argument muddied the waters, it was perfectly clear that the Senate's reservation aimed to define the CAT's concept of CIDT by using the substantive standards embodied in the constitutional rights, not to tie CAT to their jurisdictional reach. After Gonzales' testimony, three Democratic senators wrote an incredulous letter to the Justice Department requesting all legal opinions on the subject within three days.

---

[102] Gonzales's oral response, quoted in a letter to John Ashcroft from Senators Patrick Leahy, Russell Feingold, and Dianne Feinstein, Jan. 25, 2005 (www.scotusblug.com/movabletype/archives/CAT%20Article%2016.Leahy-Feinstein-Feingold%20Letters.pdf). Written response to Senator Richard J. Durbin, question 1. Confirmation Hearing on the Nomination of Alberto R. Gonzales to be Attorney General of the United States, Hearing Before the Senate Committee on the Judiciary, S. Hrg. 109-4 (2005), pp. 191–2.

The department ignored the request until two months later, after Gonzales was safely confirmed as attorney general. Eventually, the department responded in a three-page letter, which refused to release OLC opinions but cited legal authority to back up Gonzales, most prominently some 1990 comments to the Senate by Abraham Sofaer, the State Department's legal adviser during debate over the ratification of the CAT.[103] Like Gonzales, Sofaer had emphasized that "we would limit our obligations under this Convention to the proscriptions already covered in our own Constitution." If constitutional rights against CIDT do not apply to aliens abroad, then the CAT's ban on CIDT cannot apply abroad.

But this was not at all what he or the Senate meant, according to Sofaer. In a letter to Senator Patrick Leahy disavowing the Gonzales interpretation, Sofaer explained that the purpose of the reservation was to ensure that the same standards for CIDT would apply outside the United States as apply inside – just the opposite of Gonzales's conclusion.[104] The point was to define CIDT, not to create a gaping geographical loophole.[105] Apparently, however, the administration desperately wanted the geographical loophole. When Senator John McCain (a Vietnam torture victim) introduced legislation to close the loophole, the administration lobbied against it fiercely, threatening to veto major legislation rather than accede to banning CIDT by US forces abroad. When McCain's law nevertheless swept the Congress with veto-proof majorities, the administration extracted a concession: federal courts could no longer hear Guantánamo cases. CIDT might be illegal, but its Guantánamo victims would no longer have any recourse against it. And, as the final touch, President Bush attached a signing statement to McCain's CIDT ban implying a constitutional right to ignore it.

What is wrong with the torture memos?

Frivolity and indeterminacy

Kingman Brewster, asked what his years as a Harvard law professor had taught him, replied, "That every proposition is arguable."[106]

---

[103] Letter from William Moschella to Patrick Leahy, Apr. 4, 2005, note 102 above p. 3.
[104] Letter from Abraham D. Sofaer to Patrick Leahy, Jan. 21, 2005. PDF in my possession. Sofaer reiterated his views in an editorial a few months later: Sofaer, "No Exceptions," *Wall Street Journal*, Nov. 26, 2005, p. A11.
[105] It appears that the reservation was partly a response to the fact that some states declare corporal punishment to be CIDT, while the United States does not. It may also have been a response to a controversial European Court of Human Rights decision that had declared prolonged imprisonment in a US death row to be cruel and degrading. David P. Stewart, "The Torture Convention and the Reception of International Criminal Law Within the United States," *Nova Law Review*, 15 (1991), 449, 461–2.
[106] Alex Beam, "Greed on Trial," in Deborah L. Rhode and David Luban, Eds., *Legal Ethics: Law Stories* (New York: Foundation Press, 2005), pp. 287–302, at p. 291.

But not every proposition is arguable well, and not every argument is a good one. Law recognizes a category of frivolous arguments and positions, and it should. My claim is that arguments like the "organ-failure" definition of torture, Beaver's reading of *Hudson* v. *McMillian*, and Goldsmith's "contradiction" between Geneva's articles about war orphans and deportation are not just wrong but frivolous.

What makes an argument frivolous? Let me approach this question through what is, I hope, a straightforward example (unrelated to the torture memos), drawn from a 1989 case. Sue Vaccaro, a slightly built woman, attempted to use the first-class lavatory while traveling coach class with her husband on a cross-country flight. John Wellington Stephens, a large male first-class passenger, assaulted her. Stephens called her a "chink slut and a whore," told her she was too dirty to use the first-class washroom, and shoved her against a bulkhead. Vaccaro sued Stephens, and he counterclaimed, asserting that his ticket gave him a license to the first-class lavatory, and Vaccaro had trespassed on it. This harmed him, his counsel argued, because the donnybrook spoiled Stephens' flight. The judge punished his law firm for frivolous argument, and it may be hard to find a lawyer outside the firm who would disagree. The court of appeals wrote:

> To engage in a temper tantrum is not to suffer actual damage at the hands of a trespasser... The federal district court is a very hospitable court but it is not yet hospitable to entertaining law suits against people who have the misfortune to engage in argument with irascible first class passengers... The idea that if you sat in the wrong seat at a symphony, a play, a baseball game or a football game and did not get out instantly when the proper ticket holder appeared you could be sued in a federal court is not an attractive notion. It is not merely unattractive. It takes no account of the state of the law... Rule 11 is not meant to discourage creative lawyering. It is meant to discourage pettifoggery. The state of the law, whether it is evolving or fixed in well-nigh permanent form, is important in making the distinction between the plausible and the silly.[107]

No formula or algorithm exists for sorting out the plausible-but-wrong arguments from the silly, any more than an algorithm can distinguish jokes that are almost funny from jokes that are not funny at all. But a theory of frivolity is unnecessary. As the philosopher Sidney Morgenbesser once wrote, to explain why a man slipped on a banana peel you do not need a general theory of slipping.[108] Legal plausibility is a matter for case-by-case judgment by the interpretive community, and the judgment will be grounded in specific

---

[107] *Vaccaro* v. *Stephens*, 1989 U.S. App. LEXIS 5864; 14 Fed. R. Serv. 3d (Callaghan) 60, *9–12 (9th Cir. 1989).

[108] Sidney Morgenbesser, "Scientific Explanation," in David Sills, Ed., *International Encyclopedia of the Social Sciences* (New York: Free Press, 1968), vol. XIV, p, 122.

arguments like those the court of appeals offered in *Vaccaro* v. *Stephens* and – more to the point – those I have offered here about the "analyses" contained in the torture memos.

Picture a bell curve representing the number of trained lawyers who find any given legal argument plausible. Some arguments are so recognizably mainstream that virtually all lawyers would agree that they are plausible. Those arguments lie under the fat part of the bell curve. Calling an argument plausible does not mean accepting it: readers of judicial opinions often find both the majority and the dissenting arguments plausible, and situate both within the fat part of the bell curve.

Moving further out on the bell curve, we find the kind of arguments that lawyers euphemistically call "creative" (or where one might say, "Nice try!"). Litigators resort to creative arguments when unfavorable law leaves them no better option than the brief-writer's equivalent of a Hail Mary pass. The argument is too much of a stretch to be genuinely credible, but it offers a novel way to think about the law, and someday the interpretive community might get there. At the moment, though, it lies outside the fat part of the bell curve, although not far out on the arms.

Frivolous arguments, on the other hand, *are* far out. Superficially, they make lawyer-like "moves," but they take such broad liberties with legal text, policy, and sense that only someone far removed from the mainstream would take them seriously. In the definition of federal judge Frank Easterbrook, "99 of 100 practicing lawyers would be 99% sure that the position is untenable, and the other 1% would be 60% sure it's untenable."[109] Easterbrook's numbers may be too high, and in any case the numerical imagery is only a figure of speech, because nobody is actually out there surveying lawyers.[110]

---

[109] Quoted in Sanford Levinson, "Frivolous Cases: Do Lawyers Really Know Anything at All?", *Osgoode Hall Law Review*, 24 (1987), 353–78, at 375.

[110] Tax lawyers have long familiarity with numerical imagery to determine when a tax preparer can take an aggressive position without disclosing it. According to federal regulations, the preparer cannot do so unless "the position has approximately a one in three, or greater, likelihood of being sustained on its merits." 10 C.F.R. § 10.34(d)(1). This regulation derives from a 1985 American Bar Association (ABA) ethics opinion replacing an earlier opinion according to which tax lawyers could take any position for which a reasonable basis could be found. "Doubtless there were some tax practitioners who intended 'reasonable basis' to set a relatively high standard of tax reporting. Some have continued to apply such a standard. To more, however, if not most tax practitioners, the ethical standard set by 'reasonable basis' had become a low one. To many it had come to permit any colorable claim to be put forth; to permit almost any words that could be strung together to be used to support a tax return position. Such a standard has now been rejected by the ABA Committee... A position having only a 5% or 10% likelihood of success, if litigated, should not meet the new standard. A position having a likelihood of success closely approaching one-third should meet the standard." *Report of the Special Task Force on Formal Opinion 85–352, 39 Tax Law.* 635 (1986). Because of the infrequency of tax audits, tax preparation is perhaps the paradigm case where the

But the idea should be clear: the legal mainstream defines the concept of plausibility.

It might be objected that legal arguments should be judged on their merits, not on how mainstream lawyers might vote about their merits. Judging arguments by their popularity seems like a category mistake.

That may be true in fields where truths are obscure and only the deep thinkers can discern them. But law is different. Law is not written for geniuses, and it is not written by geniuses. Legal texts are instruments of governance, and as such they must be as obvious and demotic as possible, capable of daily use by millions of people with no time or taste for riddles. Even when great judges with subtle, Promethean minds write opinions, their opinions had better contain no secret teachings, no buried allusions, no symbolism, no allegory, no thematic subtleties that need Harold Bloom or Leo Strauss to tease them out. Richard Posner once described legal texts as "essentially mediocre."[111] Both words are precisely right; but Posner forgot to add that when it comes to law, "essentially mediocre" is a compliment. Within a rule-of-law regime, rules must offer clear-cut guidance to average intelligences, and that makes essential mediocrity virtually a defining characteristic of law. Law does its job properly when it is all surface and no depth and what you see is exactly what you get.[112] That is why it makes no sense to suppose that the

system depends on the honor of lawyers to give advice based on legal positions that are not frivolous. There are significant parallels between the tax adviser's role and the role of the equally unaccountable OLC.

[111] Richard A. Posner, *Overcoming Law* (Cambridge, MA: Harvard University Press, 1995), p. 91.

[112] Legal theorists might balk at this claim, pointing to the phenomenon of "acoustic separation" between the rules of conduct known by the hoi polloi and the more intricate rules of decision employed by officials. Meir Dan-Cohen, who introduced the concept of acoustic separation, pointed out that broad knowledge of available criminal defenses (for example, duress or necessity) would create perverse incentives for people to abuse those defenses. Hence it is better to keep decision rules and conduct rules acoustically separated, meaning that primary actors should not necessarily become aware of the more lenient decision rules officials actually use. Acoustic separation, with selective transmission of the law to different audiences, might actually be a useful strategy for lawmakers to adopt. Meir Dan-Cohen, "Decision Rules and Conduct Rules: On Acoustic Separation in Criminal Law," *Harvard Law Review*, 97 (1984), 625–77. The concept of acoustic separation is an interesting and useful one. In my opinion, however, legal theorists invoke the concept of acoustic separation more often than it warrants. Descriptively, the phenomenon of law intentionally tailored for acoustic separation seems like a marginal part of the legal enterprise. Normatively, there is real danger behind the idea that some law is too dangerous for ordinary mortals to know and should be left to the experts. It presupposes the superior rectitude of experts, and therefore it underrates the perverse incentives for experts to shield their own abuses from accountability. Dan-Cohen, I should add, does not make this mistake: for him, "the option of selective transmission is not an attractive one, and the sight of law tainted by duplicity and concealment is not pretty" (p. 673). Furthermore: by suggesting that society might be

plausibility of legal arguments could deviate systematically from what the interpretive community thinks about their plausibility. What could it deviate to? In law, by design, there is no hidden there there.[113]

Although the interpretive community defines the bounds of the reasonable, there remains plenty of room for interpretive disagreement within those bounds.[114] Law, we must remember, emerges from political processes, and it typically represents the compromise, or vector sum, of competing social forces.

better off if people do not know the law too well, the doctrine of acoustic separation rationalizes a system where legal services are unaffordable by tens of millions of people, and only the wealthy can buy their way around acoustic separation.

[113] The thesis I am defending is that there are no truths about what law means or requires outside the range of views that the interpretive community finds plausible. This is a weak thesis, grounded in the specific functions of law, not a general metaphysical claim that interpretive communities constitute the meaning of the objects they concern themselves with. The latter is the view of relativists like Stanley Fish, "Anti-Professionalism," *Cardozo Law Review*, 7 (1986), 645ff. I have criticized his view in *"Fish* v. *Fish* or, Some Realism About Idealism," *Cardozo Law Review*, 7 (1986), 693ff., on two grounds: first, that interpretive communities could play the role Fish ascribes to them only if they meet internal political conditions of reciprocity and freedom; and second, that the vaporous concept of "constituting" meaning buys into a metaphysical contrast between idealism and realism that we would do well to abandon.

In the present chapter, I am fishing in shallower waters. Regardless of who is right about realist, idealist, and pragmatist conceptions of inquiry and truth *in general*, it seems to me we should all agree that law contains no truths hidden from the citizens it governs and the lawyers who help them understand it.

[114] To be sure, Ronald Dworkin has argued that legal questions have a single, unique right answer – namely, that answer that displays the sources of law in the morally best light. Determining which answer that is may be something that only Judge Hercules (Dworkin's hypothetical über-jurist) can do. Ronald Dworkin, *Law's Empire* (Cambridge, MA: Harvard University Press, 1986), pp. 52–3; Dworkin, "'Natural' Law Revisited," *University of Florida Law Review*, 34 (1982), 165–88, at 169–70; Ronald Dworkin, "Hard Cases," in *Taking Rights Seriously* (Cambridge, MA: Harvard University Press, 1978), pp. 81, 105–23; Dworkin, "No Right Answer?", in P. M. S. Hacker and J. Raz, Eds., *Law, Morality and Society: Essays in Honour of H. L. A. Hart* (Oxford University Press, 1977), pp. 58–84. However, given the lack of a decision procedure or verification procedure about which people with conflicting good-faith moral views can agree (to say nothing of the unreality of Judge Hercules), it is hard to see why a Dworkinian "right answer" is anything more than a *Ding an sich*, an "as-if," that anchors a theory of objectivity without serving the basic function of law – namely, governing a community. I discuss some of the perplexities raised by the possibility of a right answer that lacks a verification procedure in Luban, "The Coiled Serpent of Authority: Reason, Authority, and Law in a Talmudic Tale," *Chicago-Kent Law Review*, 79 (2004), 1253–88.

Lacking a decision procedure does not doom us to radical indeterminacy in which anything goes. Even if we cannot settle which of several competing answers is right, we can rule out answers that are obviously wrong. To illustrate with Fred Schauer's example, "That I am unsure whether rafts and floating motorized automobiles are 'boats' does not dispel my confidence that rowboats and dories most clearly are boats, and that steam locomotives, hamburgers, and elephants equally clearly are not." Frederick Schauer, "Easy Cases," *Southern California Law Review*, 58 (1985), 399–440, at 422.

Compromise whittles down sharp edges, and legal standards without sharp edges are bound to generate interpretive disagreements. It is worth taking a moment to see why.

Some ambiguity in law results because drafters finessed a ticklish political issue with strategic, diplomatic doublespeak. To take a famous and blatant example, the UN Security Council helped end the Six Days War with a resolution issued in two official languages, English and French. The French version requires the Israelis to withdraw from all the occupied territory, while the English requires them to withdraw only from some.[115] The reason for splitting the difference is obvious: it stopped the shooting and postponed the hardest question to another day. (Unsurprisingly, for forty years Israelis have cited the English version and Arabs the French.) Likewise, US Congressional staffers admit that ambiguity in statutes often results because "we know that if we answer a certain question, we will lose one side or the other."[116]

Although strategic ambiguity is the most obvious way that politics creates legal indeterminacy, it is not the only way. Other ambiguities enter through legislative log-rolling and mutual concessions. Political give-and-take generates statutes that qualify or soften requirements, attach escape clauses to bright-line rules, or balance clauses favoring one contending interest group with clauses favoring others. None of these provisions need be unclear in itself, but taken together they generate multiple interpretive possibilities. That is because jurists interpret statutory language in the light of its purpose, and when the statute itself reflects cross-purposes, its requirements can be viewed differently depending on which purpose the interpreter deems most vital. An interpreter who views the escape clauses and qualifications as important expressions of legislative purpose will stretch them to borderline or doubtful cases; another who views the unqualified rules as the key will interpret those rules strictly and find very few exceptions. Needless to say, judges' moral and political outlooks influence their understanding of legislative purpose: it is easier to grasp purposes you agree with than purposes you do not. Every political fault line in a legal text automatically becomes an interpretive fault line as well.

Even judicially created doctrines reflect the push and pull of many outlooks. A court creates a legal doctrine that neatly resolves the case before it. Later, another court faces a case in which applying that doctrine would yield an

---

[115] UN Security Council Resolution 242 (1967). The English version calls for "withdrawal of Israeli forces from territories occupied in the recent conflict" ("territories," not "the territories," where "the" was dropped as the result of a US amendment to the British-proposed text), while the French version calls for "retrait des forces armées israéliennes des territoires occupés lors du récent conflit."

[116] Quoted in Victoria F. Nourse and Jane S. Schacter, "The Politics of Legislative Drafting: A Congressional Case Study," *New York University Law Review*, 77 (2002), 575–623, at 596. On the deliberate use of ambiguity, see pp. 594–7, 614–19.

obviously wrong outcome; so the court carves out an exception and identifies a counterprinciple governing the exception. Subsequent courts decide whether the principle or counterprinciple applies to a new case by judging whether the facts of the new case more closely resemble those of the original case or the exception – and, typically, some facts in the new case will resemble each. Which analogy seems most compelling will depend on judges' varying senses of fairness. Over the course of centuries, lines of judicial authority elaborate both the principles and counterprinciples into the architecture of the common law. As a result, legal doctrine resembles a multigenerational compromise, with principles and counterprinciples that roughly track the political fault lines of different stages of evolving society.

The result is indeterminacy in legal doctrine, a familiar theme in the writings of the legal realists and critical legal studies. But it is indeterminacy of a special and limited sort – moderate, not global, indeterminacy. Indeterminacy attains its maximum along fault lines where the law most strongly reflects a political compromise. Where political conflict was unimportant to the shape a legal text assumed, indeterminacy may be minimal or nonexistent. Brewster was wrong: *not* every proposition is arguable. Lawyers desperate for an argument will try to conjure up an indeterminacy where little or none exists, but they will have a hard time doing so honestly. The torture memos testify to that.

The ethics of legal opinions

Let me summarize. I have been suggesting that crucial arguments in the torture memos are frivolous. However, I have also insisted that no bright-line test of frivolity exists beyond whether an interpretive community accepts specific objections showing that the arguments are baseless or absurd. You know it when you see it.

In that case, why cannot the torture lawyers simply reply that their inter-pretive community sees it differently from the interpretive community of liberal cosmopolitan lawyers? One answer, perhaps the strongest, is the moral certainty that they would have reached the opposite conclusion if the adminis-tration wanted the opposite conclusion. The evidence shows that all these memos were written under pressure from officials determined to use harsh tactics – officials who consciously bypassed ordinary channels and looked to lawyers sharing their aims. An interpretive community that contours its interpretations to the party line is not engaged in good-faith interpretation.

In the case of the torture memos, the giveaway is the violation of craft values common to all legal interpretive communities. This is clearest in the Bybee memo, but the preceding discussion reveals similar problems in the other documents. What makes the Bybee memo frivolous by conventional legal standards is that in its most controversial sections, it barely goes through the motions of standard legal argument. Instead of addressing the obvious counterarguments, it ignores them; its citation of conventional legal authority is, for obvious reasons, sparse; it fails to mention directly adverse authority; and when it does cite conventional sources of law, it employs them in unconventional ways, and not always honestly.

The other memos are less transparent about it, but they, too, discard the project of providing an analysis of the law as mainstream lawyers and judges understand it. Instead, they provide aggressive advocacy briefs to give those who order or engage in brutal interrogation legal cover.

One might ask what is wrong with writing advocacy briefs. Are lawyers not supposed to spin the law to their clients' advantage? The traditional answer for courtroom advocates is yes. The aim is to persuade the judge or jury, not to write a treatise. To be sure, even courtroom advocates should not indulge in frivolous or dishonest argument. But, as Judge Easterbrook's formula indicated, the standards of frivolity leave plenty of room for pro-client spin.

But the torture memos are not briefs. They are legal advice, and in traditional legal ethics they answer to a different standard: not persuasiveness on the client's behalf but candor and independence.[117] Perhaps the most fundamental rule of thumb for legal advice is that the lawyer's analysis of the law should be more or less the same as it would be if the client wanted the opposite result from the one the lawyer knows he wants.

Other rules of thumb follow from this. First, a legal opinion ought to lay out in terms intelligible to the client the chief legal arguments bearing on the issue, those contrary to the client's preferred outcome as well as those favoring it. Unlike a brief, which aims to minimize the opposing arguments and exaggerate the strength of its own, the opinion should evaluate the arguments as objectively as possible. Second, opinions must treat legal authority honestly. (Briefs should as well.) No funny stuff: if the lawyer cites a source, the reader should not have to double-check whether it really says what the lawyer says it says, or whether the lawyer has wrenched a quotation out of context to flip its meaning. And adverse sources may not simply be ignored. Just as litigation rules require lawyers to divulge directly adverse law to courts, an honest legal opinion does not simply sweep it under the rug and hope nobody notices.

Finally, an honest opinion explains where its conclusion fits on the bell curve. While it is entirely proper for an opinion writer to favor a nonstandard view of the law, she must make clear that it *is* a nonstandard view of the law. She cannot write an opinion advancing a marginal view of the law with a briefwriter's swaggering self-confidence that the law will sustain no view other than hers.

---

[117] See ABA Model Rules of Professional Conduct 2.1: "In representing a client, a lawyer shall exercise independent professional judgment and render candid advice."

An example might help. It is only fair to use an argument in one of John Yoo's OLC memos that fulfills these requirements. A memo of January 22, 2002 (which went out over Bybee's signature) argues, among other things, that common Article 3 of the Geneva Conventions does not apply to the US conflict with Al Qaeda. That is because Article 3 applies only to "armed conflicts not of an international character." By this phrase, Yoo argues, the framers of Geneva had in mind only civil wars, like the Spanish and Chinese civil wars.[118] That would plainly exclude the conflict with Al Qaeda.

There is nothing frivolous about this argument; indeed, it is quite forceful. But there is also a powerful reply to it. In legal terminology, "international" means "among nation-states," as in the phrase "international law." An international armed conflict is a conflict among nation-states, and therefore an armed conflict "not of an international character" would be *any* armed conflict not among nation-states, not only civil wars. (This, eventually, was the interpretation adopted by the US Supreme Court in its June 2006 *Hamdan* v. *Rumsfeld* opinion.) In that case, the conflict with Al Qaeda would be classified as an armed conflict not of an international (i.e., state-against-state) character – and therefore common Article 3 would apply to it and protect even Al Qaeda captives. That conclusion would harmonize with the most obvious purpose of Article 3: protecting at least the most basic human rights of all captives, whether or not they qualify for the more extended protections Geneva offers to POWs and protected civilians in wars among nation-states. If, as a matter of policy, Article 3 aims to protect basic human rights in nonstandard wars, it would be irrational to protect human rights only in civil wars rather than all armed conflicts. Most international lawyers believe that human-rights instruments should be interpreted in a broad, gap-filling way, precisely because of the importance of human rights.

The virtue of Yoo's opinion is that he explicitly discusses all this. He sketches the evolution of the law of armed conflict in the twentieth century, acknowledging that in recent years international law "gives central place to individual human rights" and "blurs the distinction between international and internal armed conflicts."[119] He cites one of the principal cases illustrating this view, the Yugoslav Tribunal's *Tadic* decision; and in a footnote he refers to other authorities taking the same view. In response, he emphasizes that the Geneva framers were thinking principally about protecting rights in civil wars, and argues that to interpret Article 3 more broadly "is effectively to amend the Geneva Conventions without the approval of the State parties to the agreements."[120] In other words, where most international lawyers treat human-rights instruments like a "living" constitution, Yoo treats them like contracts. I think this gives him the weaker side of the argument – and, obviously, the Supreme Court rejected his position – but that is not the point. The point is that he does a respectable job of

---

[118] Greenberg and Dratel, *Torture Papers*, pp. 86–7.   [119] *Ibid.*, p. 88.   [120] *Ibid.*

sketching out the legal landscape, making it clear that his own analysis runs contrary to that of most international lawyers, and representing their positions honestly.[121] That is the kind of candid advice a lawyer can legitimately provide to the client, even if it deviates from mainstream views.[122]

The lawyer as absolver

But what happens when the client wants cover, not candid advice? – when the client comes to the lawyer and says, in effect, "Give me an opinion that lets me do what I want to do"?

Lawyers have a word for a legal opinion that does this. It is called a CYA memorandum – Cover Your Ass. Without the memorandum, the client who wants to push the legal envelope is on his own. But with a CYA memo in hand, he can insist that he cleared it with the lawyers first, and that way he can duck responsibility. That appears to be the project of the torture memos.

Notice that this diagnosis differs from Anthony Lewis' judgment that the Bybee memo "read like the advice of a mob lawyer to a mafia don on how to skirt the law and stay out of prison."[123] The torture memos are not advice about how to stay out of prison; instead, they reassure their clients that they are not going to prison. They are opinion letters blessing or koshering conduct for the twin purposes of all CYA memos: reassuring cautious lower-level employees that they can follow orders without getting into trouble, and allowing wrongdoers to duck responsibility. The fact that they emerge from the Justice Department – the prosecutor of federal crime – makes the reassurance nearly perfect.

When they write CYA memos, lawyers cross the fatal line from legal adviser to moral or legal accomplice. Obviously, it happens all the time. The journalist Martin Mayer, writing about the 1980s savings-and-loan collapse, quoted a source who said that for half a million dollars you could buy a legal opinion

---

[121] Not entirely: he neglects to mention that the drafters of the Geneva Conventions explicitly *rejected* an Australian motion to limit Article 3 to civil wars. Special Committee Seventh Report, vol. II B, p. 121. They also rejected other, similar efforts that would have had the same effect. See *Hamdan* v. *Rumsfeld*, 548 U.S. 557, 630–31 (2006).

[122] This portion of Yoo's opinion contrasts sharply with another section of the same opinion, arguing that the Geneva Conventions do not protect Taliban fighters because, under the Taliban, Afghanistan was a failed state. Here, Yoo was back in Bybee memo form. His draft opinion drew an outraged response from the State Department's legal adviser, who pointed out that "failed state" is not a legal concept; that so many states are failed states that Yoo's no-treaties-with-failed-states argument would greatly complicate US foreign relations; that if the Taliban have no rights under Geneva they have no obligations either, and therefore do not have to apply Geneva to any Americans they capture; and that Yoo's argument would annul every treaty with Afghanistan on every subject. Memo from William Howard Taft IV to John Yoo, Jan. 11, 2002 (www2.gwu. edu/~nsarchiv/torturingdemocracy/documents/20020111.pdf). The "failed-state" argument quietly disappeared.

[123] Anthony Lewis, "Making Torture Legal," *New York Review of Books*, July 15, 2004.

saying anything you wanted from any big law firm in Manhattan.[124] In the Enron case, we saw lawyers writing opinion letters that approved the creation of illegal special purpose entities, even though they knew that they were skating on thin ice. I am arguing that this is unethical. In white-collar criminal cases, some courts in some contexts will accept a defense of good-faith reliance on the advice of counsel, and presumably that defense is the prize the client seeks from the lawyer. But when the client tells the lawyer what advice he wants, the good faith vanishes, and under the criminal law of accomplice liability, both lawyer and client should go down.[125]

Giving the client skewed advice because the client wants it is a different role from either advocate or adviser. I call it the lawyer as absolver, or, less nicely, the lawyer as indulgence seller. Luther began the Reformation in part because the popes were selling papal dispensations to violate law, along with indulgences sparing sinners the flames of hell or a few years of purgatory. Rodrigo Borgia once brokered a papal dispensation for a French count to sleep with his own sister. It was a good career move: Rodrigo later became Pope Alexander VI.[126] Jay Bybee had to settle for the Ninth Circuit Court of Appeals.

It is important to see why the role of absolver, unlike the roles of advocate and adviser, is illegitimate. The courtroom advocate's biased presentation will be countered by the adversary in a public hearing. The adviser's presentation will not. In the courtroom, the adversary is supposed to check the advocate's excesses. In the lawyer's office, advising the client, the lawyer is supposed to check the client's excesses. Conflating the two roles moves the lawyer out of the limited role-based immunity that advocates enjoy into the world of the indulgence seller.

In short, if you are writing a brief, call it a brief, not an opinion. If it is an opinion, it must not be a brief. If you write a brief but call it an opinion, you have done wrong.

Government lawyers

Some might reply that in the real world outside the academy, legal opinions by government offices *are* briefs. When the State Department issues an opinion vindicating a military action by the US government, everyone understands that this is a public statement of the government's position, not an independent legal assessment. To suppose otherwise is naive.

---

[124] Martin Mayer, *The Greatest-Ever Bank Robbery: The Collapse of the Savings and Loan Industry* (New York: Collier Books, 1992), p. 20.

[125] The lawyer who okays unlawful conduct by the client has also harmed the client, and therefore been a bad fiduciary of the client. But, both as a matter of law and morality, that is a distinct ethical violation from becoming the client's accomplice.

[126] Ivan Cloulas, *The Borgias* (Gilda Roberts, Trans.) (New York: Scholastic Library Publishing, 1989), p. 38.

In that case, however, why keep up the charade? Consider, for example, a pair of documents authored by the British attorney general, Lord (Peter) Goldsmith. The first was a confidential legal memorandum to Tony Blair on the legality of the Iraq War, dated March 7, 2003, less than two weeks before the war began. The memo consisted of thirteen densely packed pages, and in my view it is a model of what such an opinion should be. It carefully and judiciously dissects all the pro and con arguments, which were closely balanced, consisting largely of interpretive debates over the meaning of characteristically soapy UN Security Council resolutions. Goldsmith concluded that while, in his opinion, obtaining a second Security Council resolution authorizing the use of force "is the safest legal course," a reasonable argument can be made that existing resolutions would suffice to justify the war.[127] It was a cautious go-ahead to Blair, larded with substantial misgivings and caveats. If Blair's request to Goldsmith was to give him the strongest argument available for the legality of the war, Goldsmith replied in the best way he could: he articulated the argument Blair wanted, advised him that it was reasonable, but also made it clear that the argument did not represent his own view of how the law should best be read. This represents the limit to which an honest legal adviser can tailor his opinion to the wishes of his client. Goldsmith's office wrote a sophisticated, honest document.

Ten days later – three days before the bombing began – Lord Goldsmith presented the same issue to Parliament, and now all the misgivings were gone. In place of thirty-one subtle paragraphs of analysis, the "opinion" to Parliament consists of nine terse, conclusory paragraphs with no nuance and no hint of doubt.[128] In place of the confidential memorandum's conclusion that the meaning of a Security Council resolution was "unclear," Goldsmith's public statement expressed no doubts whatever. It was pure vindication of the course of action to which Blair was irrevocably committed.

Two years later, Goldsmith told the House of Lords that his public statement was "my own genuinely held, independent view," and that allegations "that I was leant on to give that view ... are wholly unfounded."[129] Unfortunately for Lord Goldsmith, the confidential memorandum leaked a few weeks later, and readers could see for themselves what his genuinely held, independent view actually had been. The kerfuffle that followed fanned public suspicion about the decision to go to war, and weakened Blair in the next election.

It is obvious why Lord Goldsmith gave Parliament the unqualified opinion he did. The war was about to begin, the government was committed to it, and it was deeply controversial. An opinion laden with doubts would have had

[127] Goldsmith memo, paragraphs 27–8 (www.comw.org/warreport/fulltext/0303goldsmith.html).
[128] Hansard, 17 Mar. 2003, col. 515W.
[129] Hansard, 1 Mar. 2005, col. 112 (http://hansard.millbanksystems.com/lords/2005/mar/01/iraq-attorney-generals-opinion#column_112).

devastating repercussions for the government's policy and its relationship with the United States. Knowing this, Goldsmith wrote a brief, just as the realists think he should. But realists should notice that when he had to defend it two years later, Goldsmith continued to pretend that it was something else – a backhanded acknowledgment of the principle I am proposing: *If you write a brief but call it an opinion, you have done wrong.* In his second, brief-like opinion, he did wrong.

This is doubly true for the OLC, because in modern practice its opinions bind the executive branch.[130] That makes them quasi-judicial in character. In *Legal Ethics and Human Dignity*, I argued that legal advice from lawyers to clients is always "jurisgenerative" and quasi-judicial, but, obviously, written opinions binding entire departments of the government are judicial in a more direct way. As such, the obligation of impartiality built into the legal adviser's ethical role is reinforced by the obligation of impartiality incumbent on a judge. Two additional factors make the obligation more weighty still. First, some of the opinions were secret. Insulated from outside criticism and alternative points of view, written under pressure from powerful officials and, perhaps, from hair-raising intelligence about Al Qaeda's intentions, they were memos from the bunker. Recognizing a professional obligation to provide impartial analysis represented an essential tether to reality. Finally, the OLC is charged by statute with helping the executive discharge its constitutional obligation to "take care that the laws be faithfully executed." Fidelity to the law, not to the administration, requires impartiality.

In December 2004, nineteen former lawyers in the OLC drafted a set of principles for the office reaffirming its commitment to this standard conception of the independent legal adviser. Apparently, this is not how the Bush administration's OLC conceives of its job, for none of its lawyers was willing to sign.[131]

Conclusion

I drafted this chapter before the US Supreme Court rebuffed the Bush administration's detainee policies in *Hamdan* v. *Rumsfeld*. Among other significant holdings, *Hamdan* found that common Article 3 of the Geneva Conventions applies to detainees in the war on terror. Article 3 forbids torture and humiliating or degrading treatment – an awkward holding, because, as we have seen,

---

[130] Randolph D. Moss, "Executive Branch Legal Interpretation: A Perspective from the Office of Legal Counsel," *Administrative Law Review*, 52 (2000), 1303ff., at 1318–20. I am grateful to Dawn Johnsen, Marty Lederman, and Nina Pillard for illuminating e-mail discussions of the OLC's role and ethics. For Lederman's view, see "Chalk on the Spikes: What Is the Proper Role of Executive Branch Lawyers, Anyway?" (http://balkin.blogspot.com/2006/07/chalk-on-spikes-what-is-proper-role-of.html).

[131] The statement of principles was published as "Guidelines for the President's Legal Advisors," *Indiana Law Journal*, 81 (2006), 1345–52. They were subsequently adopted by the Obama administration OLC.

high-level officials, including the secretary of defense, the vice president, and even the president, had authorized such treatment for high-value detainees. Worse, federal law declared violations of common Article 3 to be war crimes. *Hamdan* pushed administration lawyers into overdrive, and they produced a bill, the Military Commissions Act of 2006, to respond to the court. After intense negotiations with moderate Republican senators, the final bill was approved by Congress and signed into law in October 2006.

The bill responded to *Hamdan*'s challenge in a drastic way. It stripped federal courts of habeas corpus jurisdiction over Guantánamo, defined "unlawful enemy combatants" broadly, prohibited detainees from arguing for Geneva Convention rights, retroactively decriminalized humiliating and degrading treatment, declared that federal courts could not use international law to interpret war-crimes provisions, vested interpretive authority over Geneva in the president, allowed coerced evidence to be admitted, gave the government the power to shut down revelation of exactly what techniques were used to obtain such coerced evidence, and defined criminally cruel treatment in a deeply convoluted way. For example, the bill distinguishes between "severe pain," the hallmark of torture, and merely "serious" pain, the hallmark of cruel treatment short of torture – but it then defines "serious" pain as "extreme" pain. Such bizarre legalisms call the Bybee memo to mind, of course, and they should. This bill (the worst piece of legislation I can recall from my own lifetime) was clearly inspired by the style of legal thinking perfected by the torture lawyers. In effect, the torture lawyers helped to define a "new normal," without which the Military Commissions Act would not exist.

This chapter chronicles a legal train wreck. The lawyers did not cause it, but they facilitated it. As a consequence, enmity towards the United States has undoubtedly increased in much of the world. Sadly and ironically, the net effect on US intelligence gathering may be just the opposite of what the lawyers hoped, as potential sources who might have come willingly to the Americans turn away out of anger or fear that they might find themselves in Guantánamo or Bagram facing pitiless interrogators.

This is also a chapter on the legal ethics of opinion-writing. I have focused on what Lon Fuller might have called the procedural side of the subject: the requirements of honesty, objectivity, and nonfrivolous argument, regardless of the subject matter on which lawyers tender their advice. But that does not mean the subject matter is irrelevant. It is one thing for boy-wonder lawyers to loophole tax laws and write opinions legitimizing financial shenanigans. It is another thing entirely to loophole laws against torture and cruelty. Lawyers should approach laws defending basic human dignity with fear and trembling.[132]

---

[132] I thank Christopher Kutz for emphasizing this point to me. Jeremy Waldron makes the same point in "Torture and the Common Law" (note 60 above).

To be sure, honest opinion-writing will only get you so far. Law can be cruel, and then an honest legal opinion will reflect its cruelty. In the centuries when the evidence law required torture, no lawyer could honestly have advised that the law prohibited it. Honest opinion-writing by no means guarantees that lawyers will be on the side of human dignity.

The fact remains, however, that rule-of-law societies generally prohibit torture and CIDT, practices that fit more comfortably with despotism and absolutism. For that reason, lawyers in rule-of-law societies will seldom find it easy to craft an honest legal argument for cruelty. Like the torture lawyers of Washington, they will find themselves compelled to betray their craft. Of course, they may think of it as creative lawyering or cleverness, not betrayal. I have little doubt that only intelligent, well-educated lawyers could write these memos, larded as they are with sophisticated-looking tricks of statutory interpretation. But there is such a thing as being too clever for your own good.[133]

[133] I owe special thanks to Lynne Henderson and Marty Lederman for comments and suggestions on this chapter. I do not wish to attribute any of my views or errors to them, however. (In particular, I know that Lederman disagrees with my discussion of the OLC draft memo on Article 49 of the Fourth Geneva Convention.) In addition, Jack Goldsmith raised important objections to my analysis of his Article 49 draft memo – fewer than he would have wished to raise, because his confidentiality obligations made it impossible for him to go into details. I have made some revisions based on these objections. I am grateful to him for his generosity, fairness, and objectivity in responding to my polemical comments. Obviously, remaining mistakes in my analysis are mine alone, not his – nor those of Sandy Levinson, who also offered helpful comments on an earlier draft.

Appendix: Testimony of David Luban to the Senate Judiciary Committee, Subcommittee on Administrative Oversight and the Courts: "What Went Wrong: Torture and the Office of Legal Counsel in the Bush Administration," May 13, 2009

Chairman Whitehouse, ranking member Graham, Chairman Leahy, and members of the subcommittee.

Thank you for inviting me to testify today. You've asked me to talk about the legal ethics of the torture and interrogation memos written by lawyers in the Office of Legal Counsel [OLC]. Based on the publicly available sources I've studied, I believe that the memos are an ethical train wreck.

When a lawyer advises a client about what the law requires, there is one basic ethical obligation: to tell it straight, without slanting or skewing. That can be a hard thing to do, if the legal answer isn't the one the client wants. Very few lawyers ever enjoy saying "no" to a client who was hoping for "yes." But the profession's ethical standard is clear: a legal adviser must use independent judgment and give candid, unvarnished advice. In the words of the American Bar Association [ABA], "a lawyer should not be deterred from giving candid advice by the prospect that the advice will be unpalatable to the client."[134]

That is the governing standard for all lawyers, in public practice or private. But it is doubly important for lawyers in the Office of Legal Counsel. The mission of OLC is to give the President advice to guide him in fulfilling an awesome constitutional obligation: to take care that the laws are faithfully executed. "Faithful" execution means interpreting the law without stretching it and without looking for loopholes. OLC's job is not to rubber-stamp administration policies, and it is not to provide legal cover for illegal actions.

---

[134] ABA [American Bar Association] Model Rules of Professional Conduct, Rule 2.1, cmt. 1. The identical rule and comment appears in the Pennsylvania Rules of Professional Conduct and the D.C. [District of Columbia] Rules of Professional Conduct. (I am told that Professor Yoo belongs to the Pennsylvania Bar, while Judge Bybee was a member of the D.C. Bar and is currently a judicial member. The Nevada Bar, Judge Bybee's second state of admission, has the identical Rule 2.1 but includes no interpretive comments.) The rule itself states: "In representing a client, a lawyer shall exercise independent professional judgment and render candid advice." Model Rule 2.1.

No lawyer's advice should do that. The rules of professional ethics forbid lawyers from counseling or assisting clients in illegal conduct;[135] they require competence;[136] and they demand that lawyers explain enough that the client can make an informed decision, which surely means explaining the law as it is.[137] Lawyers must not misrepresent the law, because lawyers are prohibited from *all* "conduct involving dishonesty, fraud, deceit or misrepresentation."[138] These are standards that the entire legal profession recognizes.

There is a common misperception that lawyers are always supposed to spin the law in favor of their clients. That is simply not true. It *is* true that in a courtroom, lawyers are supposed to argue for the interpretation of law that most favors their client. The lawyer on the other side argues the opposite, and the judge who hears the strongest case from both sides can reach a better decision.

But matters are completely different when a lawyer is giving a client advice about what the law means. Now there is nobody arguing the other side, and no judge to sort it out. Typically, the lawyer–client communication is confidential, and thus the lawyer is the client's only channel of advice about what the law requires. Not only is it important for the client to receive unvarnished advice, it is important for society at large that clients know their legal obligations. The ABA explains the value of lawyer–client confidentiality by pointing out its contribution to law compliance: "Almost without exception, clients come to lawyers in order to determine their rights and what is, in the complex of laws and regulations, deemed to be legal and correct. Based upon experience, lawyers know that almost all clients follow the advice given, and the law is upheld."[139] The ABA's Model Code of Professional Responsibility explains the "essential difference" between advocates and advisors:

> Where the bounds of the law are uncertain, the action of a lawyer may depend upon whether he is serving as advocate or adviser. A lawyer may serve simultaneously as both advocate and adviser, but the two roles are essentially different. . . While serving as advocate, a lawyer should resolve in favor of his client doubts as to the bounds of the law. In serving a client as adviser, a lawyer in appropriate circumstances should give his professional opinion as to what the ultimate decisions of the courts would likely be as to the applicable law.[140]

---

[135] "A lawyer shall not counsel a client to engage, or assist a client, in conduct that the lawyer knows is criminal or fraudulent." ABA Model Rule 1.2(d).

[136] ABA Model Rule 1.1. "A lawyer shall provide competent representation to a client." The D.C. Bar's rules – pertinent to Mr. Bradbury, Judge Bybee, and Professor Yoo – add: "A lawyer shall serve a client with skill and care commensurate with that generally afforded to clients by other lawyers in similar matters." D.C. Rules of Conduct 1.1(b).

[137] ABA Model Rule 1.4(b), "A lawyer shall explain a matter to the extent reasonably necessary to permit the client to make informed decisions regarding the representation."

[138] ABA Model Rule 8.4(c).   [139] ABA Model Rule 1.6, cmt. [2].

[140] ABA Model Code of Professional Responsibility (1969), EC 7–3. The Code of Professional Responsibility preceded the current Model Rules of Professional Conduct, which

Of course it is likely that the torture memos were exactly what the client wanted; according to a Senate Intelligence Committee report, "On July 17, 2002, according to CIA records, the Director of Central Intelligence (DCI) met with the National Security Adviser, who advised that the CIA could proceed with its proposed interrogation of Abu Zubaydah. This advice, which authorized CIA to proceed as a policy matter, was subject to a determination of legality by OLC."[141] In other words, the "program" had already been approved, pending legal approval by OLC.

However, the requirement of independent judgment in Rule 2.1 does not permit lawyers to shape their opinions to the client's wishes. This is common sense. Otherwise, clients might go to their lawyers to say, "Give me an opinion that says I can do what I want" – and then duck responsibility by saying, "My lawyer told me it was legal." Then we would have a perfect Teflon circle: the lawyer says "I was just doing what my client instructed" and the client says "I was just doing what my lawyer approved." The damage to law and compliance with law would be enormous.

Does that mean a client cannot come to a lawyer with the request, "Give me the best argument you can find that I can do X"? As a general proposition, nothing forbids a lawyer from doing so, but it would be deceptive to package one-sided advice as an authentic legal opinion. Emphatically this is not OLC's mission, which is to tender objective advice about matters of law, binding on the executive branch. Nor do Professor Yoo, Judge Bybee, and Mr. Bradbury claim they are simply giving, in a one-sided way, the best arguments they can find for the permissibility of the tactics. The August 1, 2002 "techniques" memo states, "We wish to emphasize that this is our best reading of the law,"[142] while Mr. Bradbury describes his May 10, 2005 "techniques" memo in similar terms: "the legal standards we apply in this memorandum ... constitute our authoritative view of the legal standards applicable under [the torture statutes]."[143]

Unfortunately, the torture memos fall far short of professional standards of candid advice and independent judgment. They involve a selective and in places deeply eccentric reading of the law. The memos cherry-pick sources of law that back their conclusions, and leave out sources of law that do not. They read as if they were reverse engineered to reach a predetermined outcome: approval of waterboarding and the other CIA techniques.

Because of time constraints, my oral statement on May 13 discussed only one example of what I am talking about; in this written testimony I include others, beginning with the case my oral statement focused on.

Twenty-six years ago, President Reagan's Justice Department prosecuted law enforcement officers for waterboarding prisoners to make them confess. The case

---

absorbed the distinction between advocate and adviser into Rule 2.1's requirement that advisers offer candid, independent advice.

[141] "OLC Opinions on the CIA Detention and Interrogation Program," released Apr. 22, 2009, pp. 3–4 (http://intelligence.senate.gov/pdfs/olcopinion.pdf).

[142] *Ibid.*, p. 18.   [143] *Ibid.*, p. 1.

is called *United States* v. *Lee*.[144] Four men were convicted and drew hefty sentences that the Court of Appeals upheld.[145]

The Court of Appeals repeatedly referred to the technique as "torture." This is perhaps the single most relevant case in American law to the legality of water-boarding. Any lawyer can find the *Lee* case in a few seconds on a computer just by typing the words "water torture" into a database. But the authors of the torture memos never mentioned it. They had no trouble finding cases where courts *didn't* call harsh interrogation techniques "torture."[146] It's hard to avoid the conclusion that Mr. Yoo, Judge Bybee, and Mr. Bradbury chose not to mention the *Lee* case because it casts doubt on their conclusion that water-boarding is legal.

In past discussion before this Committee, Attorney General Mukasey responded that *Lee* is not germane, because it is a civil rights denial case, not a torture case.[147]

---

[144] 744 F.2d 1124 (5th Cir. 1984). The Court of Appeals did not use the label "water-boarding," which had not yet been coined, but the description of the technique makes it clear that it is almost identical to waterboarding. It "included the placement of a towel over the nose and mouth of the prisoner and the pouring of water in the towel until the prisoner began to move, jerk, or otherwise indicate that he was suffocating and/or drowning." Brief of Petitioner-Appellee, *United States* v. *Lee*, No. 83-2675 (5th Cir. Nov. 9, 1984); see Evan Wallach, "Drop by Drop: Forgetting the History of Water Torture in U.S. Courts," *Columbia Journal of Transnational Law*, 45 (2007), 468ff., at 502–3.

[145] They drew sentences of two years (with three years suspended), four years, and ten years, respectively. "Ex-Sheriff Given 10-Year Sentence," *New York Times*, Oct. 27, 1983, p. A11.

[146] For example, Mr. Bradbury's May 10, 2005 opinion on individual CIA techniques cites *Hilao* v. *Estate of Marcos*, 103 F.3d 789, 790–1 (9th Cir. 1996), which describes numerous despicable tortures performed on the plaintiff, including waterboarding. Mr. Bradbury writes that "the court reached no conclusion that the technique by itself constituted torture. However, the fact that a federal court would even colloquially describe a tech-nique that may share some of the characteristics of the waterboard as 'water torture' counsels continued care and careful monitoring of the technique." Bradbury "techniques" memo, p. 44, n.57. I find it disturbing that Mr. Bradbury chooses a case where "the court reached no conclusion" that waterboarding is torture, without mentioning *United States* v. *Lee*, a case where waterboarding was the only technique at issue, and the court described it as torture in nine places. Professor's Yoo and Judge Bybee's August 1, 2002 "torture" memo includes an appendix that purports to list all "[c]ases in which US courts have concluded the defendant tortured the plaintiff." *Lee* does not appear on this list. Perhaps it is because *Lee* was criminal, not civil, and therefore had no plaintiff; or perhaps it is because the court calls the technique "torture" without formally "concluding" that it is torture. Even if these are the rationalizations for omitting *Lee* from the list, such hypertechnicality is wholly inappropriate for an opinion offering legal advice to a client. I note that Professor Yoo and Judge Bybee also did not mention *Lee* in the August 1, 2002 "techniques" memo, which actually analyzes the legality of waterboarding.

[147] "MUKASEY: Senator . . . the case to which you refer [*Lee*] was prosecuted under the civil rights law. It was not a case that dealt with whether a technique is or isn't torture under the torture statutes. That case was properly prosecuted under the civil rights laws. It would be prosecuted today under any standard under the civil rights laws. That wasn't the issue. Indeed, the issue on appeal didn't even concern the civil rights laws" (Senate Judiciary Committee oversight hearing, July 9, 2008). Judge Mukasey is correct that *Lee*

That response misses the point, however, which was not what legal issue the court was addressing in *Lee*, but the fact that the judges had no hesitation about labeling waterboarding "torture," a label they used at least nine times. They obviously could not reference the Convention Against Torture (CAT) or the torture statutes, 18 U.S.C. §§ 2340–2340A, which did not yet exist. But there is no reason to suppose that they would have reached a different characterization of waterboarding than they did in *Lee*. That might be the case if CAT and the torture statutes had transformed the meaning of the ordinary-language word "torture," making it more technical, and raising the standard of harshness so that waterboarding might not be torture under the new, technical standard.

That simply did not happen. The statutes' definition of torture as severe mental or physical pain or suffering is neither unusual nor technical. Indeed, a standard pre-CAT dictionary definition of torture describes it as "severe or excruciating pain or suffering (of body or mind)"[148] – a definition so similar to the language of CAT that it seems entirely possible that CAT's drafters modeled the treaty language on the *Oxford English Dictionary* definition. Other *Lee*-era dictionaries use formulations that do not in any way suggest that at the time of *Lee* "torture" meant something milder than the statutory standard – *Webster's Third* (1971) says "intense pain"; *Webster's Second* (1953) says "severe pain" and "extreme pain."[149]

Other significant omissions include the failure of the August 1, 2002 "torture" memo to discuss or even mention the *Steel Seizure Case*[150] in its analysis of the President's commander-in-chief power, or the highly significant early decision *Little* v. *Barreme*, 6 U.S. (2 Cranch) 170 (1804), which found that President Adams, as commander-in-chief during the "quasi-war" with France, could not authorize the seizure of a ship contrary to an act of Congress.[151] In its discussion of the necessity defense, the Bybee memo fails to mention the recently decided *United States* v. *Oakland Cannabis Buyers' Coop*, 532 U.S. 483, 490 (2001), which calls into question whether federal criminal law even contains a necessity defense if no statute specifies that there is one. Likewise, the opinion fails to mention that there is no reported case in which a federal court has accepted a necessity defense for a crime of violence – surely a crucial piece of information for a client who might be relying on the OLC's opinion in the momentous decision whether or not to waterboard detainees. In one place, the opinion may fairly be said to falsify what

---

did not concern the civil rights law – it concerned whether the trials of the sheriff and deputies should have been severed.

[148] *Compact Oxford English Dictionary* (Oxford University Press, 1971), p. 3357; likewise *American Heritage Dictionary* (Boston: Houghton Mifflin, 1976), p. 1356 ("severe physical pain").

[149] Although *Lee* was a civil rights case, Mr. Bradbury did not hesitate to refer to another civil rights case as an authority pertinent to the enhanced interrogation techniques. Bradbury "CIDT" memo, May 30, 2005, p. 33 (discussing *Williams* v. *United States*, 341 U.S. 97 (1951) (beating confessions out of subjects with a rubber hose is a violation of their civil rights).

[150] *Youngstown Sheet and Tube* v. *Sawyer*, 343 U.S. 579 (1952).

[151] 6 U.S. (2 Cranch), pp. 177–8.

a source says. Discussing whether interrogators accused of torture could plead self-defense, the memo says: "Leading scholarly commentators believe that interrogation of such individuals using methods that might violate [the anti-torture statute] would be justified under the doctrine of self-defense." The opinion refers to a law review article.[152] What the article's author actually says on the page cited is nearly the opposite: "*The literal law of self-defense is not available to justify their torture. But the principle uncovered as the moral basis of the defense may be applicable*" (emphasis added).[153] Omitting to discuss leading contrary cases, and spinning what cited sources say, is not honest opinion writing, and violates the ethical requirements of candor and independent judgment, and communication to a client of everything reasonably necessary for the client to make an informed decision.

I would like to briefly discuss other ways that the torture memos twisted and distorted the law, even though doing so requires getting even further into technicalities that, quite frankly, only a lawyer could love. The first Bybee memo advances a startlingly broad theory of executive power, according to which the President as commander in chief can override criminal laws such as the torture statute. This was a theory that Jack Goldsmith, who headed the OLC after Judge Bybee's departure, described as an "extreme conclusion," reached through "cursory and one-sided legal arguments" – a conclusion that "has no foundation in prior OLC opinions, or in judicial decisions, or in any other source of law."[154] It comes very close to President Nixon's notorious statement that "when the President does it, that means it is not illegal" – except that Mr. Nixon was speaking off the cuff in a high pressure interview, not a written opinion by the OLC. The *Steel Seizure* case I mentioned previously found that President Truman could not seize steel mills during the Korean War because doing so impinged on Congress's powers. It is a case limiting the commander-in-chief power, and it is known to every law student who has taken constitutional law.

Professor Yoo has explained that he and Judge Bybee did not discuss the *Steel Seizure* case because of a long-standing OLC tradition of upholding the President's commander-in-chief powers, central among which is the power to interrogate captives.[155] Suffice it to say, however, that nothing in either US law or US military tradition suggests that authority to torture captives belongs among the commander in chief's historical powers, any more than the authority to execute captives as a way of inducing other captives to reveal information is part of the traditional commander-in-chief power. It is perhaps for this reason that the [four] TJAGs [chiefs of the Judge Advocate General's Corps] of the Army, Navy, Marines, and

---

[152] Moore, "Torture and the Balance of Evils."

[153] There is also a world of difference between the OLC's assertive "would be justified" and Professor Moore's cautious "may be applicable," which in any event refers to his own moral argument, not to existing law.

[154] Jack Goldsmith, *The Terror Presidency: Law and Judgment Inside the Bush Administration* (New York: Norton, 2007), p. 149.

[155] John C. Yoo, *War by Other Means: An Insider's Account of the War on Terror* (New York: Atlantic Monthly Press, 2006), pp. 184–5.

Air Force all protested the torture memos when they learned of them months after they were issued. MG [Major General] Jack Rives, TJAG of the Air Force, objected that "the use of the more extreme interrogation techniques simply is not how the U.S. armed forces have operated in recent history. We have taken the legal and moral 'high ground'"[156] And BG [Brigadier General] Kevin Sankuhler, the Marine TJAG, noted sharply that "OLC does not represent the services; thus, understandably, concern for servicemembers is not reflected in their opinion."[157]

I believe Professor Goldsmith's view that no source of law supports the Bybee memo's proposition that the commander-in-chief power can override the criminal law on torture is correct; surely Professor Goldsmith, a Bush appointee, a conservative, and an intellectual ally of Professor Yoo, cannot have lightly decided to withdraw the memos. The same conclusion is reached in the definitive study of the commander-in-chief's power, the nearly 300-page articles by Professors David Barron and Martin Lederman, who conclude that "[t]here is a radical disjuncture between the approach to constitutional war powers the current President [George W. Bush] has asserted and the one that prevailed at the moment of ratification and for much of our history that followed."[158]

This is not simply a matter of scholarly disagreement; and, obviously, I am not saying that taking one side of a contested and complex constitutional issue is unethical. It is not. But omitting the leading case on the commander-in-chief power "at lowest ebb" (that is, in the face of a contrary statute) is a different matter. A lawyer writing an appellate brief on whether the torture statute encroaches on the President's constitutional authority who failed to cite or discuss *Youngstown Sheet & Tube* would be committing legal malpractice, and might face professional discipline for failing to cite directly contrary authority if, improbably, the adversary also failed to cite *Youngstown*.[159] Briefs have *more*, not less leeway to present a one-sided view of the law than advisory opinions for clients, and an omission that would be malpractice in a brief is *a fortiori* unacceptable in an opinion.

The first Bybee memo also wrenches language from a Medicare statute to explain the legal definition of torture. The Medicare statute lists "severe pain" as a symptom that might indicate a medical emergency. Mr. Yoo flips the statute and announces that only pain equivalent in intensity to "organ failure, impairment of

---

[156] Memorandum for SAF/GC, Feb. 5, 2003.

[157] Memorandum for General Counsel of the Air Force, Feb. 3, 2003.

[158] David J. Barron and Martin S. Lederman, "The Commander in Chief at the Lowest Ebb," part 2, *Harvard Law Review*, 121 (2008), 941ff., at 1112; part 1 (689ff.). I have myself examined the original understanding of the commander-in-chief power in a lengthy article, concluding that the founding generation had significant fears of a president commanding a standing army, and consequently understood the commander-in-chief authority to be narrow rather than broad. David Luban, "On the Commander in Chief Power," *Southern California Law Review*, 81 (2008), 477–571, at 507–31.

[159] "A lawyer shall not knowingly fail to disclose to the tribunal legal authority in the controlling jurisdiction known to the lawyer to be directly adverse to the position of the client and not disclosed by opposing counsel." ABA Model Rule 3.3(a)(2).

bodily function, or even death" can be "severe." This definition was so bizarre that the OLC itself disowned it a few months after it became public.[160] It is unusual for one OLC opinion to disown an earlier one, and it shows just how far out of the mainstream Professor Yoo and Judge Bybee had wandered. The memo's authors were obviously looking for a standard of torture so high that none of the enhanced interrogation techniques would count. But legal ethics does not permit lawyers to make frivolous arguments merely because it gets them the results they wanted. I should note that on January 15 of this year, Mr. Bradbury found it necessary to withdraw six additional OLC opinions by Professor Yoo or Judge Bybee.[161]

Of course, it is well known that the 2004 Levin memorandum that replaced the Bybee memo stated, "While we have identified various disagreements with the August 2002 Memorandum, we have reviewed this Office's prior opinions address- ing issues involving treatment of detainees and do not believe that any of their conclusions would be different under the standards set forth in this memoran- dum."[162] However, Mr. Levin stated in testimony to the House Judiciary Commit- tee that he "did *not* mean, as some have interpreted – and . . . this is my fault, no doubt, in drafting – that we had concluded that we would have reached the same conclusions as those earlier opinions did. We were in fact analyzing that at the time and we never completed that analysis."[163] Rather, he meant that his prede- cessors, Professor Yoo and Judge Bybee, would have reached the same conclusions based on his standards.

I have said little about the three May 2005 opinions, beyond the point I have already noted that they approve waterboarding without citing or discussing *Lee*. (Nor do they acknowledge earlier cases where the U.S. has condemned water torture – the *Glenn* court-martial from the U.S. Philippines campaign in the early twentieth century, and the *Sawada* case, in which a Japanese general was

---

[160] "We do not agree with those statements. Those other statutes define an 'emergency medical condition,' for purposes of providing health benefits, as 'a condition manifesting itself by acute symptoms of sufficient severity (including severe pain)' such that one could reasonably expect that the absence of immediate medical care might result in death, organ failure or impairment of bodily function. *See, e.g.*, 8 U.S.C. § 1369 (2000); 42 U.S.C. § 1395w-22(d)(3)(B) (2000); *id.* § 1395dd(e) (2000). They do not define 'severe pain' even in that very different context (rather, they use it as an indication of an 'emergency medical condition'), and they do not state that death, organ failure, or impairment of bodily function cause 'severe pain,' but rather that 'severe pain' may indicate a condition that, if untreated, could cause one of those results." Memorandum from Daniel Levin, Legal Standards Applicable Under 18 U.S.C. §§ 2340–2340A, Dec. 30, 2004, note 17. The Medicare statute clearly does *not* mean to define "severe pain." On the contrary, it assumes that a "prudent layperson" knows what severe pain is: that is why the statute lists it as a symptom that the prudent layperson "could reasonably expect" might indicate a medical emergency.

[161] Steven G. Bradbury, Memo for the Files, Re: Status of Certain OLC Opinions Issued in the Aftermath of the Terrorist Attacks of September 11, 2001 (Jan. 15, 2009).

[162] Memorandum for James B. Comey from Daniel Levin re: Legal Standards Applicable Under 18 U.S.C. §§ 2340–2340A, Dec. 30, 2004, note 8.

[163] Testimony to House Judiciary Committee, June 18, 2008.

condemned for forms of cruelty that included water torture.[164]) The 2005 memos are not as conspicuously one-sided as the August 1, 2002 torture memo which – again quoting Professor Goldsmith – "lacked the tenor of detachment and caution that usually characterizes OLC work, and that is so central to the legitimacy of OLC."[165] Mr. Bradbury's memos are more cautious, and contain repeated reminders that reasonable people could reach the opposite conclusion. But they too contain troubling features.

To take one example, the May 30, 2005 memo states twice that courts might reach the opposite conclusion in their interpretation of whether the CIA techniques "shock the conscience." This is an important warning, and I believe that it is perfectly ethical for a lawyer to offer a non-standard interpretation of the law in an advisory opinion, provided that the lawyer flags – as Mr. Bradbury does – that it may indeed be non-standard. However, in both places he immediately adds that the interpretation is "unlikely to be subject to judicial inquiry."[166] This is uncomfortably close to a lawyer telling the client, "it's likely to be found illegal, but don't worry – you probably won't be caught."

Other features of the memos are likewise troubling. To reach the conclusion that waterboarding does not cause "severe physical suffering," the memos rely on a specious finding from the 2004 memo, namely that to qualify as severe, suffering must be prolonged.[167] There is no such requirement in the torture statute – and indeed, there is strong reason to believe that no such requirement was intended. Congress *did* stipulate that severe mental suffering must be "prolonged" (18 U.S.C. § 2340(2)). Ordinary canons of statutory construction would lead virtually all competent lawyers to conclude that if Congress omitted the word "prolonged" in connection with physical suffering, but included it in the definition of mental suffering in the same statute, it does not exist in connection with physical suffering. In Mr. Bradbury's memo, the requirement of duration is crucial in finding that waterboarding does not induce severe physical suffering, because it does not last long enough. But, to repeat, the law itself contains no duration requirement for severe physical suffering – and it is wildly implausible that the overwhelming sensation of drowning, which is surely a form of physical suffering, is not severe.

Equally troubling is the manner in which the May 30 memo responds to bodies of law strongly indicating that the United States Government condemns the very techniques the memo is approving, which would indicate that these techniques

---

[164] These well-known cases are discussed in detail in Wallach, "Drop by Drop: Forgetting the History of Water Torture." Some commentators have tried to distinguish these because they used a worse form of water torture – namely, pouring water down the prisoner's throat. This was not true in all the Philippine cases, however; and in any event, the May 10, 2005 "techniques" memo notes that in waterboarding "the water may enter – and may accumulate in – the detainee's mouth and nasal cavity, preventing him from breathing. In addition, you have indicated that the detainee ... may swallow water, possibly in significant quantities" so that it is medically necessary to use saline solution to avoid diluting the salt content of the detainee's blood (p. 13).

[165] Goldsmith, *The Terror Presidency*, p. 149.

[166] May 30, 2005 memo, pp. 25, 38.   [167] E.g., May 10, 2005 "techniques" memo, p. 23.

are not "traditional executive behavior" or "customary practice" – as, hopefully, they are not! For example, the memo notes that our own State Department's annual Country Reports routinely condemn several of the practices the CIA used: dousing people with cold water, food and sleep deprivation, waterboarding, stripping and blindfolding them. The memo responds that "The condemned conduct is often undertaken for reasons totally unlike the CIA's."[168] But of course these countries often undertake the conduct for reasons very similar to the CIA's: learning information about terrorists. We still condemn it. In any event, the response does not even speak to the question of whether these practices represent U.S. custom or traditional executive behavior – as they surely do not. The memo goes on with an argument that is absurd on its face: the fact that the U.S. offers SERE training shows that these SERE-derived interrogation tactics are indeed traditional executive behavior.[169] It is obvious that a method of training SEALs to resist torture and cruelty is hardly traditional executive behavior in dealing with captives. In any case, the May 10 "techniques" memo notes explicitly that SERE is quite different from the CIA's program, and that the detainees were waterboarded far more often than in SERE (dozens of times instead of two).[170]

These arguments are so implausible that it seems clear that Mr. Bradbury was straining to reach a result. There are other difficulties with these three memos, which I do not wish to belabor here.[171] While I find these memoranda deeply troubling – and their conclusions are even more troubling than the Bybee memos, because the 2005 memos discuss the techniques both singly and in combination and conclude that they do not violate a lower standard than the definition of torture – they do not exhibit the one-sided and manipulative use of law to the same extent as the August 1, 2002 memos. And that is where the main problems of legal ethics in these memos lie.

Recent news reports have said that the Justice Department's internal ethics watchdog, the Office of Professional Responsibility [OPR], has completed a five-year investigation of the torture memos. OPR has the power to refer lawyers to their state bar disciplinary authorities, and news reports say they will do so.

I have no personal knowledge about what OPR has found. Presumably, investigators were looking either for evidence of incompetence, evidence that the lawyers knew their memos don't accurately reflect the law, or evidence that process was short-circuited.

---

[168] May 30, 2005 memo, p. 36.   [169] *Ibid.*, p. 38.

[170] May 10, 2005 "techniques" mem, pp. 6, 41, n.51.

[171] For example, the May 30, 2005 memo simply takes the CIA's assurance at face value that none of the interrogations will occur in the special maritime and territorial jurisdiction (SMTJ) of the United States. This is a crucial assumption to reach the memo's conclusion that Article 16 of the CAT does not apply. But this is a legal assumption, and it is properly the OLC's place to analyze the issue, which is not an easy one. According to the SMTJ statute, the SMTJ includes "the premises of United States . . . entities in foreign States" (18 U.S.C. § 7(9)). This clause was added to the statute only in 2001, and the term "entities" has never been subjected to judicial interpretation. It is entirely possible that CIA prisons in other countries are "United States entities," contrary to the CIA's opinion.

This morning I have called the torture memos an ethical train wreck. I believe it's impossible that lawyers of such great talent and intelligence could have written these memos in the good faith belief that they accurately state the law. But what I or anyone else believes is irrelevant. Ethics violations must be proved, by clear and convincing evidence, not just asserted. That sets a high bar, and it should be a high bar. Obviously, proving that lawyers were not candid in their advice, when they continue to assert publicly that they believe it is legally correct, is not easy.

In closing, I would like to emphasize to this Committee that when OLC lawyers write opinions, especially secret opinions, the stakes are high. Their advice governs the executive branch, and officials must be told frankly when they are on legal thin ice. They and the American people deserve the highest level of professionalism and independent judgment, and I am sorry to say that they did not get it here.

9

Tales of terror: lessons for lawyers from the "war on terrorism"

An astonishing feature of the "global war on terrorism" (GWOT) waged by the United States and its allies against Al Qaeda is the prominent role played by lawyers, civilian and military, representing both the US government and the people it has captured.[1] The conduct of these lawyers has been a topic of surpassing interest to many both in and out of the legal profession since the first "torture memos" were released in 2004. It is a subject of international, not merely parochial, interest. I will discuss the "torture lawyers," but also lawyers who represent the prisoners.[2] Although most of these are Americans, not all of them are. Some of the leading Guantánamo defense lawyers come from the London-based organization Reprieve. One lawyer I want to discuss, Major Dan Mori, of the US Marines, became a minor celebrity in Australia through his representation of David Hicks. The laws at issue in these cases are by and large international law; and, of course, Guantánamo has become an international symbol of the rule of law and its absence, a point central to the debate.

Lawyers and the torture team

In 1975, Richard Wasserstrom published a paper that arguably inaugurated the modern philosophical discussion of legal ethics. The paper was titled "Lawyers as Professionals: Some Moral Issues," and it began with the striking

The main text of this chapter was first published in 2010 – see Acknowledgments. I wrote the original paper as the keynote address to the Third International Legal Ethics Conference, held in Gold Coast, Australia, 14 July 2008. It was intended for an international audience, and I subsequently delivered the same address in Canada and Turkey. Although I have rewritten the paper somewhat, I have retained the style of the spoken address. I have also made stylistic revisions from the originally published version.

[1] For convenience, I will occasionally use the military abbreviation "GWOT" (pronounced "jee-wot"). In 2009, the administration of President Barack Obama abandoned the use of the "war on terrorism" terminology, although his administration continues to assert legal positions based on the theory that the struggle with Al Qaeda is an armed conflict.

[2] I have discussed at greater length the ethical difficulties facing these lawyers in "Lawfare and Legal Ethics in Guantánamo," *Stanford Law Review*, 60 (2008), 1981–2025.

assertion that "at best the lawyer's world is a simplified moral world; often it is an amoral one; and more than occasionally, perhaps an overtly immoral one."[3]

Wasserstrom illustrated his point with an anecdote from the then-recent Watergate scandal that brought down the Nixon presidency. Nixon's White House counsel John Dean was asked about a list of Watergate participants he had kept. Some had asterisks in front of their names, and the questioner wanted to know what the asterisks signified. Membership in some further conspiracy? Decision-making authority? Dean responded that the asterisks simply singled out the participants who were lawyers. He had been struck by how many there were. Dean wondered "whether there was some reason why lawyers might have been more inclined than other persons to have been so willing to do the things that were done" in Watergate and its cover-up.[4] Wasserstrom wondered the same thing. He concluded that what makes lawyers particularly vulnerable to sins of excessive partisanship is the unique "role morality" of the profession, according to which lawyers should do everything possible to advance the interests of their clients, and bear no moral responsibility for the rightness or wrongness of what the client wants. Of course, Wasserstrom's observation about the curious tension between extreme partisanship and moral detachment was hardly a novelty. A century before, the British historian Macaulay asked rhetorically why a lawyer, "with a wig on his head, and a band round his neck, [would] do for a guinea what, without those appendages, he would think it wicked and infamous to do for an empire."[5] Wasserstrom analyzed the problem as a clash between common morality and lawyers' role morality, a lead taken up a few years later by other legal ethicists, including Alan Goldman, Gerald Postema, and myself.[6]

I was reminded of Wasserstrom's paper while reading Philippe Sands' recent book *Torture Team*.[7] Sands is a British human-rights lawyer, and he set out to discover the real decision-making that went into Bush administration policies about torture, interrogation, and Guantánamo. Sands' is not the only such book – by this time there is a small library of

[3] Richard Wasserstrom, "Lawyers as Professionals: Some Moral Issues," *Human Rights*, 5 (1975), 1–24.
[4] *Ibid.*, p. 2.
[5] Thomas Babington Macaulay, "Macaulay's Essay on Bacon," in G. Trevelyan, Ed., *The Works of Lord Macaulay*, vol. VI, p. 163.
[6] Alan Goldman, *The Moral Foundations of Professional Ethics* (Totowa, NJ: Rowman & Littlefield, 1980); Gerald J. Postema, "Moral Responsibility in Professional Ethics," *New York University Law Review*, 55 (1980), 63–89; David Luban, *Lawyers and Justice: An Ethical Study* (Princeton University Press, 1988).
[7] Philippe Sands, *Torture Team: Rumsfeld's Memo and the Betrayal of American Values* (New York: Palgrave Macmillan, 2008).

them – but Sands somehow got a large number of the principals who formulated these policies to talk to him.[8]

By now you will have guessed what comes next. Going down the list of *dramatis personae* that Sands helpfully provides at the start of his book, I marked the lawyers with asterisks, and the number is astonishing. Half the members of the "torture team" were lawyers.[9] These included not only those who wrote the various torture memos, but also the highest-ranked legal officers of the US government: the president's counsel, the vice president's counsel, the attorney general, and the Defense Department's general counsel. Several of these met regularly as a self-titled "war council."[10] The lawyers included as well the Defense Department undersecretary, who urged that the Geneva Conventions should not apply to GWOT captives. And they included the first task-force commander of the Guantánamo prison – a reserve Army general who in civilian life is a state-court judge, and who shared in the initial devising of the harsh new interrogation techniques used at Guantánamo.

Lawyers waging lawfare

In one way, it was inevitable that lawyers would be deeply involved in decisions about the detention and interrogation of detainees. To a remarkable degree, contemporary armed conflict takes place amidst a dense network of laws and treaties, called the "law of armed conflict" by military lawyers and "humanitarian law" by human-rights organizations. More than a generation of US military officers has been trained in these laws, and the official policy of the United States has been one of enthusiastic support for them. Ironically, it takes considerable legal ingenuity to unwind all this law – and so the very choice to abandon the rule of law in the war on terrorism required intensive activity on the part of lawyers.

The war council consists of lawyers who are deeply suspicious of humanitarian law, for a variety of reasons. Some are enthusiasts for muscular executive power, and reject the idea that law can bind the president, particularly in a military emergency. Some of them are "new sovereigntists" – skeptics about international law who insist that it take a back seat to domestic law and who regard international law's champions as an undemocratic elite who aim to chip away at US sovereignty. All of the lawyers adhere to the theory nicknamed "lawfare": the accusation that America's enemies use humanitarian law strategically as a way to advance their own military interests by tying

---

[8] Shortly after Sands' book appeared, Jane Mayer published a magnificent book about US torture, *The Dark Side: The Inside Story of How the War on Terror Turned into a War on American Ideals* (New York: Doubleday, 2008).

[9] Sands, *Torture Team*, pp. xii–xiv.

[10] Jack Goldsmith, *The Terror Presidency: Law and Judgment Inside the Bush Administration* (New York: Norton, 2007), pp. 22–3.

American hands.[11] And, to be fair, all of them were operating in an environment of intense fear that another Al Qaeda attack might happen around the anniversary of 9/11, and that their prisoners might have important information about the attack.

Now, some of these reasons are unique to the legal outlook of the Bush administration and the legal theorists they recruited to staff their offices. But I do want to note that the "lawfare" theory comes naturally to lawyers schooled in the adversary system. The idea that parties might use law designed for peaceful purposes tactically in order to confound their enemies is simply Litigation Tactics 101. The litigator's mission has always included beating plowshares into swords. Litigators delay litigation to drive up the adversary's expenses; they try to get her counsel disqualified for a conflict of interest; they do whatever they can to obstruct her access to essential information. The novelty of the lawfare theory lies only in the fact that before it was formulated, few people thought specifically of the laws of war as weapons. But the thought comes naturally to lawyers, and it is no surprise that the military theorist who popularized the lawfare theory is a lawyer – the former number two military lawyer in the Air Force.[12]

The torture team demolished humanitarian law's protections of GWOT prisoners in three steps. The first step was the decision to use Guantánamo as a prison. In part, Guantánamo was chosen because its remoteness made it ideal from a security standpoint. But the decision was also influenced by the fact that Guantánamo would be outside the jurisdiction of US courts. Eventually, the US Supreme Court concluded that this is not so.[13] But the tactic of choosing Guantánamo and fighting bitterly in court against jurisdiction bought at least two years of freedom from law and law's scrutiny.

The second step was to strip Geneva Convention protections away from the detainees. The burden of this step fell on the Office of Legal Counsel (OLC), an elite unit of twenty lawyers within the Justice Department whose job is to provide legal advice to the executive branch of government. In a series of memos written in early 2002, OLC lawyers interpreted the Geneva Conventions to apply only to a narrow category of conflicts that excluded the GWOT.[14] The memos were also remarkable for proclaiming that customary

---

[11] *Ibid.*, pp. 58–63.

[12] Charles J. Dunlap, Jr., "Law and Military Interventions: Preserving Humanitarian Values in 21st Century Conflicts" (2001) (www.hks.harvard.edu/cchrp/Web%20Working%20Papers/Use%20of%20Force/Dunlap2001.pdf). The lawfare theory also promotes the idea that the United States can use law as its own weapon. Since this chapter was first published, General Dunlap retired from the military and entered the legal academy; as of 2013, he is at Duke Law School.

[13] *Rasul* v. *Bush*, 542 U.S. 466 (2004).

[14] These and other crucial legal memoranda and reports are reproduced in Karen J. Greenberg and Joshua L. Dratel, Eds., *The Torture Papers: The Road to Abu Ghraib* (New York: Cambridge University Press, 2005). See memo 4, pp. 38–79 (John Yoo to William

international law has no purchase on American law, and for a bizarre argument that Afghanistan is not really a state.[15] Although the State Department's
lawyer objected strenuously that the reasoning in these memos was preposterous, he lost his internal battle, and the president issued a finding that
the detainees were unprotected by Geneva.[16]

With their Geneva protections gone, the third step was to consider whether
the international Convention Against Torture (CAT) protected the prisoners
from harsh interrogation. Here, the OLC did the yeoman's work for the
torture team, crafting at least six memos that lowered the bar on what counts
as torture so that more than a dozen previously prohibited techniques could
pass muster. One of the first acts of President Barack Obama was to disavow
all the OLC memos on detainee treatment from 9/11 to Obama's inauguration.

One of them, written by OLC lawyer and Berkeley law professor John Yoo
(but issued under the name of Yoo's boss, Jay S. Bybee), has become famous
and iconic because of the extravagance of its conclusions and the boldness of
its legal arguments.[17] The "Bybee memo" claimed absolute authority for the
president to override law in wartime. Yoo sketched out criminal defenses that
torturers could use. And he defined "severe pain," the legal criterion for
torture, by looking at a healthcare statute's definition of a medical emergency.
The healthcare statute includes the unsurprising statement that severe pain
can be a symptom of a medical emergency. Yoo flipped the statute around so
that only the equivalent of a medical emergency counts as severe pain. On
Yoo's analysis, that meant that nothing short of the pain associated with organ
failure or death counts as "severe" – an argument that one critic aptly called
"textual interpretation run amok – not 'lawyering as usual,' but the work of
some bizarre literary deconstructionist."[18] Even Harvard law professor Jack
Goldsmith, a conservative and "new sovereigntist" scholar like Yoo, describes
the memos as "get-out-of-jail-free cards" for torturers, and believes that the
torture memo's "conclusion has no foundation in prior OLC opinions, or
in judicial decisions, or in any other source of law."[19] This is an amazing
assessment, because shortly after Yoo wrote the memo, Goldsmith became
the head of the OLC.

J. Haynes II, 9 Jan. 2002); memo 6, pp. 81–117 (Jay S. Bybee to Alberto R. Gonzales, 22
Jan. 2002); and memo 12, pp. 136–43 (Jay S. Bybee to Alberto R. Gonzales, Feb. 7, 2002).
[15] *Ibid.*, memo 4 (Yoo to Haynes), pp. 53–8, 71–6.
[16] See memo from William Howard Taft IV to John Yoo, 11 Jan. 2002 (www2.gwu.edu/
~nsarchiv/torturingdemocracy/documents/20020111.pdf); memo from George W. Bush
to the vice president *et al.*, Feb. 7, 2002, in Greenberg and Dratel, *The Torture Papers*,
pp. 134–5.
[17] It appears as memo 14 in Greenberg and Dratel, *The Torture Papers*, pp. 172–217.
[18] Peter Brooks, "The Plain Meaning of Torture?", *Slate*, Feb. 9, 2005 (www.slate.com/id/
2113314).
[19] Goldsmith, *The Terror Presidency*, pp. 97, 149.

Under Goldsmith's leadership, the OLC repudiated Yoo's opinion and replaced it.[20] The substitute memo no longer discussed presidential power or criminal defenses, and it criticized and repudiated the "organ-failure" definition of severe pain. But to this day, John Yoo insists that replacing his memo was a political rather than legal decision, and he points out that the substitute memo still approves all the interrogation tactics he approved.[21] My own assessment is that Yoo is more right than not about this, and that the substitute memo differs more cosmetically than substantively from Yoo's handiwork.[22] This is not to impugn the integrity of Daniel Levin, the lawyer who wrote the substitute memo. Incredibly, before writing the memo Levin reportedly had himself waterboarded to see what it is like.[23] He nevertheless built into his analysis a novel requirement that has no basis in the statutory language and which appears to permit waterboarding.[24]

The jurisprudence of legal advice

Are there lessons that lawyers can learn from this episode? For me, the crucial lesson has to do with the ethical obligations of lawyers in their role as confidential counselors, or legal advisers, to their clients. Let me set aside for a moment the most fundamental criticism of the Yoo memo – namely, that it enabled torture. The more general criticisms of the Yoo memo are two: first, that it stretched and distorted the law to reach the outcome that the client wanted, and, second, that it nowhere indicated that its interpretations are out of the mainstream. The principles behind these criticisms apply to lawyers in private practice as well as government lawyers.

They are noteworthy criticisms, because they highlight the ethical distortion that results when lawyers bring the neutral partisan role morality of courtroom advocates into the counseling role. After all, stretching the law to reach the

[20] The replacement ("Levin") memo may be found in Karen J. Greenberg, Ed., *The Torture Debate in America* (New York: Cambridge University Press, 2006), pp. 361–76, as well as on the Office of Legal Counsel website (www.usdoj.gov/olc/18usc23402340a2.htm). Abu Ghraib is, of course, a prison in Iraq where US troops tortured and humiliated Iraqi captives, to worldwide notoriety after photos of the abuse became public in April 2004.

[21] John Yoo, *War by Other Means: An Insider's Account of the War on Terror* (New York: Atlantic Monthly Press, 2006), pp. 182–3. See the Levin memo, n.8, in Greenberg, *The Torture Debate in America*, p. 362.

[22] So I have argued in Chapters 3 and 8 of this book.

[23] Jan Crawford Greenburg and Ariane Vogue, "Bush Administration Blocked Waterboarding Critic," *ABC News*, Nov. 2, 2007 (http://abcnews.go.com/print?id=3814076). Waterboarding is a form of torture in which water is poured through a cloth covering the victim's nose and mouth; it stops before the victim drowns, but the experience of drowning begins in the first few seconds.

[24] I discuss this in Chapters 7 and 8. The first to note this point is Marty Lederman, "Yes, It's a No-Brainer: Waterboarding *Is* Torture," *Balkinization* blog, Oct. 28, 2006 (http://balkin.blogspot.com/2006/10/yes-its-no-brainer-waterboarding-is.html).

client's desired outcome, and disguising the fact that stretching is going on, are exactly what advocates do every day in litigation and brief-writing. The major point, then, is that the counselor's role and the advocate's role are fundamentally different. In the words of current US ethics rules, the counselor is supposed to provide clients with independent and candid advice – telling the client what the law requires even if that is not what the client wants.[25] The reason for sharply distinguishing the advocate's pro-client tilt in stating the law from the counselor's more objective stance is straightforward. In adversary litigation, whatever exaggerations in presenting the law you introduce can be countered by the lawyer on the other side, and an impartial decision-maker will choose between the arguments. In a counseling situation, it is just the lawyer and her client, with no adversary and no impartial adjudicator. The institutional setting that justifies an advocate's one-sided partisanship in setting forth the law is completely absent in the counseling role.

For that reason, the counselor's rule of thumb should be far different from the one-sided partisanship of the advocate: it is to make your description of the law more or less the same as it would be if your client wanted the *opposite* result from the one you know your client wants.[26] That should be the litmus test of whether your advice is truly independent, or is result-driven by what you know your client wants. It seems completely clear that the torture memos flunked this test by a wide margin.

Let me add an additional wrinkle. Many of Professor Yoo's arguments about presidential power and international law were established long before he entered government; he defended them in his published scholarship. Once in the OLC, he found himself in a position to turn his views into the law of the land, simply by weaving them into opinions that carry the authority to bind the vast executive branch of the government. The fact that the most controversial of these opinions were secret insulated them from critique and pushback, until the fallout from Abu Ghraib made it expedient for the government to release them.

What should a legal opinion writer do who believes that he has the law right and the mainstream has it wrong? Here, it seems to me, the rule of thumb should be this. If your view of the law is out of the mainstream, but you believe you are right, you have the responsibility to tell your client both those things: what the law, on your own best understanding, requires, *and* the fact that your own best understanding is not one that the legal interpretive community would accept.

Professor Yoo's failing, on this argument, is that he did the first but not the second. He exceeded the bounds of a legal counselor by using his position to actually change the law in a direction he favors. Of course, it was a direction

---

[25] ABA Model Rules of Professional Conduct, Rule 2.1 (www.abanet.org/cpr/mrpc/rule_2_1.html). See Comment [1] (www.abanet.org/cpr/mrpc/rule_2_1_comm.html).
[26] See Chapter 8 of this book for expansion of this argument.

his client fervently desired; but here my point of emphasis is somewhat different: it is that a lawyer owes a duty to disclose to the client where his advice deviates from the mainstream – whether or not the client wants to hear this news.

No doubt the ability of an OLC lawyer to turn her own pet theories into law governing the entire executive branch makes the role unique. But here too, the lessons generalize to other law practice. That is because *every* lawyer who provides a client with confidential legal opinions on which the client relies is, in effect, a mini-legislator. Literally millions of lawyer–client conversations occur every week, in which a lawyer advises a client on what the client must or must not do to comply with the law. Think of these conversations as individual mosaic tiles. Put the tiles together, and the result is what the realists called "the law in action." Only a tiny fraction of such legal advice will ever be tested in a court of law, and in this respect the lawyer giving the advice is the highest legal authority the client has. That is why I call the lawyer-adviser a mini-legislator. The case of OLC lawyers, whose client is the mightiest branch of the national government, dramatically demonstrates the point – it is in macrocosm what every lawyer's legal advice on which a client relies represents in microcosm.[27]

The fact that OLC advice was delivered in secret, without an adversarial voice presenting alternative views, in what had become an echo-chamber of like-minded lawyers, is deeply troubling. It is more troubling because we now know, through the investigative efforts of Philippe Sands and Jane Mayer, that the lawyers in the "war council" deliberately froze out of the process virtually everyone who was likely to object.[28]

But on a lesser scale, the same phenomenon is no less troubling when a tax adviser, or a corporate compliance counselor, delivers a contestable legal opinion safe in the knowledge that it will never be audited or tested by outside authorities.

In a phrase, that lawyer is creating secret law. No doubt that is inevitable as long as lawyers advise clients about the law in confidential conversations. What makes this prospect bearable, it seems, is that the lawyers offering their secret advice adhere to certain standards. W. Bradley Wendel has described the operative standard as a matter of their fidelity to the law, and I find that a useful way to think about it.[29] Rather than focusing on the meaning of fidelity to law, I wish to offer two theoretical points about lawyers as microlevel lawmakers.

The first is a jurisprudential point. As we all know, the legal realists were impatient with the law in books. For them, what matters is what officials, and particularly judges, do with the law: for the realists the only real law is the law "in action." Oliver Wendell Holmes writes that "prophecies of what

[27] On this point, see "A Different Nightmare and a Different Dream," in my *Legal Ethics and Human Dignity* (Cambridge University Press, 2007), pp. 131–61.

[28] See especially Mayer, *The Dark Side*, pp. 213–37.

[29] W. Bradley Wendel, "Professionalism as Interpretation," *Northwestern University Law Review*, 99 (2005), 1167–1233.

the courts will do in fact, and nothing more pretentious, are what I mean by the law."[30] As for the law in books, Holmes' friend John Chipman Gray went so far as to hold that statutes are not law, but merely sources of law. They become law only when the judge applies them.

Later realists broadened and refined the thesis. Llewellyn and Cook pointed out that realism rightly understood should look not just at judges, but at other officials as well – sheriffs and police, for example.[31] After all, the judge's order, without police to enforce it, is simply more law on paper. But the underlying theory is the same: official actions, not words in a book, are the law.

Viewed in these terms, my claim about lawyers is that millions of times a week, the lawyer advising the client is the point where the law in books gets translated into the law in action. When I refer to lawyers in their advisory role as mini-legislators, the reader might regard this as a fundamentally realist point – a deviant strand of realism, because I relocate the lawmaking authority from judges and officials to lawyers, but realist nonetheless.

It is in a way. But I see it somewhat differently. There is a well-known objection to the realists' predictive theory of law that prevents us from simply redefining law as the law in action rather than the law in books. The objection, which has been posed by writers as varied in outlook as Felix Cohen, H. L. A. Hart, and Lon Fuller, is that the predictive theory, which seems like the plainest common sense to lawyers who analyze the law by asking what courts are likely to do, is perfectly useless from the judge's point of view.[32] If a judge is honestly puzzled about a legal question, it will do no good at all to think, "The law is whatever I say it is!" You cannot figure out what the law is by predicting your own answer to the question, "what is the law here?" The problem is not that you cannot get it right – it is that you cannot get it wrong.

An exactly analogous problem arises for a lawyer advising a client. We outside observers of the legal system may understand that the law in action is very largely the mosaic of thousands of lawyers advising their clients. But if you are the lawyer trying to figure out what advice to give, you cannot simply predict your own behavior. You must look without, not within. You must look at the sources of law – the law in books. That, it seems to me, is why Wendel's notion of lawyerly fidelity to the law is so important. Without external

[30] Oliver Wendell Holmes, Jr., "The Path of the Law," *Harvard Law Review*, 10 (1897), 460–1.
[31] Karl N. Llewellyn, "A Realistic Jurisprudence—The Next Step," *Columbia Law Review*, 30 (1930), 431–65, at 450, n.16; Walter Wheeler Cook, "'Substance' and 'Procedure' in the Conflict of Laws," *Yale Law Journal*, 42 (1933), 333–58, at 348.
[32] Lon L. Fuller, *The Law in Quest of Itself* (Chicago: Foundation Press, 1940), pp. 94–5; H. L. A. Hart, *The Concept of Law* (Oxford: Clarendon Press, 1964), p. 10; Felix S. Cohen, "The Problems of a Functional Jurisprudence," *Modern Law Review*, 1 (1937), 5–26, at 17. See also Robert Summers, *Instrumentalism and American Legal Theory* (Ithaca, NY: Cornell University Press, 1982), pp. 101–15; Yosal Rogat, "The Judge as Spectator," *University of Chicago Law Review*, 31 (1964), 213–56, at 248–9; Luban, *Lawyers and Justice*, pp. 22–4.

TALES OF TERROR: LESSONS FROM WAR ON TERRORISM   263

constraint on your powers of invention, you run the dangers of hubris and usurpation – of turning your own pet theories into the law.

My second observation about viewing lawyers as microlegislators concerns the moral rule of thumb they should follow when they write their secret law. The rule I have in mind comes straight out of Immanuel Kant. I am not referring to Kant's categorical imperative, but to a principle that he called (in his typically understated way), the "transcendental formula of public law." It says:

> All actions relating to the rights of other human beings are wrong if their maxim is incompatible with publicity.[33]

Call this the *publicity principle* for short. Kant argued that the publicity principle provides what he labels an "experiment of pure reason," which political actors perform by asking themselves, roughly, "Could I get away with this if my action and my reason for performing it were made public?" The test, in Kant's words, will rule out "a maxim which I may not declare openly without thereby frustrating my own intention."[34] That certainly encompasses lawyers who give, let us say, far-fetched tax advice, relying on the fact that it will never come to light. It encompasses the torture lawyers. And it encompasses, I think, all lawyers in the counseling role.

So, by examining the work of the OLC lawyers, we arrive at three rules of thumb for lawyers in their advisory role: asking whether your legal opinion would be the same if your client wanted the opposite result from the one you know your client wants, offering both your best interpretation of the law and an honest statement of where it deviates from mainstream understandings, and the publicity principle.

Lawyers talking torture

At this point I want to resume the story of the lawyers in the war on terrorism. John Yoo wrote the famous torture memo in August 2002. Two months later, a group of intelligence officers met in Guantánamo to discuss interrogation techniques. Present at the meeting were two lawyers, the staff judge advocate to the task-force commander at Guantánamo and the chief counsel to the CIA's counterterrorism center.

For obvious reasons, we very seldom find out exactly what lawyers say to clients in confidential meetings. This one is an exception. Detailed official minutes of the meeting exist, and in summer 2008 a US Senator released

---

[33] Immanuel Kant, "Perpetual Peace: A Philosophical Sketch," in Hans Reiss, Ed., *Kant's Political Writings* (Cambridge University Press, 1970), p. 126. I have slightly altered the translation. For analysis and discussion, see David Luban, "The Publicity Principle," in Robert E. Goodin, Ed., *Theories of Institutional Design* (Cambridge University Press, 1995), pp. 154–98.
[34] *Ibid.*

those minutes.[35] They offer a rare window into the legal counseling process. And they are, to say the least, disturbing. I am going to quote some excerpts from those minutes. But first I want to issue a caution. The CIA counsel objects that he did not say everything the minutes report him as saying.[36] I am nevertheless going to analyze the minutes as written. To the best of my knowledge, nobody else has ever come forward to say that the minutes were wrong, including the JAG at the meeting, who spoke at length with Philippe Sands, as reported in his book *Torture Team*. More importantly, the CIA counsel's objection came six years after the meeting in question. In my opinion, nobody, with the most honest intentions in the world, can possibly remember what they *did not* say at a meeting that took place six years earlier.

It is not my purpose here to launch accusations at individuals, and for that reason I am not going to use the lawyers' names. The CIA counsel will just be the "CIA counsel," and the staff judge advocate will just be "the JAG."

For example, we find the JAG saying to the group, "We may need to curb the harsher operations while the [International Red Cross] is around. It is better not to expose them to any controversial techniques." At that point, the CIA counsel helpfully adds that "In the past when the [Red Cross] has made a big deal about certain detainees, the [Defense Department] has 'moved' them away."

The CIA counsel then goes on to provide a brief exposition of the law against torture. I quote:

> [T]orture has been prohibited under international law, but the language of the statutes is written vaguely. Severe mental and physical pain is prohibited. The mental part is explained as poorly as the physical.

Pause for a moment. So far, it seems to me, he is on solid ground. He has correctly stated the legal test, and his complaints about vagueness are entirely fair. He continues:

> Severe physical pain [is] described as anything causing permanent physical damage to major organs or body parts. Mental torture [is] described as anything leading to permanent, profound damage to the senses or personality.

Pause again. Here, we find the CIA counsel quoting almost verbatim from the Bybee memo, as though it is the actual wording of the statute. Obviously, he is familiar with the memo.

---

[35] Senate document (www.levin.senate.gov/imo/media/doc/supporting/2008/Documents. SASC.061708.pdf), Tab 7. All quotations are from this document.

[36] Statement from Jonathan Fredman to Senator Carl Levin, Chair of the Senate Armed Forces Committee, and Senator John McCain, Ranking Member of the Committee (Nov. 7, 2008) (http://s3.amazonaws.com/propublica/assets/docs/05aFredman_State-ment.pdf).

Then comes the money line, as he adds his own gloss to Yoo's analysis: "It is basically subject to perception. If the detainee dies you're doing it wrong."[37]

According to the minutes, the CIA counsel answers a question about waterboarding by explaining, "If a well-trained individual is used to perform this technique it can feel like you're drowning. The lymphatic system will react as if you're suffocating, but your body will not cease to function." Then he moves to other techniques: "It is very effective to identify phobias and use them (ie, insects, snakes, claustrophobia)." The JAG asks about "imminent threats of death" – a phrase that may have stuck in her mind because the US torture statute singles it out as a form of mental torture. And the CIA counsel replies that it should be handled on a case-by-case basis. But then he adds: "Mock executions don't work as well as friendly approaches, like letting someone write a letter home, or providing them with an extra book."

At which point one of the intelligence officers pipes up, "I like the part about ambient noise."[38] Soon after that, the meeting ends. I am tempted to say nothing about this incredible script, which largely speaks for itself. But a few remarks might be useful.

First, notice the way in which the OLC torture memo percolated down through the CIA counterterrorism counsel in Guantánamo, to the judge advocate who will advise the commander, to the intelligence officers who, as it happens, will very shortly start torturing a detainee named Mohammed Al Qahtani for eight weeks. The CIA counsel reproduced John Yoo's analysis of severe pain and suffering with fair accuracy, but in his hands it quickly morphs into "if the detainee dies you're doing it wrong." A few moments' thought will show that the CIA counsel's brutal conclusion is the operational version of Professor Yoo's "organ failure or death" test of torture. Ideas have consequences. Lawyers may believe that they bear no moral responsibility for what use their advice is put to, but it seems to me that even if the OLC lawyers are not interested in moral responsibility, moral responsibility is interested in them.

Second, it seems rather clear that the two lawyers in the room have totally internalized the outlook of their clients. Talk about tough and ruthless! The JAG discusses the need to hide abusive tactics from the Red Cross. The CIA counsel speaks with an undertaker's equanimity about waterboarding, snakes, and mock executions. For him, they are all on a par with giving detainees a book to read. Snakes, books – whatever works. Although he is a lawyer and not

---

[37] The CIA counsel indignantly denies that he said the issue is subject to perception: his basic message was that the torture standard is *not* subjective or subject to perception. Rather, the standard is set out in Justice Department guidelines. However, that standard *is* subject to perception: it is the "pain equivalent to that of organ failure or death" standard in the OLC memo, which, of course, requires the interrogator to guess whether the victim is experiencing pain equivalent to that of organ failure or death.

[38] Prisoners were frequently bombarded with noise: ear-splitting rock music, round-the-clock hissing sounds, etc.

an interrogator, he offers recommendations about which tactics are most effective. He has crossed the line from legal adviser to interrogation adviser. If the clients were looking for the two lawyers to provide an independent perspective, they came to the wrong lawyers.

Three weeks later, a criminal investigator in the Pentagon named Mark Fallon read these minutes. Fallon quickly dashed off an appalled e-mail to another official. He begins, "This looks like the kinds of stuff Congressional hearings are made of" – a rather prophetic comment, given that the minutes were released at a Congressional hearing. He flags the JAG's comments about cover-ups and the CIA counsel's about torture, and describes them as "beyond the bounds of legal propriety." The comments about the lymphatic system, he writes, "would in my opinion shock the conscience of any legal body." And he ends, "Someone needs to be considering how history will look back at this."

Mark Fallon is a career criminal investigator, not a lawyer, but his phrasings make clear that he is as well trained in the legal tests of permissible interrogation as any lawyer. In any event, it seems to me that his outsider's perspective quickly enabled him to perceive what the JAG and the CIA counsel apparently could not. Their judgment had been compromised by excessive identification with their clients.

Wasserstrom, recall, fears that lawyers inhabit a simplified moral world, one that is often amoral and occasionally immoral. He believes that this phenomenon results from the neutral-partisan role morality of lawyers. But we have seen something a little different. Partisanship clearly has its place. But the simplified moral world of the partisan advocate does not belong in the counselor's role. It is too simple, and too likely to distort the lawyer's judgment and blur the line between lawyer and client. The problem is the confusion of roles, not the advocate's role itself.

The rule of law in the worldview of the Guantánamo defense bar

At this point, I want to turn to the lawyers on the other side. Detainees at Guantánamo are represented by both civilian and military lawyers. The five hundred or so civilian lawyers include professional public interest lawyers as well as hundreds of volunteers from large American law firms, many of whom consider it a badge of honor to represent Guantánamo inmates seeking habeas corpus. One of my colleagues, who studies the American criminal justice system, finds it a bit frustrating that there is so much enthusiasm for the Guantánamo cases and so little for the tens of thousands of inmates enduring worse conditions in American prisons.

The fact is that Guantánamo has taken on a significance far greater than itself, precisely because of the government's legal strategy in creating it as a law-free zone. Symbolically, the legal profession of a liberal-democratic state – a *Rechtsstaat* – simply cannot tolerate the existence of a state-created law-free zone. If the state can create one, the thought runs, then a *Rechtsstaat* is at its core nothing more than a hollow mocking promise of a system that deserves our moral and political allegiance. In that case the legal profession is nothing more than the priesthood of a false god.

To be sure, all this loads an enormous amount of symbolic freight onto Guantánamo, perhaps more than it deserves. But, having interviewed a dozen of the Guantánamo defenders, I am convinced that all of them see the stakes in the elevated terms I have just described: somehow, their professional identity is deeply bound up with Guantánamo. Guantánamo is more than a prison camp – in the eyes of the defense lawyers it is a standing affront to the political order that gives their profession meaning. That, more than any political view about the Bush administration or the detainees, is what drives so many lawyers to volunteer their time and energy to represent the prisoners.

One of the most remarkable phenomena is the role of military lawyers representing detainees, and I want to conclude by discussing them. The military lawyers, called "judge advocates" and known as JAGs, have been appointed to defend the detainees charged with war crimes before military commissions. Like the majority of American military officers, the JAG defenders are often political conservatives. David Hicks' lawyer, Major Dan Mori, described himself to me as a "pretty conservative guy."[39] Navy Commander William Kuebler (according to a newspaper profile) had never voted for a Democrat in his life, and a fellow officer described him by saying "Take the average conservative guy in the street and multiply that by a million."[40]

And yet the JAG defenders have turned out to be among the most fiery critics of the military commissions and the government that created them. Consider a closing argument made in June 2008 by Major David Frakt, representing detainee Mohammad Jawad, a teenage prisoner who had been subjected to the "frequent-flyer" program of intense sleep deprivation. Major Frakt spoke bitterly about "the civilian political appointees of this administration" who "intentionally cut out the real experts on the law of armed conflict, the uniformed military lawyers, the JAGs ... for fear that their devotion to the Geneva Conventions might pose an obstacle to their intended course of action."[41] He described the torture memos as "now disgraced, disavowed, and relegated to the scrapheap of history where they belong." He praised by name the handful of lawyers within the administration and the military who opposed the strategy of detainee abuse. And then, astonishingly, he described the

---

[39] Luban, "Lawfare and Legal Ethics in Guantánamo," p. 2017.

[40] William Glaberson, "An Unlikely Antagonist in Detainee's Corner," *New York Times*, June 19, 2008.

[41] Major Frakt's statement is available on the American Civil Liberties Union website (www.aclu.org/safefree/detention/35753res20080619.html). Outraged letters from the four TJAGs (heads of the JAG Corps) when they learned after the fact about the Bybee memo are reprinted in Greenberg, *The Torture Debate in America*, pp. 377–91.

"enablers of torture" – those are his words – as war criminals of the "home-grown variety." To make sure that the judge knew exactly whom he was talking about, he listed nine of them by name: the vice president and Secretary of Defense of the United States, and seven lawyers: three from the OLC; two from the Defense Department; the vice president's counsel; and the former attorney general of the United States. These are remarkable accusations from a major in the United States Air Force, voiced in a military court to a military judge.

In the same vein, Major Dan Mori, David Hicks' lawyer, who made eight visits to Australia, gave passionate speeches against the fairness of the military commissions and Hicks' treatment. Mori and his civilian co-counsel Joshua Dratel had concluded that the only way Hicks would ever get out of Guantánamo would be political pressure from the Australian government to cut a deal, and Mori gave his speeches to increase that pressure. Furthermore, as Dratel explained to me, both of the lawyers felt it necessary "to put David in a positive light in Australia. We knew it was likely that he would serve some time there, and we worried about how the Australians would view him when he returned in custody. We needed to help his re-entry to Australia."[42] In other words, Mori and Dratel were thinking about the case and their client the way that a sophisticated white-collar defender does.

Nevertheless, Dan Mori unexpectedly found himself threatened by the prosecutor because of his Australian speeches. Under US military law, it is a criminal offense for an officer to speak contemptuously about the civilian leadership of the country. Suddenly, Mori found himself face to face with an intense conflict between his role as a military officer, sworn to duty to his government, and his role as a defense lawyer who, in the famous words of Lord Brougham, must "separat[e] the duty of a patriot from that of an advocate, [and] go on reckless of consequences."[43] Of course, if military defenders could be stopped from criticizing the military commissions by threat of court-martial, they would all face a disabling conflict of interest, and none of them could ethically represent detainees. Sensing the stakes, Mori filed a motion to have the prosecutor disqualified for improperly coercing a defense lawyer. The issue was never resolved because the Hicks case was successfully plea-bargained before the judge ruled on Mori's motion.[44]

In a parallel case, Air Force Major Yvonne Bradley, representing Binyam Mohammed, was given a direct order by a military judge who outranked her to proceed at a hearing when she believed she had a disabling conflict of

[42] Luban, "Lawfare and Legal Ethics in Guantánamo," p. 2016.
[43] J. Nightingale, Ed., *The Trial of Queen Caroline* (London: J. Robins & Co., Albion Press, 1820–1), vol. II, p. 8.
[44] Luban, "Lawfare and Legal Ethics in Guantánamo," pp. 2014–18. For a vigorous critique of my claim of role conflict, see Major General Charles J. Dunlap, Jr., and Major Linell A. Letendre, "Military Lawyering and Professional Independence in the War on Terror: A Response to David Luban," *Stanford Law Review*, 61 (2008), 417–41, at 438–40.

interest. Like Mori, her role as a lawyer and her role as an officer were on a collision course. Bradley resolved the conflict in a startling way: she invoked her own right against self-incrimination, on the theory that if she disobeyed the order she would face charges, but if she obeyed it she would betray her ethics as a lawyer.

In both Bradley's case and Mori's, we can see something very interesting and important. Faced with a conflict between their role as officers and their role as lawyers, Mori and Bradley in effect opted for their role as lawyers. Or so I thought when I spoke with them.

Mori, however, does not see it that way. When I asked him, he replied, "I didn't have any conflict. Saying someone deserves a fair trial is what being an American and a military officer is all about."[45] Although at the time I thought the role conflict was greater than Mori believed, on reflection it now seems to me that Mori had in mind exactly what I have been talking about – the sense among many lawyers that Guantánamo poses a standing challenge to the rule-of-law values that in their eyes define the constitutional order. As Major Frakt put it in the speech I quoted previously,

> America is a nation founded on a reverence for the rule of law. We should never forget that when we take an oath to enlist or be commissioned as an officer in the United States Armed Forces, we do not swear to defend the United States, we swear "to support and defend the Constitution of the United States against all enemies, foreign and domestic."[46]

There is no role conflict, because in the eyes of these military lawyers, the country they swore to defend as officers is defined by the rule of law their profession as lawyers commits them to.

This, it seems to me, is a final lesson from the lawyers in the war on terrorism. Earlier, I focused on the integrity of the role of legal adviser and counselor, its differences from the role of advocate, and the threat that extreme partisanship poses to it. When it comes to the defense lawyers, their basic role is that of partisan advocates, and the conflict is between that role and others they might occupy, those of military officer or patriotic American. They resolve the conflict by identifying their country with its constitution, the constitution with the rule of law, and their own identities, both as officers and as lawyers, with being guardians of the rule of law. Some might criticize this chain of identifications as overly simple, and political philosophers may dispute the thought that political community can be reduced to the single value of legality.

Yet it seems to me importantly true that the *Rechtsstaat* represents a distinctive and worthy political order. *And* it is importantly true that lawyers

[45] Luban, "Lawfare and Legal Ethics in Guantánamo," p. 2004.
[46] Frakt, closing statement, June 19, 2008 (note 41 above).

play a constitutive role in defining and maintaining the *Rechtsstaat*. Even if the equation of country with constitution and constitution with legality is in a rigorous and literal sense untrue, it is a "noble lie" in something very close to Plato's sense: a myth that defines the legal profession as a distinctive calling. If we are looking for the source of moral steadfastness in the legal profession, we could do worse than start here.

10

An affair to remember

The chapters of this book focus on policies and positions adopted by the US government during the eight years of the George W. Bush administration. However, to say this does not imply that the themes are time-bound or parochial. The tension between national security and human rights, leaders' itch to maximize their power during times of emergency (real, perceived, or merely proclaimed), the morality and law of torture, and the ethical dilemmas of professionals in government are here to stay—maybe not forever, but certainly for years to come. Nor are they merely US issues, even though US policies and law raised them in an especially clear form. The threat of terrorism affects much of the world, as do the threats of torture and inflated executive power.

Nevertheless, readers will surely wonder what became of the distinctive views about rights, power, and torture in the Bush administration. The answer, I will suggest, is complex. On the one hand, the Obama administration has explicitly prohibited torture and avoided extreme assertions of executive power. As discussed in the preface to Chapter 2, Obama denies that his role as commander in chief places his decisions outside civilian law. These are major reversals. On the other hand, his administration has deliberately downplayed the torture issue, and there has been no accountability for torture. That creates problems that I shall explore in this concluding chapter.

One is a crucial philosophical, moral, and legal question: does failure to hold the previous administration accountable make the Obama administration in some sense complicit in its predecessor's wrongdoing? A principal aim of this chapter is to examine the theories under which a later administration can, through inaction, come to "own" the misdeeds of its predecessor. Whether under those theories the Obama administration is blameworthy is a very close call.

One of the theories I examine focuses on responsibility for allowing pro-torture propaganda to go largely unanswered by the organ of government most responsible for opposing it. In practice, the comparative silence of the Obama administration has had the baleful effect of allowing the friends of torture to sway public opinion in their direction. That, in turn, raises a question quite different from the Obama administration's blameworthiness: the question of broader, collective, public responsibility. Americans, I will argue, have conducted an illicit love affair with torture, even as our government has tried to forget it and make us forget it.

But amnesia was never in the cards – false memories, rosy rationalizations, and revisionist histories inevitably fill the vacuum. The American fling with torture is an affair to remember.

The end of an era?

The program of "enhanced" interrogation continued almost until 2008, despite legal efforts to stop it. In late 2005, the US Congress passed the Detainee Treatment Act (DTA), which prohibits cruel, inhuman and degrading treatment of captives outside US territory.[1] To ensure that it would not be vetoed, Congress attached the DTA to an appropriations bill necessary to fund the military. President Bush signed the bill but remained defiant: he attached a statement to his signature declaring that the DTA unconstitutionally restricted his powers as commander in chief, and he threatened to enforce it – or, rather, not enforce it – accordingly.

Then, in 2006, the Supreme Court's *Hamdan* v. *Rumsfeld* decision held that Common Article 3 of the Geneva Conventions applies to the US conflict with Al Qaeda and the Taliban – a reversal of the Bush administration's contrary position. *Hamdan* meant, specifically, that the Geneva prohibitions on humiliating and degrading treatment apply as a matter of US law. Worse still from the perspective of the interrogators, those violations were war crimes as defined in the US war-crimes statute.

Congress lost no time covering itself with glory as it acted to remove this legal embarrassment. It retroactively decriminalized humiliating and degrading treatment of prisoners back to 1997, in order to ensure that US personnel would never face charges for the abuses they had heaped on detainees.

Ironically, the details of that legislation were hammered out just a week before the sixtieth anniversary of the Nuremberg Tribunal's epoch-making judgment. In other words, just as the world prepared to celebrate the triumph of legal accountability over war crimes – an effort the United States spearheaded over the opposition of its World War II allies – Congress engineered the triumph of war crimes over legal accountability.[2] At exactly the same time, President Bush admitted that the CIA had maintained secret prisons, boasted that the interrogations saved American lives without resorting to "torture," but announced that he was closing the prisons and removing the detainees to Guantánamo.[3]

[1] 42 U.S.C. § 2000dd.

[2] See David Luban, "Forget Nuremberg," *Slate*, Sept. 26, 2006 (www.slate.com/articles/news_and_politics/jurisprudence/2006/09/forget_nuremberg.html).

[3] The White House, President Discusses Creation of Military Commissions to Try Suspected Terrorists, Sept. 6, 2006 (http://georgewbush-whitehouse.archives.gov/news/releases/2006/09/20060906-3.html).

So, grudgingly, and accompanied by a sturdy bodyguard of precautions against accountability, the US government began to inch its way out of the torture and secret prison businesses in practice, even while denying and defending them in theory.[4]

Nevertheless, old habits die hard, and the CIA kept pushing. In 2006, the Office of Legal Counsel (OLC) head Steven Bradbury answered an inquiry from the CIA about abusive conditions of confinement, and provided a memorandum giving assurance that they were not illegal.[5] As late as November 2007, the CIA inflicted six days of sleep deprivation on a detainee; the previous July, Bradbury provided a 79-page memo explaining why extended sleep deprivation does not violate the DTA and Geneva Convention prohibitions on degrading treatment. The fundamental argument was the familiar OLC assertion (criticized in Chapter 5) that the fact that it is done for vital national security purposes means that treatment cannot count as degrading.[6]

So far as we know, that was the last of the "enhanced" interrogations. In the 2008 presidential campaign, both candidates were on record as torture opponents. The Republican nominee John McCain had himself been tortured as a prisoner of war in North Vietnam.

After Barack Obama won, Bush administration officials did some last-minute housecleaning. Just five days before Obama's inauguration, Steven Bradbury – himself the author of four sweeping torture memos – wrote a remarkable

---

[4] However, there have been reports of continuing abuse well into the Obama administration. In 2010, the BBC journalist Hilary Anderson reported that the United States maintains a secret prison within the Bagram complex in Afghanistan, and that prisoners there underwent beatings, cold-cell treatment, and sleep deprivation. Hilary Anderson, "Afghans 'abused at secret prison' at Bagram airbase," BBC News, Apr. 15, 2010 (http://news.bbc.co.uk/1/hi/world/south_asia/8621973.stm); Anderson, "Red Cross confirms 'second jail' at Bagram, Afghanistan," BBC News, May 11, 2010 (http://news.bbc.co.uk/1/hi/8674179.stm). US officials denied these reports; if they are true, the mistreatment would clearly violate President Obama's directives.

[5] Letter from Steven G. Bradbury, Acting Assistant Attorney General, to John A. Rizzo, Acting General Counsel to the CIA, Aug. 31, 2006; Memorandum Regarding Application of the Detainee Treatment Act to Conditions of Confinement at Central Intelligence Agency Detention Facilities, Aug. 31, 2006, both available (www.justice.gov/olc/olc-foia1.htm).

[6] Pamela Hess, "Memos: CIA Pushed Limits on Sleep Deprivation," The Guardian, Aug. 27, 2009 (www.justice.gov/olc/docs/memo-warcrimesact.pdf). Steven G. Bradbury, Memorandum for John A. Rizzo, Acting General Counsel, Central Intelligence Agency, Re: Application of the War Crimes Act, the Detainee Treatment Act, and Common Article Three of the Geneva Conventions to Certain Techniques That May Be Used by the CIA in the Interrogation of High Value al Qaeda Detainees, July 20, 2007 (www.justice.gov/olc/docs/memo-warcrimesact.pdf). Bradbury followed up the opinion with letters to the CIA confirming this permission, dated July 24, Aug. 23, Nov. 26, and Nov. 27 (www.justice.gov/olc/docs/memo-warcrimesact.pdf). In all these documents, the detainee's name is redacted.

memo retracting nine of the most extreme OLC opinions of 2001–3, most of them by Jay Bybee or John Yoo. Bradbury explained that "in the months following 9/11, attorneys in the Office of Legal Counsel and in the Intelligence Community confronted novel and complex legal questions in a time of great danger and under extraordinary time pressure." According to Bradbury, this led the lawyers to depart from the usual OLC practice of rendering opinions only on concrete, actual policy proposals, and not on "general or amorphous hypothetical scenarios."[7]

Bradbury's excuse scarcely makes sense: if the opinions were on abstract or hypothetical legal questions rather than concrete issues, there was no extraordinary time pressure. And if the lawyers were really under time pressure to deal with specific questions, why did they take time out to write opinions on broad questions of law? In fact, the nine memos had in common aggressive assertions of executive authority, and thus the time pressure sounds suspiciously like the self-imposed desire to expand executive power before the shock of the disaster had faded. But, significantly, Bradbury went on to say that the opinions "have not for some years reflected" the OLC's views of the law.

Two days after Obama's inauguration, the new president issued a sweeping executive order forbidding torture and cruel, inhuman, or degrading treatment. Henceforth, no interrogation techniques could be employed other than those approved in the US Army's field manual on interrogation, which authorizes only noncoercive methods that comply with the Geneva Conventions and the DTA.[8] Furthermore, the executive order expressly declared that "from this day forward" no interrogators can "rely upon any interpretation of the law governing interrogation ... issued by the Department of Justice between September 11, 2001 and January 20, 2009," the date Obama was inaugurated.[9] In other words, Obama completely repudiated the legal legacy of the Bush administration on interrogation.[10]

The Obama administration took one other important step: in April 2009, responding to a freedom-of-information lawsuit, it released the hitherto-secret

---

[7] Steven G. Bradbury, Memorandum for the Files: Re: Status of Certain OLC Opinions Issued in the Aftermath of the Terrorist Attacks of September 11, 2001 (www.justice.gov/olc/docs/memostatusolcopinions01152009.pdf), p. 1.

[8] Executive Order 13491—Ensuring Lawful Interrogations, Jan. 22, 2009, sections 3(a)–(b) (www.whitehouse.gov/the_press_office/EnsuringLawfulInterrogations).

[9] Ibid., section 3(c).

[10] We should note, however, that the Army's field manual does contain one restricted method, "separation" (i.e., isolation), and adds the ominous proviso that "Use of separation must not preclude the detainee getting four hours of continuous sleep every 24 hours" – which appears to leave the gate open for the mental torture of 20-hour-a-day interrogations. US Army Field Manual FM 2–22.3, Appendix M, p. 356 (www.fas.org/irp/doddir/army/fm2-22-3.pdf). So even the Obama executive order contains one loophole for abuse.

torture memos. In doing so, President Obama countermanded his political advisers, who preferred to let bygones be bygones, and his security team, which was protective of the CIA.[11] Now the world could see for itself the memos' legal reasoning and confirm the full catalog of the CIA's "thirteen techniques," which the memos set out in graphic detail.

We learned that one detainee was kept awake for seven days and seven nights. We learned that the method for keeping detainees awake was to shackle them to the ceiling and floor in loose chains that would jerk them awake if they began to fall over; their hands would be above chest level. The memo explained that some would be naked, while those who kept their clothes would be in diapers.[12] It was from these memos that we learned how many times the detainees were waterboarded, including Khalid Sheikh Mohammed (KSM)'s 183 waterboardings in a single month.[13]

The torture memos showed us other things as well. Most notably, they revealed that torture was not a last resort after other interrogation methods failed. A detainee got only one chance to offer actionable intelligence before the "enhanced" interrogation began.[14]

Thus, the Obama administration took three vital steps against the torture legacy of its predecessor: prohibiting torture, annulling the Bush administration's legal opinions on detainee treatment, and releasing the torture memos. Obama also released other OLC memos and a fuller version of an already-released CIA Inspector General's report on torture.

But other steps went in the opposite direction. The central fact to understand is how tenaciously the Obama administration rejected any form of accountability for torture.

The president gave an early hint in an interview ten days before he took office: "I don't believe that anybody is above the law. On the other hand I also have a belief that we need to look forward as opposed to looking

[11] Daniel Klaidman, *Kill or Capture: The War on Terror and the Soul of the Obama Presidency* (Boston: Houghton Mifflin Harcourt, 2012), ch. 2.

[12] Steven G. Bradbury, Memorandum for John A. Rizzo, Senior Deputy General Counsel, Central Intelligence Agency, Re: Application of 18 U.S.C. §§ 2340–2340A to Certain Techniques That May Be Used in the Interrogation of a High Value al Qaeda Detainee, May 10, 2005, reprinted in David Cole, Ed., *The Torture Memos: Rationalizing the Unthinkable* (New York Review of Books, 2009), pp. 165–8.

[13] *Ibid.*, Re: Application of United States Obligations Under Article 16 of the Convention Against Torture to Certain Techniques That May Be Used in the Interrogation of High Value al Qaeda Detainees, May 30, 2005, reprinted in Cole, *The Torture Memos* [henceforth: Article 16 Opinion], p. 271.

[14] *Ibid.*, Re: Application of 18 U.S.C. §§ 2340–2340A to the Combined Use of Certain Techniques in the Interrogation of High Value al Qaeda Detainees, May 10, 2005, reprinted in Cole, *The Torture Memos*, pp. 203–4; Article 16 Opinion, pp. 233–4.

backwards." He added that he did not want the "extraordinarily talented people" at the CIA, who are "working very hard to keep Americans safe," to "suddenly feel that they've got to spend all their time looking over their shoulders and lawyering up."[15] In April 2009, Obama rebuffed a recommendation for a truth commission to examine the Bush-era program, repeating that he wanted to look forward and not litigate the past.[16]

"Looking forward rather than backward" became the mantra. Superficially, it sounds like common sense, but a moment's thought shows how fatuous it is. We would never say about a murderer or an embezzler, "Don't investigate or prosecute – we should be looking forward, not back." In fact, "look forward, not back" sounds more like the pleading of Shakespeare's arch-villain Richard III to the mother of the princes he had murdered:

> Look, what is done cannot now be amended...
> Plead what I will be, not what I have been;
> Not my deserts, but what I will deserve.
>
> (*Richard III*, Act IV, scene IV)

Law enforcement *demands* looking back when the law has been grievously violated. Otherwise we might as well have no law at all.

Of course, Obama had a problem: the conspiracy to torture went all the way to the top. President Bush boasts about it in his memoirs. Genuine accountability would ensnare the entire upper echelon of the Bush administration.[17] Obviously, attempting to hold the leadership accountable on an issue in which a significant part of the country agreed with the former administration would have sidelined all other issues on the new administration's agendas; it also would have failed, and no doubt Obama did not consider it for a moment. But without condemning the leadership that had approved torture, holding the followers accountable became difficult and problematic. The net result was no accountability at all.

[15] Bob Fertik, "Stephanopoulos Asks Obama About Special Prosecutor," *Democrats.com*, Jan. 10, 2009 (www.democrats.com/stephanopoulos-asks-obama-about-special-prosecutor).

[16] Shailagh Murray and Paul Kane, "Obama Rejects Truth Panel," *Washington Post*, Apr. 24, 2009.

[17] George W. Bush, *Decision Points* (London: Virgin Books, 2011), p. 170. "[CIA Director] George Tenet asked if he had permission to use enhanced interrogation techniques, including waterboarding, on Khalid Sheikh Mohamed [KSM]... 'Damn right,' I said." In 2008, *ABC News* reported that half-a-dozen top officials of the Bush administration met in the White House Situation Room to discuss and approve "enhanced" interrogations. Jan Crawford Greenberg, Howard L. Rosenberg, and Ariane deVogue, "Sources: Top Bush Advisors Approved 'Enhanced Interrogation'", *ABC News*, Apr. 9, 2008 (http://abcnews.go.com/TheLaw/LawPolitics/story?id=4583256&page=1#.UXzxW5WrrzI); Greenberg, Rosenberg and deVogue, "Bush Aware of Advisers' Interrogation Talks," *ABC News*, Apr. 11, 2008 (http://abcnews.go.com/TheLaw/LawPolitics/story?id=4635175&page=1#.UxzxBpWRrzI).

State secrets

The first courtroom clue that the new administration was unfriendly to accountability appeared in February 2009, in a California case. In 2002, an Ethiopian of British nationality named Binyam Mohamed had been rendered to Morocco by the CIA and brutally tortured. In the words of a US court that granted Mohamed's motion for a writ of habeas corpus,

> Binyam Mohamed's trauma lasted for two long years. During that time, he was physically and psychologically tortured. His genitals were mutilated. He was deprived of sleep and food. He was summarily transported from one foreign prison to another. Captors held him in stress positions for days at a time. He was forced to listen to piercingly loud music and the screams of other prisoners while locked in a pitch-black cell. All the while, he was forced to inculpate himself and others in various plots to imperil Americans. *The Government does not dispute this evidence.*[18]

After his release, Mohamed returned to the UK; he and other rendition victims sued the California-based company, Jeppesen, from which the CIA leased the airplane used in his rendition.[19] The Bush administration vaporized the lawsuit by invoking the "state secrets defense."[20] This defense declares that a case cannot be adjudicated without the risk of revealing state secrets, and therefore must be dismissed – even if the plaintiff offers to prove his case without using government sources. That is why lawyers' nickname for the state-secrets defense is "the nuclear option."[21]

Binyam Mohamed and his fellow plaintiffs appealed, and many assumed that the newly installed Obama legal team would back off from the extravagant state-secrets claim, and at least permit them to try to prove some of their claims about Jeppesen's knowing collusion with torture by using nongovernmental sources. (For example, the plaintiffs had an affidavit by a Jeppesen employee recalling that a company official admitted to him, "We do all the extraordinary

---

[18] *Mohamed v. Obama*, 704 F. Supp. 2d 1, 26–27 (D.D.C. 2009) (emphasis added).

[19] He also sued the UK government for its role in his rendition. After fruitlessly attempting to invoke a British version of the state-secrets defense, the UK government settled for an undisclosed but large amount of money. Patrick Wintour, "Guantánamo Bay Detainees to Be Paid Compensation by UK Government," *The Guardian*, Nov. 16, 2010 (www.guardian.co.uk/world/2010/nov/16/guantanamo-bay-compensation-claim).

[20] *Mohamed v. Jeppesen Dataplan, Inc.*, 539 F. Supp. 2d 1128 (N.D. Cal., 2008) (granting US government's motion to intervene and dismissing complaint because the subject matter of the case is a state secret). This dismissal was reversed on appeal, 579 F.3d 943 (9th Cir. 2009), but the government prevailed in an *en banc* rehearing, 614 F.3d 1070 (9th Cir. 2009), cert. denied, 131 S. Ct. 2442 (2011).

[21] For an encyclopedic study of the state-secrets defense, its widespread use, and its manifold abuses, see Laura K. Donohue, "The Shadow of State Secrets," *University of Pennsylvania Law Review*, 159 (2010), 77–216.

rendition flights," which the official also referred to as "the torture flights" or "spook flights."[22] This would have been powerful evidence of knowing collusion.)

Just the opposite happened. The Department of Justice's lawyer defended the Bush position that the case must be halted before it began because of the risk of disclosing privileged information. Even one of the judges hearing the argument expressed surprise.[23] The government lost, but it eventually prevailed in an *en banc* rehearing in which the government made secret submissions about the sensitive information that might be disclosed if the case were allowed to proceed. Frustratingly, we do not know exactly why the government won; the court's opinion declared that secrecy prevented it from saying even in a general way what risks the government was alleging.[24] Secret submissions about secret information resulted in a legal decision with a secret basis.

To be sure, the Department of Justice had issued assurances that the state-secrets defense would never be invoked to "conceal violations of the law" or to "prevent embarrassment to a person, organization or agency of the United States government."[25] The court agreed that in this case the state-secrets privilege was not invoked "to avoid embarrassment or to escape scrutiny of its recent controversial transfer and interrogation policies."[26]

However, it is important to see that this reassurance means less than it seems to. Suppose, as seems likely, that the privileged information consisted of whatever confidential agreements the United States made with the defendant company and with foreign governments to whom the torture victims were rendered. It is hard to imagine what else the privileged information might be. Given that the plaintiffs were offering to prove their case without government evidence, it had to have been the defendant who might need to disclose privileged information to defend itself, presumably by explaining its relationship with the government – in which case we can infer that it is the details of that relationship that the government was trying to protect.

Revealing such confidential agreements could in the government's eyes "reasonably be expected to cause significant harm to the national defense or foreign relations" – language the court quotes from the Department of Justice guidelines to explain when the state-secrets defense is appropriate.[27] That is

[22] 579 F.3d 951 n.1.
[23] John Schwartz, "Obama Administration Maintains Bush Position on 'Extraordinary Rendition' Lawsuit," *New York Times*, Feb. 9, 2009.
[24] *Mohamed* v. *Jeppesen Dataplan*, 614 F.3d, at 1086.
[25] The Department of Justice standard is Memorandum from Attorney General to Heads of Executive Departments and Agencies, Policies and Procedures Governing Invocation of the State Secrets Provision, Sept. 23, 2009 [hereinafter State-secrets memo] (www.justice.gov/opa/documents/state-secret-privileges.pdf), p. 1.
[26] 614 F.3d, p. 1090.   [27] *Ibid.*; State-secrets memo, p. 1.

because revelation might make contractors reluctant to participate in future covert operations (harming national security), or foreign governments to make secret agreements with the United States (harming foreign relations).

It would then turn out that embarrassing private corporations by breaking confidentiality agreements *is* the national-security problem, and exposing the foreign governments *is* the foreign-policy problem that led the Obama administration to invoke the state-secrets privilege. Invoking the state-secrets privilege under such circumstances would honor the letter of the Department of Justice standard: it would not be done to avoid *government* embarrassment, but rather the embarrassment of its partners. Of course, it is the same embarrassment viewed from two angles. Distinguishing them is the kind of hair-splitting argument that only a lawyer could love, but the Department of Justice and the courts are, after all, populated by lawyers.

In much the same way, one could say that preventing a prostitute's embarrassment by suppressing information about her encounters with a celebrity politician is not the same as preventing the *politician's* embarrassment – and therefore the suppression is not being done to avoid embarrassing politicians. If the distinction sounds sophistical, that is because it is. It emphatically does not mean that the information concerns anything other than the sexual encounter; and in Mohamed's case, nothing the court says compels us to conclude that the privileged information concerns anything other than the rendition program.

The Department of Justice guidelines also prohibit invoking the state-secrets privilege to "conceal violations of the law." This too means less than it seems to. The law permits the president to order covert operations as long as they do not violate US statutes or the Constitution.[28] As it happens, rendering foreign detainees to governments who torture them violates no US statute unless the US agents doing the rendition specifically intend the torture.[29] And rendering a prisoner to a foreign government, even one known to torture, does not run afoul of the Convention Against Torture (CAT), at least as the United States interprets it.[30] Once again, the anodyne-sounding Department of Justice guidelines give

---

[28] 50 U.S.C. § 413b(5) states that the president "may not authorize any action that would violate the Constitution or any statute of the United States," but international law is neither constitutional nor statutory.

[29] That is because the renderers would be liable only as aiders and abetters of the foreign government's torture, and aiding-and-abetting liability for a specific intent crime like torture requires sharing that specific intent. *Nye and Nissan* v. *U.S.*, 336 U.S. 613, 619 (1949) (holding that to be liable as an aider and abetter requires that the person "associate himself with the venture, that he participate in it as something that he wishes to bring about, that he seek by his action to make it succeed").

[30] The CAT's article 3 prohibits transferring someone to a country where they will be tortured, but the United States interprets that prohibition to apply only to transfers from the United States, not from outside the United States. Response of the United States of America to the UN Committee Against Torture, List of Issues to Be Considered During the Examination of the Second Periodic Report of the United States of

no reason to conclude that the privileged information the government was shielding concerned anything other than the rendition program.

I go into these details because they matter. The Department of Justice guidelines on the state-secrets defense are meant to reassure us that the government did not and would not use it to cover for torture. If the analysis here is correct, though, the government could maintain the guidelines with a straight face and still assert the state-secrets privilege to avoid revealing the tangled network of secret agreements and contracts that undergirded the torture program – but in real-world terms, that would be indistinguishable from covering for torture.

Accountability loses 101 to 0

What about accountability for the interrogators themselves? Let us start near the top, with Jose Rodriguez, the CIA's director of clandestine services. Rodriguez made headlines in 2005 by burning more than ninety interrogation videotapes in the aftermath of Abu Ghraib. The Bush administration's attorney general, Michael Mukasey, appointed prosecutor John Durham to investigate. In 2010, just as the statute of limitations was about to run out, Durham announced that no charges would be filed against Rodriguez.[31]

Attorney General Holder also put Durham in charge of investigating 101 torture cases. From the beginning, Holder excluded cases where interrogators followed the torture memos' guidelines.[32] To torture opponents this was a galling decision, because it allowed the discredited torture memos to reach out from the grave to set the standard of accountability. Galling as it was, the decision was probably right. Under US law, to prosecute someone for torture you must prove they intentionally inflicted severe pain and suffering, and the torture memos declared that the pain and suffering caused by the CIA's techniques was not severe. That meant interrogators could truthfully say that they lacked

America, Question 13, May 5, 2006 (www2.ohchr.org/english/bodies/cat/docs/Advance-Versions/listUSA36_En.pdf), pp. 32–7. It is not clear that the Obama administration retains this interpretation, but I am unaware of any repudiation or replacement.

[31] Jerry Markon, "No Charges in Destruction of CIA Videotapes, Justice Department Says," *Washington Post*, Nov. 9, 2010 (www.washingtonpost.com/wp-dyn/content/article/2010/11/09/AR2010110904106.html).

[32] Department of Justice, Attorney General Eric Holder Regarding a Preliminary Review into the Interrogation of Certain Detainees, Aug. 24, 2009 (www.justice.gov/ag/speeches/2009/ag-speech-0908241.html). Holder explained that intelligence professionals "need to be protected from legal jeopardy when they act in good faith and within the scope of legal guidance. That is why I have made it clear in the past that the Department of Justice will not prosecute anyone who acted in good faith and within the scope of the legal guidance given by the Office of Legal Counsel regarding the interrogation of detainees." He added, "I share the President's conviction that as a nation we must, to the extent possible, look forward and not backward when it comes to issues like these."

guilty intention because they had been told by the lawyers that the pain and suffering they intentionally inflicted did not cross the legal threshold.

In real-world terms, of course, this is absurd – it is the fundamental trick, discussed in Chapter 5, of treating "severe pain or suffering" as a legal term of art. The interrogators could see the suffering with their own eyes, and all the torture memo gave them in response was Groucho Marx' line: "Who are you going to believe, me or your lying eyes?" Nevertheless, it was an unstoppable legal defense, and prosecuting the interrogators when there was no chance of convicting them would have been unethical.

That still left plenty of interrogations for Durham to investigate: the cases where interrogators may have gone too far even by torture memo standards. Daniel Klaidman reports that Attorney General Holder "had identified at least ten instances in which interrogators had gone far beyond what had been sanctioned by the prior administration's legal team."[33] But in 2011, Holder announced, based on Durham's work, that he was closing all the cases but two – the two where the detainees died.[34] Finally, in August 2012, Holder announced that these last two cases would also be closed.[35] In the contest between torture and criminal accountability, torture won by a score of 101 to 0.

Here, however, we must understand that insufficient evidence does not mean the investigations cleared the interrogators. Indeed, the least credible conclusion to draw is that nobody tortured and nobody was tortured; tellingly, the government says nothing of the sort. Holder and the prosecutor Durham said only that "the admissible evidence would not be sufficient to obtain and sustain a conviction beyond a reasonable doubt."[36]

This might mean that government agencies succeeded in destroying or muddying the evidence – recall that Jose Rodriguez, heading the CIA's clandestine services, destroyed the videotapes of interrogations, and it is not hard to imagine that other evidence might have suffered a similar fate. Or it might mean that the evidence was stale or missing or inadmissible for any number of reasons. Or it might mean that units who tortured maintained the code of *omertà*. Or that Mr. Durham lost potential convictions because in order to get their testimony about others he immunized people who should have been

---

[33] Klaidman, *Kill or Capture*, p. 69.

[34] Department of Justice Office of Public Affairs, Statement of the Attorney General Regarding Investigation into the Interrogation of Certain Detainees, June 30, 2011 (www.justice.gov/opa/pr/2011/June/11-ag-861.html).

[35] Department of Justice Office of Public Affairs, Statement of Attorney General Eric Holder on Closure of Investigation into the Interrogation of Certain Detainees, Aug. 30, 2012 (www.justice.gov/opa/pr/2012/August/12-ag-1067.html). This announcement was issued in the late summer, a period in the annual news cycle well known for low interest in public affairs.

[36] Holder statement, note 32 above.

targets. Or that he was unwilling or unable to obtain testimony from the torture victims – who, in any case, would not willingly come to the United States to testify or would not be allowed out of Guantánamo to do so. Or that he concluded that, because the victims and witnesses are terrorists or terrorism suspects (or simply unappealing foreigners) their testimony would not be credible to an American jury. Or that he assumed – perhaps correctly – that juries would be so heavily predisposed to acquit "heroic" interrogators that the threshold for proof beyond a reasonable doubt needed to be something approaching Cartesian certainty.

Finally, it might mean that too much admissible evidence would reveal state secrets – what seems to me the most plausible explanation. There is a well-known criminal defense tactic known as "graymail," in which defendants insist that they can defend themselves properly only by revealing state secrets. We now know that the CIA had secret prisons in Poland, Romania, and Thailand, and that all of these were established with the secret cooperation of the governments of those countries. For reasons already discussed, the US government regards confidential agreements as state secrets, and would almost certainly drop criminal charges in order to avoid the risk of revealing them. In addition, the government (sometimes rightfully) regards information about the sources and methods of intelligence gathering to be state secrets. It seems likely that a great deal of the evidence Durham needed to prosecute would have fallen hostage to graymail by defendants and the state-secrets defense invoked by the government. In that case, the cover-up provided by the state-secrets defense in civil cases like Binyam Mohamed's proves equally powerful as a cover-up of criminality.

Notice that none of these hypotheses accuse Mr. Durham of conducting a sham investigation or even a shabby investigation. We should certainly not rule out the possibility of an unenthusiastic investigation, but that is more than I know or am prepared to assert. The fact that accountability came in the form of a *criminal* investigation already means the burden of proof is heavy and the rules on admissible evidence are restrictive.

Unfortunately, we know little or nothing about the Durham investigation. We do not know whom he interviewed or, equally important, whom he did not interview. We do not know whom he immunized. And we do not know how much of his evidence was blocked by state-secrets concerns – which, as I argued earlier, are only millimeters away from cover-ups.

Above all, we do not know what his evidence *did* show. That torture was more likely than not? Strongly likely? Both of these are consistent with "not provable beyond a reasonable doubt." Nor do we know what the inadmissible evidence might show. The fact of criminal investigation provides an ironclad justification to shield all these details: prosecutors are supposed to maintain tight confidentiality, to avoid smearing defendants they cannot convict.

Other forms of accountability

Truth commissions

All this suggests that criminal investigations might not be the best form for accountability to take. One alternative is a truth commission, which investigates and names names, but with no legal consequences. (In one common version, truth commissions come side-by-side with amnesty.) A truth commission would have the added advantage of avoiding the danger of "patriotic acquittals" – acquittals that might legitimize torture – by juries in no mood to convict their own intelligence personnel.

So far, the Obama administration has avoided truth commissions. The closest we have is the 577-page report by the bipartisan but private Constitution Project, based on a two-year investigation and released early in 2013. Its blue-ribbon panel unanimously concludes that the United States engaged in torture. The US Senate Intelligence Committee has also prepared a 6,000-page report on the torture program, which reportedly reaches the same conclusions as the Constitution Project but reveals far more details than have so far become public – but, as of mid-2014, it remains cloaked in secrecy.[37]

Foreign investigations

That leaves the last avenue of legal accountability, foreign investigations. For years, human-rights groups filed criminal complaints in European countries against the Bush administration officials involved in the torture program. None of these countries wanted to go up against the United States, and they all found ways to duck the cases even when their own national law gave them jurisdiction over foreign tortures and war crimes. This is hardly surprising; all these nations are US allies. The last complaint fizzled in Spain in early 2012. What might be more surprising is that the embassy cables outed by WikiLeaks showed the Obama administration secretly pressuring Spain to rein in its independent prosecutors and drop the case.[38]

---

[37] Some of these details are reportedly more grim than those previously made public. See Klaidman, *Kill or Capture*, pp. 66–7, reporting on Eric Holder's shocked reaction when a US senator showed him portions of the report.

[38] See Carol Rosenberg, "From Florida to Spain, Intrigue to Stop a Judge," *Miami Herald*, Dec. 24, 2010 (www.miamiherald.com/2010/12/24/1988022/from-florida-to-spain-intrigue. html); Carol Rosenberg, "WikiLeaks: How U.S. Tried to Stop Spain's Torture Probe," *Miami Herald*, Dec. 28, 2010 (www.miamiherald.com/2010/12/25/1988286/wikileaks-how-us-tried-to-stop.html); Scott Horton, "The Madrid Cables," *Harper's Magazine*, Dec. 1, 2010 (http://harpers.org/blog/2010/12/the-madrid-cables/). Horton provides a translation of the report in the Spanish newspaper *El País*, "EE UU maniobró en la Audiencia Nacional para frenar casos," Nov. 30, 2010 (www.elpais.com/articulo/espana/EE/UU/maniobro/Audiencia/Nacional/frenar/casos/elpepuesp/20101130elpepunac_1/Tes).

Other WikiLeaks cables revealed that the Bush administration had put similar pressure on Germany not to investigate one of the most grotesque miscarriages of justice in the war on terrorism. The CIA had snatched and rendered a German citizen named Khalid El-Masri while he was vacationing in Macedonia, but it turned out to be a case of mistaken identity. After five months of imprisonment and abuse in Macedonia and Afghanistan, it dawned on the CIA that they had the wrong man. They unceremoniously dumped El-Masri on a deserted road in Albania, and the US government never acknowledged its mistake or apologized. In fact, the WikiLeaks cables revealed that US officials warned Germany not to prosecute El-Masri's kidnappers, at the risk of US anger.[39]

Meanwhile, what happened to the CIA official who ordered the El-Masri kidnapping? A CIA counterterrorism official recalled that "she always did these cases based on her gut. She'd say 'this guy's bad, that guy's dirty', because she had a 'feeling' about them."[40] She once drew a reprimand for making a "voyeuristic" unauthorized trip abroad to watch KSM get waterboarded.[41] And her career after the El-Masri blunder? She was promoted to head the CIA's Global Jihad Unit.[42] Reportedly, the CIA reprimanded the lawyer who advised her, but she too was promoted, and by 2011 was legal adviser to the CIA's Near East Division.[43]

El-Masri sued both in the United States and in the European Court of Human Rights. In 2011, the European Court found that El-Masri had indeed been tortured and abused by the CIA in Macedonia, and ordered Macedonia to pay him compensation for its part in the operation.[44] In the United States, the Bush administration blew up El-Masri's lawsuit with the state-secrets defense.[45]

[39] Andy Worthington, "WikiLeaks' Revelations That Bush and Obama Put Pressure on Germany and Spain Not to Investigate US Torture," Andy Worthington Blog, Aug. 12, 2010 (www.andyworthington.co.uk/2010/12/08/wikileaks-revelations-that-bush-and-obama-put-pressure-on-germany-and-spain-not-to-investigate-us-torture/).

[40] Jeff Stein, "How Will the CIA Deal with 'Rendition' Supervisor?", Washington Post, May 14, 2010 (http://voices.washingtonpost.com/spy-talk/2010/05/how_will_the_cia_deal.html).

[41] Jane Mayer, The Dark Side: The Inside Story of How the War on Terror Turned into a War on American Ideals (New York: Doubleday, 2008), p. 282.

[42] Adam Goldman and Matt Apuzzo, "CIA Officers Make Grave Mistakes, Get Promoted," NBC News, Feb. 9, 2011 (www.nbcnews.com/id/41484983/ns/us_news-security/t/cia-officers-make-grave-mistakes-get-promoted/#.UX0_6ZWRrzI). The article details other examples of CIA officials who participated in illegal or even fatal interrogations and who were promoted or who, after being reprimanded and leaving the agency, came back on board as contractors.

[43] Ibid.

[44] El-Masri v. The Former Yugoslav Republic of Macedonia, Application No. 39630/09, Judgment, Dec. 13, 2012 (http://hudoc.echr.coe.int/sites/eng/pages/search.aspx?i=001-115621#{"itemid":["001-115621"]}).

[45] El-Masri v. United States, 479 F.3d 296 (4th Cir. 2007).

Firings and internal discipline

Even without a truth commission or criminal prosecutions, accountability could take the form of internal discipline in the CIA, including firings. Indeed, one form of accountability that would not run into the obstacles faced by criminal prosecutions would have been a wave of firings and demotions in the CIA of those who promoted the torture program and – especially – interrogators who exceeded the permissions even of the torture memos. There is no evidence that this took place. Instead, we saw promotions.

The lawyers

Next consider the fate of the Bush Department of Justice lawyers who wrote the secret torture memos. Only two of them (out of four) were investigated by the Office of Professional Responsibility (OPR), the Department of Justice's internal ethics watchdog. The OPR wrote a scathing report and recommended that both lawyers should be referred for professional discipline.[46]

But under Obama, the report was given to a senior Department of Justice official, who recommended reversing the recommendation.[47] Criticizing the OPR's report on nitpicky grounds, he announced that the torture lawyers had been guilty only of "poor judgment."[48] The attorney general followed his recommendation. There would be no referrals for disciplinary action.

As other chapters in this book have detailed, the lawyers were at the heart of the entire torture program, as well as the firewall of nonaccountability surrounding it. Not only did their opinions provide what Jack Goldsmith labeled get-out-of-jail-free cards to interrogators, they cleared the upper reaches of the Bush administration (including the president himself) to authorize and approve it – which in turn made the quest for accountability harder. The fact that the lawyers were doing what their clients wanted, while the clients were insulated

---

[46] Department of Justice Office of Professional Responsibility Report: Investigation into the Office of Legal Counsel's Memoranda Concerning Issues Related to the Central Intelligence Agency's Use of "Enhanced Interrogation Techniques" on Suspected Terrorists, July 29, 2009 (http://cdm16064.contentdm.oclc.org/utils/getfile/collection/p266901coll4/id/2317/filename/2318.pdf).

[47] David Margolis, Associate Deputy Attorney General, Memorandum for the Attorney General and Deputy Attorney General, Memorandum of Decision Regarding the Findings of Professional Misconduct in the Office of Professional Responsibility's Report of Investigation into the Office of Legal Counsel's Memoranda Concerning Issues Related to the Central Intelligence Agency's Use of "Enhanced Interrogation Techniques" on Suspected Terrorists, Jan. 5, 2010 (http://judiciary.house.gov/hearings/pdf/DAGMargolis-Memo100105.pdf). I have analyzed and criticized this memorandum in David Luban, "David Margolis Is Wrong," Slate, Feb. 22, 2010 (www.slate.com/articles/news_and_politics/jurisprudence/2010/02/david_margolis_is_wrong.html).

[48] Ibid., p. 68.

by the legal advice the lawyers tailored to the measures of their desires, created what in the appendix to Chapter 8 I labeled a perfect Teflon circle.

Censorship

The US campaign against accountability extends even to the literary realm. There is now an impressive library of memoirs by former interrogators and officials. By law, these must be reviewed by the CIA, to make sure that they do not reveal any precious state secrets.

One of them was written by a former FBI agent named Ali Soufan. In 2009, Soufan and I were both witnesses at a Senate Judiciary Committee hearing about the torture program. Soufan was the star witness, although none of us ever laid eyes on him. To protect his personal safety, he testified from behind a black curtain and a wooden screen – a rather unforgettable sight.

What Ali Soufan had to say was remarkable. He was the interrogator of Abu Zubaydah, and it was Soufan who extracted the most valuable information Zubaydah had to give, without resorting to torture or coercion. Then the CIA took over and tortured Zubaydah, who promptly shut down. He was briefly returned to Soufan and his partner, who re-engaged him and got the most important piece of information Zubaydah had to give, the identity of Jose Padilla. Then the CIA took over again, and Zubaydah shut down again. After one more such cycle, Soufan protested at the "borderline torture" Zubaydah was undergoing, at which point the FBI pulled Soufan out. Zubaydah was ultimately transferred to Guantánamo.[49]

In 2011, Soufan published a book about all this, titled *The Black Banners*. But when the CIA vetted the book, they imposed scores of cuts and redactions. They made Soufan take out information that was already in his public Senate testimony. They made him take out the words "I" and "me" when he was describing interrogations he conducted. Just as the book was going to press, CIA demanded 30 additional days to review the index – so the book was published without an index.[50]

---

[49] What Went Wrong: Torture and the Office of Legal Counsel in the Bush Administration: Hearing Before the Subcommittee on Administrative Oversight and the Courts of the Senate Committee on the Judiciary, 111th Congress (2009), pp. 22–5 (testimony of Ali Soufan); see his full written statement (www.judiciary.senate.gov/hearings/testimony. cfm?id=e655f9e2809e5476862f735da14945e6&wit_id=e655f9e2809e5476862f735-da14945e6-1-2).

[50] Scott Shane, "C.I.A. Demands Cuts in Book About 9/11 and Terror Fight," *New York Times*, Aug. 25, 2011 (www.nytimes.com/2011/08/26/us/26agent.html?pagewanted=all); Michelle Shepard, "Terrorism, Waterboarding and CIA Censorship: Ex-FBI Agent Ali Soufan Talks to The Star," *Toronto Star*, Sept. 15, 2011 (www.thestar.com/news/world/2011/09/15/terrorism_waterboarding_and_cia_censorship_exfbi_agent_ali_soufan_talks_to_the_star.html).

Compare this with the experience of Jose Rodriguez, the head of CIA clandestine services who burned the videotapes. Rodriguez is quite a colorful character. He once bragged to a *60 Minutes* reporter that "we are the dark side," and it was Rodriguez who demanded that government officials "put their big boy pants on and provide the [legal] authorities that we needed."[51] Rodriguez's book *Hard Measures* discussed some of the same interrogations that were redacted out of Soufan's book. The subtitle of Rodriguez's book is *How Aggressive CIA Actions After 9/11 Saved American Lives.* Apparently the CIA has no objection to revealing "secrets" when they are spun to make the agency look good; they only injure national security when they embarrass the CIA. Eventually, discrepancies like these became glaring enough that the CIA launched an investigation into the biases of its publication review board.[52]

The facts I have just recited are not world-shattering except to the victims. Like other ephemeral scandal news, they will soon be forgotten, and they will almost certainly be out of date by the time this book is published. Yet the utter lack of accountability for torture raises issues of broad and lasting moral significance, as I now hope to show.

Owning the past

After the government defended the broad state-secrets defense in Binyam Mohamed's case, the journalist Andrew Sullivan warned that "with each decision to cover for their predecessors, the Obamaites become retroactively complicit in them."[53] Interestingly, during the 2009 White House debates over whether to release the torture memos, Attorney General Eric Holder issued a similar caution to President Obama, warning that "if you don't release the memos, you'll own the policy."[54] Call this *Holder's maxim.*

Holder's maxim sounds even stronger than retroactive complicity. The latter may refer simply to the traditional legal concept of an accessory after the fact: someone who, "knowing that an offense ... has been committed, receives, relieves, comforts or assists the offender in order to hinder or prevent his apprehension, trial or punishment."[55] Holder's terminology of "owning"

---

[51] Leslie Stahl, *60 Minutes* transcript, "Hard Measures: Ex-CIA Head Defends post-9/11 Tactics," Apr. 29, 2012 (www.cbsnews.com/8301-18560_162-57423533/hard-measures-ex-cia-head-defends-post-9-11-tactics/).

[52] Greg Miller and Julie Tate, "CIA Probes Publication Review Board over Allegations of Selective Censorship," *Washington Post*, May 31, 2012 (http://articles.washingtonpost.com/2012-05-31/world/35455152_1_publications-review-board-harsh-interrogation-cia-critics).

[53] Andrew Sullivan, "The Binyam Mohamed Case," *The Daily Dish*, Feb. 9, 2009 (www.theatlantic.com/daily-dish/archive/2009/02/the-binyam-mohamed-case/205864/). See also David Luban, "You Cover It up, You Own It," *Balkinization Blog*, Feb. 10, 2009 (http://balkin.blogspot.co.uk/2009/02/you-cover-it-up-you-own-it.html).

[54] Klaidman, *Kill or Capture*, p. 61.   [55] 18 U.S.C. § 3.

the policy implies something stronger than a detachable after-the-fact wrong-doing. It suggests taking over the actual perpetrator's responsibility.

Holder's maxim has intuitive resonance, but is it true? Responsibility ordinarily implies direct or indirect causation of an act, but outside of science fiction and theoretical physics no such thing as retroactive causation exists. In what sense can someone acting after the fact come to own the prior fact?

Perhaps all that Holder meant was the tautology that if Obama chose to perpetuate secrecy, he would thereby take aboard the policy of secrecy. But "if you don't release the memos, you'll own the policy" becomes even more significant if "the policy" meant the entire Bush administration program of torture and denial. In that case, "you'll own the policy" means something like "if you continue the secrecy and concealment, you'll own not merely the coverup, but the policies you are covering up." That would be a way of saying that prohibiting torture and rescinding the Bush-era legal memos would not sufficiently cleanse Obama of responsibility for the torture policies.

This seems to be exactly what Holder meant, for he also told his assistants, "It's not enough that we stopped doing these things. If we don't look into this and hold people responsible, then we become morally culpable."[56] In saying this, Holder echoed a warning from US Senator Sheldon Whitehouse when Whitehouse showed Holder portions of the Senate's confidential report on the interrogation program – portions about mock executions, about threats that detainees' children would be killed and their wives raped, and about interrogators waving a gun and a power drill in front of the prisoner's head. "Eric," Whitehouse said, "right now the Bush administration is responsible for what happened... But if we don't do what's right and investigate these allegations, we will be responsible."[57]

Let us consider what Holder's "ownership" metaphor means. It might mean one or both of two things. First, ownership of an act might mean quite literally that the act is one's own. Second, it might mean ownership of moral responsibility for an act done by someone else. Call these *act-ownership* and *responsibility-ownership*. I take it that Holder's maxim means the latter – not that the Obama administration would have retroactively become perpetrators of the Bush administration's torture program, but that failure to account for it would take ownership of moral responsibility.

I do not mean that it is impossible for a latecomer to take ownership of an act after it has been performed. Suppose that four thieves commit a jewelry heist together, and the next day a fifth man offers to fence the jewelry and launder the proceeds in return for a cut of the profits. It seems natural to regard him as a participant in the overall robbery. He shares the group's intention, and his role completes and consummates their plan. The fact that

[56] Klaidman, *Kill or Capture*, p. 68.   [57] *Ibid.*, pp. 67–8.

he did not sign on until the day after the jewelry had been stolen, rather than the day before, seems morally irrelevant, and would be treated as irrelevant in most systems of criminal law. The entire scheme forms a single joint criminal enterprise, and each participant, including the latecomer, could be charged as a principal perpetrator.

This, I take it, would be an unfair analogy to the kind of cover-up in which Holder feared continued concealment would embroil the Obama administration. There was no shared intention to torture or to profit from the torture program; and lax accountability would not obviously count as the completion and consummation of the plan – although the latter point is more debatable, given that the torture policy always included shielding the participants from liability. But the new administration had very different motives for concealment than consummating or profiting from the policy, so the jewelry-heist analogy would stretch the concept of act-owning the torture program too far. It seems far more likely that Holder's maxim refers to responsibility-ownership, not act-ownership, and that is how I will interpret it. That still leaves the question how a nonparticipant in a policy can take over moral responsibility for it.

In what follows, I will suggest three ways that ignoring and downplaying a predecessor's wrongful policy might entail moral responsibility for the policy. One is based on the commonplace assumption of continuity of government through political change. The second comes from the expressive character of government action, including inaction: when a subsequent administration signals acquiescence in or approval of a prior administration's wrongdoing, it associates itself with it. And the third is an argument that by failing to impede the downstream consequences of prior wrongdoing, the later administration takes responsibility for those consequences.

On each of these theories, I will argue, the Obama administration comes out with a mixed report card – not as the owner ("free and clear") of the Bush administration's policies or moral responsibility for them, but not exactly as *not* the owner, given the gravity of failure to provide accountability in any of its forms for the torture program.

Sovereign moral debt

Distinct from the culpability and responsibility of individuals, organizations can be liable as corporate bodies for their individual agents' misdeeds. This familiar notion of corporate responsibility applies straightforwardly to governments and their departments. In international law, the default assumption is *continuity of the state* even when administrations change. Lawyers insist on it even when a revolution replaces one regime with its sworn enemies. And not only lawyers: international credit markets live and die by the continuity assumption, which guarantees that borrower governments must repay their debts regardless of internal political change. That is why postrevolutionary regimes remain responsible for the sovereign debts of their predecessors, no matter how odious.[58]

The continuity assumption is not a novelty in international law. Medieval jurists distinguished between the sovereign's "body natural" and "body politic": the king's body natural would age, sicken, and die, but the body politic survived unaltered even as a new body natural ascended the throne.[59] The concept of a continuous body politic was an indispensable legal fiction that would (for example) allow the monarchy to enter into binding contracts even if the monarch's "body natural" was that of a small child.

Is the continuity assumption anything more than a legal fiction useful for purposes like government contracts? We might strenuously object, after all, to the assertion that in the real world a revolutionary regime perpetuates the old regime it shed blood to overthrow. There is force to this objection. But when the form of the state remains intact, and power transfers lawfully and smoothly from one administration to the next, the continuity assumption seems plausible in common-sense terms. In such cases it amounts to little more than the acknowledgment that collective agency is possible and that collective agents maintain their identity through turnover of personnel. That is how we ordinarily think about corporations and governments.

Under the continuity assumption, a change in regime or administration does not change the state itself, and successor administrations automatically inherit their ancestors' policies, laws, and obligations. Sovereign debts and treaty obligations offer the most conspicuous examples, but there is no reason to limit the effect of the continuity assumption to these.

States can bear a burden of sovereign *moral* debt as well as sovereign financial debt. A state that commits injustice owes a duty of rectification – a moral debt to its victims and, in cases of international crime, to humanity at large. That sovereign moral debt does not melt away when the regime changes, any more than a state's financial debt to its bondholders melts away. In concrete legal terms, when the United States joined the CAT it took on sovereign obligations to prevent, investigate, and punish torture – and, of course, we may suppose that it would have had a parallel moral obligation even if the CAT had never existed.

The continuity assumption creates a presumption that a new administration *always* owns the policies of its predecessor. Viewed in light of the continuity assumption, Holder's maxim thus takes on a different hue. In this light, Holder's maxim does not say anything mysterious, or tie ownership of the predecessor policy to retroactive causation. Presumptively, the US government already

---

[58] I do not mean to defend this rule of international law. There are reasons to think it is a rule that great powers and other foreign creditors imposed on post-colonial regimes for venal reasons.

[59] The classic discussion is Ernst H. Kantorowicz, *The King's Two Bodies: A Study in Medieval Political Theology* (Princeton University Press, 1957).

owned the Bush administration's policies, and the real question is what it would take for the Obama administration to break with them.

Notice that this is act-ownership – ownership of the policy itself, not of moral responsibility for the policy. Indeed, one might doubt that a corporate entity like a government is the sort of being to which we can intelligibly ascribe moral responsibility. As a British jurist famously quipped, corporate entities have no soul to damn or body to kick.[60]

But individual corporate and governmental agents do. They bear moral responsibility for the decision whether the government will continue to own the act, or will, quite literally, disown it. Responsibility-ownership of government policies by the officers of government is the counterpart to act-ownership by the government viewed as a corporate body, and vice versa. They come as a package.

A new government can disown predecessor policies only by (1) discontinuing them and (2) explicitly and officially disavowing them – and even then it continues to owe whatever sovereign debts the predecessor accrued, moral debts included. On this reading, Holder's maxim means two things:

(1) that without going further than the executive order prohibiting torture, the Obama administration would not break sufficiently with the Bush administration to overcome the presumptions that the United States owns the Bush policies and that the new administration's officers own moral responsibility for them, and

(2) that going further than the executive order was needed to discharge the US sovereign moral debt.

Both seem right. The point of the first idea is that even though Obama's executive order *ended* the Bush torture program – which, as we have seen, was already largely gone in practice – he needed to explicitly disavow the principles and policies behind it and explain why.

Fortunately, Obama did this. He not only prohibited torture and CIDT, he admitted publicly that what the United States had engaged in was, in fact, torture, and condemned it in principle. In a much-noted national security

---

[60] I am grateful to Amy Sepinwall for clarifying discussion of the distinction between ownership of an act and ownership of moral responsibility for it, and of whether corporate entities can own acts without being the kind of entity that can be the subject of ascriptions of moral responsibility. The seemingly paradoxical idea that a corporate or governmental entity can (nonmetaphorically) be said to *act* but cannot be said to have *moral responsibility* for its acts – responsibility lying solely with the human beings who compose the corporate entity – is one that I have taken from Sepinwall. It is less paradoxical than it sounds. Consider that a trained animal can act, and can even act intentionally, but is not the sort of being to which it makes sense to ascribe moral responsibility. The moral responsibility lies with the animal's human master. On the view defended here, corporate entities are analogous to trained animals, and their officers to the animals' master.

speech in May 2009 – delivered at the National Archives (a symbolically appropriate venue for moral retrospection!) shortly after the torture memos were released – Obama said this:

> Instead of strategically applying our power and our principles, we too often set those principles aside as luxuries that we could no longer afford. And in this season of fear, too many of us – Democrats and Republicans; politicians, journalists and citizens – fell silent.
>
> In other words, we went off course. And that is not my assessment alone. It was an assessment that was shared by the American people, who nominated candidates for President from both major parties who, despite our many differences, called for a new approach – one that rejected torture... And that is why I took several steps upon taking office to better protect the American people.
>
> First, I banned the use of so-called enhanced interrogation techniques by the United States of America... We must leave these methods where they belong – in the past. They are not who we are. They are not America.[61]

Obama echoed the same themes in his Nobel Prize lecture a few months later: "I believe the United States of America must remain a standard bearer in the conduct of war... That is why I prohibited torture."[62] And again in a 2011 press conference: "Waterboarding is torture. It's contrary to America's traditions. It's contrary to our ideals. That's not who we are... And we did the right thing by ending that practice."[63] Finally, in a much-heralded 2013 speech, Obama said, straightforwardly, "I believe we compromised our basic values – by using torture to interrogate our enemies." He added that his administration "stepped up the war against al Qaeda, but also sought to change its course... We unequivocally banned torture."[64]

The important point about all these statements is that they not only admit that "enhanced interrogation" is torture, but they also explicitly disavow it as a matter of principle. This is precisely the kind of public disavowal, expressed in official, on-the-record statements, that it takes to overcome the presumption that Obama's administration owns the predecessor's policies.

The other meaning of Holder's maxim – that the United States continues to owe its sovereign moral debt – is far less comfortable for the Obama administration and the United States. For that debt has never been discharged.

---

[61] Remarks by the President on National Security, May 21, 2009 (www.whitehouse.gov/the-press-office/remarks-president-national-security-5-21-09).

[62] Remarks of the President at the Acceptance of the Nobel Peace Prize, Dec. 10, 2009 (www.whitehouse.gov/the-press-office/remarks-president-acceptance-nobel-peace-prize).

[63] News Conference by President Obama, Nov. 21, 2011 (www.whitehouse.gov/the-press-office/2011/11/14/news-conference-president-obama).

[64] Remarks of President Barack Obama, The Future of Our Fight Against Terrorism, National Defense University, May 23, 2013 (www.whitehouse.gov/the-press-office/2013/05/23/remarks-president-barack-obama).

Discharging it would require accountability, apology, and compensation to innocent victims like Maher Arar and Khalid El-Masri.

Here, Obama's "look forward, not back" theme was a culprit. For example, in his statement when the torture memos were released, Obama praised the US commitment to the rule of law and to (unspecified) ideals and "core values," but insisted that "this is a time for reflection, not retribution... Nothing will be gained by spending our time and energy laying blame for the past."[65] That is patently untrue: what would be gained by laying blame is, precisely, acknowledging that what was done in the past is *blameworthy* and identifying on whom the blame falls. That seems essential to paying down the sovereign moral debt.

Obama took a step in that direction in the previously quoted speech where he acknowledged that "too many of us – Democrats and Republicans; politicians, journalists and citizens" fell silent in the face of torture, and "we went off course." But without any other form of accountability, apology, and restitution beyond a few scattered presidential remarks, the sovereign moral debt remains unpaid (and apparently uncollectible).

Noticing these two corollaries of sovereign continuity – that overcoming the presumption of policy continuity requires public, principled disavowal of past policies, but also discharging the sovereign moral debt – allows us a more precise way to identify the partial achievement and partial failure of the Obama administration's efforts to disown torture. He accomplished the first, but failed on the second.

Symbolic affiliation

The question whether officials' failure to investigate and punish wrongdoing makes the officials "owners" of the wrongdoing is a familiar one in military law's doctrine of command responsibility. Although the military context differs markedly from its civilian counterpart, the analogy is instructive, and reinforces the conclusions of the preceding section.

In its modern formulation, a military commander is culpable if she knowingly fails to punish her subordinates' war crimes – if, in the formulation of the Rome Statute of the International Criminal Court, she fails "to submit the matter to the competent authorities for investigation and prosecution."[66] Failure to punish is a generic offense meaning, more inclusively, failure to investigate, report, or discipline war crimes by subordinates under the superior officer's effective command.

---

[65] The White House Office of the Press Secretary, Statement of President Barack Obama on Release of OLC Memos, Apr. 16, 2009 (www.whitehouse.gov/the_press_office/Statement-of-President-Barack-Obama-on-Release-of-OLC-Memos).

[66] Rome Statute of the ICC, art. 28(a)(2).

Command responsibility is a centuries-old doctrine, as is the criminalization of failure to punish troops' crimes. The chief unsettled legal question is whether or not failure to punish makes the commander responsible for the subordinates' crimes – whether, in our terms, the commander retroactively *owns* the subordinates' crimes (in either the act-ownership or responsibility-ownership sense). The alternative interpretation is that failure to punish is a separate, self-standing crime, like dereliction of duty or conduct unbecoming an officer. In that case, the commander's failure to punish would be a far less serious offense than the war crimes themselves, and would not entail ownership. Call these two readings of the failure to punish the *ownership reading* and the *separate wrongdoing* reading. Over the years military law has vacillated and split between the two readings, with the United States currently using the ownership reading to punish its enemies and the more lenient separate wrongdoing reading to punish its own.[67]

Of course, the analogy between a commander's responsibility to punish troops' misconduct and an administration's responsibility to punish misdeeds by its

---

[67] In brief, the ownership reading appeared in the rules governing George Washington's army. See American Articles of War of 1775, article 12, quoted in William Winthrop, *Military Law and Precedents*, 2nd edn. (Boston: Little, Brown, 1920), vol. II, p. 1480. But it disappeared from the Civil War Lieber Code and subsequent US articles of war, up to and including their replacement in 1951 by the Uniform Code of Military Justice (UCMJ). Indeed, the entire doctrine of command responsibility is absent from those codes. All these versions of the US Articles of War may be found online (www.loc.gov/rr/frd/Military_Law/AW-1912-1920.html). Commanders who fail to investigate or punish their troops' war crimes can now be punished only for the separate and lesser offenses of dereliction of duty or conduct unbecoming an officer. That means, in practice, that the UCMJ has adopted the separate wrongdoing interpretation of command responsibility. Yet the United States punished Japanese military and even civilian commanders under an ownership interpretation of command responsibility that had disappeared from its own military law. See Trial of General Tomoyuki Yamashita (8 Oct.–7 Dec. 1945), 4 L.R.T.-W.C. 24 (1948); Trial of Koki Hirota, in R. John Pritchard and Sonia Magbanua Zaide, Eds., *The Tokyo War Crimes Trial: The Complete Transcripts of the Proceedings of the International Military Tribunal for the Far East* (Lewiston, NY: Edwin Mellen Press, 1981), vol. XX, p. 49,791. History repeated itself when Congress enacted the Military Commissions Act of 2006, establishing military tribunals to try alien enemy combatants: Congress incorporated the ownership reading of failure to punish, although that interpretation does not apply to US commanders even if their troops commit the same crimes: 10 U.S.C. § 950q(3) (declaring that an alien enemy commander who fails to punish war crimes is to be charged as a principal in those war crimes). International tribunals have also been divided between the ownership reading and the separate wrongdoing reading: the International Criminal Tribunal for Former Yugoslavia (ICTY) has adopted the separate wrongdoing reading, while the International Criminal Court (ICC) uses the ownership reading. The ICTY cases are *Prosecutor* v. *Hadzihasanovic*, Case No. IT-01-47-T, Trial Judgment §§ 1777–80 (Mar. 15, 2006) and *Prosecutor* v. *Halilovic*, Case No. IT-01-48-T, Trial Judgment §§ 91–100 (Nov. 15, 2005). The ICC's doctrine appears in article 28 of the Rome Statute.

predecessor's leadership is a distant one; but the distinction between the ownership and separate wrongdoing readings of failure to punish is similar to the issues we have been exploring.

How should one choose between the ownership and separate wrongdoing readings? I am especially attracted to a proposal by Amy Sepinwall, in the leading scholarly article on failure to punish. Sepinwall suggests that the ownership reading should apply when the failure to punish expresses the same disregard for the crime victims as the original act, for in that case the commander has acquiesced in or endorsed the subordinates' behavior.[68] Ownership arises from the expressive context of the failure to punish. When the context expresses *symbolic affiliation* with the wrongdoers who are not punished, the commander takes ownership of their misdeeds (or, in our alternative conception of ownership, of moral responsibility for the misdeeds).

Sepinwall's idea is the individual counterpart to the collective continuity of government we have just examined. In the same way that one administration (collectively) owns responsibility for the policies of its predecessors unless it explicitly breaks with them, a commander who culpably fails to punish wrongdoing by his troops (individually) owns their deeds, if the import of his failure is affiliation with them.

"Symbolic affiliation" is a rather abstract concept, and we need to see what it means concretely. Obama administration acts of symbolic affiliation with the Bush policies include tolerating the CIA's censorship of books criticizing the CIA; using the state-secrets doctrine to block courtroom accountability for torture; the heavy-handed diplomacy to stop foreign investigations of US torture; the refusals to apologize to torture victims; and the promotion of the CIA officials who masterminded – an odd word – the kidnapping and rendition of El-Masri. Every one of these steps is a form of symbolic affiliation with the torturers. On the other side of the ledger, acts of disaffiliation include all Obama's antitorture statements and actions quoted previously.

Somewhere in between affiliation and disaffiliation lies Obama's cautious approach to accountability, expressed in his desire to look forward and not back, and his distaste for the prospect that CIA employees might have to look over their shoulders and "lawyer up." These are not exactly sentiments of affiliation, but they are far from disaffiliation. It is instructive to contrast Obama's cautious tiptoeing around accountability for torture with his angry reaction to a survey reporting a large number of sexual assaults in the US military.

> "The bottom line is, I have no tolerance for this," Mr. Obama said in answer
> to a question about the survey. "If we find out somebody's engaging in this

---

[68] Amy J. Sepinwall, "Failures to Punish: Command Responsibility in Domestic and International Law," *Michigan Journal of International Law*, 30 (2008–9), 251ff., at 289–90. Sepinwall is deeply critical of the ICTY's rejection of the ownership reading.

stuff, they've got to be held accountable, prosecuted, stripped of their positions, court-martialed, fired, dishonorably discharged. Period."[69]

In the sexual-assault scandal, the president does not fret that negligent military commanders who fail to punish sexual assaults might have to look over their shoulders and lawyer up. Here, therefore, he symbolically and expressively *disaffiliates* from military personnel who commit or ignore sexual assaults. The contrast with personnel who may have committed torture could hardly be more striking.[70]

Unimpeded downstream consequences

A final way in which a later administration can come to own the policies of its predecessor, even though those policies were formulated "upstream," is if it makes no effort to impede or interrupt dangerous downstream consequences of those policies that can reasonably be foreseen.

In general, moral agents are responsible for the reasonably foreseeable consequences of their intentional actions unless those consequences are unwanted byproducts ("collateral damage") resulting from the intended action. In the latter case, many philosophers accept the view that the agent is exonerated from blame for the unwanted and unintended collateral damage, at least if it is not disproportionate. This is the "doctrine of double effect." In its classic formulation by Thomas Aquinas, "Nothing hinders a single act from having two effects, only one of which is intended, while the other is beside the intention. Now moral acts get their character in accordance with what is intended, but not from what is beside the intention, since the latter is incidental."[71]

Michael Walzer offers a plausible refinement of the doctrine of double effect: merely *not intending* the collateral damage is insufficient to exonerate an agent; the agent must *intend not* to inflict it, where the latter requires active efforts by an agent to avoid the damage.[72] Otherwise, agents could avoid moral

---

[69] Jennifer Steinhauer, "Sexual Assaults in Military Raise Alarm in Washington," *New York Times*, May 7, 2013, p. A1.

[70] This is not to deny important differences between military sexual assault and torture. The former, if undeterred, might continue because failure to punish would establish a climate of assault, whereas Obama ended torture; and, of course, the top leadership of the United States never ordered sexual assault. So there are reasons other than symbolic affiliation or disaffiliation explaining Obama's very different reactions. Regardless of the reasons, however, the fact remains that Obama denounced one vile practice far more strongly than the other. I am grateful to Rachel Luban and Marty Lederman for pressing me on this point.

[71] Thomas Aquinas, *Summa Theologiae*, II–II, question 64, article 7.

[72] Michael Walzer, *Just and Unjust Wars: A Moral Argument with Historical Illustrations* (New York: Basic Books, 1977), pp. 150–2. I discuss Walzer's treatment of double effect at greater length in the context of military ethics in Luban, "Risk Taking and Force Protection," in Itzhak Benbaji and Naomi Sussman, Eds., *Reading Walzer* (London: Routledge, 2013), pp. 277–301.

culpability merely by narrowing the scope of their intentions without changing their actions, which is clearly a cheat. As Elizabeth Anscombe testily observes, "someone who can fool himself into this twist of thought will fool himself into justifying anything, no matter how atrocious, by means of it."[73] Blamelessness for an action cannot be won merely by changing your thoughts about it, any more than you can release yourself from a promise by mentally crossing your fingers when you make it.

One of the reasonably foreseeable consequences of the Obama administration's decision to "look forward, not back" is a continued shift in public opinion in a pro-torture direction, as former officials of the Bush administration and commentators sympathetic to their viewpoint filled the vacuum with the argument that torture saved American lives, and were not rebutted with any energy. Presumably, the shift in public opinion is exactly what those officials and commentators intend. They would, in that case, happily accept responsibility for that outcome. Obama and his administration, on the other hand, presumably would reject the drift in favor of torture as, in Obama's words, "not who we are."

Of course, permitting the shift in public opinion was not the Obama administration's intention. The intention was to promote an ambitious domestic agenda that would become sidetracked by partisan politics if the new administration revisited the torture issue; the shift in public opinion was merely unwanted collateral damage. But remember Walzer's refinement of the doctrine of double effect: *not intending* is not enough. The new administration would have to do something more active in order to *intend not* to cede the field of public opinion to the friends of torture. By failing to do that, it comes to own the unimpeded, reasonably foreseeable consequences of the decision to do nothing. Let us see what those consequences are.[74]

Figure 10.1 is a summary of polls taken by the Pew Research Center since the year 2004. Each poll asks the same question: "Do you think the use of torture against suspected terrorists in order to gain important information can be often justified, sometimes be justified, rarely be justified or never be justified?" Before discussing the answers, let me point out something striking about the question. Pew does not ask about the use of torture against *proven* or *known* terrorists. They ask about torturing *suspected* terrorists. And the question does not say torturing them might gain "life-saving" information, only "important" information.

---

[73] G. E. M. Anscombe, "War and Murder," in Walter Stein, Ed., *Nuclear Weapons: A Catholic Response* (New York: Sheed & Ward, 1961), n.2. Anscombe's full comment is this: "The idea that they [attackers] may lawfully do what they do, but should not *intend* the death of those they attack, has been put forward and, when suitably expressed, may seem high-minded. But someone who can fool himself into this twist of thought will fool himself into justifying anything, no matter how atrocious, by means of it."

[74] The information on this graph is drawn from Pew Research Center surveys from 2004 to 2011; the graph itself was drawn by Luke Mitchell, and is reproduced with his permission.

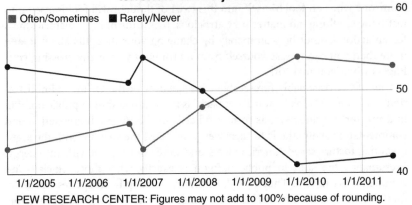

Question: Torture to gain important information from suspected terrorists can be justified ...

Figure 10.1   Question: torture to gain important information from suspected terrorists can be justified.

Of course, it may be that people responding to the poll miss these subtleties. Maybe they see only the word "terrorist," and maybe they assume that "important" *means* life-saving. But the fact remains that a significant number of Americans went on record in favor of torturing people for information on the mere suspicion of being terrorists.

How significant a number? The first Pew poll is dated less than three months after the revelations at Abu Ghraib, presumably a moment when public revulsion against torture was high. It shows a 53 percent majority of Americans who believe torture can rarely or never be used. Even then, 43 percent said torture can often or sometimes be used.

Seven years later those numbers were reversed. Now 53 percent favored torture and only 42 percent thought it should rarely or never be used. The graph shows largely unbroken, steady rise in support of torture from 2004, and a steady decline in opposition to torture with only one significant but brief reversal in late 2006. It was sometime during the first years of the Obama administration that public support for torture passed the 50 percent mark.

The most striking speed-up in pro-torture sentiment took place between February and April of 2009, when it rose five full points.[75] What happened then? Crucially, these were the early months of the Obama administration. As we saw, in his third day in office, President Obama signed a sweeping executive order banning torture. Immediately, former Bush administration figures like Dick Cheney, John Yoo, and Marc Thiessen began a full-throttle public relations

[75] This is more easily seen in Figure 10.2.

campaign on behalf of torture, hammering home the twin themes that torture works and torture saved American lives – along with their third theme, "it isn't really torture."[76]

Obama responded with the National Archives speech I quoted earlier, in which he disowned torture as a matter of principle. Furthermore, he added, "I know some have argued that brutal methods like waterboarding were necessary to keep us safe. I could not disagree more. As Commander-in-Chief, I see the intelligence. I bear the responsibility for keeping this country safe. And I categorically reject the assertion that these are the most effective means of interrogation."[77]

But beyond that statement, the administration abandoned the field to the nonstop propaganda of the friends of torture. This is the major practical drawback of looking forward, not back: it leaves the interpretation of the past in the hands of those who have no scruples about using it to advance their own agenda. So we are stuck with a national debate in which the friends of torture are full of passionate intensity, while the government apparently lacks all conviction.

America's illicit affair with torture

I have criticized the Obama administration for lax leadership in ceding the struggle over public opinion to the friends of torture. But, of course, public opinion is formed by democratic citizens with minds of their own; and the new administration's fear of adverse public reaction if they took a powerful antitorture stand clearly influenced their "look forward, not backward" approach as much as the other way around. This story will not be complete without considering our collective responsibility for torture.

The fact is that for the past decade, the United States and We The People have carried on an illicit love affair with torture. It moved from flirtation to seduction, from seduction to consummation, from consummation to deception and self-deception. As we saw in Chapter 3, the flirtation started within days of 9/11, when newspapers already reported that torturing terrorists had become a topic of conversation throughout the country. Like other flirtations, this one may not have

---

[76] The campaign reached a fever pitch in April 2009, after the Obama Department of Justice released the torture memos. For a useful summary of torture defenses that release provoked, see Dan Amira, "Who Defends Torture?", *Daily Intelligencer*, Apr. 21, 2009 (nymag.com/daily/intelligencer/2009/04/who_supports_torture.html). The article includes useful links to articles and broadcasts defending the Bush program and criticizing Obama, by former Vice President Dick Cheney, former Attorney General Michael Mukasey, former CIA Director Michael Hayden, former US Senator Mike Huckabee, Republican strategist Karl Rove, and the journalists Christopher Buckley, Steve Doocy, Abe Greenwald, Brian Kilmead, Charles Krauthammer, William Kristol, Rush Limbaugh, Bill O'Reilly, Joe Scarborough, and Mark Thiessen, as well as the editorialist of the *New York Post*.

[77] Remarks by the President on National Security (www.whitehouse.gov/the-press-office/ remarks-president-national-security-5-21-09).

been serious. It is hardly surprising that in the aftershock of 9/11 our fantasies turned to vengeance, but that does not make them anything more than fantasies.

But soon fantasy and flirtation turned to genuine seduction. The seduction was less public, as seductions always are. Vice President Cheney told us we would have to turn to the "dark side," and we nodded. Nameless officials commented that "if you don't violate someone's human rights some of the time, you probably aren't doing your job."[78] We chuckled. Before the year was over, the Washington Post reporter Dana Priest reported on the first torture stories from Afghanistan, which turned out to be true but which we completely ignored at the time.[79] The signs and warnings were there, but We The People chose to wink at them. By the end of 2001, the psychologists James Mitchell and Bruce Jessen were peddling their ideas about enhanced interrogation to the CIA, and they found a willing buyer.[80]

As a nation, we do not admit our illicit affair with torture in public – that is what makes it illicit. We proclaim our own righteousness, our democratic values, our moral stature in the world. And yet, gradually, torture is winning over our hearts and minds. Or so the public opinion polls tell us.

A breakdown of the Pew data (Figure 10.2) shows that absolute opposition to torture has never been a popular view: in July 2004 fewer than a third of surveyed Americans answered "never" to the question, "When can torture be justified?" Today, it is fewer than a quarter. Furthermore, the line graphs in Figure 10.1 show that pro-torture sentiment rose steadily and uninterruptedly from Abu Ghraib until it leveled out in the fall of 2009 at higher than 50 percent.

One symptom of our collective attitude can be seen in the terms in which we debate torture. It is not a debate about morality, but about efficacy, because it revolves almost entirely around the question, "Does torture work?"

Of course, that is the wrong question. Nobody asks, "Does murder work?" If they did, we would have to answer, "of course, murder works." It stops your enemies forever. In its own way, murder works a lot better than torture, where every true needle of information the victim gives up is buried in a haystack of lies. But we do not debate the question, "Does murder work?", because we know murder is wrong. It seems to follow that if we debate whether torture works, we have not concluded that it is wrong.

[78] Dana Priest and Barton Gelman, "U.S. Decries Abuse But Defends Interrogations; 'Stress and Duress' Tactics Used on Terrorism Suspects Held in Secret Overseas Facilities," Washington Post, Dec. 26, 2002, p. A1.

[79] Ibid.

[80] Scott Shane, "2 U.S. Architects of Harsh Tactics in 9/11's Wake," New York Times, Aug. 12, 2009. For fuller discussions of the role of Bruce Jessen and Jim Mitchell, and the psychological theories of learned helplessness they used, see M. Gregg Bloche, The Hippocratic Myth: Why Doctors Are Under Pressure to Ration Care, Practice Politics, and Compromise Their Promise to Heal (New York: Palgrave Macmillan, 2011), chs. 7 and 8, and Mayer, The Dark Side, ch. 7.

Can Torture Be Justified Against Suspected Terrorists To Gain Important Information?

Torture can be justified	July 2004 %	March 2005 %	Oct. 2005 %	Oct. 2006 %	Jan. 2007 %	Nov. 2007 %	Feb. 2008 %	Feb. 2009 %	April 2009 %	August 2011 %
Often	15	15	15	18	12	18	17	16	15	19
Sometimes	28	30	31	28	31	30	31	28	34	34
Rarely	21	24	17	19	25	21	20	20	22	18
Never	32	27	32	32	29	27	30	31	25	24
Don't know	4	4	5	3	3	4	2	5	4	4
Often/Sometimes	43	45	46	46	43	48	48	44	49	53
Rarely/never	53	51	49	51	54	48	50	51	47	42

Source: Pew Research Center Surveys (2004–2011)

Figure 10.2 Can torture be justified against suspected terrorists to gain important information?

Apparently, we are indifferent to our own stringent laws against torture; we carry on the debate over whether torture works without even mentioning the law. In this book I have suggested that we became distracted and infatuated with ticking-bomb mythology, no doubt amplified by post-9/11 rage and vengefulness. Whatever the explanation, the fact is that US public opinion fell remarkably out of synch with the antitorture commitments of US law. It is also out of synch with public opinion in peer states. In 2006, public opinion in the UK polled 12 points below the United States in agreement with the proposition that "terrorists pose such an extreme threat that governments should now be allowed to use some degree of torture if it may gain information that saves innocent lives." On the same question, Spain polled 20 points below the United States. I single out these countries because both had suffered recent terrorist bombings in their capitals' commuter railways; the Madrid bombing killed or wounded two thousand people. Yet only 16 percent of Spaniards agreed with the pro-torture side, while 65 percent agreed that "clear rules against torture should be maintained because any use of torture is immoral and will weaken international human rights standards against torture." These numbers come from a BBC poll of 27,000 people in twenty-five countries. Twenty of these countries polled pro-torture responses lower than the United States, and fourteen polled 5 or more points below the United States.[81]

---

[81] *BBC News*, "One-Third Support 'Some Torture'", Oct. 19, 2006 (http://news.bbc.co.uk/2/hi/6063386.stm). At that time, only 36 percent of Americans agreed with the pro-torture view (a lower number than the contemporaneous Pew poll's 46 percent who supported torture of terrorist suspects often or sometimes). The countries that polled 5 or more

There is an additional reason "Does torture work?" is the wrong question. As I noted in the preface to Chapter 4, the Bush administration adviser (and torture opponent) Philip Zelikow cogently pointed out that "the elementary question would not be: did you get information that proved useful? Instead it would be: did you get information that could have been usefully gained only from these methods?"[82] As I noted, Zelikow's elementary question is hardly ever asked.

In 2011, the question "Does torture work?" took concrete form, when US Navy SEALs killed Osama bin Laden in Pakistan. As we saw in Chapter 4, torture supporters immediately proclaimed that the trail to bin Laden would never have been followed without torture – but that turns out to be untrue. Not only was torture not needed, but also it did not work. Hassan Ghul gave up the name of bin Laden's courier before he was tortured; and the decisive clue about the courier that torture extracted from KSM was not a revelation, but rather a denial of the courier's importance that aroused the interrogator's suspicions – a lie that KSM would undoubtedly have told whether or not he had been tortured.

This should come as no surprise. For years, former interrogators like Soufan and Matthew Alexander have hammered on the theme that skilled, culturally knowledgeable interrogation based on building rapport is far more effective than brutality at producing accurate information.[83] Ignorant interrogation produces little information, after which frustration may turn the interrogators to brutality. The result may be a great flood of revelation, most of it false, as the victim says anything to make the brutality stop. The misinformation is a net security cost, because it needs to be checked out, which eats up security resources. If there are also nuggets of true information in the mountain of lies, they will be taken as "proof" that brutality works. A US Army interrogator told me that in Iraq he interrogated men who had previously been beaten by Special Forces, and always got information through building rapport that the previous interrogations failed to get. I asked him why his superiors did not notice, and his answer was simple: determined as they were to "take the gloves off," enamored of the toughness of Special Forces, and desperate for actionable intelligence, his superiors treated whatever information brutality extracted as golden, which "proved" to them that brutality works, and

---

points below the United States were Australia, Canada, Chile, Egypt, France, Germany, the UK, Italy, Mexico, Poland, South Korea, Spain, Turkey, and Ukraine. Those that polled higher than the United States in support of torture were China, Indonesia, Iraq, Israel, and Russia; only Iraq and Israel were 5 or more points higher.

82 Philip Zelikow, "Legal Policy in a Twilight War," *Houston Journal of International Law*, 30 (2007–8), 89, 105.

83 Matthew Alexander, *How to Break a Terrorist: The U.S. Interrogators Who Used Brains, Not Brutality, to Take Down the Deadliest Man in Iraq* (New York: Free Press, 2008).

therefore that whatever information it produces is golden. The interrogator summed up the dynamic as "a giant self-licking ice-cream cone."[84]

In late 2012, the issue surfaced again with the release of Kathryn Bigelow's film *Zero Dark Thirty*, a fictionalized retelling of how the CIA found and killed Bin Laden. The film contains graphic and horrifying torture scenes that leave little doubt that "enhanced interrogation" is, in fact, torture. It also strongly suggests that it was torture that led to the discovery of bin Laden's courier. Most readers of this book will have already read and heard far too much about *Zero Dark Thirty*, and I do not have much to add. Viewers can decide for themselves whether the film is an advertisement for torture, or an advertisement against torture, or both, or neither.

At the very least, director Kathryn Bigelow and her screenwriter based their script on a selective and untrue version of reality. But a more important omission is that the film fails even to hint that there was any internal opposition in the government to the torture program – let alone fierce opposition outside. That leaves a story so one-sided that it is objectively false, because it falsely suggests near unanimity among the professionals, and opposition only from the ignorant. Airbrushing away the antitorture movement in and out of government, such a story would be objectively false even if all the events in the film were true (which no one claims they are).

Would the film have been made this way if the Obama administration had fought the antitorture fight in the public sphere for four years, instead of abandoning the field to the friends of torture? Imagine that Obama administration officials had singled out for praise such Bush administration torture opponents as Zelikow, the US Navy general counsel Alberto Mora, the CIA inspector general John Helgerson, and military officers like Antonio Taguba (the Army general who investigated Abu Ghraib and subsequently accused the Bush administration of war crimes) and Stuart Couch (an Air Force lawyer who refused to prosecute a Guantánamo detainee because he had been tortured). Would a nonideological filmmaker still ignore the internal opposition? Would the film be the same if lawyers had been referred for discipline, if torturers had been fired or demoted, or if civil lawsuits had been allowed to proceed and expose the workings of the program? I find it hard to believe that the answer is yes.

Of course, I cannot say for sure. Hollywood knows its audience. So does Washington. That returns us to the uncomfortable topic of collective responsibility. Even as public opinion has been shaped by the friends of torture operating with at best listless opposition by the Obama administration, it shaped the

---

[84] Personal interview, Sept. 2006. See also Douglas A. Pryer, *The Fight for the High Ground: The U.S. Army and Interrogation During Operation Iraqi Freedom, May 2003–April 2004* (Fort Leavenworth, KS: Command and General Staff College Foundation Press, 2009).

administration's fear of stepping further into the torture debate. What remains is a vicious circle (or self-licking ice-cream cone) in which comforting lies about the benefits of torture and the heroics of torturers fill the vacuum, and public opinion – which was never resolutely antitorture – drifts in a direction that cements the lies into our collective memory.

In the decades following the fall of the Soviet Union, the end of apartheid in South Africa, and the transitions to democracy in South America, a discipline known as "transitional justice" emerged. Transitional justice studies the way in which societies come to terms with their own guilty past, and by now its literature is vast. Some nations have used criminal trials to expose and condemn past wrongdoing, while others have experimented with truth commissions and reconciliation mechanisms. Official apologies and reparations schemes have also figured in transitional justice. Different societies have chosen different models. In each case, the challenge has been forging a collective memory that allows a society to come to terms with its own guilty past without dissolving into cycles of vengeance and vendetta.

Transitional justice focuses on transitions from tyranny or civil war to democracy. It is jarring to talk about transitional justice in a democratic society with a continuous government and peaceful handovers from one administration to another. Yet I suggest that the United States also needs a mechanism for coming to terms with its descent into torture. Otherwise, the hard-won norm against torture stands in jeopardy. Our affair with torture must be an affair to remember.

I argued earlier that criminal investigations are not always good mechanisms of transitional justice, because the very important protections of the rights of defendants and targets may work to conceal truth rather than revealing it. Civil lawsuits might do better, except that invocations of the state-secrets doctrine and official immunities from tort actions prevent them from getting to court.

What would a truthful collective memory look like? By now, the general contours and many of the specifics of the torture program are public knowledge. But we have yet to knit them together into a story that might go something like this:

After 9/11, we were frightened and angry. We wanted to protect ourselves but we also wanted revenge. Fighting a fanatical, cruel, and lawless enemy, we concluded that tougher is better, and that rules of restraint are red tape that must not stand in the way of tougher. We are pragmatists, and pragmatists do not believe in letting rules get in the way of solving problems. We dismissed antitorture principles with ticking-bomb fantasies, and dismissed antitorture scruples with the vengeful response that our prisoners were "the worst of the worst" and had it coming. Self-protection and punitive fury danced together in happy harmony. The two motivations converged on torture. To the extent that we cared about our own laws and our high-minded international rhetoric, we indulged in doublethink: yes, it is torture but it is justified; and no, it is not torture. We narrowed the "torture debate" to waterboarding alone, and completely ignored the hundreds of abuse victims who were not waterboarded; we forgot as well about those who died under US interrogations.

As the years of "tougher is better" stretched towards a decade, our pre-9/11 ideas of right and wrong adjusted accordingly. The economic crisis displaced war and torture as issues deserving attention; with millions out of work, the torture of a few "terrorists" seemed kind of trivial. With no stomach for accountability in the new administration, it seemed only natural to conclude that torture is nothing that needs to be accounted for – from which it is a short step to thinking that torture is sort of OK. The partisan and unapologetic advocacy of torture by the former administration made opposition to torture seem like an equally partisan position rather than moral bedrock. Little by little, being mildly pro-torture came to seem to many of us like the moderate, sensible, and nonpartisan position. With actual facts cloaked in secrecy, dueling pronouncements by ex-officials about whether torture had produced bad information, or valuable information, or life-saving information allowed us to believe whatever we wished – and many of us wished to believe that torture kept us safe, perhaps because the belief made it comfortable to be mildly pro-torture. As for Zelikow's "elementary" question about whether information could have been obtained without torture, we never bothered to ask it.

A concluding thought

I am reminded of a powerful and famous speech delivered fifty years ago by a great American champion of social justice, Rabbi Abraham Joshua Heschel. The speech was Heschel's prophetic protest against racial segregation. One of his thoughts was this:

> There is an evil which most of us condone and are even guilty of: *indifference to evil*. We remain neutral, impartial, and not easily moved by the wrongs done unto other people. Indifference to evil is more insidious than evil itself; it is more universal, more contagious, more dangerous. A silent justification, it makes possible an evil erupting as an exception becoming the rule and being in turn accepted.
>
> The prophets' great contribution to humanity was the discovery *of the evil of indifference*. One may be decent and sinister, pious and sinful.[85]

Unlike Heschel, I am temperamentally unsuited to speaking in the words of a prophet. I lean to the pedantic. But the American torture debate – including

[85] Abraham Joshua Heschel, "Religion and Race" Speech Text, Jan. 14, 1963, Voice of Democracy: The U.S. Oratory Project (http://voicesofdemocracy.umd.edu/heschel-religion-and-race-speech-text/).

the torture that we do not debate because of our indifference and ignorance – does seem to me like the sign that we have become both decent and sinister, pious and sinful.

As I have argued in this book, the prohibition of torture is a hard-won achievement of civilization. It stands side by side with the abolition of slavery, the criminalization of military massacres, and the condemnation of female subordination. All these moral revolutions of the past two centuries have this in common: they unexpectedly drove underground practices as old as history itself. Practices routinely accepted became unacceptable, and eventually they became unthinkable (which is not to say that they stopped). We might have supposed from the success of the CAT that the same had happened with torture. To find an advanced democracy treating this milestone of civilization so cavalierly should remind us that no achievement of civilization can ever be taken for granted.

Still, in the words of the novelist David Grossman, we cannot afford the luxury of despair.[86] Public opinion has changed, but not greatly, and it can change back. In any event, public opinion is often more brutal than public norms. At the end of World War II, a Gallup poll reported that 13 percent of Americans wanted to kill all the Japanese.[87] Happily, the Obama executive order ending torture may prove very hard to undo. Sadly, the fight for accountability was lost. But I have suggested that the fight against torture is not merely a legal fight. It never was, and it never should be.

---

[86] Rachel Cooke, "David Grossman: 'I cannot afford the luxury of despair,'" *The Guardian*, Aug. 29, 2010 (www.guardian.co.uk/books/2010/aug/29/david-grossman-israel-hezbollah-interview).

[87] George Gallup, Ed., *The Gallup Poll: Public Opinion 1935–1971* (New York: Random House, 1972), vol. I, pp. 477–8.

MAIN INDEX

24 (television show), 87–8

abortion, 216
Abu Ghraib. *See also* Schmidt report
  and Guantánamo techniques, 72–3,
    148–9, 165, 220
  as example of torture culture,
    64–6
  dog-handlers, 150
  exposed, 198
  government response to, 211
  punishment for, 43, 83
acoustic separation, 232
act-ownership, 288–9, 291–2, 294
Addington, David, 210–11, 220–1
Al Qaeda
  1995 bomb plot, 16, 57–8
  applicability of Geneva Conventions
    to, 4, 6
  fighters, 211–12
  suspects, 11–13, 33–4, 36–9
al Shibh, Ramzi bin, 92
Ali, Omar Abu, 72
al-Kuwaiti, Ahmed, 78–9
Allhoff, Fritz, 79–84
al-Qahtani, Mohammed, 78, 148–9,
    161, 164–5, 188–9, 219
al-Zari, Mohammed, 9
American Bar Association (ABA),
    243–5
Améry, Jean, 97–8, 151
Anscombe, Elizabeth, 297
Aquinas. *See* Thomas Aquinas, Saint
Arar, Maher, 72
Authorization for the Use of Military
    Force (AUMF), 4
axis of evil, 18

Bagram prison, 8, 207
Beaver, Diane, 68, 218, *See also* torture
    memos: Beaver memo
Beccaria, Cesare, 51–2, 201
behavioral science consultation teams
    (BSCTs), 163
ben Yochai, Shimon (Rabbi), 143
Bennett, Jana, 62
Bentham, Jeremy, 29
Berenson, Bradford, 208
Bible, 140, 142–3
Bigelow, Kathryn, 303
bin Laden, Osama, 78–9, 302–3
bloodless torture. *See* enhanced
    interrogation techniques
Borgia, Rodrigo, 238
Bork, Robert, 30
Bosnian Human Rights Chamber, 12
Bradbury, Steven, 115, 197, 273–4,
    See also torture memos
Bradley, Yvonne, 269
Brandom, Robert, 132–3
Brooks, Mel, 27
Brooks, Peter, 69, 215
Bush administration
  acknowledgment of detainee torture,
    165
  and executive power, 23–5
  and mental torture, 155
  approving Abu Ghraib techniques,
    148–9
  involvement of top officials in
    approving CIA torture, 241, 276
  pressuring Germany to drop torture
    investigation, 284
  resisting prohibition on CIDT, 85–6
  retraction of OLC memos, 273

humanitarian law, 256-8
humiliation
    and torture, 50, 140, 146-51
    as horror-multiplier, 96-7
    in Judaism, 142-6
    of Mohammed al-Qahtani, 165, 219
    sexual, 167
Humphrey, John, 138
Huntington, Samuel, 23
hybrid war–law approach, 3-9
    case against, 14-16
    case for, 13-14
    law model, 10-11, 13-15
    war model, 9-13, 15-16
hypothetical cases, critique of, ix, 58-9,
    98-9, 104-6

institutional competence, 21, 23, 39-40
international armed conflicts (IACs),
    5-6, 236
International Committee of the Red
    Cross (ICRC), 5, 225, 264
interrogation, psychology of, 62-6
Iraq, 23-4
isolation, 166, 274

Jackall, Robert, 64
JAG Corps, 209-11, 263-70.
    See also US military
Jamadi, Manadel, 207
Jawad, Mohammad, 267
Jeppesen, 277
Jessen, Bruce, 163, 300
Justice Department, 25, 33, 85, 155,
    172-3, 227-8, 278-80, 285.
    See also Office of Legal Counsel
    (OLC)

Kant, Immanuel, 263
KGB, the, 163, 206
Kiriakou, John, 92
Krauthammer, Charles, 87, 89-90, 93,
    100

Langbein, John, 52
law in action, 261-2
law of armed conflict. See humanitarian
    law
lawfare, 256-7

learned helplessness, 132, 163-4, 166,
    192-3
legal advice, 231, 234-45, 259-63,
    266
    from government lawyers, 238-40
legal archetypes, 111. See also moral
    archetypes
legal ethics. See legal advice;
    Wasserstrom, Richard
legal indeterminacy, 232-4
legal opinions. See legal advice
legal realism, 261-3
Levin, Daniel, 259. See also torture
    memos: Levin memo
liberalism, 43-5. See also torture:
    abhorrence of
liberty. See fallacies about liberty and
    security
Libya, 25
Lieber Code, 126
Lincoln, Abraham, 26, 33
Lindh, John Walker, 10
Louima, Abner, 204
LOVEINT, 20

Macaulay, Thomas Babington, 255
Mackey, Chris, 63
Maimonides, Moses, 140-1, 143-4
Malik, Charles, 138
Margalit, Avishai, 144
Margolis, David, 115, 285
Maritain, Jacques, 138
materialist bias, 154, 171-3, 175, 182
Mayer, Jane, 87, 210
McCain, John, 228, 273
McCoy, Alfred, 188-9
mental torture, 153-94.
    See also forensic fallacy; materialist
    bias; pain and suffering: mental;
    substitution trick
    effectiveness of, 191-3
    forms of, 166-7
    prolonged harm, 171, 264
    restricted conception of in US
    torture statute, 167-86
    specific-intent requirement, 179-80,
    185
military commissions, 5, 7-8, 165,
    266-9

Solum, Larry, 138
Soufan, Ali, 74, 92, 286–7
sovereign moral debt, 289–93.
    See also moral responsibility
Stanford Prison Experiment, 65–6
state secrets defense, 20, 72, 277–80,
    282, 284
Stephens, John Wellington, 229
Stewart, Mark, 21
Stockholm syndrome, 132
substitution trick, 154, 169–71, 176,
    178–9
suicide terrorists, 14
Sullivan, Andrew, 287
Sunstein, Cass, 138
Survival, Evasion, Resistance, and
    Escape (SERE) program, 96, 133,
    163, 252
Suskind, Ron, 92, 209
Sussman, David, 48, 97, 129
symbolic affiliation, 293–6
Syria, 25

Take Care Clause, 26–7, 69, 240,
    244
Taliban, 4, 6, 237
Talmud, 143–6
Taylor, "Chuckie," 184
terrorism, material support for, 19–20,
    28–9
Thiessen, Marc, 298
Thomas Aquinas, Saint, 296
Thompson, Fred, 153
ticking-bomb scenarios, 56–60
    Allhoff on, 79–84
    and the one-percent doctrine,
    209
    apparent cases, 76–9, 90–3
    Gäfgen case, 76–8
    how it cheats, 93–5
    implausibility of, 89–90, 101
    Murad case, 90–1
    Osama bin Laden case, 78–9
    pitfalls of, ix, 46, 98–9, 104–5,
    152
    power of, 86–9
    stakes of, 99–101
    West case, 91
    Zubaydah case, 91–2

torture
    abhorrence of, 46–50, 95–8, 133–5,
    150–1, 186–90, 193–4
    absolute prohibition of, 55, 57, 101,
    124–5
    accountability for, 277–99
    and Argentina, 62
    and division of labor, 62–4, 66
    and Israel, 61, 81–3, 101
    and public opinion, 44–5, 74, 86,
    151–2, 297–304, 306
    and the American people, 44–5,
    299–306
    and the UK, 124
    and the US, 74, 85–6
    and tyranny, 48, 50–1, 55
    as a practice, 60–6, 80–4, 101–2
    as punishment, 51–2, 120
    as second resort, 152, 275
    as terror, 51
    communicative conception of, x,
    127–36
    custodial, 117–18, 127–8
    effect of 9/11 on, 44–5, 55
    end of US program, 272–3
    for extracting confessions, 52–3
    for intelligence gathering, 53–6
    for victor's pleasure, 50–1
    foreign investigations of, 283–5
    history of criminalization of,
    201–5
    legal definition of, 112–26
    mental. *See* mental torture
    purposes of, 47–53, 55–6, 119–20
    state-sponsored, 118–19
    terminology for, xiv, xv, 112
    US techniques, 205–8
torture culture, 65–73
torture lawyers
    actions of, 207–13
    and the fundamental trick, 114–17
    and torture culture, 66–73
    at Guantánamo meeting, 263–6
    Bradbury's excuse for, 273–4
    failure to discipline, 285–6
    legal justification of CIDT, 121–3
    legal justification of enhanced
        interrogation techniques,
        147–9

INDEX OF LEGAL AUTHORITIES